Praise for *Social Customer Experience: Engage and Retain Customers through Social Media*

"Social technology applied to business is at once an aspiration and a requirement for business: Given the speed with which consumers are adopting social technology, this book is a must-read for any professional seeking to connect the two."
—AARON STROUT, Managing Director at W2O Group

"Dave and Joe take social media from concepts and theory to concrete, simple steps that make it easy to implement social technology in your business."
—MARCO RONCAGLIO, Sr. Director Online Marketing & CRM, Personal Care, Philips, Amsterdam, the Netherlands

"Dave Evans and Joe Cothrel have been working in this space longer than most. So it's no surprise that this book is likely to become the authoritative guide to everything you need to know for this Age of Customer Engagement. Read it now if you want to understand how to turn customers into your most valuable collaborators. Otherwise, your customers will do the job without—or against—you. Or, to say it in Dave and Joe's words, 'Your customer is now a part of your organization.'"
—MARTIN OETTING, Managing Director at trnd, Milan, Italy

"Innovation is not a one-way street where you walk alone! Take your customers on the journey, and see the difference. Social technologies, clearly explained in this book, enable you and your customers to work as a team."
—KAUSHAL SARDA, CEO, Kuliza, Bangalore

"Rigorous, measurable quality improvement is critical for getting social media and word-of-mouth working for your business. This book highlights quality programs that work and shows you how to implement them in your business."
—JEFF TURK, CEO, Formaspace, Austin, Texas

"What's so appealing about social media is its power to reach not just one consumer at a time but a huge network of friends through the open graph. Businesses must learn to do this or risk losing their connection with consumers altogether. Social Customer Experience: Engage and Retain Customers through Social Media *shows you how.*

, Friend2Friend,
Barcelona, Spain

Social Customer Experience

Engage and Retain Customers through Social Media

Dave Evans

Joe Cothrel

SYBEX®
A Wiley Brand

Senior Acquisitions Editor: WILLEM KNIBBE
Development Editor: RICHARD MATEOSIAN
Production Editor: REBECCA ANDERSON
Copy Editor: LINDA RECKTENWALD
Editorial Manager: PETE GAUGHAN
Vice President and Executive Group Publisher: RICHARD SWADLEY
Associate Publisher: CHRIS WEBB
Book Designer: FRANZ BAUMHACKL
Compositor: MAUREEN FORYS, HAPPENSTANCE TYPE-O-RAMA
Proofreader: KIM WIMPSETT
Indexer: JOHNNA VANHOOSE DINSE
Project Coordinator, Cover: TODD KLEMME
Cover Designer: RYAN SNEED/WILEY
Cover Image: BACKGROUND ©GIOADVENTURES/ISTOCKPHOTO.COM; GRID WILEY

Copyright © 2014 by John Wiley & Sons, Inc., Indianapolis, Indiana

Published simultaneously in Canada

ISBN: 978-1-118-82610-2

ISBN: 978-1-118-82609-6 (ebk.)

ISBN: 978-1-118-92712-0 (ebk.)

Dear Reader,

Thank you for choosing *Social Customer Experience: Engage and Retain Customers through Social Media.* This book is part of a family of premium-quality Sybex books, all of which are written by outstanding authors who combine practical experience with a gift for teaching.

Sybex was founded in 1976. More than 30 years later, we're still committed to producing consistently exceptional books. With each of our titles, we're working hard to set a new standard for the industry. From the paper we print on to the authors we work with, our goal is to bring you the best books available.

I hope you see all that reflected in these pages. I'd be very interested to hear your comments and get your feedback on how we're doing. Feel free to let me know what you think about this or any other Sybex book by sending me an email at contactus@ wiley.com. If you think you've found a technical error in this book, please visit http:// sybex.custhelp.com. Customer feedback is critical to our efforts at Sybex.

Best regards,

Chris Webb
Associate Publisher, Sybex

For our family and friends and the business executives and organizational leaders we've had the pleasure to work with. We've learned from all of you. Thank you.

Acknowledgments

This book is, first and foremost, an acknowledgment to the collective contributions of professionals, business executives, organizational leaders, and an entire social media industry that has dedicated itself to delivering on the opportunities that the Social Web offers: the opportunity to understand, first-hand, what markets are saying; the opportunity to identify specific influencers and to quantify the impact that social media has as a result on markets and the businesses and organizations that serve them; and the opportunity to learn faster, to adapt more quickly, and to build and bring to market the next generation of globally acceptable, sustainable goods and services.

Following the founding principles of the Web, we've built on shared knowledge: There is barely a page that is 100 percent ours. Instead, this book is our point of view based on our insights—shaped by our experiences *as customers*—in the context of a growing, collective body of knowledge that is itself available to all via the Social Web. For the professionals whose names appear inside we are indebted.

In particular, we'd like to acknowledge the efforts of the professionals working within the firms whose products and services are referenced in this book. We are customers of nearly every one of the brands mentioned, for good reason.

The work by individuals and firms implementing social technology programs that has resulted in superior customer experiences is inherently a part of any book like this. The work they've done stands as testament to what can be accomplished when customers and their points of view and willingness to collaborate toward the betterment of the brands they love are fully recognized. As well, it is an acknowledgment to our colleagues at Lithium Technologies, to our customers, and to each of the professional services and consulting firms who support us in the work we do.

Social technology has been, for us, a truly collaborative learning experience. As you read this book you'll find dozens of references to the people who are helping to take the founding concepts of the Web and bring them to strategically sound, quantitatively expressed tactical implementations that create genuine, long-term competitive advantage. Take the time to explore their work and their points of view as you strengthen your own understanding of how social customer experience and its related concepts can help you build your business. For they are the experts; we are simply the narrators.

About the Authors

Dave Evans is the vice president of social strategy at Lithium Technologies, based in Austin, Texas. Dave was a cofounder of Austin-based Social Dynamx, acquired by Lithium in 2012. Dave is the author of the best-selling *Social Media Marketing: An Hour a Day* as well as *Social Media Marketing: The Next Generation of Business Engagement.*

Dave has worked in social technology consulting and development around the world, including HP, BSkyB, Yahoo!, Swisscom, DISH, Comcast and Time Warner.

Dave is a regular writer for ClickZ, where he publishes his column on the business application of social media and social technology.

Previously, Dave was a product manager with Progressive Insurance and a systems analyst with NASA | Jet Propulsion Labs. Dave cofounded Digital Voodoo, a web technology consultancy, in 1994. Dave holds a BS in physics and mathematics from the State University of New York/Brockport and has served on the Advisory Board for ad:tech and the Measurement and Metrics Council with WOMMA.

You can contact Dave via Twitter (@evansdave) and LinkedIn (www.linkedin.com/in/evansdave) and read more about customer care and its impact on marketing at his blog, ReadThis.com.

In almost two decades of work, **Joe Cothrel**, chief community officer at Lithium Technologies, has arguably touched more customer-facing social efforts than anyone in the world. More than 300 companies on four continents—including AT&T, British Telecom, Best Buy, IBM, SONY, and PayPal—have benefited from his advice and guidance, and he has trained nearly 500 social media managers in the certification program he created and runs.

A specialist in social media management and measurement, Joe calls on 10 years of prior experience in management consulting at Arthur Andersen and Ernst & Young. He has shared the results of his work in such publications as *MIT Sloan Management Review, Strategy & Leadership*, and the *Journal of Computer-Mediated Communication.*

In addition to his work with clients, Joe has devoted significant time to advancing the understanding of online communities in business: Joe has been quoted in *CIO, Computerworld*, the *New York Times*, the *Wall Street Journal, Forbes, Fortune*, and other publications, and his work has been cited in more than 50 books on the subjects of online communities, collaboration, commerce, and knowledge management.

You can contact Joe via Twitter (@cothrel) and LinkedIn (www.linkedin.com/in/cothrel).

Contents

Foreword

I've had the pleasure of working with Dave Evans on three books now; first as an editor on *Social Media Marketing: An Hour a Day*, then as a supporting author on *Social Media Marketing: The Next Generation of Business Engagement*, and now writing the introduction to this newest book by Dave and coauthor Joe Cothrel. It's been a fascinating journey over the last five years as we've all watched this social media thing turn from a small line item to a major component of marketing budgets. And customer care budgets. And product innovation budgets. And human resources budgets. The world has embraced social media, and most brands are struggling to keep up.

The steady evolution and adoption of social technology in business—whether by small, local businessess or large, incredibly complex enterprises—is undeniable. Consumers the world over are looking to each other to validate the promises of marketing and to make the smart choices that enable them to live their lives with a high degree of, call it consumption satisfaction, and all the while doing so on a budget that works for them.

This evolution has been massive and rapid, causing most companies to struggle, in some way, to keep up. Just about the time that brands feel like they've reached a comfortable spot with social, there's something new to challenge them. And the biggest issue we face today is *scale*.

No longer is it acceptable to simply have a few social tools in place or to have some minor level of engagement in social channels. Customer expectations have changed in a significant way, and these changes apply to all the brands they do business with, large or small. Customers are constantly asking themselves, "If my local mom-and-pop business can reply to my tweets, why can't a major business with thousands of customer service reps do the same?" And in turn, they are asking, "If a major brand with tons of overhead and structure can figure out how to engage me directly on Facebook, why can't the small business around the corner do the same?"

Any small-business owner, any brand employee, understands the complexity inherent in either of these questions, of course. Social technology enables conversation and engagement opportunities like no other time in business history. But as my dad has always said, "There's no greater burden than a golden opportunity."

How we think about scale, how we adjust our processes, and how we crack the code on engaging customers where they are, when they want, and how they want will be the way we succeed in the coming years. Customer expectations have changed, whether we see it or accept it. We all must look at how to challenge ourselves and our colleagues to scale our social channel, social technology, and social engagement efforts to become what my company calls a fully engaged enterprise.

The biggest challenge we all face in our journey to the fully engaged enterprise is that we are fighting an inherent business culture bias: optimization. As organizations scale, there's a need and a pull toward depersonalization. We all struggle with the cultural and historical desire to restrict personal connection with customers because it seems expensive, risky, or unscalable. The truth is, however, personal connection and an understanding that we are in a new market environment require us to figure out how to best address these concerns without letting them hinder or restrict us from staying competitive. We can, and must, find ways to meet the growing customer expectations of engagement and connection in ways that can scale. And that scale is certainly going to come from a better collaboration across the organization. It will come from better advanced strategic planning. It will come from a better understanding of and a constant engagement with your customers.

Dave Evans and Joe Cothrel are two of my favorite social media practitioners and all-around great guys. I'm excited that they are continuing the long, always-unfinished effort to help you and the larger business world understand this crazy thing called "social."

JAKE McKEE

Introduction

"If you have questions, go to the store. Your customers have the answers."

Sam Walton, founder, Walmart

Arriving at Bengaluru International Airport in India, coauthor Dave Evans found his checked bags on the luggage carousel within seven minutes of landing. A "wow" experience to be sure. He tweeted that. Arriving late at night in Austin after a weather-related flight delay, he was greeted by a driver arranged by United Airlines for transportation to his home so that his wife and son would not have to wait alone for him in a darkened airport. Another "wow" experience. He wrote a blog post and follow-up article about that.

This is social customer experience management in action: running your organization in a way that generates the conversations you want people to see. It's the way that savvy business are using social media, not just as a publishing channel for their own gain but as a transformational theme that recognizes the role that customers and employees, connected by social technology, can play in business.

In 2008, Dave wrote *Social Media Marketing: An Hour a Day* expressly for marketers wanting to make the leap into social media and its use in building demand. The follow-up to the book, *Social Media Marketing: The Next Generation of Business Engagement*, was first published in 2010. Dave and coauthor Jake McKee pushed social technology beyond marketing proper and asked the question "What does a social *business* look like?" The answer is, of course, "It looks like the experiences Dave shared after landing in Bangalore and Austin." The question, of course, is how do these businesses do it?

The World Wide Web—described by Sir Tim Berners-Lee as "an interactive sea of shared knowledge...made of the things we and our friends have seen, heard, believe or have figured out"—has dramatically accelerated the shift to consumer-driven markets and with that shift has come an unprecedented transformation in the relationship between a business and its customers. For millennia, power has rested with those in control of essential resources: first with land, then capital, and, most recently, media. In a socially connected marketplace, *shared knowledge* is now emerging as the ultimate essential resource. "Information wants to be free," the saying goes, and in these new social marketplaces it is: free of constraints on place, free of control on content, and free of restrictive access on consumption.

Social technology is now powering a new kind of relationship, a new kind of *customer experience*. How you manage this customer experience on the Social Web is increasingly central to your achievement of your business objectives. Whether listening to what customers have to say, inviting them to share ideas on how they see your product or service evolving, or connecting your customers and employees directly in the process of co-creation, social technology is now part of your business platform. In writing *Social Customer Experience: Engage and Retain Customers through Social Media* we set out to take the foundations established in *Social Media Marketing: The Next Generation of Business Engagement* and place them in a current context. Social media marketing was aspirational in 2008; by 2010 it was mainstream. The same holds true for social customer experience: Aspirational in 2010, it is core to business success now. As you read this book, compare the cases we've left in from our earlier work (Starbucks, Dell, and Intuit, for example) with the businesses that have picked up the ball and run with it (companies like HP, Skype, giffgaff, JoeMobile and Barclay's that have rebuilt their businesses on SaaS to deliver social technology). It's an accelerating trend, and your timing in considering this for your business or organization is perfect.

How to Use This Book

This book has three parts. Building on the ideas provided by readers of our other works, we've written this book so that *you don't have to read it all!* Here's how the book works.

Part I: Social Customer Experience Fundamentals

At just over 100 pages, Part I will get you up to speed quickly on what you really need to know about social customer experience: why it matters and how to manage it. Its four chapters span the defining elements of social customer experience management and the ecosystem in which you can build your business platform. If you simply want to know why social customer experience matters, read Part I.

Part II: Your Social Presence

Part II takes you deeper into the application of social technology to your business or organization, showing you how business decisions are informed through collaborative software and surrounding processes. Part II provides a starting point for measurement and, like Part I, includes references and pointers that quickly take you further as you develop your specific social business programs and initiatives. Part II concludes by covering five big trends that you need to be aware of and how these trends—real-time engagement, mobile computing, co-creation, crowdsourcing, and gamification—can help you build your business. If you are part of a team considering a social customer experience program, read Parts I and II.

Part III: Social Customer Experience Building Blocks

Each of the five chapters in Part III—covering customer engagement, social CRM, social objects, the social graph, and social applications—presents one key concept, in depth and again with hands-on exercises and additional pointers to online references and thought leaders. Part III provides a detailed treatment of the individual components of a solid, business-backed platform for social customer experience management. If you are designing or collaborating on the development of your firm's social customer experience program, you'll want to read Part III as well.

What This Means

If you read Part I, you'll understand the basic concepts well enough to participate on a team that is suggesting, planning, or otherwise requesting your involvement in a social business initiative for or within your organization. Part I is highly recommended for executives wanting a quick, comprehensive treatment of the fundamentals of social customer experience. If that's you, you can stop at the end of Part I. Of course, you may not want to, but then that's your choice.

If you read Part II, you'll be informed well enough to question or guide a specific implementation of social business practices and in particular to specify the required metrics relevant to your business. If you are a process leader who is championing a social business initiative within your organization, you should consider reading at least through Part II.

If you read Part III, you'll have a solid handle on the underlying concepts along with the resources and pointers to actually plan and implement social technologies as you build your social customer experience platform. You'll be prepared to actively participate in the design of social-technology-based solutions for your business or organization. If you are responsible for such an implementation or if you are planning to undertake a project like this yourself, you should read through Part III.

The Appendixes

Appendix A (key definitions), Appendix B (thought leadership resources), and Appendix C (hands-on exercises) *are applicable to anyone reading this book*. They provide a handy way to quickly locate key terms, find thought leaders, and revisit the hands-on exercises presented at the end of each of the individual chapters.

Above all, enjoy this book. Use it as a starting point and reference as you define and specify the way your firm or organization will adopt social technologies and use them to *engage* your customers and stakeholders.

Social Customer Experience Fundamentals

I

In the new world of the Social Web, social media marketing is already an established discipline, linking marketing with the important conversations that customers are leading on the Social Web. But there's another wave just beginning, and its impact is sure to be bigger. Companies are rethinking not just marketing but customer care, product development, basic business processes, and more—all with the goal of driving real business outcomes through a new discipline: social customer experience.

Social Media and Customer Engagement

Social technology is now part of business: The growing role of online social interaction in people's lives has made social a must-have for anyone making or providing a product or service. After all, if our customers are social, then business and the way it is run must be also.

The unfortunate result is a sort of land rush to build brand outposts in places like Facebook and Pinterest, too often without fully understanding the range of options that exist for social efforts and the business opportunity that social technologies—implemented in a strategic and systematic manner—actually offer. This chapter tackles the basics of what makes a social strategy work.

1

Chapter contents:

The Social Feedback Cycle

For a lot of organizations—business or non-profit—social media use begins in Marketing, Public Relations, or Communications. This makes sense, too, given the compelling events that typically drive interest in social media at a senior level, such as:

- A slew of negative comments online.
- Messages—good or bad—that have gone "viral."
- Signs of a new generation of customers increasingly out of reach of traditional media.
- A general concern about "loss of control" of "brand voice"—what happens when the inmates really do run the asylum?

In a word, many organizations have focused on getting the right messages to customers, and they see social media in a split view: on the one hand, social media is a way to tell an existing story to an audience that has to some degree "detached" from traditional channels. On the other, it a channel where the power balance is decidedly tipped toward consumers: whether this a good or bad depends largely on factors *outside* of the control of Marketing.

Given this, it's not surprising that social media projects end up being treated like traditional marketing campaigns—often seen as a relatively safe place to start the journey—rather than the efforts aimed at unlocking revolutionary experiences, like a climb up the north face—that they truly are. Too many social efforts end up pigeon-holed in short-term efforts aimed at building awareness or managing brand reputation. While laudable, the real objective of most any successful business—engagement and development of loyal customers—is missed. Is it any wonder that so many social media campaigns run their course and then fizzle out?

To be fair, there are many successful and innovative social media marketing programs. But approaching the Social Web from the perspective of "what can *I* tell *you*" predictably fails to produce the significant business outcomes that are possible given this new and ubiquitous, real-time, two-way communication medium. Missing this opportunity is unfortunate because social technology and the ability to step beyond pure marketing efforts are within the reach of nearly everyone. The technologies that now define a contemporary online-enabled marketplace—technologies commonly called social media, the Social Web, or Web 2.0—offer a viable approach to drive change deep inside business *to produce better experiences for customers.* There is something here for most any organization, something that extends beyond marketing and communications.

This chapter, beginning with the social feedback cycle, provides the link between the basics of social media marketing and the larger idea of social technologies applied at a whole-business level. Social technologies make it easy for people to create and publish content, to share ideas, to vote on and curate the contributions of others, and to recommend things based on their own experience. As a sort of simple, early definition, you can think of this deeper, customer-driven connection between operations and marketing as *social business*.

Customers have always done these things, of course. But now they do them at scale, in public. No longer satisfied with advertising and promotional information as the sole source for learning about new products and services, consumers have taken to the Social Web in an effort to share their own direct experiences with brands, products, and services to provide a more real view of their experience. At the same time, consumers are leveraging the experiences of others *before* they actually make a purchase themselves. All this has forced a change on the well-established norms of business marketing and management. In short, the management of these customer experiences—not just the experience at the point of sale or traditional point of service—is as a result your primary challenge.

Figure 1.1 shows the classic purchase funnel, connected to the Social Web through digital word of mouth (aka social media). This loop—from expectation to trial to rating to sharing the actual experience—is now a part of almost every purchase or conversion process; people are turning to people like themselves for the information they need to make smart choices. These new sources of information are looked to by consumers for guidance alongside traditional media, combined with advertising and brand communications, which are still very much a part of the overall marketing mix. The result is a new vetting that is impacting—sometimes positively, sometimes negatively—the efforts of businesses and organizations to grow their markets.

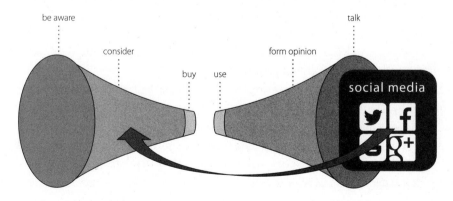

Figure 1.1 The social feedback cycle

Open Access to Information

The social feedback cycle (hereafter referred to as the *feedback cycle*) is important to understand because it forms the basis of your ability to manage the social customer experience. What this feedback cycle really represents is the way in which Internet-based publishing and social technology have connected people around business or business-like activities. This new social connectivity applies three ways: between a business and its customers (B2C), between businesses (B2B), and between customers themselves (C2C, also known as peer-to-peer).

This more widespread sharing has exposed information more broadly. Information that previously was available only to a selected or privileged class of individuals is now open to all. Say you wanted information about a hotel or vacation rental property: Unless you were lucky enough to have a friend within your personal social circle with specific knowledge applicable to your planned vacation, you had to consult a travel agent and basically accept whatever it was that you were told. Otherwise, you faced a mountain of work doing research yourself rather than hoping blindly for a good experience in some place you'd never been before. Prior to visible ratings systems—think TripAdvisor, HomeAway, or AirBnB—you could ask around but that was about it, and "around" generally meant nearby friends, family, and perhaps colleagues.

The travel agent, to continue with this example, may have had only limited domain expertise as well, lacking a detailed knowledge of rental versus hotel properties in the specific location you were interested in. This knowledge, or lack of it, would be critical to properly advising you on a choice between renting a vacation property and booking a hotel. An entire travel vertical—rental vacation properties—was created by the simple ability to post rental properties online, organize the listings for easy browsing, and overcome consumer hesitation by providing actual ratings and reviews. These services now provide tens of thousands of rated and reviewed options in both popular spots and off-the-beaten-path locations within reach of a click.

An entire business around empowering consumers looking for vacation options has been created by a shift in technology. In that spirit, ask yourself: What is social technology doing—or about to do—to your business? Consumers turn to social technology in part for *more* information and in part for *better* information. Access to information has long been an issue—correctly or incorrectly—that has dogged financial services, pharmaceutical, and insurance sales to name just a few: Is the recommendation based on the needs of the customer, the incentive offered by the equities broker, the drug's manufacturer, or the insurance underwriter, or some combination? From the consumer's perspective, the difference is everything, and in these types of industries it can be difficult for customers to get answers needed to properly evaluate complex purchases. So, they turn to each other.

Progressive Insurance, where this book's co-author Dave Evans worked for a number of years as a product manager, implemented a direct-to-consumer insurance product as an alternative to policies sold through agents. Progressive created this product specifically for customers who wanted to take personal control of their purchases. This made sense from Progressive's business perspective because the degree of trust that a customer has in the sales process is critical to building a long-term *trusted* relationship with its insured customers. While many insurance customers have solid and long-standing relationships with their agents, it is also the case that many consumers are seeking additional information, second opinions, and outright self-empowered alternatives. Customers universally want to make smart choices, and this desire is fueled by the access and choice that easily accessible web-based information brings.

Whereas information beyond what was provided to you at or around the point of sale was relatively difficult to access only 10 years ago, it is now easy. Look no further than the auto sales process and your smartphone for an indication of just how significant the impact of scalable, connected self-publishing—ratings, blog posts, and photo and video uploads—really is. This access to information and the opinions and experiences of others, along with the outright creation of new information by consumers who are inclined to rate, review, and publish their own experiences, is driving the impact of social media deeper into the organization.

Social Customer Experience: The Logical Extension

Social customer experience follows right on the heels of the wave of interest and activity around social media and its direct application to marketing. It's the logical extension of social technology throughout and across business, inclusive of the community and marketplace in which the business operates. It takes social concepts—sharing, rating, reviewing, connecting, and collaborating—to *all* parts of the business. From customer service to product design to the promotions team, social behaviors and the development of internal knowledge communities that connect people and their ideas can give rise to smoother and more efficient business processes. If this seems a lot to grapple with, add one more reality to the mix: The adoption of social technology—viewed in the context of business—quickly becomes more about change management than the technology itself. That's a big thought.

The Contribution of the Customer

It's important to understand the role of the customer—taken here to include anyone on the other side of a business transaction. It might be a retail consumer, a business customer, a donor for a nonprofit organization, or a voter in an election. What's common across all of these archetypes—and what matters in the context of social business—is that each of them has access to information, in addition to whatever information you put into the marketplace, that can support or refute the messages you've spent time and money creating.

"But wait," as we say in sales, "there's more." Beyond the marketing messages, think as well about suggestions for improvements or innovation that may originate with your customers. As a result of an actual experience or interaction with your brand, product, or service, your customers have specific information about your business processes and probably an idea or two on how your business might serve them better in the future. Tap into that and your brand advocates will self-identify.

Consider the following, all of which form the basis for a customer experience associated with a transaction, an experience this customer will quietly walk away with unless you take specific steps to collect this information:

- Ideas for product or service innovation
- Early warning of problems or opportunities
- Awareness aids (testimonials)
- Market expansions (ideas for new product applications)
- Customer service tips that flow from user to user
- Public sentiment around legislative action or lack of action
- Competitive threats or exposed weaknesses

This list, hardly exhaustive, is typical of the kinds of information that customers have and often share among themselves—and would readily share with you if you asked—*provided that they trusted you, were offered the means to talk directly with you, and had reason to believe that you would act on the information they shared.*

Ironically, this idea-rich information rarely makes it all the way back to the product and service policy designers where it would do some real good. Whether due to "not invented here" or "not on our roadmap" or "legal advised us not to take customer suggestions" or simply "our departments don't collaborate that way," the result is the same: The information that you need to innovate and compete is lost. In the marketplace, this means you are fighting with one hand tied behind your back. Collecting this information and systematically applying it is, in this view, in your best interest.

Here's an example: Suppose a customer finds that your software product doesn't integrate smoothly with a particular software application that this customer has also installed. How would you even know? If you have a high-cost enterprise product, you may have a field team that picks up on this. But what if your product is a small, cloud-based plug-in? Enter social: This information is something you can collect through peer support channels—aka support communities—and associated analytics. It can then be combined with the experiences of other customers, as well as your own process and domain knowledge, to improve a particular customer experience and then offered generally as a new solution. This new solution can then be shared—through the same community and collaborative technologies—with your wider customer base, raising your firm's relative value to your customers in the process and *strengthening your relationship* with the customers who initially experienced the problem.

The resultant sharing of information—publishing a video or writing a review—has value beyond public social forums: It is useful *inside the organization,* where it forms the stepping-off point from social media marketing and social customer care into social business. From a purely marketing perspective—as used here, meaning the MarCom/advertising/PR domain—this shared consumer information can be very helpful in encouraging others to make a similar purchase. It can enlighten a marketer as to which advertising claims are accepted and which are rejected, helping that marketer tune the message. Beyond that, however, this same information can also create a bridge to dialogue with the customer—think about onsite product reviews or support forums—so that marketers, product teams, your Legal department, and sales teams—can all understand in greater detail what is helping to build loyal customers and what is not. Taken to its ultimate end, this information can drive process change that results in better products, improved margins, and the general sorts of measurable gains that are associated with primary business objectives.

Prior to actually making process changes, you'll of course want to vet this information. Listening and information gathering—treated in depth in Chapter 6, "Social Analytics, Metrics, and Measurement"—falls under the heading of more information and so drives a need for enhanced social analytics tools to help make sense of it. It's work, but it's worth pursuing. Access to customer-provided information means your product or service can adapt faster. By sharing the resulting improvement and innovations while giving your customers credit, your business gains positive recognition and brand advocates, customers who as a result of your recognition feel a stronger tie to the brand.

The Importance of Identity

Although customers can prove an invaluable source of information, much of this value comes from your ability to understand who this particular customer is and therefore how to evaluate or consider this feedback. Is a specific voice within a conversation that is relevant to you coming from an evangelist, a neutral, or a detractor? Is it coming from a competitor or disgruntled ex-employee? You need to know so that you can plan your response. And while the overall trend on the Social Web is away from anonymity and toward identity, it's not a given—at least not yet—that any specific identity has been verified. This means you need tools that help you to dig deeper.

Anonymity opens the door for comment and rating abuse, to be sure. But social media also provides for generally raising the bar when it comes to establishing actual identity. More and more, people write comments *in the hope that they will be recognized* so as to build personal social capital.

As people take control over their data while spreading their Web presence, they are not looking for privacy, but for recognition as individuals. This will eventually change the whole world of advertising.

—Esther Dyson, 2008

With this growing interest and importance of actual identity, in addition to marketplace knowledge, social business and the analytical tools that help you sort through the identity issues are important to making sense of what is happening around you on the Social Web. Later sections tie the topics of influencer identification back to your business objectives. For now, accept that identity isn't always what it appears, but at the same time the majority of customer comments are left for the dual purpose of letting you know what happened—good or bad—and at the same time letting you know that it happened to someone in particular. They signed their name because they want you (as a business) to recognize them.

Social Customer Experience Is Holistic

When you combine identity, ease of publishing, and the desire to publish and to use shared information in purchase-related decision-making processes, the larger role of the feedback cycle and its connection to business emerges. Larger than the loop that connects sales with marketing—one of the areas considered as part of traditional customer relationship management (CRM)—the feedback cycle wraps the entire business.

Consider an organization like Freescale, a spin-off of Motorola. Freescale uses YouTube for a variety of sanctioned purposes, including as a place for current employees to publish videos about their jobs as engineers. The purpose is to encourage prospective employees—given the chance to see inside Freescale—to more strongly consider working for Freescale. Or, look at an organization like Coca-Cola, reducing its dependence on branded microsites in favor of consumer-driven social sites like Facebook for building connections with customers. Coke is also directly tapping customer tastes through its Coca-Cola Freestyle vending machines that let consumers mix their own Coke flavors. Music service Spotify invites customers to help them determine what artists and songs belong on the service; Verizon FIOS does the same with cable channels. In the United States, DISH, Time Warner Cable, and Comcast all use Twitter as a customer-support channel. Computer-maker Lenovo does them one better—customers actually write the help articles that you find on the Lenovo website. The direct integration of social technologies in business—beyond marketing—is growing rapidly.

These uses of social technology in business are explored in greater detail in subsequent chapters. For now, the simple question is, "What do all of these uses have in common?" The answer is that *each of them has a larger footprint than marketing.* Each directly involves multiple disciplines within the organization to create a customer experience that is shared and talked about favorably. These are examples *not* of social media marketing but of social technology applied to business practices.

Importantly, these are also examples of a reversed message flow: The participation and hence marketplace information is coming *from* the consumers and is heading *toward* the business as well as other customers. With TV, radio, and print—mainstays of advertising—it's the other way around: strictly from the business to the customers. In each of the previous examples, it is the business that is listening to the customer. What is being learned as a result of this listening and participation is then tapped internally to change, sustain, or improve specific customer experiences.

The Connected Customer

The customer is now in a primary role as an innovator, as a co-contributor, as a source of forward-pointing information around taste and preference, and as such is *potentially* the basis for competitive advantage. We say potentially because recognizing that your customers *have* opinions or ideas, actually *collecting* this useful information, and *using* the information to build your business are three different things. Here again, social technologies step in. Where social media marketing very often stops at the listening stage, perhaps also responding selectively to directly raised issues in the process, social customer experience management goes further.

First, experience management practices are built on formal, visible, and transparent connections that externally link customers with business and internally link employees to each other and back to customers. This is a central aspect of a truly social business: The "social" in social business refers to the development of connections between people, connections that are used to facilitate business, product design, service enhancement, market understanding, and more. Second, because employees are connected and able to collaborate—social technology applies internally just as it does externally—the firm is able to respond to what its customers are saying through the social media channels in an efficient, credible manner.

Before jumping too far, a point about your fear of the unknown, the unsaid, the unidentified, or even the uninformed saying bad things about your brand, product, or service that aren't even correct! Fear not, or at least fear *less.* By engaging, understanding, and participating, you can actually take big steps in bringing some comfort to your team around you that is maybe more than a bit nervous about social media. Jake McKee—partner at PwC, a colleague of ours, and the technical editor for this book—attended one of Andy Sernovitz's way-cool social media events. The group toured an aircraft carrier *while it operated in the Pacific.* One of the things Jake noted was that even though the deck of an active aircraft carrier—considered among the most dangerous workplaces on Earth—was to the untrained eye loud, chaotic, and therefore scary, in reality it was surprisingly fear-free. Everyone knew their place and everyone watched out for each other (and especially for Andy's tour group). F-18s were launching 100 feet away. Average age of the crew? 19. Fear? None.

The point is this: You can overcome fear with structure and discipline—on the deck of an active aircraft carrier or in business on the Social Web. Chapter 5, "Social Technology and Business Decisions," Chapter 6, "Social Analytics, Metrics, and Measurement," and Chapter 7, "Five Key Trends," provide insights into the organizational adoption of social technology along with the best practices and essential quick-start tips to put you at ease.

The Social Web and Engagement

Adopting social technology and its supporting processes can enable the critical activities of engagement and response. This section provides a starting point for understanding how. But beware: It's a different viewpoint than that which applies to engagement in traditional media. Engagement is redefined by consumers when acting in an open, participative social environment. This is a very different context from the read-only setting in which traditional media practitioners typically define engagement, so take the time here to understand engagement as it is used in this book.

Engagement on the Social Web means that customers or stakeholders become *participants* rather than viewers. It's the difference between *seeing* a movie and participating in a screening of *The Rocky Horror Picture Show. The difference is participation.* Engagement, in a social sense, means your customers are willing to take their time and energy and talk *to you*—as well as *about you*—in conversation and through processes that impact your business. They are willing to participate, and it is this participation that defines engagement in the context of the Social Web.

The engagement process is, therefore, fundamental to successful social marketing and to the establishment of successful social customer experience management. Engagement in a social context implies that customers have taken a personal interest in what you are bringing to the market. In an expanded sense, this applies to *any* stakeholder and carries the same notion: A personal interest in your business *outcome* has been established. Consider the purchase funnel shown in Figure 1.1. As customer conversations enter the purchase cycle in the consideration phase of the sales process, there is a larger implication: Your customer is now a part of your Marketing department. In fact, your customers and what they think and share with each other form the foundation of your business or organization.

The impact is both subtle and profound—subtle in the sense that on the surface much of social customer experience management amounts to running a business the way a business ought to be run. Businesses exist—ultimately—to serve customers through whose patronage the founders, employees, shareholders, and others derive (generally) an economic benefit and are therefore ensured a future in running that business. At times, however, it seems the customer interest gets dropped. The result can be seen on Twitter most any day by searching for the hashtag #FAIL.

The Social Web also drives profound change in the sense that the stakes in pleasing the customer are now much higher. Customers are more knowledgeable and more vocal about what they want, and they are better prepared to let others know about it in cases of over-delivery or under-delivery. On top of that, not only are customers seeing what the business and the industry are doing, but they are building their own expectations for *your* business based on what *every other* business they work with is doing. If Walmart can quickly add dynamic ratings and reviews to any product it sells, the expectation is that American Airlines will prominently place customer ratings on every flight it flies. Ask yourself: If flight attendants, by flight, were rated according to service and demeanor by past fliers and that information were used to make future flight choices in the same way as on-time performance, how would the overall flying experience change? It happens in restaurants. We all have a favorite waitperson and frequently ask for that person or book a table on the night when he or she is working. Airlines like Delta now ask in their surveys, "If you had a business, would you hire this person?" Like their competitors Southwest, Alaska Airlines, and United, they have placed emphasis on service quality; all four enjoy higher than average Net Promoter scores partly as a result.

By the way, the rating of service employees as the basis for making purchase decisions cuts both ways: What would happen if patrons were also rated? Car-share services like Uber and Lyft took a page out of eBay in the way that ratings are applied to both *buyers and sellers*: If you gain a reputation on Uber *as a passenger* for being a bit of a jerk, expect to stand on the street corner longer. Patrons now protect their reputations as a way of guaranteeing future consideration when conducting business in these markets or requesting services of these providers, ironically lowering the costs of doing business and boosting margins as a result; dealing with jerks is expensive!

The Rules of Engagement

If social media is the vehicle for success, the Social Web is the interstate system on which it rides into your organization. Social customer experience management, therefore, is about equipping your entire organization to listen, engage, understand, and respond directly, specifically, individually, and measurably through active conversation and by extension in the design of products and services in a manner that not only satisfies customers but also encourages them to share their delight with others.

Share their *delight*? What scares a lot of otherwise willing executives is the exact opposite: sharing dismay or worse. The fact is, negative conversations—to the extent they exist, and they do—are happening right now. Your participation doesn't change that. What does change is that those same naysayers have company—you. You can engage, understand, correct factual errors, and apologize as you address and correct the real issues. But do watch out for what Paul Rand has labeled "determined detractors." See the sidebar "Respond to Social Media Mentions" for a response flow chart. It's simple, and it works.

Respond to Social Media Mentions

Wondering how to handle a negative mention or whether or not to say "Thank you" for a nice compliment? The United States Air Force developed a flow chart that formed the basis of social technology consultancy Altimeter's recommended responses in various social media scenarios. You'll find the chart here:

www.web-strategist.com/blog/2008/12/31/diagram-how-the-air-force-response-to-blogs

In Chapter 8, "Customer Engagement," and Chapter 9, "Social CRM and Social Customer Experience," you'll see how the basic principle of incorporating the customer directly into the marketing process extends throughout the product life cycle. In this opening chapter the focus is limited to the supporting concepts and techniques by which you can build customer participation and consideration of customer experience into your business processes. For example, encouraging participation in discussion forums or helping your customers publish *and rate* product or service reviews can help you build business, and it can put in place the best practices you'll need to succeed in the future. Social business includes product design, pricing, options, customer service, warranty, and the renewal/re-subscription process and more. All told, social business is an organization-wide look at the interactions and dependencies between customers and businesses connected by information-rich and very much discoverable conversations.

So what gets talked about, and why does it matter? Simply put, anything that catches a consumer or prospective customer's attention is fair game for conversation. It may happen among three people or three million. This includes expectations exceeded as well as expectations not met and runs the gamut from what appears to be minutiae ("My bus seems really slow today.") to what is more obviously significant ("My laptop is literally on fire…right now!").

How do these relate to business? The bus company, monitoring Twitter, might tweet back, "Which bus are you riding on right now?" and at the least let its rider know that it noticed the issue. Or the bus operator's social care team may go further and ask for additional info; it may even communicate with others via Twitter and in the process discover a routing problem and improve its service generally. As for the laptop on fire, the brand manager would certainly want to know about this as soon as possible and by whatever means. That includes Twitter.

News travels fast, and nowhere does it travel faster than the Social Web. In his 2009 *Wired* article "Twitter-Yahoo Mashup Yields Better Breaking News Search," writer Scott Gilbertson put it this way: "Whenever there's breaking news, savvy web users turn to Twitter for the first hints of what might be going on." What's important in a business context is this: In both the bus schedule and laptop fire examples, the person offering the information is probably carrying a social-technology-capable, Internet-connected mobile device. As noted recently by *Advertising Age* and others, it is very likely that Twitter or a similar mobile service *is also this person's first line of communication about any particular product or service experience!*

Brand managers connected to these information streams can track feedback using real-time social media analytics tools and thereby become immediate, relevant participants in customer conversations. This kind of participation is both welcome and expected to be present by customers. The great part of all of this is that by connecting, engaging, and participating, as a business manager you tap into a steady stream of useful ideas. See Chapter 12, "Social Applications," for more on idea-generation platforms and their application in business. Take the time to understand the rules as well as the technologies that will help you build a successful social strategy.

Assessing Engagement

The Social Web revolves around conversations, social interactions, and the formation of groups that in some way advance or act on collective knowledge. The earliest analytics tools focused on listening and on understanding and managing specific attributes of the conversation: sentiment, source, and polarity, for example. Now, social technology built for engagement takes this a step further: By connecting directly with specific customers, a social care team not only can keep tabs on and respond to basic issues as they are raised on social channels, but it can also dig in and ask, "How or why did this conversation arise in the first place?" For example, is the conversation rooted in a warranty process failure? With that information the team can respond in a better manner and take measurable steps toward building brand advocates.

The adoption of social technology in business is helpful in determining how to respond to and address the detailed issues that often drive online conversations about brands, products, and services. Is a stream of stand-out comments being driven by a specific, exceptional employee? Being able to identify and measure the contributions and performance of specific social care agents will help your organization create more employees like that one. From a business perspective—and Marketing and Operations are both a part of this—understanding how conversations come to exist and how to tap the information they contain is key to understanding how to leverage your investment in social technology, to move from "So what?" to "I get it!"

Business processes based in social technologies allow organizations to capture and share insights generated by customers, suppliers, partners, or employees through social technologies in ways that actually transform a conversation into useful ideas and practical business processes. Social customer experience is built around a composite of technologies, processes, and behaviors that facilitate the spread of experiences (not just facts) and engender collaborative behavior.

An easy way to think about social technology and its application to business is in its conveyance of *meaning* and not just attributes such as polarity or source or sentiment, and in what a business can do in response to this information. Social customer experience is built around collaborative processes that link customers to the brand by engaging them as a part of the product development cycle. Consider the social business framework now in place at Dell.

Dell, hit hard by Jeff Jarvis's August 2005 "Dell Hell" reference in his Buzz Machine blog posts, needed to become a brand that listened and engaged with customers, employees, and suppliers across the Web. Dell employees like Bob Pearson, now President, Austin consultancy W2O Group, and Sean McDonald, now a managing director with PwC Advisory, believe that people spend a lot of time on the Web but not necessarily on *your* domain buying *your* product. So, the engagement strategy has to begin with going out onto the Web and meeting them on their terms and on their turf. In other words, it's better to fish where the fish are, not where you wish the fish were.

The team at Dell built on the strength it found in its customers. There were 750,000 registered users in the Dell Community at the time, with a good portion highly engaged. *These customers wanted Dell to participate.* Dell quickly realized that engaged users were stronger contributors and more vocal advocates of the brand. This realization was the breakthrough for the wide range of social media programs that Dell offers today. Dell's programs are built around its customers (not just the brand), and they actively pull customers and their ideas into Dell where Dell employees collaborate and advance the product line, completing the information cycle between businesses and their customers.

Social customer experience requires the design of external engagement processes in which participants are systematically brought into the processes that power, surround, and support the business. This is achieved by implementing social technologies, but not by that alone. It also requires changes to internal roles, responsibilities, and business processes. As Joe always says, if people's jobs haven't changed—if someone in support isn't doing something differently today, and also in communications, product development, web development, and so on—then you're really not doing social at all.

The Engagement Process

What if you threw a party and nobody came? What if they came, but no one talked, ate, drank, or laughed? Engagement makes the world go round, no less in social media than anywhere else. Unlike traditional media, social technologies push toward engagement and collaboration rather than exposure and impression. Engagement is defined here to mean an intentioned interaction. But not all interactions are alike. The social engagement process moves customers in brand, product, or service-related conversations beyond consumption (reading an article) and toward active collaboration in a series of distinct steps, each built around a specific interaction type.

The hierarchy of engagement, shown in Figure 1.2, shows a typical progression toward increasing participation for communities associated with larger businesses. Note that creation—asking a question—often precedes curation—rating or improving the usefulness of content. In communities associated with more casual members, curation may well occur first, and can in fact be the driver of content creation.

Regardless of your actual application, you'll see in detail how the stages of the engagement hierarchy, always starting with consumption, fit together.

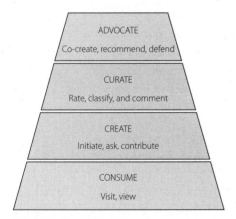

Figure 1.2 Hierarchy of engagement

Consumption

The first of the foundational blocks in the process of building strong customer engagement is *consumption*. Consumption, as used in the context of social media, means downloading, reading, watching, or listening to digital content. Consumption is the basic starting point for nearly any online activity, and especially so for social activities. It's essentially impossible (or at least unwise) to share, for example, without consuming first: Habitually retweeting without first reading and determining applicability to your audience will generally turn out badly. More practically, if no one knows about a particular piece of content, how can anyone share it? Further, because humans filter information, what we share is only a subset of what we consume.

As a result, consumption far outweighs any other process on the Social Web: It's that cliché that says that the majority of people on the Web are *taking* (consuming) rather than *putting back* (creating). There's even a rule for it, called 90-9-1 (see sidebar).

People often think that mere browsing is not a valuable activity. But if you're creating social channels for your business, much of your value will come from browsing. Think about it: If you use social channels for support, it's the *viewing* of solutions that generates value, not the creation of solutions. If you use social channels to help sell product or build your brand, it's the *viewing* of social content that drives commerce clicks, not the creation of the content. The fact that the majority of users are not creating content is not the bad part of social—it's the good part! It means that most people are using social channels to buy, use, learn, and get the most from your products and services.

Participation Inequality: 90-9-1

Way back in 2006, web designer Jakob Nielsen noted the proliferation of social sites on the Web and made an interesting observation: "All large-scale, multi-user communities and online social networks that rely on users to contribute content or build services share one property: most users don't participate very much. Often, they simply lurk in the background." Citing research conducted by Will Hill at Bell Labs in the early 1990s, Nielsen said that user participation "more or less follows the 90-9-1 rule." As he defined the rule, 90 percent of users are lurkers, 9 percent participate from time to time, and 1 percent of users "participate a lot and account for most contributions."

Was Nielsen right? We look in detail at that question in Chapter 3. The short answer is participation almost never breaks down in exactly that way. But it's almost always that unequal, or more. The value of the rule is not its precision, but its thrust—to get engagement in a community or network, you almost always need many more people to come than you might think.

You can read the Nielsen's original article. His newsletter, *Alertbox*, is also one of the most valuable sources of ongoing insight into interface usability and web design.

www.nngroup.com/articles/participation-inequality/

Having said that, you can't create a great social customer experience without moving your customers up the hierarchy of engagement. At a minimum, you need customer-created content to provide the trusted content that customers today want and expect. More importantly, if you don't try, you'll never get the rewards that come from responding to your customers desire to contribute to, and collaborate with, your business.

Creation

Creation is the act of contributing content you created. At the earliest stage, this content can be as simple as a question in a forum. A question is content, too! At more advanced stages, it can include contributing a blog article, a product review, or a video. Creation involves contributing something that others can respond to.

How do you encourage creation? Just saying "You can upload your photos!" is generally not enough. You need a good call to action. People need to know it's OK to contribute. You need to "prime the pump" with content similar to that which you hope people will contribute. Usually you start by reaching out to customers you know and asking them to help create that starter content. Most important, however, is one key principle: You have to make it easy. Ease trumps all other values and benefits when trying to engage users.

Thinking about adding photo or video sharing to your site? Take a look at Tumblr, now owned by Yahoo. Tumblr hosts more than 160 *million* blogs, and there's a good reason for that: Tumblr is absolutely simple. Will your application require a file of a specific format, sized within a given range? You can count on a significant *drop* in participation because of that. When someone has taken a photo on a now-common tens-of-megapixels smartphone or camera, your stating "uploads are limited to 100 Kbytes" is tantamount to saying "Sorry, we're closed." Instead, build an application that takes *any* photo and then resizes it according to your content needs and technology constraints. Hang a big "All Welcome" sign out and watch your audience create.

Getting members to participate for the first time is the tough part. Think of a topic that would be easy for everyone to comment on. In the early days of their community, UK telecommunications company BT started a thread to invite comments on a series of ads featuring an attractive couple, Adam and Jane. Most people in the UK had seen the ads, which had run for almost five years. The company asked "Where do you think this relationship will go?" Customers responded with more than 900 suggestions over 30 days, from the cheeky ("They will go back to their respective spouses") to the far out ("Adam turns out to be an alien who crash landed thousands of years ago."). While the community itself was focused on technical support, the thread gave newcomers the chance to participate in a fun, low-effort way. When the event was over, daily participation rates sustained that marked increase that never went away.

The business rationale for encouraging content creation is simple: People like to share what they are doing, talk (post) about the things that interest them, and generally be recognized for their own contributions within the larger community. Reputation management—a key element in encouraging social interaction—is based directly on the quantity *and quality* of the content created and shared by individual participants. The combination of easy content publishing, curation, and visible reputation management is the cornerstone of a strong community.

Curation

Curation is the act of rating, classifying, and commenting on content contributed by others. *Curation makes content more useful to others.* When someone *creates* a product review, the hope is that the review will become the basis for a subsequent purchase decision. However, the review itself is only as good as the person who wrote it and only as useful as it is relevant to the person reading it. Reviews become truly valuable when they can be placed into the context, interests, and values of the person reading them and when those reviews are *recommended* to others.

This is what curation does. By seeing not only the review but also the reviews of the reviewers or other information about the person who created the review, the prospective buyer is in a much better position to evaluate the applicability of that review given specific personal interests or needs. Hence, the review is likely to be more useful (even if this means a particular review is rejected) in a specific purchase situation. The result is a better-informed consumer and a better future review for whatever is ultimately purchased, an insight that follows from the fact that better informed consumers make better choices, increasing their own future satisfaction in the process.

Curation is an important social action that helps shape, prune, and generally increase the signal-to-noise ratio within the community. Note as well that curation happens not only with content but also among members. Consider a contributor who is rewarded for consistently excellent posts in a support forum through member-driven quality ratings. This is an essential control point for the community and one that, all other things being equal, is best left to the members themselves: curation of, for, and by the members, so to speak.

Curation is, therefore, a very important action to encourage. Typically, curation is done by people who are regular users and care about the quality and usefulness of the information. In casual communities, assigning ratings can be the small, low risk step that encourages content creation and participation. It's a lot like learning to dance: Fear, concern of self-image, and feelings of awkwardness all act as inhibitors of what is generally considered an enjoyable form of self-expression and social interaction. Introducing your audience to curation makes it easy for them to become active members of the community and to then participate in more substantive creative and collaborative processes that drive community membership and health over the long term.

Advocacy

At the top of the ladder of the core social customer experience building blocks is *advocacy*. Advocacy is the act of co-creating, recommending, and defending on behalf of a product or a brand. Advocacy is about exerting influence—on other customers, to encourage them to embrace the products you love, and on the company, to help them create the best products and experiences for their customers.

Advocacy is commonly equated with positive word-of-mouth, and that's obviously key in an online world. In defending the brand, customers can say things that brands can't say themselves, or can't generally say with the same credibility and trust. To achieve such a level of relationship with a customer is indeed a profound thing. Consider the Net Promoter score, or NPS: Companies that embrace the methodology believe that likelihood to recommend is in fact the most important indicator of a customer's satisfaction. A high-valued NPS is a clear step toward realizing advocates.

But advocacy doesn't stop at word-of-mouth. Advocates want to participate in your business. They'll let you know when you don't meet your usual high standards. They'll insist not only that you fix a problem for them but fix it for everyone else as well. They see themselves as your partner. They want to work with you—to *co-create*, in the current parlance—to make things better.

Like other social behaviors, there is a scale against which social activity can be viewed in perspective: The collective use of ratings aside, consumption, curation, and creation can be largely individual activities. Someone watches a few videos, rates one or two, and then uploads something. Someone asks a question or posts a reply. It's a two-way conversation, it's social, but it's fairly low on the collaboration value scale.

Activities like blogging are a bit more collaborative. Take a look at a typical blog that you subscribe to, and you'll find numerous examples of posts, reinterpreted by readers through comments that flow off to new conversations between the blogger and other readers. Bloggers often adapt their "product" on the fly based on the inputs of the audience, correcting or rewriting the original post.

Wiki or knowledge base articles take the process further. Several customers contribute to the same article. A customer may collaborate with a company employee. Neither one owns the end result; the outcome is collaborative, not individual. Ideation tools do something similar: An idea contributed by an individual is refined by comments from other users and then rated by other users to reflect its importance. The outcome—a refined and prioritized set of ideas—is again a collaborative product, not an individual one.

In some ways, what we just described—encouraging basic interaction and participation—is the *easy* part. The hard part is taking *direct input* from a customer and *using it* in the design of your product. Take bloggers for example: Many effective bloggers take direction from readers' comments and then use these contributions to build a new thought based on the readers' interests and thoughts. This is actually a window into how a socially enabled business can operate successfully by directly involving customers in the design and delivery of products and services. How so? Read on.

Consider a newspaper where a journalist writes an article and the subscribers read it. The primary feedback mechanism—letters to the editor—may feature selected responses, but it's certainly not *all* responses, and it's generally the end of the line. The original journalist may never again come back to these individual responses and is even less likely to build on these comments in future stories. Traditional media is as a result very often experienced as a one-way communication.

Now move to a blog or a blog-style online paper, something like the Huffington Post or Mashable. With the online publications of these businesses, audience participation is actually part of the production process. The comments become part of the product and directly build on the overall value of the online media property. The product—news and related editorial and *reader* commentary—is created collaboratively. As content consumption moves to smart devices, news will increasingly find its way back to the living room where it may again be discussed socially—even if in the online living room—with the (also digital) social commentary as an increasingly important part of the content.

How does this relate to business? Taking collaboration into the internal workings of the organization is at the heart of social business. This is equally applicable to the design of physical products, long-lived (multiyear) services, and customer relationship and maintenance cycles. By connecting customers with employees—connecting parents with packaging designers for kids' toys, for example—your business can leapfrog the competition and earn favorable social press in the process.

The Engagement Process and Social Customer Experience

Taken together, the combined acts of consumption, creation, curation, and advocacy carry participants in the conversations around your business from readers to talkers to co-creators. Two fundamentally important considerations that are directly applicable to your business or organization come out of this.

First, your customers are more inclined to engage in collaborative activities—sharing thoughts, ideas, concerns—that include you. It may be a negative process: Your customers may be including you in a conversation whose end goal is forcing a change in your business process in response to a particular (negative) experience they've had. Or, it may be "We love you…here's what else we'd like to see." The actual topics matter less than the fact that your customers are now actively sharing with you their view of the ways in which what you offer affects them and therefore *what they are likely to say if asked*. By considering social behaviors and inviting customers into these processes, your business or organization is in a much better position to identify and tap the evangelists that form around your brand, product, or service.

Second, because your customers or other stakeholders have moved from reading to creating and collaborating, they are significantly closer to the steps that follow collaboration as it leads to engagement: trial, purchase, and advocacy. The engagement process provides your customers with the information and experiences needed to become effective advocates and to carry your message further into their own personal networks. *People talk about how companies need to change and learn in the new social era; they forget that customers are changing and learning too!*

As examples of the value customers and organizational participants will bring as they share their experiences and ideas, consider the following:

- You don't get to the really good results until you go through the necessary venting process by people you've previously ignored: Opening up a dialogue gives you a natural way to enable venting and healing.

- The way you deal with negative issues is an exhibition of your true character: Become a master at accepting critical feedback and turning it into improved products and services and then reap the rewards.

- It's your job to understand what was really meant, given whatever it was that was actually said. "I hate you" isn't always as simple as it sounds: This kind of seemingly intense negativity may arise because the customer involved *likes you enough* to actually *feel* this way when things go wrong.

- Ultimately, your *customers* want to see you do well: They want your product or service to please them.

Shown in Figure 1.3, there are distinct benefits to engagement and advocacy that apply well beyond the immediate customers involved. Advocates gather around your brand, product, or service to spread their experiences for the purpose of influencing others. For you, it's a double payoff: Not only does it make more likely the creation of advocates through social technologies, but because these and other social applications exist, the advocates that emerge are actually *more able* to spread their stories.

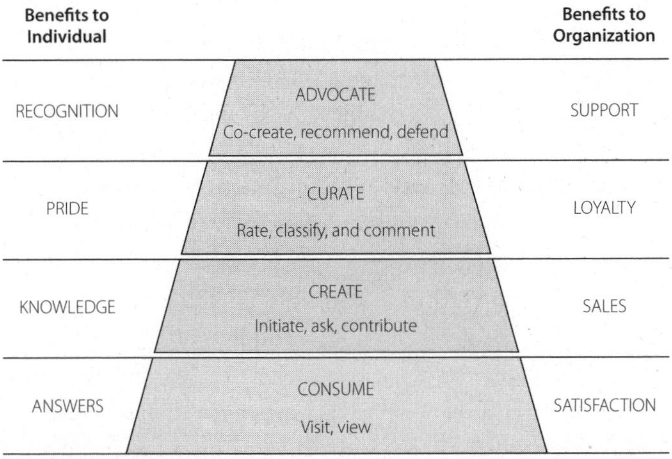

Figure 1.3 Benefits of engagement

In the end, the engagement process, delivered via the thought-out application of social technology, is about connecting your customers and stakeholders with your brand, product, or service and then tapping their collective knowledge. It's about connecting and conveying what you learn into your organization to drive innovation and beneficial change. With this linkage in place, the larger social feedback loop is available to you for use in ways that can—and do—lead to long-term competitive advantage.

The Operations and Marketing Connection

So far this chapter has covered two primary topics: the importance of understanding the mechanics of the social feedback cycle and the *collaborative* inflection point within the larger *social* engagement process. Engagement has been redefined in a social context as a more active (participative) notion compared with the decidedly more passive advertiser's definition of engagement—reading an ad or mechanically interacting with a microsite—typically applied in traditional media, where the term *engagement ad* literally means "an ad you can click to see more." That's not what participants on the Social Web generally think of when they think of engaging.

The final section ties the mechanical processes of the social technologies together with the acts of participation and collaboration and establishes the foundational role of the *entire business or organization* in setting up for success on the Social Web. The social feedback cycle—the loop that connects the published experiences of current customers or other stakeholders with potential customers or other stakeholders—is powered by the organization and what it produces. This is a very different proposition from a traditional view of marketing where the message is controlled by an agency and the experience is controlled—often in relative isolation—by the product or services teams and others even more distant.

Figure 1.4 shows the alignment that needs to occur between what can loosely be called operations and the marketing team as they contribute to the effort of managing customer expectations and experiences. Included in operations are the functional areas that control product design and manufacturing, customer service and support policies, warranty services, and similar. In other words, if marketing is the discipline or function within an organization that defines and shapes the customer's expectation, then operations is the combined functional team that shapes and delivers the actual customer experience. Looked at this way, it's clear that operations has a major stake in the management of the social customer experience.

The connection between the disciplines of marketing and operations and social media—and in particular the conversations, ratings, photos, and more that carry as content the stories and evidence of distinct customer experiences—is this: The majority of conversations that involve a brand, product, or service are those that arise out of a difference between what was expected and what was delivered or experienced. Disappoint customers, and they'll talk about that. Exceed their expectations, and they'll talk about that too. Basically delivering as promised isn't typically talk-worthy.

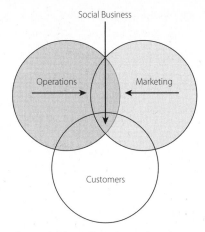

Figure 1.4 The marketing-operations connection

If this sounds vaguely familiar, think about the underpinnings of the Net Promoter methodology: We tend to talk more about what was *not* expected than what was expected. Note too that in this simple relationship between expectation and actual experience, the folly of trying to control conversations on the Social Web after the fact becomes clear: Conversations on the Social Web are the artifacts of the work product of someone else—a blogger, a customer, a voter, and so forth—who typically doesn't report to the organization desiring to gain control! You can't control something that isn't yours to control.

Instead, it is by changing the product design, the service policy, or similar in order to align the experience with the expectation or to ensure the replicable delivery of delight, for example, as Zappos does when it upgrades shipping to Next Day for no other reason than to delightfully surprise a customer. At Zappos, it's not just a story of an occasional unexpected upgrade that got blown out of proportion in the blogosphere. When bloggers—and customers—rave about Zappos, it's for good reason: Zappos creates sufficient numbers of moments of delight that *many* people have experienced them and gone on to create and share content about them. It's expensive—and Zappos isn't always the lowest cost shoe retailer. But in the end, delight wins. Zappos set out to build a billion-dollar business in 10 years. As a team, they did it in 8. Ultimately, it is the subsequent customer experiences—built or reshaped with direct customer input— that will drive future conversations and set your business or organization on the path to success.

Connect Your Team

Social media marketing is in many ways a precursor to operating as a social business. Social customer experience is most effective when the entire business is responsible for the experiences and everyone within the organization is visibly responsible for the overall product or service. When engagement is considered from a customer's perspective— when the measure for engagement is the number of new ideas submitted rather than the time spent reading a web page—the business operates as a holistic entity rather than a collection of insulated silos. The result is a consistent, replicable experience that can be further tuned and improved over time.

When it comes to rallying the troops to support your organization-wide effort, there is no doubt that you'll face some pushback. Very likely, you'll hear things like this:

- We don't have the internal resources and time.
- We lack knowledge and expertise.
- Not till you show me the value and ROI.
- We don't have guidelines or policies.
- It's for young kids—not for our business.
- Our customers will start saying bad things.

One of the first tasks you are likely to face when implementing a social media marketing program and then pushing it in the direction of social business is the organizational challenge of connecting the resources that you will need. The good news is that it can be done. The not-so-good news is that it *has to be* done.

When you're a marketer, one of the immediate benefits of a social media program is simultaneously gaining access to a large audience and being able to understand by listening to what people are saying as it relates to you and your business objectives. Through listening you can analyze what you find that is relevant to your work and then use this to develop a response program (active listening) coordinated or delivered through customer care. This information can be presented internally and done in a way that is inclusive and draws a team around you. Listening is a great way to start, though it will quickly become clear that this is best done through an effort that reaches across departments and draws on the strengths of the entire organization. Anything you can do to get others within your business or organization interested is a plus.

Basic listening and analysis can be done without any direct connection to your customers or visible presence with regard to your business or organization on the Social Web. In others words, it's very low risk. While it may not be optimal, the activities around listening and analyzing can be managed within the marketing function. As you grow beyond that, however, into actively responding to individual customers (social customer care) or implementing a support forum (peer-based care), you'll want both to invest in a platform built for measurable engagement and to enlist functions and resources across your organization. With workflow-enabled engagement platforms—for example, using a social customer care platform that automatically routes tweets about warranty issues to customer service—you can certainly make it easier to oversee all of this and therefore gain confidence in your ability to consistently provide excellent social customer care.

Building on this approach, when you move to the next step—responding to an individual customer about a policy question, #FAIL experience, or product feature request—you'll be glad you pulled a larger team together and built some internal support. Otherwise, you'll quickly discover how limited your capabilities inside the Marketing department *to respond directly and meaningfully to customers* actually are, and this will threaten your success. How so?

Suppose that you see negative reviews regarding the gas mileage of a new model car you've introduced, or you see posts about an exceptional customer service person. In the former case, you can always play the defensive role—"True, but the mileage our car delivers is still an improvement over…." Or, you can ignore the conversation in hopes that it will die out or at least not grow. (Note: It probably won't just die out.) In the case of the exceptional employee, you can praise that particular person, but beyond the benefit of rewarding an individual—which is important, no doubt about it—what does it really do for your business?

Ignoring, defending, and tactically responding in a one-off manner doesn't produce sustainable gain over the long term. What would really help you in building a successful, enduring business is delivering more miles per gallon or knowing how to scale the hiring, training, and retention of exceptional employees. You need to get control of the process issues that define customer experience—and doing that requires a larger team. This means building a team that is inclusive in membership beyond any single discipline within your organization.

Who is that larger team, and how do you build it? The answers may surprise you: Your best allies may be in unlikely or previously unconsidered places. Consider, for example, the following:

- Your legal team can help you draft social media and social computing policies for distribution within the organization. This is great starting point for team-building because you are asking your legal team to do what it does best: to keep everyone else out of trouble.

- You can connect your customer service team through social analytics tools so that they can easily track Twitter and similar conversations.

- You can champion the implementation of a social customer platform within your customer care department to more effectively respond to customers raising questions on social channels and the answers provided in response.

- Enlist your own customers. Most business managers are amazed at how much assistance customers will provide when asked to do so. Read on.

Your Customers Want to Help

While it may surprise you, your customers are part of the solution. They are often the biggest source of assistance you have. Flip back to the engagement process: consumption, curation, creation, collaboration. At the point that your customers are collaborating with each other, it is very likely that they are also more than willing to provide direct inputs for the next generation of your product or service or offer tips on what they think you can quickly implement now. Starbucks customers have been busy offering such ideas on the "My Starbucks Idea" platform. In the two years that followed its implementation in 2008, about 80,000 ideas were submitted with over 100 direct innovations as a result. While 100 out of 80,000 may not seem like a lot, consider that Starbucks's own customers did most of the filtering, and 100 ideas implemented translates into one customer-driven innovation introduced in a retail context every week. That's impressive, and it paid off in business results.

Ideation and support applications are discussed in Chapters 9 and 12. They are among the tools that you'll want to look at, along with social media analytics and influencer identification tools covered in Part II of this book. However you do it, whether planning your social customer experience program as an extension of an in-place marketing program or as your first entry into social technology and its application to business, take the time to connect your customers (connection fuels engagement) to your entire team (so that collaboration between customers and employees is possible).

Review and Hands-On

This chapter provided a foundation for thinking about social customer experience, providing a framework for building a sufficient team inside your organization to successfully implement a social customer experience management effort. Chapter 1 connected the current practice of social-media-based marketing—a reality in many business and organizations now—with the fundamental application of the same technologies at a whole-organization level aimed at managing the social customer experience, thereby setting up next generation of customer engagement.

Review of the Main Points

This chapter focused on social media and social technology applied at a deeper business level for the purpose of driving higher levels of customer engagement. In particular, this chapter established the following fundamentals:

- There is a distinct social engagement process. Beginning with content consumption, it continues through creation, curation, and advocacy. These reflect increasing stages of collaboration, creating stronger links between you, your colleagues, and your customers.

- Operations and marketing teams must work together to create the experiences that drive conversations. The social feedback cycle is the real-world manifestation of the relationship that connects all of the disciplines within your organization and drives the customer experience.

- Collaboration—used to connect customers to your business—is a powerful force in effecting change and driving innovation. Collaboration is, in this sense, one of the fundamental objectives of a socially aware *business* strategy.

Now that you've gotten the basics of the engagement process and understand the usefulness of social applications along with the ways in which you can connect your audience, employees, and business, spend some time looking at the following real-world applications. As you do, think about how the engagement process is applied and about how the resultant interactions leverage the larger social networks and relevant communities frequented by those who would use these applications.

Hands-On: Review These Resources

Review each of the following, taking note of the main points covered in the chapter and the ways in which the following resources demonstrate or expand on these points:

- Search the Web for "Dell Hell" to understand what happened at Dell and how it inspired other companies to start on the social journey.

- Read the Nielsen Norman Group's report on Social Media User Experience.

  www.nngroup.com/reports/social-media-user-experience/

- Review Starbucks's "My Starbucks Idea" ideation application:

  http://mystarbucksidea.com

- Read the Altimeter State of Social Business Report to understand how companies are responding to the needs of their social customers.

  www.altimetergroup.com/research/reports/the_state_of_social_business_2013

- Look at the blog of Peter Kim, on the topic of social business:

  www.beingpeterkim.com

- Look at the work of Jeremiah Owyang, focused on the topic of social technology and collaboration applied to business:

  www.web-strategist.com/blog/

  http://crowdcompanies.com/

Hands-On: Apply What You've Learned

Apply what you've learned in this chapter through the following exercises:

1. Define the basic properties, objectives, and outcomes of social applications that connect your customers to your business and to your employees.

2. Define internal processes that enable efficient resolution of customer-generated ideas.

3. Map out your own customer engagement process, and compare it with the engagement process defined in this chapter.

The Social Customer

2

The Social Web connects your organization and its stakeholders—customers, employees, suppliers, and influencers, all of whom have defined new roles for themselves. This chapter explains these new roles in business terms, showing you how to determine which connections matter, who is influencing whom, and where the next great ideas are likely to originate.

Chapter contents:

Who Is the Social Customer?

In the early days of the Web, the marketing debate centered on the question "*who* is the Internet user?" Much effort went into characterizing the members of this new segment. They were, it was said, young, tech-savvy, and early adopters. Many wondered if the Web was truly for the mass market.

Today, it's clear who the Internet user is: It's everyone.

Likewise, with the arrival of the Social Web, a new and similar debate centers around "who is the *social* user?" A late 2012 study by the Pew Research Center's Internet & American Life Project (`http://pewinternet.org/Reports/2013/Social-media-users.aspx`) found, predictably, that social network users were more likely to be young, urban, and more educated than the general population. As with Internet users, it's a fair certainty that those distinctions will fade as the Social Web is knitted more tightly into the business world.

But Social Web users are very different in one important respect: how they behave as customers. It starts with the fact that they are better informed than any previous generation. Google has put the world—its information and to a large extent its population—at their fingertips. But the impact is much broader than that.

Chris Carfi was one of the first to document this shift, way back in 2004, in his "Social Customer Manifesto":

- I want to have a say.
- I don't want to do business with idiots.
- I want to know when something is wrong and what you're going to do to fix it.
- I want to help shape things that I'll find useful.
- I want to connect with others who are working on similar problems.
- I don't want to be called by another salesperson. Ever. (Unless they have something useful. Then I want it yesterday.)
- I want to buy things on my schedule, not yours. I don't care if it's the end of your quarter.
- I want to know your selling process.
- I want to tell you when you're screwing up. Conversely, I'm happy to tell you the things that you are doing well. I may even tell you what your competitors are doing.
- I want to do business with companies that act in a transparent and ethical manner.
- I want to know what's next. We're in partnership...where should we go?

This is indeed a new kind of customer, looking for a new kind of customer experience. For a company, succeeding in social requires more than a different kind of web presence; it requires a different kind of company.

The Motives for Social Interaction

The "social" in Social Web is really two things: social content and social connections. First, in relation to social content, the Social Web allows users to participate in a discussion, comment on an article, contribute a product review, post a photo or video, or contribute in myriad other ways to the user-generated content (UCG) that makes up the Social Web. If Web 1.0 was written by companies, Web 2.0 is being written every day by individuals. This has transformed the Web in many ways—not the least is that it's bigger, more varied, and more rapidly changing than ever before. The very architecture of the Web is being transformed by the fact that it now has billions of potential authors. Heard about big data? In a very real sense, you created it!

The term *social* usually refers less to content and more to people, though in this book we will cover both content and people. And that's where connections come in. Connections, like content, come in various forms. Someone might favorite a photograph you've contributed to the photo-sharing site Flickr—that's a kind of connection. Someone else might enjoy one of your tweets on Twitter and decide to follow you—that's a connection too. If that person already knows you—or knows of you and would therefore like to know you—she might even friend you on Facebook. Note that such "friending" is a higher order of connection, since it requires a two-way agreement: two people become friends on Facebook only if both agree. The Social Web is a vast network of connections, even a network of networks: Most people are members of many networks.

As you can tell from these examples, content and connections are deeply intertwined. While people connected online are often connected offline as well—neighbors, co-workers, or relatives—some connections arise purely from content. A research subject quoted in the *Journal of Business Research* in 2011 describes how this happens:

"I think consumer engagement in the blog starts by somebody needing some information. And so they come, they find the site maybe through Google. They read about it, but they don't want to read it all, or it's just easier to come in and ask a question, and they're welcome to do that. It goes from there. They might stay engaged for a period of time."

Content often precedes or prompts a connection. And you can't forget that when people connect, they usually do so for a *reason*: perhaps to learn something, to share an experience, or to collaborate on a project, but in all cases to achieve something that they can't achieve alone.

Thus, a great place to start learning about the Social Web and its connection to business is with the basic relationships that are created between participants in social networks and social applications and to then look at the types of interactions between them that follow.

Relationships and interactions between individuals define the *social graph*— a term of art that means simply who you are (that is, your profile), who you are connected to (for example, your friends or followers), and what you are doing (for example, contributions, actions, status updates). The social graph is to building relationships what ordinary links between websites are to building an information network: These links define the social connections. Without the social graph—and without the profiles and friends, followers, and similar relations that form as a result—online social communities are reduced to task-oriented, self-serve utilities much as a basic website or shopping catalog might present itself in isolation.

A quick way to see this is to visit Yelp. Yelp provides reviews, ratings, venues, and schedule information—all of the things needed to plan an evening or other outing. This is the kind of activity that an individual might do or an individual might do on behalf of a small, known group of friends with a specific personal goal in mind: find a good restaurant and then see a show and so forth. That's the basic utility that Yelp provides, and by itself it appears to be a site full of social *content*, but nothing more.

Go one step further, though, and it becomes clear that Yelp is also about *people*, about social connections. When someone builds a Yelp profile and connects with other Yelpers—that's what people using Yelp call each other—the transactional service becomes a relationship-driven community. Rather than "*What* would I like to do this evening?" the question becomes "*With whom* would I like to do something this evening?" This is a distinctly social motive, and it is the combination of utility value (information and ratings) along with the other Yelpers' own profile and messages (the social elements) together with whom they are connected to that makes the social aspects of Yelp work. Social—and not purely transactional—tools power Yelp.

By encouraging the development of relationships within a collaborative community—or across functional lines within an organization or between customers and employees of a business—the likelihood of meaningful interaction, of collaboration, is significantly increased. This kind of collaborative, shared experience drives the production and exchange of information (experiences) within a customer community and just as well within an organization. Without connections, there is no sharing of content. It works for Yelp, and it works in business networks connecting manufacturers with suppliers and employees with each other. The key to all of these is building relationships and providing relevant, meaningful opportunities for personal interaction.

The Social Graph

The *social graph* is the collection of links, relationships, interactions and other connections that comprise a social network. In this book the term *social graph* refers to the links and connections, while the term *social network* refers to the collection of connected individuals. Wikipedia has more on social graphs, and the comparison of these terms, here:

```
http://en.wikipedia.org/wiki/Social_Graph
```

A Means to Connect: Friending and Following

Good relationships require three things: a *means* to connect, a *motive* to connect, and an *environment* in which the relationship can grow. In the next sections, starting here with the means to connect, you'll see how each of these is enabled on the Social Web.

Whether it's the more intimate connection of friending—the mutually acknowledged linking of profiles within or across defined communities—or the casual connection of a reply to a thread, connections are the cornerstone of the Social Web. Just as in real life, the various relationships that exist between profiles (people) often imply certain aspects of both the nature of the expected interactions and the context for them. Relationships at a club or church are different in context—and therefore in expectation—from relationships in a workplace, for example: When someone elects to follow another on Twitter, there is likewise an expectation of value received in exchange for the follower relationship, all within the context of the network in which this relationship has been established. People create connections to exchange value, at some level, with the others in and through that relationship.

Of course, all connections are not alike. On many sites, people can post content, rate submissions, and similar—but to what end? YouTube is a great example of exactly this sort of content creation and sharing. The result is a highly trafficked site and lots of buzz, but with a depth of social interaction that is less than a brand should expect from a community they create for their customers. Compare this to communities where the majority of sharing involves thoughts, ideas, and conversations and occurs between members who have a true (albeit virtual in many cases) friendship link in place.

Moving from a personal to a business context, connections drive the creation and refinement of knowledge. Collaborative behaviors emerge in environments of linked friends as the recognition of a joint stake or shared outcome becomes evident between participants. Working together—versus alone—almost always produces a better end product. Think about the corporate training exercises that begin with a survival scenario: The group nearly always develops a better solution given the stated scenario (meaning, the group members are more likely to survive!) than do individuals acting alone. And like Carfi's social customer referenced in the opening of this chapter, members begin to act not just on their own behalf but for the benefit of the community as a whole.

In communities built around shared content, the process of *curation* (touched on in Chapter 1, "Social Media and Customer Engagement") and its associated activities such as rating and recommending a photo improve the overall body of content within the community and thereby improve the experience and raise the value of membership. This type of public refinement and informal collaboration results in a stronger shared outcome. The process of curation applies to individuals just as it does to objects like photos. Just as a photo is rated, so are the contributions of a specific community member, providing a basis for the *reputation* of that member. This sense of shared outcome—of content and contribution driving value and hence reputation—is what you are after when implementing social technologies within the enterprise or when creating an active, lasting customer or stakeholder community that wraps around it.

Ultimately, the acts of friending, following, and similar formally declared forms of online social connections support and encourage the relationships that bond the community and transform it into an organically evolving social entity. As these relationships are put in place, it is important that the participants in the community become more committed to the care and well-being of the community. Plenty of social networking services have failed even though lots of members had lots of friends. There needs to be an activity or core purpose for participants to encourage them to engage in peer-to-peer interaction. Chapter 10, "Social Objects," Chapter 11, "The Social Graph," and Chapter 12, "Social Applications," offer in-depth discussions on how to ensure that these essential relationships form.

An Environment for Connection: Moderation

When talking about communities, networks, and other social sites, there's a fundamentally important connection: the connection between the individual and the community or network as a whole, or more simply *membership*. In general, to contribute to a community or network you must become a member. Membership typically involves a registration process in which you contribute information about yourself, and you also agree to the rules that have been defined for that community or network.

The preceding discussion of relationships and interactions and their importance in the development of a strong sense of shared purpose within a community left aside the question of how the social norms or rules of etiquette are established and maintained within a community. Cyberbullying, flame wars, and the general bashing of newbies clearly work at cross-purposes with developing a vibrant online community. In the design of any social interaction—be it as simple as posting on Twitter or as complex as driving innovation and collaboration in an expert community—the policies that define and govern the conduct of participants, also known as *Terms of Service*, are of utmost importance.

By the way, almost every website has *Terms of Use*, but don't get confused— these aren't Terms of Service. Terms of Use usually govern the use of content found on the site. Terms of Service, by contrast, come into play when you register to use a service, not just read content. Communities and networks are services, ergo, Terms of Service.

Typically, the Terms of Service provide for the following, each of which contributes directly to the overall health of a collaborative community:

- An expectation of participation, perhaps managed through a reputation system that rewards more frequent and higher-quality contributions
- A requirement that participants stay on topic within any specific discussion so that the discussion remains valuable to the larger community *and so that the topics covered are easily found again at a later date*

- The prohibition of any form of bullying, use of unacceptable (e.g., hate) speech, posting of spam, and similar behaviors that are counterproductive within a typical business (or related) community

Always read the Terms of Service for network and communities you use. Not only will they explain your obligations in using these sites, they will also give you a good idea of what you should include when creating your own terms of Service.

Of course, successful networks and communities don't stop at writing good rules: They think hard and creatively about the question "what will we do when the rules aren't followed?"

It is the function of moderation that takes over when rules aren't followed: Moderators, among other duties, watch for unexpected issues or problems that require some sort of review or escalation. At a basic level, moderation enforces the Terms of Service by warning members about inappropriate posting, language, or behavior. Moderation provides a sense of comfort for newer members who may be unfamiliar with more subtle rules or expectations that exist within the community. Moderation is typically guided by a brief document called a Moderation Guideline.

While members themselves typically do not see this document, your social agents, moderators, or others charged with maintaining your community use it to guide every step of the moderation process, from identifying issues to warning members. Moderation Guidelines, Terms of Service (governing external communities—for example, a customer or supplier community), and social computing policies (governing internal use of social technology—for example, by company employees) together provide an organizational safeguard when implementing social media and social technology programs. Terms, guidelines, policies, and more are all part of an effective social effort.

Social Computing Policies

A clear policy for organizational adoption of social computing is essential. You can think of social computing policies as the Terms of Use governing social media within a business. IBM offers its social computing policies for review. Spending some time with these is highly recommended.

http://www.ibm.com/blogs/zz/en/guidelines.html

Before leaving moderation—and do visit Jake McKee's resources (see sidebar "Community Moderation: Best Practices") for further discussion on moderation best practices—there's one last point with regard to ensuring community health: Moderation provides an important relief valve for seasoned members. By guiding conversations in the proper course and keeping discussions on track, skilled moderators actually make it easier (and more pleasant) for the experts in a community to stay engaged and to continue contributing in ways that benefit everyone. This too contributes to the overall development of effective social community programs.

A Motive for Connection: Reputation

In this final section you'll learn about the establishment of "motive"—about why people want to connect.

Curation, touched on previously, is often presented in the context of *content*, rating a photo or commenting on or scoring an article. As noted, curation also occurs between community participants: In the context of the community participants, curation occurs between members with regard to contributions and behavior. Members are voted up and down or otherwise ranked according to the relative value of the quality of their contributions and impact or value of their participation as individual community members. This is directly analogous to the way personal reputations are built (and sometimes destroyed) in real life.

Reputation systems—formalized manifestations of the curation process when applied to profiles and the acts of the people represented by them—are essential components of any brand community or network. Without them, all sorts of negative behaviors emerge, ranging from unreliable posts being taken as fact (bad enough) to rampant bullying and abuse (which will kill a community outright).

Reputation systems and content curation work together to help you manage and grow your social presence. Unlike your ad or public relations (PR) campaign, which you can start, stop, and change at will, on the Social Web it's generally not your conversation in the first place, though you may well be a part of it. Rather, the conversation belongs to the collective, *which includes you but is typically not yours alone.*

On the Social Web the actual customer experiences, combined with your participation and response to them, drive the conversations and hence provide the key to managing them. Management in the social context depends on *authority*—manifested through *reputation*—and that authority has to be earned rather than assumed. *Reputation,* which applies at the individual level just as it does to the brand or organization, accrues over time in direct response to the contributions of specific members associated with that brand or organization. A declaration of "guru" means relatively little without the collective nod of the community as a whole.

Reputation management works on the simple premise of elevating participants who behave in ways that strengthen the community and by discouraging the behaviors that work against community interests. Posting, replying, offering answers or tips, completing a personal profile, and similar are all behaviors that typically result in elevated reputations. HP's Support Forum ranking structure, shown in Figure 2.1, is an excellent structure that is patterned on the hierarchy of a university. Each level is based on not just one kind of activity but a range of activities organized in a formula. Participation is rewarded, but quality is emphasized. Members can clearly see where they rank in relation to the overall hierarchy.

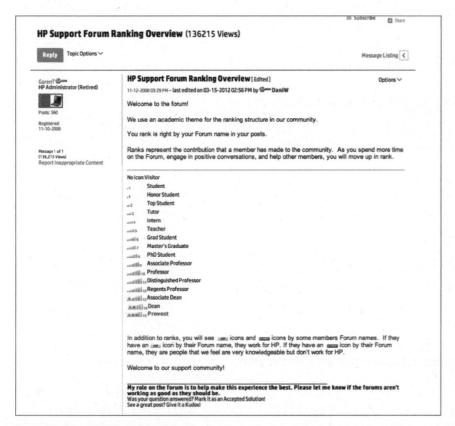

Figure 2.1 HP Support Forum ranking structure

The importance of the reputation system in a social community cannot be over-stated. Absent reputation management, individual participants are essentially left on their own to assess their own value and that of the participants around them, which rarely leads to a satisfying experience. It is this satisfaction that is at the root of the motive for connecting in the first place! Simply put, people do what people like to do; they do things that feel good.

Beyond the work of a skilled moderator and a well-designed reputation system, tips and guidelines should be presented clearly. Helping your community members do the right thing on their own—rather than simply telling them to do it—is a direct benefit of a reputation management system. Rather than prescriptive rules, a dynamic reputation management system provides feedback that guides members—in the moment and in the context of specific activities—in the direction that supports the collective need of the community.

When implementing any collaborative social program, pay specific attention to the design of the reputation management system. Technical help communities like HP's Support Forum or Stack Overflow (http://meta.stackoverflow.com/help/badges) are well worth studying as examples of how reputation systems may be implemented. Reputation systems can incorporate badges, medals, or points in addition to ranks and make contribution rewarding and also fun. Social customer experience platforms like Lithium Technologies allow you to reward and incent the kinds of participation that helps communities grow and thrive.

Web Reputation Systems: What They Do

Randy Farmer and Bryce Glass, authors of *Building Web Reputation Systems* (O'Reilly Media, 2010), neatly summarize the diverse problems that reputation systems solve on the Social Web:

Problems of scale (how to manage—and present—an overwhelming inflow of user contributions)

Problems of quality (how to tell the good stuff from the bad)

Problems of engagement (how to reward contributors in a way that keeps them coming back)

Problems of moderation (how to remedy the worst stuff quickly and effectively)

See Randy's presentation in Google's Tech Talk series:

www.youtube.com/watch?v=Yn7e0J9m6rE

The Customer Experience and Social CRM

As we noted in Chapter 1, CRM was envisioned as a data-driven understructure to power great customer interactions, particularly in the sales cycle. Based on historical transactions, insights into what a customer may need next, or when a particular customer may be ready for an *upsell,* offers are generated based on past data and the known patterns of purchase or use that exist across the entire customer base.

In a social world, however, guesses based on past transactions aren't enough. Customers are now expressing their wants and needs directly, online. When CRM is adapted to support this new customer role, it is called Social CRM, or SCRM for short. Think here about the social feedback cycle and the role of a brand ambassador, or an advocacy program that plays out in social media. In each of these, there is a specific development process—from tire kicker to car owner to loyal customer to brand advocate—that can be understood in terms of available behavioral data. Posts on social sites, collected through social analytics tools, for example, can provide real clues as to the likelihood of building brand advocates or spawning brand detractors at any given moment.

This new customer role can be effectively understood and managed by borrowing some of the ideas and practices of CRM and then weaving into them the essential social concepts of shared outcomes, influencer and expert identification, and general treatment of the marketplace as a social community.

On the Social Web, individuals participate for many reasons: to learn, to have fun, to gather facts or answers that help them accomplish their own goals. As a social customer, motivations include becoming smarter about a favorite product or service, contributing to the improvement of loved brands or companies, or earning recognition for knowledge or abilities. In the course of participating, customers share their experiences, opinions, ideas, aspirations, and intentions. This information can be used to design better products, understand unmet needs, or even identify customers who should receive discounts or incentives. When SCRM extends from gathering data and shaping interactions to transforming business processes and creating customer experiences, we're in the realm of social customer experience management (SCEM).

The Role of Influence

Both SCRM and SCEM draw on the interactions between people, on relationship management and influence, and on how conversations relevant to the business can be used to drive sales. But what makes one particular reviewer more influential than another?

For example, a potential customer looking at a review is actually looking at the net result of the business process that resulted in an individual customer being moved to write this review. If you can understand the business decisions that drove the content of the review—your store opening at 9 a.m. instead of 8 a.m., your return policy requiring an original receipt, or choosing to offer gluten-free dining options—from the perspective of the individual who actually wrote the review, you can sort out the real business impact of your operational decisions in a social context. Simply put, knowing who is talking about you and why—and being able to relate this to your specific business decisions—is fundamental to building brand advocates on the Social Web. Social

CRM—data driven and focused on the feedback cycle—extends across your entire business and wraps the entire customer experience, *including external influencers*. An understanding of the present role of the customer in your business, *along with the role of influencers and a resulting ability to connect with them just as with customers*, is what makes social CRM powerful.

Very important—and a big insight into what separates social customer experience management from social media marketing—is taking note that SCEM is often used by operations in addition to informing marketing about customer trends and business issues. As used here, operations refers to the departments and functions inside your organization that deliver the actual customer experiences. Beyond product promotion or brand messaging, SCEM data and related analytical tools are often used in customer support to estimate phone unit staffing levels, in product management to spot potential warranty issues, or in product design to identify potential innovations. SCEM is therefore an approach to business that *formally* recognizes the role of the customer and external influencers as a key in understanding and managing conversations around the brand, product, or service. If the reference to conversations seems to narrow the definition, consider this: The conversation in the contemporary business context is a holistic, digital artifact that captures and conveys the sum total of what your firm or organization has delivered. Markets *are* conversations, right?

Social CRM and Customer Engagement

We highly recommend that you download and study Paul Greenberg's whitepaper on social CRM, "Social CRM Comes of Age." You can also follow Paul, a thought leader around social CRM and its application, on Twitter (@pgreenbe) and via his blog, which you can find here:

www.zdnet.com/blog/crm/

Kira Wampler, formerly of Intuit where social brand building is a highly refined practice, provides great insight into the new role of the customer: She points out that most organizations know ahead of time where their next "Dell Hell" (the online forum that led to Dell's breakthrough response and adoption of social technology) or "United Breaks Guitars" is going to come from, so why not be proactive and fix things ahead of time? Kira recommends a basic set of questions and activities:

- Audit existing voice-of-customer channels: How many are in use, what is being said, and what is the process for analyzing, responding, addressing, and closing the loop with a solution?

- Map the customers' end-to-end experiences: Understand in detail each step that a customer undertakes when doing specific tasks that relate to your product or service. Create cross-functional teams to relate what you learn to each point in your process that impacts the customer experience at that point.

- Overlay the moments of truth with a feedback channel audit: Where are the gaps? Where do the channels overlap? What feedback do you have that shows how you are performing at these points?

- Establish a baseline of customer experience and priorities to improve: Based on these, align efforts with your business objectives and set out a plan.

- Establish a regular process for reporting: Use the associated metrics for each step in the process along with your plan to keep your larger (cross-functional) team updated. "No surprises" is the best surprise.

Put these ideas together and you have the basic value proposition for social CRM, in the context of a new role for the customer, in a participant-driven business: By understanding *who* among your customers is influential, by noting who is at the center of a specific conversation, and by developing relationships with these people, you create the opportunity to more deeply understand why they feel—positively or negatively—the way they do. You can use this information in a forward-looking (proactive) rather than reactive manner to drive innovation and to ultimately shape the conversations in ways that benefit rather than hinder your business.

Looking at Figure 2.2, you can see that the product or service experience creates a conversation, one that is often directed or intended for a specific audience and that often exposes or suggests an opportunity for innovation. This is the new role of the customer, expressed through its impact via the traditional CRM process, integrated now with a social component.

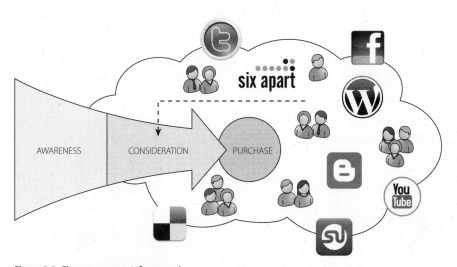

Figure 2.2 The new customer influence path

The Social Graph

Just as you are able to track your communication with an existing customer through the relationship life cycle, you can track customers and other influencers through that same relationship when they create content and converse on the Social Web. This can be very enlightening and is really useful when pulled into the product design process.

You can apply this same discipline internally, too, and connect customers and external influencers to your employees, to the customer service manager, to brand managers, and to others. Once connected, your customers and employees can bond further and move toward collaboration. Collaboration drives customer-centric product and service innovation and leads to the highest forms of engagement with your customers.

How do you encourage collaboration? Start with your data gathered through customer registration or collected as a result of online social engagement. You can use this to understand what your current and prior customers are saying about your product or service or about your brand, firm, or organization in the context of actual purchases and experiences. You can then extend this effort to bring the views of external influencers—bloggers, for example, who may not be customers—into your business decision process as well. All of this adds up to information you can use to drive change and innovation just as HP, United, Starbucks, Dell, and others are doing.

How do you integrate influencers into the way you do business? One example is what companies are doing with a tool called BuzzStream. BuzzStream helps you connect with, and manage your relationship with, the influencers in your marketspace. BuzzStream contains basic social CRM and social graph capabilities centered on influencer identification and contact management. Figure 2.3 shows the BuzzStream console and the social linkages identified for a typical influencer and the corresponding profile of interest. Scanning the figure, note that a basic Twitter listening tool was used to spot an interesting post and that this information was then used to look in further detail via BuzzStream at the person who created that post. The result was a specific action (sending a book) in response to that post.

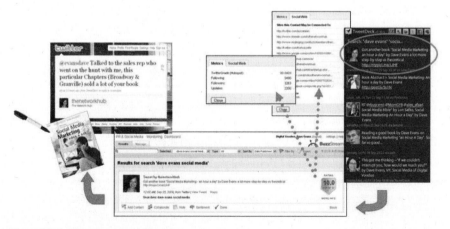

Figure 2.3 BuzzStream and the social graph

BuzzStream and similar tools include influencer dashboards that allow the easy monitoring of conversations based on keywords and the conversion of source data in much the same way as basic social web listening tools work. With influencer-monitoring tools like BuzzStream, the profiles and links of people directly contributing to the conversation you are following are converted into contacts in an influencer database that can be managed alongside your other customer data. Note that BuzzStream provides one component of a larger social CRM effort: Combined with your business data, deeper social analytics, and an internal collaboration platform, BuzzStream's contact information provides an easy way to manage subsequent conversations with the influencers around your brand, product, or service as you track issues, look for opportunities, and introduce innovations driven in part by these same conversations.

BuzzStream: Who Matters and Why

BuzzStream offers a set of tools that automate the process of building a relationship with influencers:

- When you find someone who's writing about the topics you care about, BuzzStream evaluates their social graph for you, discovering the other places they write or create content.

- BuzzStream keeps track of your communications with the people you've identified and does so for you and for other members of your team.

- BuzzStream provides tools that make it easy to manage the people you are most interested in (for example, food bloggers with more than 500 Twitter followers).

You can find out more about BuzzStream, and the larger class of related tools, by visiting these links:

    www.buzzstream.com

    www.targetinternet.com/seo-tools-comparison-raven-seomoz-
    buzzstream/

At the heart of tools like BuzzStream is the social graph. Social influence and social CRM tools work by crawling the personal and profile links in your online conversations to find information about the source of the conversation in much the same way as a searchbot crawls page links to find related or supporting content. Starting with a comment or a blog post, BuzzStream looks for a reference to a website or email or Twitter handle that may be present in or near that post. As it finds contact information, the social graph crawler will organize and return potential or contact points.

As these contact points are discovered, a list of potential links and identities are grouped together and presented through the dashboard. As a human (yes, we are still needed!) you can review this information and pick out the bits that actually seem related. Then, click a button and create your influencer contact. A typical contact may have a profile name, a Twitter handle, and perhaps an email address or phone number.

Over time you'll add to it, as your *actual* relationships with these influencers develop. Once this contact is created, its tweets, emails, or similar will be logged, just as with a traditional CRM system. You can then build and manage your relationship with these influencers just as you would any other contacts.

Engaging the Social Customer: Two Cases

Let's look at two cases in order to understand where and how social CRM and similar concepts can be applied in business. Note in these examples that breakthrough ideas are often the product of small teams, focused on customer issues. Decades ago, famed GE CEO Jack Welch used to say that every successful company should have a small group of people working on the question "what would our business look like if we blew it up and started from scratch?" What he didn't know was that, one day, that small group of people would be your customers!

Barclaycard Ring

If customer insights can help you improve your products and services, why not ask customers to help you create products in the first place? That was the inspiration for Barclaycard Ring, a new credit card product based on strong collaboration between the company and its customers.

The effort was founded on three core beliefs, articulated by Barclay's as follows:

- Customers deserve a simple credit card that's also a great deal.
- The bank needs customers' ongoing feedback to make Barclaycard Ring even better.
- Members should have a real say in how their credit card evolves over time.

These were radical ideas—particularly in an era when trust in banks and financial services companies was at an all-time low. Would customers respond?

Remember the "Social Customer Manifesto"? If so, you'll know that the answer was a resounding yes. And the results weren't just reflected in the number of registered members or volume of participation. Barclaycard found that the new card has a higher retention rate than traditional cards as well. Retention matters, because attracting new customers is expensive, and *all (other) customers benefit from the reduced churn* because the underlying cost of this card—and hence the cost to customers—is lower. Products that are built through direct collaboration typically have another benefit as well: fewer complaints. In the case of the Barclaycard Ring, the new card generates half as many complaints as a traditional credit card product, which further generates cost savings. The result for customers? An attractive annual percentage rate and the absence of fees that otherwise make customers crazy.

So, the business benefits are clear, but what keeps customers engaged? To some extent, it's the same force that united the old-time credit union: Barclaycard Ring customers are part of a community, in other words, the *environment* in which connection can occur. On the Social Web, participation can be recognized and rewarded in visible ways. The Barclaycard Ring community has a reputation system that reflects many dimensions of a member's interactions with the company and the community. To use the popular term, the community is *gamified*: points are earned for helping others with useful information, and badges are awarded for taking positive actions such as paying on time and going paperless. This is the blend of social CRM and social customer experience management in action: the marriage of business systems and social systems to create a holistic social customer experience.

In 2012, Barclaycard's success was recognized with the Forrester Business to Consumer Groundswell Award.

For more information on Barclaycard Ring, see the following:

www.barclaycardring.com/

http://player.vimeo.com/video/70438563

Autodesk

It might seem from what we've discussed that social is all about consumer-facing businesses (B2C) and not so much concerned with the world of business-to-business (B2B). In practice, social customer experience management is equally applicable in business-to-business.

A great example is the customer community at Autodesk. Autodesk makes the software that designs and shapes much of the world around you. Their best-known product, AutoCAD, is the world's leading 3D design and engineering software. But when Autodesk helped launch the computer-aided design revolution in the 1980s, it was a small group of engineers who foresaw the need to move from pencil-and-paper design to CAD tools.

John Walker, Founder, Autodesk

Looking for an insight into the kinds of people who lead small teams and create significant innovations? Check out the personal site of John Walker, founder of Autodesk, Inc., and co-author of AutoCAD.

Among other things, you'll learn the French word for "ant" and why "CH" is the country code for Switzerland. Take 5 minutes for a great brain recharge.

www.fourmilab.ch

The AutoCAD movement grew through the use of early social tools: newsgroups and commercial online services like CompuServe. That makes Autodesk's community one of the oldest continuous social efforts in the world of business.

As a pioneering and innovative firm, Autodesk was also one of the first companies to see the power of marrying social technologies to CRM systems: providing its customers with the *means* to collaborate (social) and the business platform (CRM) to capture, organize, and facilitate the development of relationship. CRM is of particular importance in business-to-business, where the lifetime value of the customer is high and customers expect a high-touch experience. With a mature online social effort Autodesk asked the question "how can we create a social customer experience that has the same qualities as the 1:1 relationship we enjoy with our customers?"

To serve a customer well, you first need to understand who that customer is. To do this, the CRM connection is critical. CRM systems contain information like customer type, purchase history, and current service subscriptions. Social systems contain rich customer-contributed content, but often it's associated with little more than an email address. Clearly, the two needed to be combined, but how?

By linking their Salesforce CRM system to their Lithium social platform, Autodesk creates an experience that is specific to that customer. A simple example: some Autodesk customers have support contracts that entitle them to direct support and advice from Autodesk engineers and support professionals. With the CRM integration those customers—even when participating in the general support forums—can be identified and provided with specific assistance according to the provisions of their contracts. Customers who have asked questions in the community yet have not received answers may escalate their question directly to an Autodesk engineer. Even better, unanswered questions from support subscribers can be automatically escalated if they remain unanswered for 24 hours. The combined power of customer data (CRM) and social data (from the social customer experience platform) enables these types of meaningful and rewarding business processes. The result? A systematic development of brand advocates.

For more information on Autodesk's efforts, read the Gartner Group case study written by Michael Moaz:

www.lithium.com/customer-stories/autodesk

Or, just search the Web for "lithium autodesk case study."

Outreach and Influencer Relations

The prior sections covered the role of the customer as an influencer and the impact of this influence on business through disciplines like CRM. You saw how social CRM can fit into your organization's business intelligence and relationship management programs and how it ties the response-driven foundation of traditional CRM to the Social Web's customer experience management process.

This section focuses on very specific conversation makers: your customers who—through their own efforts in blogs, forums, and social networks—effectively speak with authority. These customers may cover your particular market as a part of their profession or, as in the case of passionate hobbyists, purely out of interest in what you do or what you make. Because these customers speak with authority, they play a nontrivial role in landing your product or service into shopping carts.

Influencer Relations

Influencer relations extend the basics of customer outreach, taking your outreach as it relates to customer relationship management to the individual level. In an early AdWeek post covering the release of Accenture's 2010 Global Content Study, columnist Marco Vernocchi summarized one of the key findings this way:

Target individuals, not audiences. The days of thinking about audiences in broadly defined demographic buckets are over. As consumers abandon analog and consume more and more content on digital, connected platforms, media companies have been handed an opportunity—an obligation, even—to engage with customers as never before.

Almost five years on, engagement of customers across social channels is just now becoming a reality. For large brands, the task is daunting: To respond to the thousands of posts created each day that mention these brands, an efficient process built around capable engagement tools is required. Note that while you do not have to physically meet and greet every single customer, you do need a way to identify those customers for whom a response is required given your business objectives. Individual customer engagement pushes you beyond listening and analyzing broad trends and sentiment into engagement platforms that would be more recognizable in a call center than in a marketing group.

Individual engagement is the challenge now: without it, it's nearly impossible to support the collaborative processes your customers crave. This ability to scale across tens or hundreds of thousands of individual customers is perhaps the most important requirement as you plan your overall social customer experience management program. How big is big? In its first year using a true engagement platform—Lithium Social Web—DISH Network engaged with customers, parsing, routing, prioritizing, and responding to over 1,000,000 separate posts.

Why such massive scale? The Social Web is open to all comers: There is a place for everyone and therefore the requirement to engage with large numbers of customers as individuals. Today's one-off customer interaction may just turn someone into tomorrow's evangelist and may well create your next round of enthusiastic influencers. Your social customer experience program combined with an engagement platform will identify and help solidify relationships at a near-grassroots level.

Here's why: Aside from reaching and building relationships with people who may be influential to large groups of people important to you—a customer-turned-blogger with a following, a customer viewed as an industry expert, or similar—consumers are increasingly making their purchase decisions based on information, tips, and recommendations from people like themselves. Take a look at the sidebar on the Edelman Trust Barometer, and download that free report. The Trust Barometer, itself from a trusted source, makes a very convincing case for social media listening programs and for taking the step to individual engagement, thereby giving you the edge and the insight you need to position your business for long-term success.

The Edelman Trust Barometer

The Edelman Trust Barometer is a measure of the relative trustworthiness of various sources of information. Over the past 10 years there has been a significant shift, corresponding first with the mainstream adoption of the Internet and more recently with the use of social tools. In short, traditional sources of trust—people like CEOs, analysts, and news reporters—have been replaced with "people like me," with word-of-mouth and curated social media. It is a significant shift that you cannot ignore.

You will find the current Edelman Trust Barometer report here:

www.edelman.com/trust

Influencer Relations: A Representative Case

Following is a quick case study on influencer outreach. In this case the primary challenge was assembling a cross section of influencers from a very large and distributed set of individuals who are each an influencer of relatively small numbers of people but in total add up and therefore possess a significant voice.

McDonald's Family Arches

Fast-food giant McDonald's has long been the subject of attention for the nutritional value of its food. In the media, the reporting on the subject is often harsh and sometimes, in McDonald's view, unfair. A wider range of opinion is found on the Social Web, where customers themselves share the practical, day-to-day needs that are served by low-cost, well-prepared convenience foods.

Recognizing the value of the Social Web in shaping opinion, McDonald's in 2010 reached out to women who were blogging on the subject of food, families, and nutrition with an interesting proposal: Would they be interested in participating in a community where they could discuss these topics with others like themselves? The results would help McDonald's better understand the needs and opinions of these increasingly influential individuals and help those individuals be better informed about the subjects they care about. A typical reaction to McDonald's "Family Arches" is shown in Figure 2.4.

Figure 2.4 Reactions to Family Arches

Why would people volunteer time and effort in a program like McDonald's Family Arches? Participants saw benefits—a *motive*—including the following:

- The opportunity to share questions and feedback with McDonald's
- The chance to earn cool swag from McDonald's and invitations to exclusive events
- Access to exclusive info straight from McDonald's leaders and executives
- Connections with trendsetters, creative thinkers, and influential parents from around the country
- The opportunity to help build and shape the community from the ground up

The activities aren't just online: The creative moms who author the Mommy Warriors blog (www.mommywarriors.com/), for example, were invited to attend a star-studded product launch in Hollywood, where they became some of the first members of the public to sample the new Chicken McBites product. Jokingly wondering whether two tired moms could stay awake for a 9 p.m. event, they ended up having a great time—and writing about it, of course, online: "To all the folks at McDonald's and the Chicken McBites Brand, thanks for a great evening, you made two moms feel young again!"

Take a larger view of the Family Arches program: Beyond the celebrity events, the shared purpose of the program, for members and for the company, is a serious one. In an era of increasing attention to health, food quality, and significant issues like obesity, the need for informed dialogue is more important than ever. A partnership between McDonald's and caring moms is making it happen. If you're a mom and a blogger, join in!

www.familyarches.com

Review and Hands-On

This chapter defines the new role of customers and stakeholders—the recipients of the experiences associated with the product or service you are providing—and then connects those customers and stakeholders into your business. Social CRM and social customer experience management are the larger operational and analytical processes that wrap all of this and help you understand how to respond in a dynamic, conversation-driven marketplace.

Review of the Main Points

This chapter explored the more participative role of the customer and the tools that support the new expectation of an opportunity to talk back to the brand and shape future experiences and interactions. In particular, this chapter covered the following:

- Social relationships develop when three elements are present: a *means* to connect, a *motive* to connect, and an *environment* in which a relationship can grow.
- Social CRM is a business philosophy. It refers to the tools and technologies used to connect your customers and influencers into the forward-looking, collaborative processes that will shape your business or organization as you move forward.
- Social customer experience management (SCEM) is about engagement and innovation, getting at "what's next" from your customers' point of view. SCEM is most useful when applied at the business (operational) level.
- Influential customer engagement programs that capture, prioritize, and route relevant conversations directly into your organization are an essential component of your customer engagement program. Look for automation, workflow, contact management, and robust analytics when selecting social engagement tools.

In summary, social customer experience management involves the entire organization and the complete management team in response to the newly defined role of the customer *as a participant* in your business. Some of the concepts and technologies have evolved from marketing, while others are straight out of high-scale customer care. Unlike the adoption of social media tools and techniques for campaign efforts, however, picking up on and implementing ideas generated through social customer engagement requires the participation of the *entire* organization.

Hands-On: Review These Resources

Review each of the following, combining the main points covered in the chapter and the ways in which the following resources expand on these points. Then tie each into your business or organization:

- Paul Greenberg's "Social CRM Comes of Age"

  www.oracle.com/us/036062.pdf

- Jeremiah Owyang's listing of social CRM tools

  www.web-strategist.com/blog/2009/12/08/list-of-companies-providing-social-crm

- The Edelman Trust Barometer

  www.edelman.com/trust

Hands-On: Apply What You've Learned

Apply what you've learned in this chapter through the following exercises:

1. Find examples of where your customers are behaving like the new social customer today. What are they telling you about what they want and expect?

2. Find examples of bloggers or other social participants who are influential in ways related to your product or industry? Was it easy or hard to find these people?

3. Review the tools and platforms you use today to manage customer information and customer interactions. How "socially aware" are they? Where are the gaps?

Social Customer Experience Management

3

Customer experience is the hottest topic in business today, and it should be. Research clearly shows that customer experiences, positive and negative, have a direct impact on the bottom line. It can be a challenge to put together all the pieces that make a customer's experience great, and in this context social technologies represent both a threat and an opportunity: They simultaneously empower customers to share experiences as well as find alternatives with just a few clicks. This chapter explains how the notion of customer experience emerged and what it means today, in a social world.

Chapter contents:

Understanding Customer Experience

At first blush, customer experience might seem just a fancy term for good, old-fashioned customer service. In fact, it's a radically different way to think about how customers relate to companies and how satisfaction, loyalty, and other business benefits really come about.

Where did the notion of customer experience come from? Not too long ago, the dominant model for understanding customers and the decisions they make was the *rational actor* model. In this model, customers make rational decisions based on a kind of informal cost/benefit analysis. The products that sell best are those that customers believe to offer the maximum benefits for the lowest costs. To make rational choices, customers need information, and so in the rational actor model, the process of evaluating and selecting products is a matter of gathering and processing information. *Consumer Reports*, the magazine of ratings and reviews, was the de facto embodiment of the information essential to the rational customer.

In the mid 1980s, an alternate model of the customer emerged—the *experiential* model. In this model, many factors—emotional as well as rational—influence a customer's choices. The experiential model was first articulated in an academic paper written by Morris B. Holbrook and Elizabeth C Hirschman. The paper's title says it all: "The Experiential Aspects of Consumption: Consumer Fantasies, Feelings, and Fun." In the late 1990s, Joseph Pine and James Gilmore took a further step; in their book *The Experience Economy* they argued that every company, whether Walt Disney Company or Progressive Insurance, should think of itself as selling experiences, not just products or services.

Customer experience management is now a discipline, embraced by many of the world's largest brands. Frameworks and models abound. Hearing a lot lately about the customer journey? That's part of the movement too. In 2011, Bruce Temkin, a pioneer in the field in his time at Forrester Research, cofounded the Customer Experience Professionals Association (CXPA) for people whose role in their organization focuses on customer experience. Some of these people, bearing titles like vice president of customer experience or even chief customer officer, report directly to the CEO.

Customer Experience Professional Association

Cofounded by Bruce Temkin, the Customer Experience Professionals Association (CXPA) offers resources and reference material for those interested in understanding the processes and technologies applicable to customer experience management.

www.cxpa.org/

Forrester Research continues its leading work in this area: Harley Manning and Kerry Bodine detail this in their 2013 book, *Outside In: The Power of Putting Customers at the Center of Your Business*. Notably, they are helping to quantify company performance in customer experience in their annual surveys. In their 2011 report, they quantified the potential dollar benefit of great customer experience, by industry. For example, they found that hotels that offer superior customer experience could tap into $495 million in revenue from additional night's stays by satisfied customers.

As the customer experience movement shows, businesses are responding to the reality that experiences drive customer behavior. And just in time, too: In the era of the Social Web, the experiential life of customers is on full display—in comments on social networks like Facebook and Google+, in questions posted on Twitter and in ratings and reviews appearing on almost every retail website.

Fortunately, the power of companies to create and respond to experiences is greater than ever before. The combined result of these transformed markets where experiences play a more significant role, together with widely available social technology, is the emerging practice of social customer experience management (SCEM).

Are You Ready for SCEM?

Creating great customer experiences is not just about new channels and new platforms. Companies that think of social as a new kind of website are bound to fail. Rather than a web makeover, getting the social customer experience right takes a new kind of company. The following sections establish the ground rules.

Social Businesses Are Participative

At the heart of your social customer experience program is a simple idea: that operating a business on the Social Web revolves around *participation with and by* your customers. Underlying this idea are two fundamental modes of behavior: collaboration *with your customers* and collaboration *between individual customers.*

Collaboration between customers offers organizations the invaluable crowd wisdom that is one of the unique benefits or social technologies. When businesses and organizations adopt holistic social customer experience management, including both customer-company and customer-customer collaboration, everyone wins. By bringing customers in and by directly involving stakeholders in the design and operation of the organization, constructive ideas built around fundamentally measurable processes inevitably emerge.

To serve social customers you need to see your organization as a *social business*. A social business is one that is prepared—with vision, culture, business processes, and technology—to participate in an ongoing dialogue with customers and to understand its place in the markets and communities that surround these conversations. Companies that can collaborate, inside and outside the organization and with the marketplace and surrounding *physical* community as a whole, are often better able to respond to marketplace dynamics and competitive opportunities than a traditionally organized and managed firm.

The takeaway is this: Efforts leading to the creation of a social business often begin with identifying or creating an opportunity for participation with (or between) customers, employees, or stakeholders and then pursuing those opportunities effectively.

Common Misconceptions

One of the biggest misconceptions about online customer opinion—learning about what your customers want is certainly part of building a social business—is that it consists mostly of complaints and rants. Not so. A 2013 study by Adobe found that social mentions online are actually slightly positive in the United States—an average of 5.07 on a scale of 1 (highly negative) to 10 (highly positive)—and trending upward. Results from other English-speaking countries were 5.04, 5.24, and 5.36 for Australia, Canada, and the UK, respectively. So while your efforts initially focus on the negative—helping those who are dissatisfied or needing assistance—it is important to understand that social comments overall are much more balanced than you might think. This is important when you move from resolving problems to developing advocates.

Another common misconception is that great internal collaboration is a prerequisite for collaborating successfully with customers. There's no disputing the fact that good internal information sharing helps you present a more consistent, high-quality experience to customers across channels. Good internal collaboration also makes it easier to *innovate*, to implement great ideas that customers suggest or inspire. But beware: internal collaboration efforts are in many ways more complex and difficult than external, customer-facing efforts. A 2013 study by Gartner, for example, found that *only 10 percent of internal social networking efforts succeed*. This isn't a reason not to undertake such efforts, but it does suggest *not holding off* on customer-facing efforts that can pay real dividends right now until some distant day when internal efforts are perfected.

The experience of one high-tech company we know illustrates what's potentially lost when "perfect internal collaboration" becomes the gating factor for all other social business efforts. The company began internal and external social efforts at the same time, with (as is typical) different teams, departments, and technologies being deployed. Eighteen months later, the internal effort was finally ready for launch, having navigated the shoals of HR policy, IT standards, the goals of different department heads, and various mid-flow organizational changes. In that same timespan, the customer-facing social customer care effort, which launched in just 90 days, had already attracted 250,000 customers to join and participate. How much time would have been lost in building customer care if it had not been started until after the internal efforts were sorted out? In competitive markets, 18 months is forever!

Successful external social efforts often begin by thinking about the natural communities that exist around your brand. Consider support communities as one starting point: Different communities might exist around different product lines or different geographies. Existing customers might have different needs than prospects. In addition to customers, a company's partners or distributors typically offer additional opportunity for external social efforts. Successful efforts begin by prioritizing your objectives and first-steps based on likelihood of success, understanding that it's easier to move forward from success than to try again after a failure.

Speaking of moving ahead from success, you might be tempted to create a social effort aimed at customer groups you *don't* currently address, for example a younger demographic then you currently serve. That's certainly a valid and legitimate aspiration: You can use social technology to broaden your existing audience. But here's a word of caution: It's usually much better to start with those who already know and engage with you—we call it an addressed audience—and then branch out to new audiences once your initial efforts are successful.

Autodesk, a provider of business software, first created a community for design and engineering professionals who use its tools in the workplace. This was a natural audience that was eager for places to share knowledge and tips on how to use the software successfully. Today, with the burgeoning maker movement, Autodesk's community is also used by a new generation of consumers and hobbyists. The company, in turn, has begun to craft products with those consumers in mind, including apps available on the Apple App Store. It's unlikely that Autodesk would have enjoyed the same success path if they started by trying to attract the maker communities first.

Build around Customer Participation

Regardless of who the members of your community are, strong communities are built around the things that matter deeply to the members of that community: Skills, problems, passions, and causes are common engines of social efforts.

The strongest communities often are powered by more than one of these. Consider the community created by French beauty-products retailer Sephora. The Sephora BeautyTalk community (`http://community.sephora.com`) is powered by the passion for high-quality beauty products, the skills and knowledge required to select and use those products, and the confidence and pride that people gain by using those products appropriately. Regardless of your company or industry, you'll find parallels in the types of discussions, the ways that members interact with each other and with the brand, and the way in which BeautyTalk links customers to each other and to Sephora.

BeautyTalk is what our friend Sean O'Driscoll at PwC calls a "help and how-to community." You may think of how-to as limited to things like home improvement, but many products and services generate how-to questions. Communities and social networks, in turn, are great ways to connect customers so they get the how-to help they need. It's important here to recognize that successful communities are not defined by your motive as an organization, whether business or nonprofit, but rather by the needs and desires of the *participants* within these communities.

Brand Communities Are Everywhere

Everyone knows that passionate customers exist but companies often doubt that they have passionate customers of their own. In fact, brand-passionate customers are everywhere. This was first demonstrated in 2001 in a study conducted by Albert M. Muniz and Thomas C. O'Guinn, who added the term *brand community* to our lexicon. Muniz and O'Guinn randomly selected a small neighborhood in Bloomington, Illinois, to conduct their research, the goal of which was, in part, "to search for evidence of the existence" of brand communities.

Beginning with interviews in this neighborhood of 14 households, they discovered a rich set of affiliations with brands including Saab, Michelin, Ford, Apple, Zippo, Coca-Cola, and Star Trek. Their findings reveal how brand passion has become part of everyday life.

Participation Is Driven by Passion

Getting the activity focused on something larger than your brand, product, or service is critical to the successful development of social behavior within the customer or stakeholder base and as well within the firm or organization itself. After all, if narrowly defined business interests take center stage, if the social interaction is built purely around business objectives, then what will the customers of that business find useful? What's in it for them?

Further, how will the employees of that business rally around the needs of customers? At Southwest Airlines, *employees* are bound together in service of the customer, through a passionate belief that the freedom to fly ought to be within the grasp of anyone. So much so that when times are tough or situations demand it, the employees don the personas of Freedom Fighters and literally go to work on behalf of preserving the right to fly for their customers. As Freedom Fighters, they keep the characteristic Southwest energy up. This translates directly into the experiences that drive positive conversations about Southwest Airlines.

Being a Freedom Fighter is the kind of powerful ideal that unites businesses and customers and the kind of passion—for travel, exploration, or the ability to go out and conquer new markets as a business executive—that powers Southwest. It's the kind of passion around which a business traveler's community can be built.

While we focus here on networks and communities, in a more general sense customer experience management as a whole is built around your understanding of the passions and aspirations of your customers. What experiences do they want? What experiences will surprise and delight them? What will make their life easier, more productive, and more meaningful? Of these, which are most relevant to the realities and aspirations of your brand? If you can answer these questions, you can avoid the missteps that derail otherwise well-intentioned efforts. You'll have a community that will grow by organic interest generated by and between the participants themselves, rather than by high-cost advertising or promotional efforts.

In Search of a Higher Calling

The surest way to avoid this trap is to appeal to the core interests of your members—in other words, to anchor your initiatives in something larger than your brand, product, or service. Appeal to a higher calling, one that is carefully selected to both attract the customers you want to attract and provide a natural home or connection to your brand, product, or service.

Figure 3.1 shows the traditional business model: You make it, you tell your customers about it, and they (hopefully) buy it. Figure 3.1 is largely representative of the basic approach that has defined business for the past 50 years.

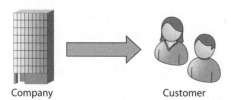

Company   Customer

Figure 3.1 Traditional business

This works well enough provided your product or service delivers as promised with little or no need for further dialogue. It helps too if it is marketed in a context where traditional media is useful and covers the majority of your market. Traditional media has wide reach, and it is made for commercial interruption. This provides a ready pathway to attentive customers and potential markets. The downside is that traditional media is also getting more and more expensive—TV advertising costs have increased over 250 percent in the past decade—and it's harder to reach your entire audience. What took three spots to achieve in 1965 now takes in excess of 100. Another problem is that some customers, like some members of the millennial generation, can't be reached at all by traditional media.

Figure 3.2 shows an evolved view of business and the beginning of a move away from a purely transactional view of the customer. The customer receives (or consumes) marketing messages, for example, and buys the product or service. But the customer's journey doesn't stop there. They go on to ask questions, share experiences, provide feedback, and share ideas, either directly with you or among their peers. The difference is that there is a feedback loop. Compliments and concerns can flow your way. Concerns, because they can be expressed, don't turn into frustrated rants—provided of course that something is done about them. Recall that this opportunity to listen and understand, and thereby craft a response, is a direct benefit of participation with customers, whether through traditional methods or as now, on the Social Web.

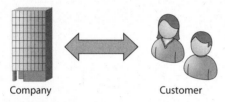

Company   Customer

Figure 3.2 Evolved business

Finally, Figure 3.3 shows the business-customer relationship when the idea of a higher calling is introduced. The higher calling forms a common bonding point for both the business or organization and the customers and stakeholders, in particular in the context of social participation with a business. To be sure, savvy marketers have tapped this best practice even through their traditional campaigns: At GSD&M Idea City, where author Dave worked with clients ranging from the Air Force to Chili's to Land Rover, Walmart, and AARP, brands were connected with customers through a shared value and purpose, something larger than the brand itself and to which both the brand and customer simultaneously aspired. This created a very powerful linkage that transcended the basic brand-consumer relationship. This same type of appeal to a common purpose or value that is larger than the brand itself can be applied in an analogous manner on the Social Web.

Social media takes this practice to the next level. Social media inherently revolves around passions, lifestyles, and aspirations—the higher calling that defines larger social objects to which participants relate. The social media programs that are intended to link customers to communities and shared social activities *around the business*, and thereby around the brand, product, or service, must themselves be anchored in this same larger ideal. Compare Figure 3.3 with Figures 3.1 and 3.2: Simple in concept, getting this larger social object identified and in place is critical to the successful realization of a social customer experience effort.

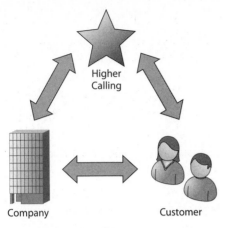

Figure 3.3 The higher calling

Here is an old-school example: Tupperware, and more specifically Tupperware parties. Having seen more than a few of these first-hand as a child, Dave recalls that Tupperware parties seemed to be little more than a dozen or so women getting together to spend a couple of hours laughing and talking about plastic tubs. Obviously, there was more to it: There was a higher purpose involved, a much higher purpose. Tupperware had tapped into the basic human need for socialization, and a Tupperware party provided the perfect occasion to link this need with its product line. The combination of great products and meeting its customers' human needs (social interchange) as well as their practical needs (efficient and organized food storage, the perennially favorable economics of left-overs, etc.) has helped Tupperware build a business as timeless and durable as the products it sells.

Personal transformation is another common higher calling. In the case of Sephora's BeautyTalk, members become more proficient at creating great looks for themselves and their friends. Similarly, in the Barclaycard Ring community presented in Chapter 2, "The Social Customer," members become more sophisticated at managing their use of credit, avoiding credit problems, and maintaining their financial security. The McDonald "Family Arches" social business effort helps members mother in an aspirational sense, feeding their kids nutritious foods even when they're on the go.

The list goes on. Personal transformation is an increasingly powerful trend on the Web at large: Think of the quantified-self movement—think "wearable devices that measure bodily functions"—where web-connected products like running shoes and iPhone apps help members track their achievements and share them with others in a community.

Look back at the brands and associated experiences just covered, ranging from selling products to creating experiences to creating a platform by which customers achieve their dreams. Is that powerful, or what? It is, and these are exactly the kinds of experiences you can add to your brand in support of your online presence.

$pend Your Way to a Social Presence

The appeal to a higher calling—to a lifestyle, passion, or aspiration—is what drives organic participation and growth in brand communities. The payoffs are more engagement, better engagement, and lower costs over time.

Why lower costs? Ask yourself: If you don't have a higher calling, what powers participation? If you lack the aspiration, passion, or lifestyle connection you see in communities like Barclarycard Ring and Sephora, how do you get people to join and engage?

The answer is typically spending. You invest in advertising and promotional efforts that generate attention and buzz. This is not to overlook the great creative work that goes into promotional campaigns but rather to note that spend-driven programs versus purpose or values-aligned programs often lag in the organic growth that powers social media and long-term activity on the Web. And, they cost more!

To understand why this is so, compare the social appeal of the Old Spice deodorant social media campaign shown in Figure 3.4 with the basic appeal of the brand communities we've discussed. The Old Spice campaign was part of television ad campaign created by ad agency Wieden+Kennedy and introduced during the 2010 Super Bowl. Following the event, the ad was viewed more than 3 million times on the Old Spice YouTube channel. To capitalize on the ad's success, Old Spice staged a 36-hour social media event in which questions posed by fans on Facebook, Twitter, and YouTube received responses in the form of videos featuring the star of the ad, Isaiah Mustafa. Old Spice posted more than 180 new videos to YouTube over the course of the event, directly in response to questions and comments from fans. The videos were viewed 5.9 million times and generated 22,500 comments from viewers.

Figure 3.4 Old Spice "The Man Your Man Could Smell Like" campaign

The Old Spice social media campaign included many of the same platforms that would be used in a social customer experience effort, including Twitter, Facebook, and YouTube. But attention and participation in efforts like this die out unless continually primed by more ads, promotions, and contests. From purely a traditional marketing and advertising standpoint, the campaign was a brilliant success. But while social, it's a very different thing than creating an ongoing, collaborative relationship with customers that grows, organically, over time. Here again, your business objectives are critical: If you are seeking current market awareness, then spending to build your social presence makes sense. But if you are after long-term, sustained participation, then ultimately you'll need to connect with members at a more fundamental level.

Three Levels of Social Activities

Jake McKee has created a nice articulation of the views on building a social presence advanced by Chris Brogan and others. Following this view, the activities that surround social media and social business can be thought of in three layers:

A Home Base

Your home brand or organizational home base consists of your website, related properties, and associated microsites.

Outposts

The outposts are the properties or sites that you do not own or control but in which you participate and create connections. Twitter, Facebook, and LinkedIn are examples of outposts. Importantly, brands can have an official presence in these outposts, which can be managed as a part of a larger, integrated marketing and business effort.

Passports

Passports are the places where you are invited or otherwise welcomed to participate: a guest blogging program or a blogger outreach program, for example. Note that you should disclose any connection between your participation and your business.

You can read more about the concepts and best practices around the use of a home base, brand outposts, and passports here:

www.chrisbrogan.com/a-simple-presence-framework

Truth is, you probably need a blend: In social customer channels participation and organic growth occur naturally. Promotion may be needed at launch, or when major additions or changes occur, but it's not required to drive daily activity. Great social efforts grow organically based on an individual's realization of a reason to be there: Members see the value in more members, so they actively encourage their friends to join. The obvious purpose and basic appeal of these sites combine to drive organic growth.

When charting your course in social customer experience, be sure that you distinguish between social media campaigns—like the Old Spice campaign—and social programs that more tightly link the personal aspirations, lifestyles, passions of customers with the business and its products and services, like Barclaycard, Sephora, or Autodesk. Social-media-based marketing efforts like the Old Spice campaign can drive awareness—and there is value in that. But social customer experience efforts develop long-term, ongoing relationships with customers, and there's compelling (and measurable) value to the brand in that, too.

Build Your Social Presence

Campaign-centric communities are *not* the focus of an SCEM program. If you find yourself thinking "campaign," you are heading for either social-media-based marketing or traditional/digital marketing that is made to look like social media. Beware: The focus of social customer experience—distinct from social media marketing—is on the application of the Social Web to business in ways that are driven fundamentally through organic versus paid processes and that are intended to benefit your business generally versus sell products specifically.

Organic communities and Social Web activities built around a business are designed to exist independently of marketing campaigns, with the possible exception of initial seeding. They are intended to inform the business, to connect it to its audience, to encourage collaboration between customers and employees toward the objective of improving the business, and to sustain this over time for the purpose of driving superior business results. The preference for organic growth rather than spend-driven growth is not to say that there is no value in spend-driven communities. Significant promotional value can arise out of measured fulfillment against marketing and advertising goals.

Instead, this preference arises out of the economic value of organic growth, as an alternative to paid growth. Social technology programs are centered on core business objectives and expressed through an appeal to the aspirations, lifestyles, passion, and of customers. These types of programs are specifically put in place to encourage collaborative participation. The collaboration that occurs between customers and between customers and employees is the root focus of SCEM.

Social Customer Experience Management: Elements

The following elements are helpful when considering an SCEM strategy. Taken together, and built around a central alignment between marketing and operations, they support an organic approach to the application of social technology to business. The chapters of this book that focus on each are also indicated.

Customers, Stakeholders, and Employees

Beginning with the conversations occurring on the Social Web, actively listening, responding, facilitating collaboration, and retaining customers are among the primary objectives of a successful social customer experience implementation. Chapter 5, "Social Technology and Business Decisions," Chapter 6, "Social Analytics, Metrics, and Measurement," and Chapter 7, "Five Key Trends," in Part II along with Chapter 8, "Customer Engagement," and Chapter 9, "Social CRM and Social Customer Experience," in Part III provide tips, best practices, and examples of how this is accomplished.

Communities and Networks

Built around a marriage between your products and services and the customer's aspirations, lifestyle, or passion, communities encourage deep, long-term engagement that results in collaboration and advocacy. Social networks, on the other hand, provide an entry point for customers who are not yet engaged with you or aren't deeply engaged as members of your community. Chapter 10, "Social Objects," and Chapter 11, "The Social Graph," provide insights and cases supporting the development of strong communities and social network efforts.

Social Applications

Social applications are the components of a social customer experience implementation that connect participants within existing communities or networks to which they belong. Social applications deliver on a specific need or utility, for example, an ideation application in an on-domain community, or a photo-sharing app like Instagram off-domain. Chapter 12, "Social Applications," provides a deeper dive into social applications and how to plan your use of them.

Figure 3.5 shows the fundamental relationship between experiences that are talked about (word of mouth), community participation, and the function of the brand outpost. Unlike social media marketing, the application of the Social Web to the business itself views the participants as an integral component of the business, rather than simply participants in a campaign. In this context, the naturally occurring (nonpaid) activities of participants are the most valuable. The design of the social business components is powered by the activities that are sustained through participant-driven interest.

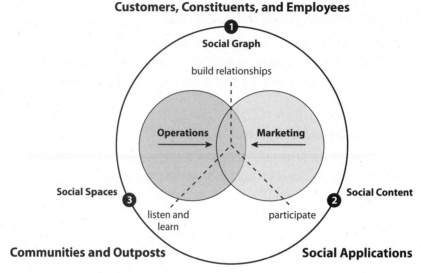

Customers, Constituents, and Employees

Social Graph

build relationships

Operations → ← Marketing

Social Spaces ❸ — listen and learn — participate — ❷ Social Content

Communities and Outposts   **Social Applications**

Figure 3.5 The social business

Your Business as a Social Trigger

People gather around a shared aspiration, lifestyle, or passion in pursuit of a sense of collective experience. As the early research into brand communities showed, these people are often motivated by a desire to talk about a brand, product, or service experience with each other, relating this to what they have in common. What they have in common may in part be that brand, product, or service, but it is generally also something deeper. Apple products—and the customer following they have created—are a great example of this: Apple owners are seemingly connected *to each other* by Apple products, and in a deeper sense they are also connected by the ethos of Apple and the smart, creative lifestyle associated with the brand.

For LEGO enthusiasts—and in particular adult LEGO enthusiasts—there is a gathering that occurs on LEGO's owned (more technically referred to as "on-domain") community along with a variety of other fan-created websites, forums, and blogs such as LUGNET.com. Conversations appear to revolve around LEGO products, but in reality the higher calling is the shared passion for creation, which LEGO (as a product) facilitates. While LEGO creation may bring members to the community, and while it may be the common thread that unites a seemingly disparate group, the camaraderie is what keeps members together year after year.

A business or organization is itself in many respects a social place. In much the same way, the social business is a place where employees and customers gather together around a common purpose of creating the products and services that define—and are often subsequently defined by—the brand and its higher purpose. Employees and customers, together through collaboration, create the experiences they want. Together they are responsible for the business. When the conversations that result are a reflection of this shared interest of both customers and employees, the conversations themselves are very likely to be powerful expressions that carry the business or organization forward.

This kind of end result—an expressed passion around a brand, product, or service—is associated with the higher stages of engagement. Beyond consumption of content, the activities leading to advocacy are engagement in the form of curation, creation of content, and collaboration between participants.

LEGO.com and LUGNET.com

Organizations often think, "I'd like to create a place for customers to engage, but it's already happening—over there." Don't let the presence of a vibrant, third-party community or network deter you from creating your own. In reality, third-party efforts often help support similar brand efforts, and vice versa. For a great example of this, check out LEGO's communities. You'll find them here:

```
http://lugnet.com/

http://community.lego.com/
```

Brand Outposts

Communities like those referenced from LEGO and Sephora are an important part of these companies' SCEM strategies. Because they are part of the brands' own websites—on-domain—the brand has the ability to craft the experience exactly as they want, to manage it effectively, and to measure the results very precisely.

As a result of the growth in social activities on the Web there is a natural expectation on the part of consumers to find the brands they love in the social sites they frequent. As a matter of course, customers expect this kind of presence and participation off-domain as well. So in addition to the branded community efforts just described, an alternative (or complementary) approach to connecting a brand or organization with an *existing* community also exists: the creation of a *brand presence*—known as a brand outpost—within an established social network or online community such as a Facebook business page, a Twitter account, or a YouTube channel, to list just a few.

In creating a brand outpost—in comparison to an on-domain community—there need not be any reason other than the expectation for the brand to be present and a tie back to business objectives that are served by such a presence. There does, of course, need to be a relevant contribution by the brand, product, or service *to the network or community it wishes to join*. Simply posting TV commercials to YouTube is in most cases not going to produce engagement beyond the firm's own employees and perhaps their families watching these commercials. New content created for YouTube—for example, the videos that Freescale encourages its employees to post—is the kind of content that is both welcomed and appreciated, since it is created specifically for this venue and with a social objective in mind.

Members expect to find their favorite brands on their favorite social networks. Sometimes this means bringing functionality from the website out to the social network. For example, Aircel, an Indian telecom provider, created a Facebook application that gives Aircel customers the ability to recharge—in this case, meaning to add minutes to their prepaid plans. The Aircel recharge application is shown in Figure 3.6.

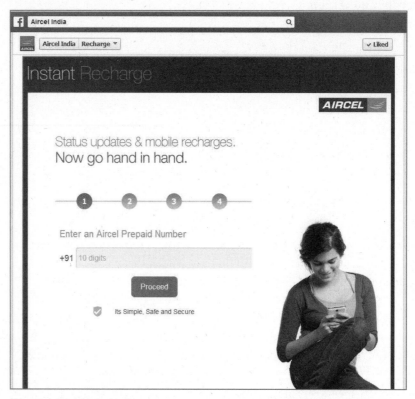

Figure 3.6 Aircel: Facebook recharge

More often, however, companies are bringing live engagement rather than just functionality. Citing its own business objectives around improving customer service and customer satisfaction, Australia's Telstra uses its Twitter presence (@telstra) to answer customer questions. Telstra did this partly out of recognition that Twitter is a burgeoning customer service channel and partly because—as is the case with Facebook and other leading social networks—its own customers expect it to be there. The Twitter account is part of Telstra's crowd support efforts, which also include on-domain elements such as product reviews, support forums, and an idea exchange.

Presence in existing social networks is welcomed because it makes sense from the perspective of consumers. Most brands are present in all of the other places where people spend time: on TV, on the radio, in movies (before the show and integrated into it), in all forms of outdoor advertising, and at sports events and more. Social sites—the new gathering place—are no exception. Movie studios, soft drink brands, auto manufacturers, and more are all building brand outposts on Facebook and other social sites because their audience spends significant time on those sites. Many of the brands and organizations participating in the Social Web are coincidentally skipping the development of dedicated product microsites and even major TV brand campaigns in favor of a stronger presence in these social sites.

As a part of your overall social business strategy, don't overlook the obvious: Facebook, Google+, Twitter, LinkedIn, Pinterest, and SlideShare. All offer places where your business or organization can add value to the larger social communities that naturally form around these social sites.

SCEM and Measurement

Concerns about the measurability of social efforts and the benefits thereof are somewhat paradoxical. In fact, the migration to the Web has made business far more measureable than ever before, and social is no different. Chapter 6 explores measurement and metrics in depth. As an initial step into the integration of metrics within your SCEM programs, however—and to get you thinking about this aspect of undertaking a social business effort—consider measuring conversion and participation.

Conversion

Conversion is a concept often left to ecommerce specialists, but it's relevant to every social business and Social Web effort. Think of the kinds of conversion you need to achieve to make your social efforts successful:

- Target audience to visitors
- Visitors to return visitors
- Visitors to contributors
- Participants to repeat contributors

Conversion doesn't end there. You may want to convert contributors to different types of contributions: from forum answers to product ideas, from text comments to video, from contributing content to curating. Further, there are probably conversion events outside your social channels that you want to encourage as well: conversion to a purchase, membership in a loyalty program, subscription to marketing email lists, and so forth. Adopting the language of conversion can help you convey progress and value to your stakeholders. Your boss may not know why a page view matters, but every businessperson understands conversion.

Participation

Participation is one of the easiest things to capture and track. Comments, replies, new topics, reviews, ratings, and so forth—every contribution represents active participation. Individually, they indicate what each user values and wants to do. Collectively, they can be used to assess the overall levels of interest and activity within the community or network.

Foursquare—Gaming Drives Participation

Foursquare is a location-based service that provides users with tips left by others when they check in at a specific location. To help spur participation, Foursquare uses a game-like point system—which itself is a useful metric for the Foursquare development team—that directly rewards participants for checking in, adding new venues, and leaving tips about venues, which are exactly the activities that increase value for the Foursquare community. Location-based tagging is increasingly part of many social applications on the Web. A Pew Internet research study in October 2013 found that 30 percent of Internet users have at least one of their social media accounts set to automatically tag their posts with current location.

http://foursquare.com

There are also measures of what is sometimes called passive participation. A visit to the community that does not involve a contribution is still a useful metric. Similarly, metrics like unique visitors, page views, video views, or topic views can help you understand what is of greatest interest to your members. Given that most members at any given time are participating passively, one could argue that passive metrics are in fact the most important starting point for understanding the value your social efforts are creating.

Reputation systems are designed to incent participation, but they are also a great way to measure participation. Participants in on-domain communities, for example, are often rewarded through increasing social rank based on contribution to the community. Upon joining, you may be assigned the rank of visitor and then over time earn your way to expert status as you contribute content and earn positive ratings from other members. Behind the scenes, the platform is calculating your rank based on a formula defined by the community manager. Related metrics include the following:

- Number of members who have achieved top ranks
- Percentage of members who have achieved top ranks
- Percentage of content contributed by top-ranked users
- Percentage of top-ranked users who have participated in the past 30 days (retention)

If the reputation system includes badges, medals, points, or other rewards, you might measure and report them similarly to the way you measure and report rankings.

In addition to reputation, there is an equally important related concept: distribution. Companies active on the Social Web need to understand not only who is influential or has ranked up in the eyes of fellow community members but also how these members and others in the community are distributed. Here's an example: Suppose a certain thread in your support forum collects 100 contributions. It's important to understand the makeup in the origin of these comments; did you get 10 posts each from 10 people or 100 posts from a single user?

Community participation, like participation in social groups offline, is typically not equally distributed. As noted in Chapter 1, "Social Media and Customer Engagement," the general principle known as 90-9-1 is often invoked to convey the idea of participation inequality in communities: At any given time, 90 percent are merely browsing, 9 percent are participating casually, and 1 percent are participating frequently. The 1 percent are often referred to as "superusers" or "superfans."

Community managers and the organizations they work for often conclude that a more equal distribution would be better: Wouldn't it be better to have most people participating modestly than to have some people participating a lot and most people not participating at all? But do you even know how participation in your community is divided? And more important, how does this relate to your underlying business objectives and the objectives of your customers? In reality, the numbers rarely break down exactly in this proportion, but to be sure participation is almost always unequal. Keep this in mind as it's something you should measure.

The Gini Coefficient

Developed in the early 1900s as a statistically sound measure of distribution, the technique has been applied to the problem of understanding participation in a social community context by Lithium chief scientist Dr. Michael Wu.

http://en.wikipedia.org/wiki/Gini_coefficient

For more about Dr. Wu's work on the distribution of participation in social communities, use this suggested search term: "Gini coefficient participation Dr. Wu."

Or visit the following link:

http://lithosphere.lithium.com/t5/science-of-social-blog/The-Economics-of-90-9-1-The-Gini-Coefficient-with-Cross/ba-p/5466

Like other social measures, there are more advanced and technically grounded approaches to understanding who is participating and how participation is distributed: Lithium Chief Scientist Michael Wu has used a statistical concept called the Gini coefficient to quantify participation inequality. Analyzing communities in the Lithium database of enterprise communities—the largest such database in the world—Dr. Wu has uncovered some interesting insights, among them that communities consisting of business customers are much less unequal than communities of consumers.

If you'd like to use the Gini coefficient for yourself, social media strategist Bud Caddell has outlined a very straightforward way of doing so. While his method assumes the presence of a point system, you can just as easily use a simple metric such as posts or comments for doing the calculation yourself. Using this method, you can measure very precisely the progress you are making in creating a community that is less unequal—and therefore more representative—over time.

Measure Relative Participation

Bud Caddell's insightful measurement technique for assessing inequality of participation not only is useful but also shows the ways in which existing, well-understood statistical techniques can be applied to behavioral analysis when setting up measures of participation for your online community. You can follow Bud on Twitter: @Bud_Caddell.

www.seomoz.org/ugc/measuring-participation-inequality-in-social-networks

Business Value

Except for sales conversions, none of the metrics we've discussed are direct measures of business value. Some may therefore suggest these metrics be disregarded, that they are soft or squishy metrics. Measure return on investment, they say, not posts or registrations!

"Measure ROI" is a certainly a great rallying cry, but that said, it also misses an important point: Just as there is a role for ROI, there is a role for indicators of conditions that lead to ROI. "Measure (only) ROI" is comparable to telling a manufacturer "Don't measure output from your assembly line! Measure sales!" Most manufacturers know better: After all, if the assembly line stops, you can't have sales because you have nothing to sell.

Similarly, companies with successful SCEM programs have found that customers who engage in the brand's social channels will buy more, buy more often, and remain customers longer than customers who don't. They know that getting customers to engage is a process that creates better relationships, more satisfaction, and more sales over time. They measure their ROI, yes. But they also measure the engagement that makes ROI possible.

Other Measures

In addition to the measures of *what* is happening within the community or brand outpost, *where* the activities are occurring also lends itself to measurement.

Relationships themselves are worth tracking. To what extent is a community driving the creation of relationships? How many are being formed and between which community members? This can be understood by tracking the number of unidirectional (think following on Twitter) relationships as well the number of mutually affirmed friendships or other similar connections that exist. Add to this the relative number of communications that flow between mutually connected users to create a measure of the importance of relationships in day-to-day activities.

Outposts and communities—the places where brand-enabled social activity happens—are a source of quantitative data that leads to an assessment of value. Within these social spaces, tracking the number of member versus nonmember interactions (if the latter are permitted), the number of times members log in, and membership abandonment (for example, members who have not logged in for 90 days or more) all provide a basis to understand—quantitatively—what is happening inside social communities and by extension with the organizations that implement social-media-based business programs.

Chapter 6 provides an in-depth treatment of these and additional metrics. As you work through the next sections, keep these initial measurement techniques and sources of data in mind. Rest assured that when you're implementing social computing and social media techniques as a part of a business strategy, the outcomes can most certainly be held to quantitative performance standards.

The Essential Role of the Employee

Ultimately, getting SCEM right depends on more than understanding what your customers or stakeholders are talking about and how that relates to your firm. It depends as well on connecting your employees into the social processes. For example, the insights collected from social channels may be routed to and applied in marketing, to operations areas like customer support, or to other departments *within* the organization where it can be acted on.

The final link in the chain—and remember the conversation about ordering internal versus external efforts at the opening of this chapter—is therefore to connect employees (organizational participants in the more general sense) to each other and into the flow of customer information. This completes the customer collaboration cycle, shown in Figure 3.7, and enables the business to capitalize on the implementation and use of social technologies.

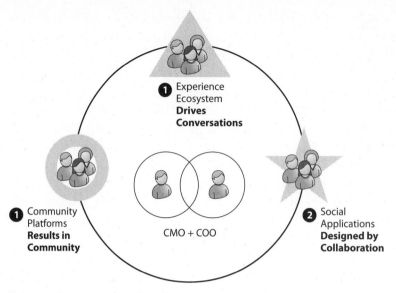

Figure 3.7 The customer collaboration cycle

Empower an Organization

Consider the following scenario: Imagine that your employer is a major hospital chain. Clearly, this is a complex business and one that customers readily talk about. Health care in a sense is one of the "this was made for social" business verticals: It cries out for the application of social technology.

Taking off on social media marketing, imagine that you are in the marketing group—perhaps you are a CMO, a VP of marketing, or a director of communications or PR or advertising for a community hospital. You're reading through social media listening reports, and you find conversations from a new mother that reflects a genuine appreciation for the care and attention she received during the birth of her child. You also find some pictures uploaded by the people who attended the opening of your newest community health care center. Along with that you find other conversations, some expressing dissatisfaction with high costs, unexplained charges, a feeling of disempowerment—in short, all of those things outside of the actual delivery of quality health care that make patients and their families nuts.

In health care, or any other business vertical for that matter, what you're discovering is the routine mix of conversations that typify social media. So you get interested, and you begin monitoring Twitter in real time, using a free tool like TweetDeck. One day you notice that a patient and her husband have checked in: They seem to like your hospital, as you note in the tweets you see in real time via TweetDeck as they enter your hospital. By the way, this is an entirely reasonable scenario (and in fact actually happens). When Dave flies on United, he routinely posts to @United on Twitter—as often to ask a question as to simply say thanks for a great experience—and very often hears back soon after. People do exactly the same thing when they enter a hospital and many other business establishments. Remember that if a mobile phone works on the premises, so do Twitter, Facebook, and Foursquare.

A few more tweets from your newly arrived patient and spouse pop through as they head from your hospital check-in to the waiting area and finally to pre-op. And then you see the following actual tweet, posted from inside your hospital, shown in Figure 3.8.

Figure 3.8 An actual hospital tweet: What would *you* do?

Looking at Figure 3.8, if you saw this tweet, in real time, what would you do? By clicking into the profile data on Twitter and then searching your current admittance records, you could probably locate the person who sent it inside your hospital in minutes. Would you do that, or would you let the opportunity to make a difference in someone's life, right now, just slip away?

It's these kinds of postings that take social business to a new level. Beyond outbound or social presence marketing, social business demands that you think through the process changes required within your organization to respond to the actual tweet shown in Figure 3.8. It's an incredible opportunity that is literally calling out to you. Don't let it slip away, which in the case above is what happened. That is not only an opportunity lost but a negative story of its own that now circulates on the Social Web.

The conversations that form and circulate on the Social Web matter to your business, obviously through the external circulation they enjoy and the impact they have on customers and potential customers as a result. But they also have a potential impact inside your organization: Each of these conversations potentially carries an idea that you may consider for application within your organization, to an existing business process, a training program, or the development of delight-oriented key performance indicators (KPIs). You are discovering the things that drive your customers in significant numbers to the Social Web, where they engage others in conversations around the experiences they have with your brand, product, or service. As such, these would be considered talk worthy, and if you were to tap the ideas directly and incorporate them into your business, you'd be onto something. You are exploring the conversations that indicate a path to improvement and to competitive advantage, but only if you can see the way to get there.

Too often, though, instead of taking notes, marketers sit there frozen in panic. As a marketer, *what are you going to do* in response to posts like that of Figure 3.8?

Your hospital Facebook page, your New Parents discussion forum, and your connection to the community through Twitter are of basically no help in this situation. Marketing outreach through social channels is designed to connect customers to your business and to give you a voice alongside theirs, a point of participation, in the conversations on the Social Web. All great benefits, they are certainly the core of a social media marketing program. Problem is, you've already done this. Yet the challenging conversations—and opportunities lost—continue.

Distinctly separate from social media marketing, the challenge facing marketers in health care and near any other consumer-facing business, B2B firm, or nonprofit is not one of understanding or being part of the conversations—something already covered through your adoption of social media analytics to follow conversations as they occur. Rather, the challenge is *taking action* based on what customers are saying and then bringing a solution to them to close the loop. The challenge here is getting to the root cause of the conversation and rallying the entire organization around addressing it. That's why the panic sets in, and that's what makes social business so hard.

It's at this point that social media marketing stops and social customer experience begins. Going back to the health care example, billing systems, in-room care standards, and access to personal health care records all require *policy changes*, not a marketing program. Hospital marketers are certainly part of the solution, but only a *part*. Social customer experience extends across the entire organization and typically requires the involvement of the C-suite or equivalent senior management team. Connecting employees, tapping knowledge across departments, and conceiving and implementing holistic solutions to systemic challenges is difficult. What is needed is a methodology that can be consistently applied. Touchpoint analysis—discussed in more detail in Chapter 5 is extremely useful in this regard. Touchpoint analysis helps pinpoint the root causes of customer satisfaction as well as dissatisfaction. Social customer experience takes off from this.

In short, connecting employees in ways that encourage knowledge sharing converts whole teams from "I can't do this in my department" paralysis into "As a collaborative business, we can solve this." It allows employees to more fully leverage learning, by being aware of what is going on all around them in the business and in the marketplace. Customers are often more than willing to share their ideas, needs, and suggestions and even to put forth effort. The problem is, as the "Knowledge Assimilation" sidebar shows, most organizations aren't set up to hear it. Some are actually built—or so it seems—to outright *suppress* it.

If the degree to which businesses fail to assimilate knowledge is even close to what Socialtext CEO Ross Mayfield has noted in his blog—that only about 1 percent of all customer conversations result in new organizational knowledge while 90 percent of the conversations never even reach the business—the actual loss through missed opportunities to innovate and address customer issues is huge. Turned around, if only a small gain in knowledge sharing and assimilation were made—if every tenth rather than every hundredth customer (the current assessment of typical practices) who offered up an idea was actually heard and understood and welcomed into the organization as a contributing member—the change in workplace and marketplace dynamics would be profound. In a practical sense, you'd have uncovered a source of real competitive advantage. As noted in a previous chapter, Starbucks has been implementing, on average, two customer-driven innovations per week since 2008. Take a look at its stock price over that period and ask yourself if these are perhaps related.

This is exactly what is happening with the ideation tools used by an increasing number of businesses and nonprofit organizations. Tapping customers directly, and visibly involving them in the collaborative process of improving and evolving products and services, is taking hold. Chapter 12 treats ideation and its use in business in detail.

Knowledge Assimilation

Ross Mayfield, founder and CEO of Socialtext, a social collaboration platform for businesses, presents his adaptation of the 90-9-1 rule as follows:

- One percent of customer conversations are assimilated as organizational knowledge.

- Nine percent of customer conversations touch the organization, but no learning occurs.

- Ninety percent of customer conversations *never touch the organization*.

This data is excerpted from Greg Oxton at the Consortium for Service Innovation (CSI). You can review the entire blog post here:

```
http://ross.typepad.com/blog/2009/08/crm-iceberg.html
```

Employees in Customer Communities

It's funny to recall that in the dawn of enterprise communities, the conventional wisdom was that employees should *not* participate. In fact, businesses were taught that their customers didn't want to see them show up. The community belongs to the customer, they were told; stay out. Companies even created customer online communities under completely new brand names, thus beginning their voyage into the new world of social by casting their most valuable asset—their brand—overboard!

Fortunately, businesses learned over time that the customer not only wanted them to show up—they expected it. And so they tentatively began to join in the conversation. In how-to communities employees provided advice that no one else could supply—after all, they made the products! In marketing channels, employees supplied the latest news on new products and services, guided by social media policies appropriately created and delivered within the organization by the legal and finance groups, working with HR. Slowly, companies began to find their role—and a role for their employees—in the new social world.

Then, Twitter arrived. Early adopters like Comcast showed that responding to customers online could generate real customer delight and earn the brand enormous goodwill. Hundreds of companies followed. Social support became not just customers helping customers in communities but company agents helping customers on off-domain social channels. Suddenly, companies are participating everywhere. If this were a movie, it would be called *Return of the Company*!

Amid the flood of new participation—most of it needed, much of it very good—has come a new awareness that employee participation online needs to be well managed.

Clear Policies

Most companies today have a social media policy. This policy provides guidance to employees on what they may say online in their role as company employees. The purpose of the document is two-fold: to protect the brand from damage that may result from inappropriate or unauthorized activities undertaken by employees online and to protect employees by making them aware of the risks of online blunders.

Social media policies generally do not address the challenges faced by employees whose jobs involve regular participation online on behalf of the company. When the decision is made to participate, many questions arise:

- *Where should we participate?* On our home base (on domain) only? On social outposts like Facebook and Twitter, and if so, on which ones? Or on passport sites as well? And which regions of the world? Most companies are selective, understanding that each channel or region can represent a significant commitment.

- *When should we participate?* During business hours or 24/7? Immediately or after peers have had the chance to chime in? On all topics or just on topics only we can answer? Participation sets expectations; you need to make sure you can maintain any presence you establish.

- *Who should participate?* Can our customer support agents simply add social participation to their duties? If so, will they need additional training? What about our product experts? What about employees who have the knowledge and are eager to help, even on their own time? Most companies require training for any employee who wants to participate under the company's brand online.

Rules like these help companies create an experience online that customers can depend on, every time.

Specific Business Objectives

The final step in connecting employees to your SCEM program is ensuring clarity around business objectives. Understand what you hope to accomplish by participating and how you will measure whether participation has been successful.

Social efforts sometimes suffer from the "everyone else is doing it, and so I should do it too" syndrome. Advice to better define business objectives is often brushed off in the rush to deploy in Internet time. Inevitably, however, the day arrives when the investment must be justified, usually by measuring the return. A hunt ensues for ways to measure impact—any impact.

The objectives of participating online should be well defined ahead of time. Joe, whose past life in management research included a significant study of leadership development practices at companies including Levi Strauss and Royal Dutch Shell, likes to say that while great leadership can be difficult to define, there's one thing leadership is not. Leadership is not a boss who comes to his subordinates in a panic and says, "Quick! We have to justify why we're doing this!" Before undertaking any new effort, ensure that it is grounded in your stated, agreed-to business objectives.

Review and Hands-On

This chapter covered the concepts of social customer experience management (SCEM) and some of the demands it places on an organization. This chapter sets a foundation for the processes, cases, and specific solutions covered in detail in upcoming chapters in Part III, "Social Customer Experience Building Blocks." For now, focus on how your customers and employees use social media today, and ask yourself, "Where are our best opportunities for connecting customers in networks and communities? What will it take on the company's part to make this happen?" Digging into these questions will lead right into the remaining chapters.

Review of the Main Points

This chapter provided an overview of the considerations when moving toward SCEM. In particular, this chapter covered the following:

- SCEM is a natural extension of the customer experience movement, recognizing that social technologies have fundamentally changed the way customers experience brands and products.

- SCEM requires that companies view customer relationships as two-way, collaborative conversations that are broader than just the brand or its products.

- Social media marketing and the activities associated with social business are fundamentally measurable. Because the activities are expressed digitally, integrating social media analytics with internal business metrics produces useful, valuable insights that can guide product and service development efforts.

- Your employees have a major role to play in the success of your SCEM efforts, by embracing collaboration both with customers and among themselves.

With the basics of social business defined, you're ready to begin thinking through what this might look like in your own organization and how connecting your own working team with customers through collaborative technologies can speed and refine your business processes that support innovation, product and service delivery, and similar talk-worthy programs.

Hands-On: Review These Resources

Review each of the following, taking note of the main points covered in the chapter and the ways in which the following activities demonstrate these points:

- The Temkin Group website, including the Customer Experience Matters blog

  www.temkingroup.com/

- Michael Wu's books, *The Science of Social* and *The Science of Social 2*

  http://pages.lithium.com/science-of-social

  http://pages.lithium.com/science-of-social-2.html

- Chris Brogan's A Simple Presence Framework, which we adapted for this book

  www.chrisbrogan.com/a-simple-presence-framework/

- Consortium for Service Innovation website, how the practice of customer service is changing

  www.serviceinnovation.org/

Hands-On: Apply What You've Learned

Apply what you've learned in this chapter through the following exercises:

1. Arrange a meeting with senior executives in your organization to talk about their views on collaborating with customers.

2. Create an inventory of your current social media programs. List home bases, outposts, and passports (see the "Three Levels of Social Activities" sidebar earlier in this chapter for definitions of each) and then define the metrics and success measures for each.

3. Meet with the leadership of your customer service and product design teams, and meet with legal and HR to review the requirements or concerns about connecting employees more collaboratively or engaging more fully on the Social Web.

The Social Customer Experience Ecosystem

This chapter concludes Part I and the introduction to social technology and its impact on customer experience. It pulls together the elements of the social customer experience ecosystem—profiles, applications, communities and forums, and more—and thereby provides the basis for understanding how to connect current and potential customers with the inner workings of your business or organization, where collaborative processes can drive long-term benefits.

Chapter contents:

Social identities and profiles
Social applications
Social channels
Brand outposts and communities
The social ecosystem

Social Identities and Profiles

At the center of the Social Web and the shared activities that define it are the online *identities* of participants. Participants reveal their identities directly, by selecting usernames or populating profiles. They also express them indirectly, through the facts, experiences, and opinions they share. Observing and analyzing these identities is key to creating an effective social customer experience.

Not too long ago, when contributing anything online, people used pseudonyms. This was due, in part, to system limitations; usernames typically consisted of a single word, not a first name and a last name. Even if you were satisfied compressing your first name and last name into a single unit, character limits often prevented it. Concerns about privacy also drove the use of pseudonyms. After all, the Internet for the first time allowed an individual to create something that could potentially be seen by millions of people. Before then, only media companies had that power. People no doubt regarded their new power with some degree of caution.

Until the mid-2000s, the popular online social sites drew members, true enough, but those members were identified all too often with names—or handles—like blueangel12 or lotusflower. Then came social networks like Facebook. On Facebook and similar networks built around real identities people used their actual names. And that changed everything.

Facebook began as a way to share content—and hence experiences—with people you already knew: your classmates. As adoption spread, Facebook allowed members to add friends, family, and co-workers. The networks were private, limited to the people you chose and those who chose you. In that context, using your own name was obvious. And as a result, this collection of private networks grew very large—larger, in fact, than any social sites had ever become.

The arrival of massive real-name networks in a heretofore almost exclusively pseudonymous online world attracted surprisingly little comment among Internet watchers in media and academia. Those who did comment merely noted that real names might bring more civility to online discussions because participants would no longer be able to hide behind a masked identity.

From the perspective of social customer experience, however, the change is much more profound. Businesses could, as a result, identify their customers online and so could deliver more relevant offers and service to those customers. Just as important, they could identify those who are not their customers and begin to build relationships with them too. Real names presented an opportunity to bring the power of CRM to the Web, which must, by necessity, begin with a real identity.

Still, although hundreds of millions of people still interact using pseudonyms online every day, current trends suggest that real-name participation will continue to spread, well beyond the private, semi-private, or ambiguously public-private places that networks like Facebook have become. Consider Twitter, for example, where even those who choose non-real-name handles typically also provide their real name in their profile and often a photo as well. Sharing your real identity is part of the online social experience.

Speaking of profiles, while usernames and identity are in flux, there's no such confusion about profiles. Profiles are where people display the personal information they choose to share with others. Profiles include information such as name, city of residence, hometown, employer, personal interests, hobbies, and favorite brands and products. Often, they also display, in an activity feed, the user's most recent contributions or actions on the Social Web. Today's profiles give individuals plenty of control over who sees what on their profile. Though detailed personal information is (still) generally not available except to trusted friends or colleagues, almost any profile provides a business with a basis for understanding who is actually participating and thereby potentially connecting that person to your business.

The existence of user identities—whether a simple username or a rich profile—is, in this sense, what differentiates social platforms and applications from everything else on the Web. Other websites can still be interactive, of course, but the interaction is between the application and the user: navigate to a file, download a PDF, or place an item in a shopping cart. In each of these, the primary activity occurs between a user and an application and is designed to facilitate a specific task. Identity—beyond basic security or commerce validation requirements—is of relatively little importance in this context. Because the individual participant is steering the entire process and because this is typically a task-oriented transaction, the identity of the participant matters little.

In a social context, by comparison, the interaction occurs between the participants as much or more than it does (overtly) between a specific participant and the application or platform. In fact, the less the software gets in the way, the better.

The Profile as a Social Connector

The role of the social profile as a *connector* cannot be understated in business applications of social media. Following on the prior discussion, the social profile provides two essential social elements:

- A tangible personal identifier around which a relationship can be formed
- A framework for accountability for one's actions, postings, and roles taken in the relationship that forms

Taken together, the significance of the profile is its central role in establishing *who* is participating. In any relationship, the more knowledge you have about a person, the more likely you are to trust and share. For businesses, it's even more critical. By connecting a business with its customers—or a nonprofit with its members or supporters—social profiles form the basis for an accountable, productive relationship.

Profiles on social networks function somewhat differently from profiles on more specifically focused communities. Social networks are people-centric: The profile is therefore a critical element. Communities are content-centric: People become known by what they contribute. Accordingly, profiles have a more limited role in communities than they have in social networks. In social networks, people tend to share their tastes and preferences; in communities, the profile is mostly an activity feed. In communities, few people take the time to complete optional fields or upload pictures. So much so that, a few years ago, when community platform provider Telligent introduced a design that highlighted photos of users, sites were covered by the gray silhouettes that stand in for real photos rather than the colorful portraits Telligent had assumed would be posted. One user waggishly commented, "What's with the ghosts? Halloween is over."

Of course Telligent wasn't wrong—just early. Photos of actual members are now common on social networks. The shifts in member behavior being driven by social networks are making their way into communities too. Just as real names are showing up more and more often, profiles with real data are starting to receive more attention.

Corporate Blogs and Identity

The connection between companies and their customers is not about loyalty to a logo. It's about a personal connection to the people behind the brand. Among social applications, blogs are uniquely suited to the voice of an individual, which is why they have assumed such an important role today.

At the center of the relationship with a reader is the identity of the writer: When humans read something, they imagine that some*one*—not some*thing*—wrote it. They connect with that person, so it's important that the personality and voice be both genuine and consistent.

For these reasons, a generally recommendation is that corporate blogs be written by company employees rather than by an outside agency. Ask yourself: Who would you rather build a relationship with around a product or service, the CEO or head of customer service or a project engineer. . .or someone at the firm's public relations agency? Understanding what the firm is doing—the kinds of things you can learn by reading the PR communications, for example—is worthwhile. At the same time, if you want to engage the business when suggesting an alternative product or service policy, it is more satisfying to do it through a direct link to the company rather than through its agent.

When weighing the cost of direct participation against the value of the relationships created, management and representation of the corporate identity are worth more than passing thought.

Premiere Global: A Practical Example of Profiles

Dave witnessed the demand for and value of real identity in his work with Atlanta-based Premiere Global (PGi) on the implementation of a community for developers working with PGi's API suite. The community was intended to bring independent developers and internal PGi experts together in a collaborative venue that would spur the development of new and innovative communications applications.

The PGiConnect Developers Community, shown in Figure 4.1, was built on the Jive Software community platform.

Implemented for PGi by Austin's FG SQUARED, Jive's toolset could have been used right out of the box. One of the advantages of building on a platform like Jive, rather than developing a custom application, is the speed with which a fully functional community can be launched. But PGi saw the need for something Jive didn't have. They were convinced that profiles could be a powerful force for bringing developers together. But they also knew that most community members never bother to complete the optional fields. Taking a page from LinkedIn, PGi's digital agency had an idea: If they made profile updating easier and more obvious, they'd probably get more completed profiles. FG SQUARED developed a customer profile component for use with the Jive core toolset to do just that. Now when users visit the community, they get a quick indication of "what to do next" to help them move to the next level of completeness. In a nod to customer-driven improvement, Jive now includes this capability in its platform.

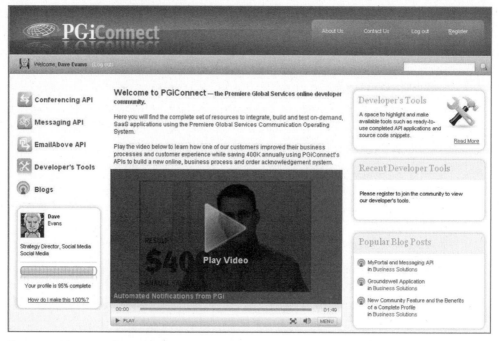

Figure 4.1 PGiConnect: profile completeness

The Profile and the Social Graph

Recall the discussion of the social graph in Chapter 2, "The Social Customer." Looking ahead, Chapter 11, "The Social Graph," provides an in-depth treatment. For now, understand that the social graph includes the set of profiles that describe the members of a social network and the interactions, activities, and relationships that connect specific profiles on the Social Web. In perhaps the simplest view, the social graph defines the way one profile is connected to another, through a friendship relationship or membership in a group. Because the profile itself is tied to a person—however vaguely that profile may have been defined—there is a sense of accountability and belonging that translates into shared responsibility between those so connected. This relationship might be highly asymmetric: Blogger Robert Scoble's individual fans may get more from him, as he is both an aggregator and an originator, than he gets from any *one* of them. Nonetheless, there is a set of rules and expectations that define these relationships and in doing so set up the value-based transaction and knowledge exchange that ultimately occurs between participants on the Social Web.

Understanding the construction of the social graph in the context of the profiles (people) collecting around your brand is essential in creating an organic social presence. Go back to the core challenge of effective participation on the Social Web: How do you participate without being branded as self-interested *only*? Your firm or organization needs to assert its relevance and then deliver through utility, emotion, or gained knowledge some sort of tangible value if it is to develop a strong bond with your customers that outlasts contests, advertising spending, and other direct incentives aimed at driving early involvement with the online social presence of the brand, product, or service.

What are the first steps in developing a social presence where this can happen? You go where your customers are, communities such as LinkedIn or Facebook, and create *an appropriate* place within them for your business or organization. As you work your way into these communities you'll discover (or confirm) what or where you can add value. By participating, actively listening, and understanding and tracking influencers, you'll see the relationships, interactions, and needs that exist within the community and intersect with the value proposition of your business or organization. That is your entry point and one on which you can build your presence.

Social Applications

In Chapter 2 we discussed the four basic building blocks of engagement: consumption, curation, creation, and collaboration. How do these processes happen online? They happen through *social applications*.

Whether a social network like Facebook or an online community like Autodesk's, every social site is a collection of applications that allow users to interact and share. These applications fall into five basic categories:

- Discussions
- Articles
- Assets
- Metadata
- Activity streams

Let's look at each category in detail.

Discussions

Two-way text-based communication is a fundamental element of social interaction on the Web. There are several social applications that help accomplish this type of interaction.

Forums were the first discussion application on the Web. As a result, the word *discussion* has become interchangeable with forums in the parlance of web professionals. The essential element of the forum is a discussion thread, typically a series of back and forth exchanges (or posts) between two or more users. A forum is a collection of discussion threads.

Comments are arguably the most common discussion application on the Web today. Comments are themselves discussion threads attached to an article or asset.

Messages are typically private texts exchanged between two individuals. Messaging is usually provided as a subsidiary feature in a set of social applications and is often called direct or private messaging.

Chat is typically discussion that is conducted among users who are online at the same time. It is sometimes referred to as a synchronous application, as distinguished from asynchronous applications like forums, comments, and messaging.

Needless to say, the boundaries between these applications can be fuzzy, particularly the boundaries between messaging and chat, depending on the constraints or affordances the application offers with regard to public versus private, individual versus group, and synchronous versus asynchronous.

Articles

Articles, like discussions, are content contributed by users. They are distinguished from discussions primarily by length and format. Discussion posts tend to be short and free-form; articles are longer and typically must conform to a format or structure specific to the type of article. Articles almost always permit comments to be posted in response. Following are a few examples.

Blogs are articles that are presented in order of date of authoring and often (though not always) address a subject of current interest: Most bloggers post *today* and things that are relevant *today*. They are usually written from the point of view of an individual author rather than a corporate identity as might be the case for the About Us page on a company website.

Wiki pages are articles usually written collaboratively by one or more authors and capture a subject in detail. They usually include links to other pages and often include assets (see the next section) as attachments.

Knowledge base articles generally contain how-to information for readers trying to accomplish a specific task.

Status updates are brief articles of a timely nature, generally bearing on what the author is feeling, thinking, or doing. These updates often relate to what the author is reading or viewing online and therefore contain links to social articles or discussions like those previously mentioned or articles and assets from official media sources.

Reviews are articles that consider and evaluate products or services that the author has personally used or experienced. Reviews used to be perhaps the most common type of social article on the Web, until social networks made status updates so ubiquitous.

Assets

Assets are items that exist in forms other than HTML text, such as videos, document files, images, code samples, and so forth. While text is still the most common social medium, images and video sharing are growing, spurred by the growth in smartphone use. And of course, video site YouTube and pinboard photo-sharing site Pinterest are among the largest social sites on the Web.

Metadata

Metadata is perhaps an arcane word to use for something so common: the assignment of scores, ratings, tags, or bookmarks to the content encountered on the Web. Sometimes the items rated are social, like marking a review on Amazon.com as helpful or not. Sometimes the items rated are not in themselves social, like giving a five-star rating to a computer printer. Regardless, both kinds of action are deeply social, since our action is visible to others, and they can and do use this information to make their own decisions about what to read, believe, or buy.

While large social sites exist purely for the purpose of rating customer experiences—think Reddit—we focus mostly on how companies are using metadata features to help gain the customer's help in evaluating their experience and organizing the social content they contribute and use.

Activity Streams

You'll often hear terms like *newsfeeds*, *status updates*, and *activity streams* used to describe the dynamic nature of social content and metadata as it flows between people on the Social Web. Of primary importance are newsfeeds and activity streams. Consider Wikipedia's definition of an activity stream:

An activity stream is a list of recent activities performed by an individual, typically on a single website. For example, Facebook's News Feed is an activity stream.

If you're still confused about the difference between newsfeeds and activity streams—which get merged in this definition—you're not alone. In the context of the Social Web, it's important to distinguish between a *newsfeed* and an *activity stream*. A newsfeed doesn't have to be social; you can get a newsfeed from any news or similar content website. An activity stream, by contrast, *is always social* and always composed primarily of entries *composed by you for consumption by others*. (We say "primarily" in recognition of Facebook's suggested posts and Twitter's sponsored tweets.) In this this sense, status updates—which are really links to the profiles or pages of other members in your chosen social network—are considered components of a feed. Here is a simplified definition:

A feed *consists of links to the work or contributions of others;* a stream *consists of the actual content associated with those contributions.*

In this book, we reserve the term *feed* for things like the list of links to others' activities that might appear on a profile page, and we use *activity stream* to refer to a listing of your contributions and that of other members within your network so you can read them at a glance.

Social Channels

When you engage your customers on the Web, rather than providing random, isolated experiences, you are generally better served by organizing these touchpoints within defined *social channels*.

As used in business and particularly in marketing, the term *channel* refers to the way that a company provides products or services to customers. Businesses typically use many channels within their marketplace to convey information. They use marketing channels (for example, television advertising, billboards, and direct mail) to deliver marketing messages to prospects. They use support channels (for example, phone, email, or service people in the field) to provide service to customers. And they use distribution channels (retailers, wholesalers, value-added resellers, and so forth) to get their products into the hands of customers.

Needless to say, the Internet sparked a revolution in the channels employed by business. According to the Internet Advertising Bureau (IAB), in just its first decade of mainstream use, online advertising grew to exceed advertising on cable television and nearly exceeded advertising on broadcast television, a 70-year-old advertising medium. Now, yet another revolution is reshaping business channels. This revolution is driven by social technologies, through channels characterized by ownership.

When characterizing social channels, we distinguish them according to the ownership of the social channel itself. We call channels that a brand or business uses for its own purposes *on-domain*, citing the typical association of that channel with the company's own Internet domain (for example, `http://supportforum.mybrand.com`). By comparison, we refer to channels built around online properties that *someone else owns* as *off-domain* (for example, `http://facebook.com/mybusinesspage`).

An off-domain *social customer experience occurs on a social network or with an application that you participate in as a business but that you do not control directly; an* on-domain *social customer experience occurs within a platform or application that you directly control.*

The following sections cover off- and on-domain channels in detail.

Off-Domain Channels

Recall the discussion of home base, outposts, and passports in Chapter 3, "Social Customer Experience Management." There's an important distinction between home base versus outposts and passports: Home base is *on-domain* while passports and outposts are both off-domain. Your home base is generally your website and the associated properties. Social applications used on your home base are ones that you choose, implement, and manage. You determine who the members are, what they do, and what rules they abide by. Outposts and passports, by contrast, are *off-domain*. Someone else chooses the applications; someone else manages the platform. You have a presence on their platform. That presence may be a branded space where you have some control over design and features, or you may simply be participating as any other named member, interacting but not controlling the environment.

Off-domain channels are the ones that most people think of when they say *social media*. And particularly, they think of off-domain outposts like Facebook and Twitter. Like other outposts, these networks permit firms to have their own presence, branded in some way. On Facebook, companies can develop custom applications that no other company on the network has. Companies can create their own look and feel and even create multiple Facebook pages to accommodate different objectives or support different products or brands. Companies don't own the network, but they own the experience that they create within that network. Table 4.1 shows some of the major outposts used by companies along with their reported member bases. Keep in mind that *registered* does not necessarily mean active, real people. That's a discussion for another day.

▶ **Table 4.1** Social customer experience outpost

Site	Core Applications	Users (2013)
Facebook	Activity stream	1.15B registered users
YouTube	Video	1B users
Twitter	Status updates	500M registered users
Google+	Activity stream	343M active users
LinkedIn	Profiles	238M registered users
Instagram	Photo sharing	130M users
Pinterest	Photo sharing	70M users

There are many more outposts that may be of interest to a company, depending on industry, location, or target audience. For example, if you're in China, then Sina Weibo (500M users in 2013) is of greater interest than Twitter. Business-to-consumer firms rarely consider SlideShare (50M users) a priority, but for business-to-business use, SlideShare can be quite significant in its ability to generate leads.

Social passports are related to off-domain social outposts. Passports differ in many ways from outposts in that the largest outposts are relatively few in number, and most companies use the same ones, such as those listed in Table 4.1. Passports are extremely varied, range widely in size, and tend to differ by industry. Outposts permit you to essentially own a piece of the network, branding and (often) customizing it as you see fit. Passports permit you to participate but without a dedicated branded space. Instead, companies send their employees to participate in these spaces or contribute content. That content is branded but appears alongside content created by other users.

Whereas outposts can support very different kinds of businesses, passports tend to be more industry specific. Intercontinental Hotels Group (IHG) can use Facebook as an outpost as effectively as Verizon Communications can. However, when looking for a passport, Verizon wouldn't use TripAdvisor, any more than IHG would use the community at Broadbandreports.com. Microsoft and HP might each invite the other to participate in their social channels as a passport; American Idol and Caterpillar would not.

For all these reasons, there is no list of major passport sites. However, in Table 4.2 we provide examples of representative passport sites by industry.

▶ **Table 4.2** Example passport sites by industry

Site	Industry	Focus
Broadbandreports.com	Telecommunications	Cable TV and Internet services
CrackBerry	Mobile devices	BlackBerry phones
FlyerTalk	Airlines	Air travel and airline loyalty programs
TripAdvisor	Travel and hospitality	Hotels, restaurants, travel destinations

On-Domain Channels

Accepting that social applications are an adjunct to social networks and online communities, the starting set of applications—support forums—is built around the white-label social technology platforms offered by more than a few software providers. As used here, *white label* means a software application that can be branded to your specification but is otherwise ready to use. The platforms may be delivered as software for you to install or as a SaaS (software as a service) application from providers like Lithium Technologies, among many others. Table 4.3 shows a representative set of these platform providers.

Provider	Core Strength	Examples
Lithium Technologies	Influencer identification, social customer experience	DISH, Comcast, Skype, Lenovo, Sephora
Jive Software	Internal collaboration	Premier Global's iMeet
Salesforce.com	Ideation	My Starbucks Idea, Dell IdeaStorm
SharePoint	Enterprise workflow	KraftFoods.com, content management
Small World Labs	Niche communities	American Cancer Society
Socialtext	Enterprise collaboration	TransUnion, internal employee collaboration

On-domain social applications built using the tools referenced in Table 4.3 are designed to facilitate *accomplishing something in the context of a shared or collaborative goal* and thereby to provide a specific and generally visible value to a given group of participants. And because these are on-domain applications, this activity occurs on your site, where you can manage and build on the relationships that result.

On-domain social applications are rooted in the task orientation of customers but then extend beyond that into more general social activities: Customers seeking assistance with printer support on the HP support forum may end up sharing stories about the events leading up to the pictures they wanted help printing. By delivering a service and then encouraging people to share their results, you create interpersonal relationships. In this way, on-domain social applications drive their own longevity and usefulness.

This is a very beneficial attribute when you are trying to encourage repeat visits and you don't have an unlimited supply of funds to make up for organic interest and participation.

There is another aspect of social application design that warrants attention. *A utility-oriented application by itself is not social.* This means that unless you design your social application to be a part of the larger social framework—the ecosystem—in which your audience spends time, you'll end up with an island.

What makes the social application social is its connection to the participants' communities. For example, if a customer is interested in tips on how to enhance photos, a FAQ built out as a wizard-style assistant can suggest filters and related techniques. That will earn you one visit. But if you also add photo sharing and add the ratings or collaborative features to that same application, the resulting social interaction around the photos will earn you repeat visits and word-of-mouth that drives membership in your on-domain social application when the original member posts those photos and invites friends to your site to comment.

Manage On- and Off-Domain Activity

Deciding how to implement and manage on- and off-domain social sites can be difficult. Both are valuable, but for different reasons. Off-domain social networks like Facebook can be a significant source of traffic. On-domain social applications like support forums or product ratings and reviews can significantly enhance the customer experience and thereby enhance business results. Connecting on- and off-domain activity is therefore an area where you'll want to dig in.

Consider the following use case: You'd like to manage off-domain activity—respond to people talking about or to you on social networks—and then draw some part of this traffic toward your on-domain support forum. But how do you accomplish this? The tools you may need to manage and measure interactions to the level of speed and quality you prefer may or may not be available within the native toolset on either or the off-domain network or within your on-domain application.

An entirely new category of tools has emerged to equip companies to get the most out of their off-domain social network outposts. Though many of the tools in this category reflect the relative immaturity of social networking itself, the newest tools support a broad range of social activity management. In the early days of social networks, companies focused more on listening than on engagement, so the early tools were good at listening but not so good at doing anything else. Now, it's the demand for response that is central.

Customer support teams in particular were poorly served by tools originally designed for the very different objectives of the marketing organization. This situation is changing for the better as companies once struggling to engage and respond using a marketing platform take advantage of the newer social customer care platforms purpose-built for enterprise-class engagement. Table 4.4 lists some of the most popular tools used by companies today for listening, publishing, and social engagement.

Company	Product	Focus
HootSuite	HootSuite	Social engagement
Lithium Technologies	Lithium Social Web	Social support and engagement
Salesforce.com	Buddy Media	Social publishing
Salesforce.com	Radian6	Social listening and engagement
Spredfast	Spredfast	Social publishing
Sprout Social	Sprout Social	Social publishing and engagement

Build a Vibrant Presence

Importantly, the social applications are not necessarily communities per se, though some amount to as much: They are more generally enablers of an activity or outcome that is useful to the members of a community with which an application is associated. Simply put, and critical to understanding how to build an effective social presence, this means recognizing that most brands, products, or services *cannot* support a community by themselves.

Why not? Think about the products that you use, the organizations that you support, and the real-world community around you. What among them constitute the things you think about daily and regularly and that you obsess over? These—and only these—are the things that are candidates for long-lived, organically developed communities.

Despite a lot of time and effort spent to the contrary, some brands, products, and services still do not command sufficient daily mindshare to sustain a community of their own. To see why this is so, make a quick mental list for yourself of the real-world organizations of which you are a member. The typical individual has one, three, perhaps five, or even a few more organizations. After that, most people run out of *bandwidth*, that is, the combination of an individual's time and attention. There are only so many social organizations one person can effectively participate in. Online it's no different: How many social communities can you really belong to? More importantly, how many will you actively participate in? For most, the answer is surprisingly similar (or perhaps not surprising at all) to the capacity for participation in real life.

Against that, ask yourself how likely you are to join a deodorant, toothpaste, or laundry detergent community. Yet, more than a few consumer goods brand managers have undertaken to build just these types of communities. Make no mistake: As long as the advertising spending is happening, people join, take advantage of offers, and maybe even engage in light social activities. But understand that membership is being driven by ad spending and not organic social interaction. Organic growth—versus ad spending and incentive-driven growth—is what you need to build long-term participation in a community.

This is not to knock awareness communities or the application of social media technology to drive awareness. These communities may well be important parts of overall awareness and marketing programs and often do deliver on some of the surface promises of the Social Web. Content consumption certainly happens, and to an extent curation—people voting or ranking what they see or do in these communities—may also be happening. But above that, in the more important behaviors of content creation and collaboration, activity generally starts to drop off. And as noted, when the ad spending stops, the community generally stops growing as well.

Think back to the laundry detergent site, and set aside the media-driven *awareness* uses of the site. How might this site look if it were to be built as a social application?

The typical laundry site probably has a stain-removal chart, right? There is clear utility value in knowing what types of pretreatments are effective on what types of stains. To this end, there are literally dozens of these types of sites. The problem is, specific products can be recommended for all sorts of reasons, and among them is because someone paid for the recommendation. This is, of course, the underlying issue with traditional and marketer-driven communications versus social or collective/consumer-driven communications. As a consumer, the only thing you *know* is that the marketer is trying to sell you something. The rest is based on the combination of brand reputation, your experience, and the shared experience of those you trust.

Enter social media, part one. The first element of the social application—and the first use of the engagement processes associated with it—is curation. Consumers are often more candid (issues of transparency and disclosure noted) in their reviews than marketers. Reviews are part of the solution, and the reviews of reviews go further and help others interested in the specific product or service to sort out and make sense of specific reviews by identifying those considered most helpful.

The contemporary social application takes it one step further: Building on the connectivity afforded by social technologies, the social application makes its results available to others, outside of the social application itself. In the context of the present example, where the basic consumer-driven reviews on the laundry site makes relevant information available to people who visit the site, the well-connected social application makes the results of trying a specific solution available to everyone. This can dramatically impact the spread of useful information (and sometimes not-so-useful information from the brand's point of view).

Here's an example of how this might work: Suppose someone discovers a particular stain-removal technique to be useful and posts this onto the stain-fighting social application. The application then sends a message to Twitter—with the contributor's explicit permission—alerting the contributor's followers that an effective stain-removal technique has been found. The member's social graph takes over from there, spreading and amplifying the underlying consumer-generated content.

In this example, not only has the social application shown the customer how to better use a cleaning product, but it has encouraged the customer to post a new review and then facilitated its sharing through that customer's larger (online) social community. Now those friends of friends have this information, and if confronted with a similar stain, or queried by someone they know, they can point back to the original source and benefit from it. This is how information traverses the social graph and adds value to participants.

Central to the social customer experience is the act of sharing, facilitated by the connectedness of the application to the communities around it. This is what creates the real value to a marketer. Sharing has a significant impact on the spread of positive (or negative—watch out!) information that amplifies and drives marketing at no cost beyond the construction of the application and its maintenance. Miss out on this aspect of social applications—build a social application that is more like an island than a shared space—and you will surely decrease the potential return on your investment.

The GoodGuide app shown in Figure 4.2 is a customer-driven, shared, and socially connected shopping application, available for both Android and Apple smartphones. GoodGuide is a great example of how the Social Web is beginning to exert an impact on business units within the enterprise *outside of the marketing department.* GoodGuide is a business application built around the social customer experience. Read on to see how it works.

Figure 4.2 GoodGuide

Mobile applications for smartphones that scan a barcode and present pricing data and customer reviews are common. When Dave was looking for a portable spin-style toothbrush in Target, he was confronted with over two dozen competing models of semi-disposable, single-user (versus family applications) brushes in the under-$5 category. Dave recalls the experience, "I had zero information other than "Buy me!" to go on. So, I used my Android-based smartphone to scan the barcodes, right there in the aisle. Sure, I got a few odd stares (normal for me), but I also got access to independent product reviews, instantly through Google's shopping guides. Based on the combination of independent reviews and manufacturer's information, I made my decision." This was a classic use of social media in a business (commerce) context. For the most part, as a consumer Dave was working with the marketing data, evaluating things like price and promoted feature set, and then extending this with a mix of company and *consumer-generated product reviews.*

GoodGuide moves beyond this core review data, which is now largely considered cost-of-entry for consumers nearing the point of actual purchase. It also moves *well beyond the marketing department* and into the core values and purpose of the business itself. GoodGuide serves up health, environment, and societal impact ratings: A score of 10 on Society, for example, means the product in consideration is offered by a *manufacturer* with responsible investment policies, equitable hiring practices, an appropriate commitment to philanthropy, and a firm policy toward workplace diversity. As noted, this goes way beyond the purview of the marketing and communications departments.

Compare this with ratings, reviews, prices, and features. Investment policy, hiring practices, and environmental impact are decidedly outside the marketing domain in most businesses, although social business certainly suggests that this is likely to change. Customers are now armed with a much more holistic view of the countries of origin, manufacturers, suppliers, retailers, and even taxing entities that make up the entire purchase chain. This is all part of the decision-making process now.

Social applications such as GoodGuide bring visibility to the larger business process and with it an entirely new set of considerations that reach across departments and functions. If you are looking to enable more of your organization to create favorable conversations, this is the starting point.

The combination of on-domain social applications—your support forums, communities, knowledge stores, and similar—along with your off-domain presence in places like Twitter, Facebook, and Google+ can be quite powerful. When compared with building a stand-alone community around a brand, product, or service—go back to the toothpaste or deodorant community examples—a highly integrated social implementation results in a more widespread and free-flowing interchange of information between consumers and your organization. This, of course, brings up one of the aspects of the Social Web and its use by consumers that causes some marketers sleepless nights: the prospect of negative conversations circulating outside of their control but very much visible to potential customers.

Unfortunately, there is no easy answer when negative conversations arise, unless you consider fixing the problem at its source as being easy. Take time to review the "Respond to Social Media Mentions" sidebar in Chapter 1 as you develop your basic response process.

Here too, however, social technology provides relief. Support forums—properly managed—can go a long way toward improving the customer service experience (lowering the incidence of negative conversations) and reducing the costs of customer service delivery in the process. At the very least, support forums can be used to quickly spot common problems so that root-cause corrective action can be taken. Once the problems are corrected, the very customers raising the objections can be connected back into the process, creating a more favorable relationship.

Here again you see the larger connection between the Social Web and *business*: Beyond social media marketing and monitoring conversations, the integration of social applications that connect your business to the larger (customer) ecosystem provide you with the data, solutions, and basis for relationships that can help you fix what needs fixing and preserve what's already working.

Much of what we just covered sounds simple—and in theory it is—but beware: Stepping up and actually implementing social customer experience management— directly connecting your engineers to your customers so that they can learn first-hand the pain points of customers—is challenging. That said, getting it right creates both a barrier to entry and a competitive differentiator that is difficult for slower-off-the-mark competitors to counter. If you move first, you get the advantage, and that can pay measurable benefits down the road.

Content Sharing

If support forums and similar social applications provide the connections between communities and your business, what is actually shared? Recall the engagement building blocks—consumption, creation, curation, and collaboration. Sharing first emerges in the curation phase of engagement as people rate the works of others in a public setting. Content creation, moving up another step, is almost universally done for the purpose of sharing.

Given this, social applications are typically built with the idea of members creating and sharing something. That something might be a rating, a photo, a solution, a story, an idea, or any number of other things. Expert communities are examples of sharing, wherein the content being shared relates to a specific problem posed by the community. On a different scale—and typically serving many times the number of people—support forums operate in this same way: Customers share problems in the hopes that by sharing they will find a solution.

Where the challenge in building a compelling social application is identifying the *purpose* of the application, the challenge in driving shared content is encouraging participation in the first place. The degree to which content is created and shared is almost purely a function of how easy it is to do and in the rewards for having done it. By rewards, we don't mean cash; we mean social recognition. If someone is contributing *quality* content, ensure (as a moderator or through moderation policies or your reputation management system) that this person is recognized. Identifying and developing experts/influencers by watching content production and subsequent content sharing is one the keys to building a powerful social application.

Purpose-Built Social Add-Ons

Purpose-built add-ons—small software components that you add to increase or fine-tune application functionality—can provide a way to quickly implement social behavior. Like communities and social applications in general, these small, purpose-built software add-ons are designed to facilitate specific interactions within communities or between stakeholders. Contests, gifting, and content-sharing applications are examples of the kinds of things that you can add to your overall social presence to increase visitor participation. Further examples include advertising modules or "Share this with friends" blocks of code that you drop into a page template on your site to enable an external sharing or publishing service.

Table 4.5 lists a set of leading, proven, purpose-built social tools and add-ons that can be implemented quickly on Facebook and Twitter. They range from the simple—photo or video sharing—to the complex. Providers such as Friend2Friend and Buddy Media offer a range of full-featured add-ons that support contests, gifting, sharing, and more. *Disclosure: Dave is a board advisor with Friend2Friend.*

▶ **Table 4.5** Easy Social Solutions on Facebook and Twitter

Provider	Core Strength	Examples
Buddy Media/Salesforce	Ready-to-use Facebook applications	Budweiser and Samsung Facebook tabs
Disqus	Comments and discussions	Droid Life (www.droid-life.com)
Friend2Friend	Social amplification	New Belgium Brewing's Facebook Mobile Photo and Story Contest

One of the more popular Friend2Friend-based solutions for New Belgium Brewing was based on people's natural behaviors around sharing and story-telling. Figure 4.3 shows the campaign home screen inside Facebook.

What is notable about the New Belgium applications is how easy it is to build a compelling social program *without* building a complete community. Using the Friend2Friend platform along with Facebook, the app leverages the participant base that is already there by providing a small, well-defined activity that has meaning and relevance to a precise audience. The additional solutions shown in Table 4.5 from Buddy Media and Disqus are all great examples of promotional programs with a decidedly social element.

Figure 4.3 New Belgium mobile story contest

It is exactly this kind of smart approach to social media marketing and the larger area of social technology applied to business that makes obvious the way in which the Social Web is maturing. While Web 1.0 was typically implemented as competing islands (large portals going for traffic dominance in the hopes of selling ad space) Web 2.0 brought shared experiences and mashups (the "mashing together" of independent software apps to produce a complete solution) to the table. Savvy marketers picked up on this by building applications that connected their brands to the existing communities where their target audience spent time. The Social Web, the subject of this book, continues the shift toward *shared* versus *competing* experiences by integrating the audience and the business through a set of applications that facilitate collaboration, knowledge exchange, and consumer-led design.

Use Brand Outposts and Communities

It's time to connect the basics to put in place the beginning of a framework for a social customer experience. Chapter 1 covered the basics of engagement. Chapter 2 covered the new role of the customer as a potential participant in your business. It also touched on the social graph and social CRM, highlighting tools that help you identify and build relationships with people who are talking about your brand, product, or service and influencing others in the process.

Chapter 3 framed social applications in the context of a business or organization that is being run based on direct collaboration with its customers. The basic interactions—creating relationships between community members and creating shared knowledge—come about through specific, replicable actions that can be designed into the organization itself.

In this section, the social behaviors described so far are applied in specific social spaces—think online communities here—where the actual interactions, discussions, and conversations take place.

Recall from Chapter 3 that communities are built around things like passions, lifestyles, and causes, the *significant things* that people choose to spend their time with. Sometimes, a brand, product, or service by itself does not warrant a community of its own; even when it does, that particular community is typically participated in by only a fraction of the total potential audience. For most businesses and organizations, the places where customers willingly spend time—often engaged in conversation about the business or organization—is a social network or online community that is dedicated not to brands, products, or services but rather to other people like themselves, with interests like their own.

So how do you participate as a business? Even more pressing, how do you get your customers to spend time doing real work with your team, contributing ideas and insights that will help you better define products or innovate in ways that will lower costs or differentiate you from your competitors? In short, how do you become part of the communities your customers or members belong to and begin to realize the promised benefits of social computing? You participate in the activities they are involved in—with full disclosure and transparency—in order to build the levels of trust that that will elicit their contributions of knowledge back to you.

To make the most of the Social Web, recognize two accepted facts:

- People often turn to their friends before they turn to a brand for help.
- The brand is, all other things being equal, probably in the better position to help.

So, the challenge is drawing from the places where people naturally spend time asking questions of each other and bringing them to a place where they can find specific help.

In an interview with *Businessweek,* author and blogger Jeff Jarvis noted three common mistakes that many companies make when adding social-media-based marketing programs to their overall communications mix. Of the three mistakes (see the "Jeff Jarvis: Three Mistakes to Avoid" sidebar for a complete reference), one in particular applies to brand outposts: The mistake is expecting customers to always come to you *on their own* for information. Jeff points out that it is essential for you to go to them instead. Look at the following list of the typical places where brand outposts are established: In each of these cases, *you* are going to *them*.

Twitter Support Handle
Google+ Business Presence
Facebook Business Page
YouTube Brand Channel

What defines a successful brand outpost? Given the shift from social engagement to advertising sales as the core *business* of most social networks, success is best measured in acquired attention, just as you'd measure success in any other advertising context.

Jeff Jarvis: Three Mistakes to Avoid

In an interview by *Businessweek*'s Diane Brady, Jeff Jarvis cited the three avoidable mistakes that companies sometimes make when implementing social-media-based programs and how to avoid them:

- Talking in a corporate or institutional voice. Instead, use the language that your customers use, appropriately.

- Expecting your customers to always come to *your* website. Instead, go to where they are and join them in their activities.

- Trying to control the conversation. Instead, recognize that you (as the brand participant, for example) are one voice among many.

You can quickly find the interview by searching for "Jeff Jarvis Diane Brady."

Coca-Cola: Facebook

At about 10 million fans, Coke's original outpost—its Facebook page—is one of the most successful examples of a brand outpost. Even more remarkable, it wasn't created by Coke; it was built by Dusty Sorg and Michael Jedrzejewski, two passionate Coke fans. When confronted with a site built on Facebook but outside of Coke's control, Coke chose to empower the fans who created the site and embraced the work they'd done.

Coke's Facebook brand outpost, shown in Figure 4.4, is now a valued element of its online marketing program, so much so that in 2010, Coke deemphasized the use of one-off online campaigns in favor of extended social-media-based efforts, in part built around its brand outposts at Facebook and YouTube. In an interview at the time of the announcement, Prinz Pinakatt, Coke's interactive marketing manager for Europe, said,

"We would like to place our activities and brands where people are, rather than dragging them to our platform." Coke may have additional opportunities for on-domain interaction, but they're spot-on in meeting customers where they are!

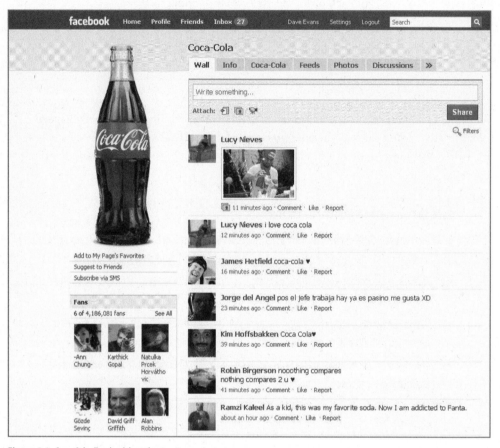

Figure 4.4   Coca-Cola: Facebook brand outpost

Take a tip from Coke, Starbucks, Dell, and dozens of other brands: Approach the Social Web as a *consumer* and understand how you relate to it in that context. What do you find useful? Why are you using Facebook? What do you like about your business blog or internal company intranet? What utility do these provide and why are they useful to you? Apply the answers to these questions to the design of your social programs, and let them guide your participation in the online communities where the people you are interested in choose to spend their time.

The Social Ecosystem

The social ecosystem, taken as a whole, provides three fundamental opportunities for understanding and leveraging the behaviors associated with collaborative interaction.

These opportunities—the social graph, social applications, and social platforms—are shown in Figure 4.5.

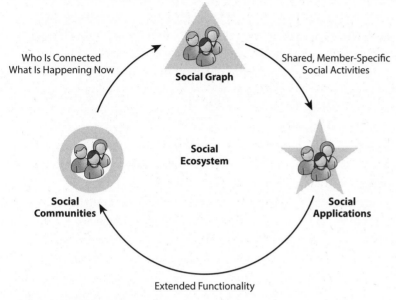

Who Is Connected
What Is Happening Now

Social Graph

Shared, Member-Specific
Social Activities

Social Ecosystem

Social Communities

Social Applications

Extended Functionality

Figure 4.5 The social ecosystem

The *social graph*—the connective elements that link profiles and indicate activities through status updates and the like—provides a framework for understanding who is related to whom, who is influential, where to look for potential advocates, and what is happening right now. This framework is important for participants: The social graph and the applications that rely on it facilitate friending and the sharing of content and experiences throughout a social network.

Behind the scenes, the social graph supports the programming techniques that allow social applications to discover relationships and to navigate the links that define them, suggesting potential friends or helping to spot influencers and generally providing an indication as to how participants in a social network are connected to each other and what they are sharing among themselves.

Social applications—extensions to the core capabilities of the social platforms and software services that support social networks—provide the additional, specific functionality that makes the larger community and platforms useful to *individual* participants. The Aircel recharge application shown previously in Figure 3.6 that extends the functionality of Aircel's Facebook presence is an example of a smart, simple social application.

Social applications are also important in that they can facilitate overall membership growth. By incorporating specific applications into your community, that community becomes more useful to members, increasing the member stickiness and referrals in the process.

Finally, communities and other social platforms—built around passions, lifestyles, aspirations, or similar higher callings—provide the gathering points for individuals interested in socializing and collaborating in pursuit of the specific activities they enjoy together. These communities, support forums, and related social platforms are all places where the attention you have acquired on brand outposts can be collected and organized around specific topics, interests, or shared needs. By building a community around a passion, lifestyle, or cause and by looking for likely members among the participants in your brand outposts, you can foster and strengthen the relationships between the brand, product, or service and your customers and influencers. The progression from casual association (brand outpost) to collaborative participation and higher-level engagement (on-domain community) is thus enabled.

Importantly, the social graph, off-domain social applications, and your on-domain community applications drive each other. Take any one of them away and the value of business or organizational participation drops. This follows from the interconnections between these three. Without the social graph, for example, relationships between participants do not form and the community becomes transactional and self-oriented rather than social and collectively oriented. Without the communities and larger social objects (passions, lifestyles, and causes), the participants lack a sufficient motive to drive organic social growth. And without the social applications that extend the functionality of the core social platform, the activities within the community are limited to the broad activities of larger demographic groups, missing the highly engaging and very specific activities of small groups or even individuals. As a result, the social graph fails to develop in the way it would otherwise.

Review and Hands-On

This chapter showed how social applications connect members within communities and thereby facilitate social interaction. By behaving as a value-added member of these communities and then always participating from that position, you can establish a basis for trust. You'll have to deliver, or course. Where fine print and high-speed voice-over can legally disclaim whatever expectations an advertisement may have set, in a social setting walking the talk is required. If you say it, you have to do it.

The benefits are significant: The combination of trust and relevance drives engagement and encourages people to share the information that leads to long-term success through the delivery of a superior experience. This applies within your organization—where the goal is instilling in everyone an attitude and empowered commitment to customer satisfaction—as well as outside, in the store, where as Sam Walton said, "Your customer has the answer."

Review of the Main Points

Implementing social customer experience initiatives challenges many of the accepted norms in traditional top-down management systems. It requires rethinking some aspects of running a business and in many ways involves the not-so-obvious discipline of running your business as if you were a customer.

The tools and techniques covered in this chapter pull together the connection points between an organization and its stakeholders and in particular accomplish this in a way that facilitates knowledge sharing. The main points are these:

- Businesses connect socially to customers through visible relationships and useful, collaborative applications.

- Participation, knowledge transfer, and social activity can be measured.

- Friending and reputation management are important aspects of social behavior that lead to strong communities.

- Effective moderation and clear policies spur community growth.

- Brand outposts created within communities popular with your audience are ideal places to connect your business.

By recognizing the components of the Social Web and the ways that your customers or stakeholders use them, you can adapt your business or organization to a more participative, collaboration-oriented audience. This closer connection comes at a cost: Accepting customers as collaborative partners imposes an obligation to consider what they offer and to act on it. Not all businesses can do this, and even fewer can do it easily. That said, there is a clear process for accomplishing this, and there are plenty of cases and best practices from globally recognized firms that have been successfully building their own businesses using social computing and related techniques.

Hands-On: Review These Resources

Review each of the following, ensuring that you have a solid understanding of the concept being shown in the example:

- Brand outposts like Coca-Cola's Facebook page are sometimes viable alternatives to one-off microsites and branded communities:

  www.facebook.com/cocacola

- New Belgium Brewing's Facebook-based mobile photo and story contest taps readily available passions and interests. You don't have to reinvent wheels to create great social media points of presence. Check this and other social marketing efforts based on sharing and content collaboration created by Friend2Friend for New Belgium Brewing:

  www.friend2friend.com/client/new-belgium/

- Clearly articulated policies create a strong platform for collaboration and the adoption of social computing:

  www.ibm.com/blogs/zz/en/guidelines.html

Hands-On: Apply What You've Learned

Apply what you've learned in this chapter through the following exercises:

1. If you use Twitter or LinkedIn, bring your personal profile up to 100 percent completion.

2. If your office or organization has a profile-driven knowledge-sharing application, repeat exercise 1 for your profile on that network. Then, get three colleagues to do the same.

3. List your favorite social communities, and describe an application that your business or organization might offer within that community. Connect it to your business objectives.

Your Social Presence

II

Part II leads you into the development of your own social presence. It begins by showing how strategies built to take advantage of social technologies relate to your goals, audience, organization, and business processes. It then looks at analysis and measurement—key topics that organizations often mistakenly neglect until after efforts are underway. Wrapping up, we look at other five key trends that are reshaping social customer experience.

Social Technology and Business Decisions

5

You might think, after reviewing the ecosystem in Chapter 4, that your starting point in creating a social presence is obvious: You just need to decide where *to engage and* what *technologies to employ. In fact,* where *and* what can *come only after you consider two other key questions:* why *and* who. *Why is your organization undertaking social efforts? With whom in your base of customers and prospects will you engage, and who within your organization will be involved in or affected as a result of this process? Knowing* why *and* who *provides the basis for the* where *and the* what, *enabling you to build a social technology plan for success.*

Chapter contents:

Three reasons for social customer experience

Prioritization: getting to the conversations that matter

Social technology and decision support

Three Reasons for Social Customer Experience

There are many reasons why organizations undertake social efforts. Certainly not least among them is that customer behavior has changed; customers are themselves forcing many organizations to move onto the Social Web. Customers increasingly insist on engaging on social channels. But in an era of shrinking margins and competing priorities, that may not be enough. Getting the organization behind a social customer experience effort will take more than just saying "the customer wants it." And that's good, because more specific goals will better equip you to measure success and justify investment going forward. So let's get more specific.

In general, there are only three reasons any organization invests in social customer experience:

- To sell something (to increase revenue)
- To save something (to reduce expenses)
- To learn something (to innovate faster)

That's it. It's that simple. Let's look at each in detail.

Selling with Social Channels

Sales and marketing may be the most common reasons organizations get involved in social channels today. The ways in which social technologies support sales and marketing are more varied than you might think.

First, consider social channels as a means of acquiring new customers—what are sometimes called top-of-the-funnel strategies. This is the first pillar of a social sales and marketing strategy. Remember Table 4.1? The fact that outposts like Facebook, Twitter, and others have gained hundreds of millions of members has led marketers to view them as attractive channels for delivering offers and other marketing messages to both customers and prospects. One expression of this sentiment is the ever-increasing use of Facebook as a channel for delivering coupons. In September 2013, blogger Craig Smith scanned Facebook for offers from U.S. retailers and restaurants and found more than 150 companies—from Ace Hardware to Ziploc—offering coupons.

Examples of Social Selling

Craig Smith offers this look at the use of the Facebook as a marketing channel for U.S. retailers and restaurants.

```
http://expandedramblings.com/index.php/nov-2012-update-the-
ultimate-list-of-brand-facebook-coupons/2/
```

While coupons are a tried and true way to attract new customers, they are hardly the most creative use of the world's first ubiquitous, many-to-many, real-time, multimedia communication medium. More creative are efforts that tap the viral potential of social networks, like Burger King's Whopper Freakout campaign in 2008 or the Man Your Man Could Smell Like from Old Spice in 2010. With humor and wit, these efforts captured the attention of millions of viewers both online and on television, with the online audience driven largely through individuals sharing their favorite video from the series on social networks.

Don't underestimate the usefulness of basic techniques, like coupons, adapted for social media. Producing a video that receives wide attention through sharing—aka a viral video—takes a bit of genius, a fact often missed by those who aspire to success through virality. Even in the social era, genius is in short supply. And, with all their creativity, viral ads are still ads and coupons are still coupons, both imports of traditional marketing methods to the Social Web. Be sure you balance your efforts and take full advantage of all of the tools in your marketing toolbox.

You can expect top-of-the-funnel efforts to continue to be a focus. The message here is that these strategies need to be part of your social customer experience strategy but cannot be all of your strategy. In fact, recent experience shows that equally powerful impacts can come from engaging with customers in activities that go beyond deal-hunting and video sharing.

Social Media Marketing: An Hour a Day

If some of the core social media marketing concepts are unfamiliar to you as you head into Part II, you may find Dave's earlier book helpful. *Social Media Marketing: An Hour a Day*, 2nd Edition (Sybex, 2010) covers the basics of social media marketing and provides a solid introduction to the connection between the marketing purchase funnel and the Social Web.

Organizations are increasingly looking at how the behaviors of customers who engage in their social channels differ from those who do not. Invariably, they find that social customers buy more, buy more often, and remain customers longer than customers who don't use social channels. When companies can quantify that difference, the impact of engaging each additional customer in social channels is clear. For example, if you know that a social customer spends 20 percent more than a non-social customer on average, then driving adoption in social channels also drives spend. We'll look at some specific cases and metrics in Chapter 6, "Social Analytics, Metrics, and Measurement," a discussion that will lead to an important second pillar of marketing and sales: ROI related to the use of social technology.

In addition to ROI, important pillars for social selling include loyalty and satisfaction. Many organizations know the economic value that a single percentage point increase in customer satisfaction or single point on the Net Promoter Score scale represents in terms of future revenue. Those organizations look to social customer experience to contribute that future revenue, and they use long-term measures—combined with near-term KPIs (key performance indicators)—to keep on track. In other cases, for example, products or services sold on a subscription basis, shorter or repeating sales cycles mean that measuring loyalty is more direct. Wonder why cable operators and telecommunication companies are so active in social? Now you know.

In summary, if the answer to "why" for your organization is to more effectively market and sell, think about which of these pillars—ROI, loyalty, or satisfaction—is most important or the easiest to impact by social efforts. Use that insight as the starting point and then expand as you prove your case.

Save with Social

Want to know the biggest secret in social media as it's applied to business? The majority of the organizations that have adopted social technology *and can prove a positive ROI* are using social technologies not to drive sales but to reduce costs. In a very simple sense, a business can improve its margin either by increasing revenue while holding costs constant or by reducing expenses while holding sales constant. Companies often use cost savings to justify spending on social programs: They know that such programs can have a broad and deep impact on the business, and they know that they can measure it directly. Cost savings are often easier to quantify—providing a clearer path to dollars—than other kinds of return on social technology investments.

When considering the use of social technology for cost reduction, one of the immediate differentiators is where this technology is applied. Sales and marketing tend to focus on off-domain channels, offering campaigns built around coupons on Facebook or promoted offers on Twitter that might be run at a lower cost as compared to a traditional channel like a newspaper. But on-domain cost savings can also be significant. Support communities, where customers directly help other customers, are one example of cost reduction achieved through social technology.

Like sales and marketing, a savings strategy has pillars. The first pillar is traffic generation. Most companies spend a lot of money trying to build awareness, the first step in the marketing purchase funnel. Often, this means attracting people to your off-domain social outposts and then converting that traffic into on-domain visits and orders. Your website is typically where people learn about the details (beyond the ad) in your offerings, request a sales contact, or make purchases. So how do you do this?

It's no secret that for most companies, a majority of website traffic comes not from ads or affiliate sites or partners but rather from search engines. To see just how fundamental search has become, think about how you actually visit most websites:

Using the search bar, what Google Chrome users recognize as the anywhere bar, you use a search engine even when you know or could easily guess the web address you're seeking! Recognizing this, organizations collectively spend billions every year on search engine marketing programs like Google's AdWords. An entire discipline has grown up around managing and measuring search engine marketing spend, and it's an important part of being in business today.

Search engine marketing isn't going anywhere—except perhaps up in cost and volume. So organizations have developed effective alternatives to bring in traffic: robust social content is often considered to be "search gold." Search engines give preference to social content, because it changes frequently (it's fresh) and because lots of people reference and link to it (it's authoritative.). Here's the insight:

To keep the promise that search engines make to those who use them—delivering the most complete and current information on the Web—search engines must index social sites continuously. And no matter how many people you have developing content for your website, your customers can do more, and can do it faster.

The benefits of social technology—and in particular communities, support forums, and similar applications—are substantial. Consider HP, Adidas, or Sephora, whose customer communities typically receive 60–70 percent of their total traffic from search engines. In other industries, too, like entertainment, the social areas of the website attract more traffic than all the other areas combined. Across most industries, organic search developed as a result of on-domain community sites is sufficiently powerful that these communities are designed as gateways to relevant content and features located elsewhere on the site. The result is both a revenue opportunity and a savings opportunity, with many companies actively trading some of their search engine marketing budget for investments in social customer experience applications because it accomplishes the same goals at a lower cost.

The second pillar of a savings strategy is cost savings in customer care and support. The support communities mentioned earlier aren't just a better, more social experience for customers. They are typically less expensive ways of providing support. Think about it: When a customer solves another customer's problem, it costs less than having a customer service agent do it. Because customers are adopting social channels in such large volumes, the savings can be massive. Social support applies to both peer-to-peer support—customers answering other customers' questions—and support by social agents, whose organizational role is similar to that of agents who answer customer calls. Whether peer-to-peer or agent/expert focused, social tools can help companies respond faster and more efficiently.

There's another reason why social support is so common: It's the easiest channel for customers to use. Historically, phone-based customer care has been the primary place for customer interaction with a company. In many organizations the support team effectively owns the relationship with customers, owing to the frequency and intimacy of support processes. So, an opportunity exists to connect marketing and customer care through the support process. The result is an additional path to engagement that is perceived as easier by customers. What's not to love about that?

The third pillar in a savings strategy consists of cost savings that exist in other functions where customers are willing to engage and help out. The most common example is market research. Historically, when companies wanted to learn what customers thought, they hired an agency to convene a focus group, often an expensive and time-consuming undertaking. Worse, the pure logistics (to say nothing of the expense) limits the size and often requires additional analysis, delaying results by days or weeks. By contrast, social channels provide a way for companies to get real-time information on customer experiences and opinions and to open these sessions to as many customers as are interested in participating. The cost of doing so can be much less, and the results can be considered in real time. The time-tested best practice of customer research hasn't gone away; the methods, however, have changed to take advantage of technology and customers' inherent desire to socialize.

Learn with Social

Learning may sound like a soft benefit, one of those labeled indirect or hard to quantify in ROI models. In fact, it's the most powerful benefit of all, because it helps transform the organization in ways that enable it to thrive in the future. Learning, as used here, actually contains two elements: listening and collaborating. *Listening* is the process by which information is gathered, analyzed, and put in the right form and locations so that it can be acted upon. *Collaboration* is the process of acting on what you hear; typically, in social efforts, it involves cooperative work by multiple parties inside and outside the walls of your organization.

Too often, what starts as an obvious great idea—tapping social technology to enhance your business—gets hung up in the processes of organizational change, of breaking down silos, and of appropriately sharing and exposing information quickly and widely. It is critically important not to repeat the business mantra that goes "Our customers are at the center of everything we do" *while operating largely without their input* and without formally integrating their experiences, thoughts, and ideas into your internal business processes.

The key to combining listening data—posts pulled from selected off-domain social networks—with the rich on-domain conversations found in your support forums and similar social applications is that all of this needs to be connected to your business strategy and the processes that surround it. Given the hyper-transparency of the Social Web, what you do (in practice) needs to be absolutely aligned with what you claim.

For example, an outbound marketing message may claim your product has been "created for working mothers like you!" If it also turns out that your firm does not equitably promote women within the workplace, this contradiction will inevitably become known, very likely being spread through social channels. The need for aligning actions with claims raises the requirements for *listening* and incorporating customer feedback into your business processes. Without a strategic basis for participation, any involvement in the Social Web will be limited to listening (but not responding) and using platforms such as Twitter or Facebook for talking (as opposed to participating). Neither of these is optimal, and neither will result in the desired business outcomes.

The Innovation Cycle

The combination of social-media-based marketing and applying social technology to engage customers is powerful. Connecting customer intelligence and what is learned through active listening deeply into your business results in a customer-driven innovation cycle and in creating an organization that consistently delivers on what it claims to stand for.

What all of this adds up to is a new view of the customer in the context of engagement. Figure 5.1 offers a view of the innovation cycle, co-developed with Kaliza CEO and Dave's 2020 Social colleague Kaushal Sarda, that combines the engagement processes of social customer experience management. The primary loop—Learn, Abstract, Do, Offer—provides a framework for engagement that is based on an understanding of the endpoint use or application of the product, service, or cause-related program that you deliver. By closing the loop—by iterating—you set up a continuous cycle that drives long-term innovation through listening and collaboration.

The use of social technologies to create a presence for your brand on the Social Web—whether though a smart application that a community finds useful or a space of your own built around your customers' needs—creates a durable, relevant connection to the Social Web. On-domain tools like ideation platforms and support communities encourage customers to provide insights, thoughts, and ideas on how you can better serve them. This is precisely the information you need to succeed over the long term.

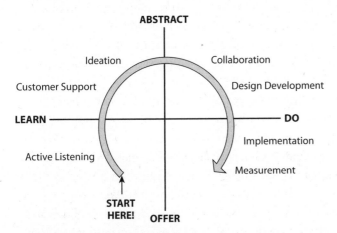

Figure 5.1 Innovation and social engagement

Kaushal Sarda

Kaushal Sarda is CEO of the enterprise applications and products firm at Kaliza, based in Bangalore. You can follow Kaushal on Twitter (@ksarda).

Social technology and the disciplines of social CRM and social customer experience management sit at the core of this cycle. It is *repeated innovation*—not one-off hits—that drives success. The Apple iPod is a great example. The first models launched in the early 2000s bear only passing resemblance to the wide range of devices that compose the iDevice family of Apple products now available.

The relationship between innovation and social engagement is directly applicable to building your social presence. This relationship spans the stages of learning, applying the ideas gained to design, and then iterating to steadily improve (sometimes in radical steps) what is offered to customers or cause-related constituents in the marketplace. This is what makes social customer experience management different from traditional approaches to customer and market development. It's the addition of customer-powered *collaborative* experiences that enhance the value of customer engagement. Without collaboration, *engagement* quickly devolves to a more standard company-driven marketing and business development effort.

It is important to understand the requirement for collaboration in creating effective channels for engagement. It's easy to fall into the trap of "this is the same as what we've been doing, only now our customers are talking too." The problem with this kind of thinking is not that there aren't analogies to existing processes—there are, just as there would be in any business process evolution. Rather, it's because "the same as" is exactly the excuse used to avoid substantive change inside your firm or organization, an excuse that inertial forces within your firm will desperately seek. Does this sound like an overstatement? It's not. As with any other aspect of business transformation, moving toward a social mindset *with the customer at the center* involves fundamental process change and recognition of the need for collaboration across many fronts. This *may be different from what you've been doing*, and it is important to set expectations of fundamental change early on.

Getting your social customer experience strategy right, and successfully applying it to your business, depends more on creating an internal culture around change, around collaborative workflow, and around processes like ideation than on implementing any particular toolset. In our social media workshops, for example, we don't begin with social media tools: we *end* with them. The workshops begin with an explanation of business objectives and customers and the dynamics of the Social Web. With such an understanding in place, it's easy to choose the particular tools that are most likely to produce the desired results. Starting from the point of view of tools would result in an endless chasing of me-too ideas. Sometimes this approach works, fair enough, but more often it leads to #FAIL.

Adoption of technology follows the same rules; social technology may impact management and decision-making, for example. Product and service innovation, where ideas become reality, is certainly impacted. So are customer-support processes, where the post-purchase issues that inevitably occur are sorted out. The ripple will touch your HR department, your supply chain, and your delivery network. You get the idea.

When choosing a social technology, start with your business, your culture, and your internal processes to create a strategy for an overall platform that provides connections to your customers, supports the formal processes of active listening, and encourages your customers to share their ideas, based on their experience with your product or service, about how they'd like to see your business evolve.

We hope this discussion on the whys of social customer experience helps you see the full spectrum of opportunities companies pursue when they undertake social efforts. With luck, it also helps you recognize that you can't do everything; success is a matter of focusing on the most immediate, practical, and relevant goals for your business. In other words, it requires prioritization.

Prioritization: Getting to the Conversations That Matter

The prior section dealt with why—selling, saving, and learning—so now it's on to who. Too many times this fundamental question doesn't get asked or gets asked in a cursory, almost rhetorical way: "'Who' is our customer—that's who! That's why it's called social customer experience!" In practice, a detailed understanding of "who" matters. "Who" isn't an easy question, nor is it even a single question.

As a starting point, think about who in two ways:

- Members: Who is the target audience, or audiences, for your social channels?
- Makers: Who within your organization will need to be involved, in any way, to make your investment in and use of social channels successful?

The following sections cover members and makers.

Members

Who are the people you want to engage with in your social channels? You may think of channels as representing different audiences—your Facebook audience, your Twitter audience, your website audience, and so forth. While it may seem logical, viewing "who" solely by channel leads to challenges with diversity and overlap: with the fact that not everyone on Facebook is the same, and many people who use Facebook also use Google+, Twitter, and other social channels. Your largest channels are likely to be very diverse. They'll include long-time customers and new prospects; highly profitable customers and bargain hunters; those who buy your most popular products but also those using niche products, or older models, or even products you no longer make.

At the same time, while the channel won't decide for you, you still need to decide for yourself: With whom do I want to engage and cultivate a relationship? Who can I influence, and who can influence others? Which parts of my business are ready to engage socially, and which need more time? *Which parts of my customer base are ready to engage in the ways that will support my goals?*

Almost every action you take in social channels will be more relevant to some than others. Think of this as an opportunity rather than a constraint; you get to shape your audience by what you offer them.

Think back on the coupon examples. Coupon mavens are legion, and a coupon offer is likely to attract new customers, for sure. But some of these customers are there for the coupon, and when the coupon is gone, they'll be gone too. Even those you keep may be difficult to migrate to more expensive and profitable products (you've effectively taught them that "price" is "35 percent off"), preferring to stick to the bargains. Meanwhile, the social channel you use for coupons may turn away those in search of the latest news on new products and new ways to interact with your brand.

The same applies to engagement on your website. Many early adopters of social technology listened to the gurus who told them that a real community was a place where customers could talk about anything they wanted—not just topics related to your products or brand experience. So they created off-topic forums on their website and got what they asked for: conversations that were far afield from the goals of the business or even most customers. Eventually, executives asked, "why are people talking about puppies on our travel website?"

Co-author Joe Cothrel's experience with a large U.S. insurance company was typical. Customers, they said, will decide what to discuss. The community was structured not by subject but by customer segment—recent grad, empty nesters, new parents, and so forth. The company knew that different people had different insurance needs at different times of life, true enough, but they didn't reflect on needs that these members, across life-stage segments, had in common: the need for security, compliance with the law, economics and affordability, and more.

As a result, the community quickly wandered away from business objectives and toward an unstructured collection of random conversations. A few hours after community launch, for example, a long conversation developed on the subject of potty training. The company quickly understood where this would lead and rightfully concluded that a little guidance would be a good thing.

Most companies have an engaged audience around their brand or products; many have more than one. When launching social effort, think about whom you want to engage, and then shape your content and activities and offers accordingly, all within the context of your business objectives.

It's important when thinking about target audiences to keep in mind your business objectives and the common, shared needs of your customers that relate to those objectives. The most successful social efforts begin with an addressable audience with a common bond or need. An *addressable* audience is an audience that already engages with you on a regular basis, preferably online. They visit your website or your Facebook page. They subscribe to your email newsletter. In some way, they have signaled their interest in what you offer. In the process, they have also given you a way to reach them—an address.

A successful social effort will ultimately attract a larger, unaddressed audience, but it's important to begin with those you can easily engage. Take the insurance company as an example: They have a much better chance of engaging with new parents than with recent graduates, since most people don't consider insurance products—and therefore engage with insurance companies—until they have children. For this company, new parents would readily self-select and form an addressed audience. Other forms of mass-reach campaigns might then be used to attract unaddressed recent grads.

A final key point on customers and conversations: For most companies, any channel to the public will attract two kinds of conversation: feedback (including complaints) and requests for service and support. It doesn't matter how clear you are about the purpose of the channel; those topics will arise. That doesn't mean you should morph every channel into a customer service channel, but you must have a plan for addressing those requests successfully. Often it's a simple escalation to a more appropriate channel.

Makers

To ensure a great social customer experience, someone has to create that experience. As you learned in Chapter 1, "Social Media and Customer Engagement," this responsibility does not rest solely within the social team. Nor can it rest with the digital team or even with the customer care team. A great social customer experience is the product of a great business.

Listening to the conversations in your marketplace is the starting point in becoming a great business. The application of more rigorous analytics to these conversations yields clues as to how an organization might use this input to improve a product or service. It also reveals *why* the highly recommended cross-functional work team approach to managing the Social Web is so essential.

The basic process of listening—whether using a marketing-style dashboard offering like Salesforce's Radian6 or your own informal methods built around search and the underlying social networking tools themselves—is an intuitively sensible starting point. One caution, though: While listening can provide anecdotal clues as to what your customers do and don't appreciate about your brand, product, or service, at some point you'll need to move to customer engagement. Why?

Unless you make it known otherwise, no one knows you're listening except you—so that makes it a safe starting point. However, unless you are also responding in a meaningful way, your customers and other stakeholders will almost surely recognize that you are *only* listening. If you've ever hollered for help in an empty room, you know how obvious it is—and what it feels like—when no one responds. Even worse, customers who are nearby—in the social sense, meaning part of the conversation or closely connected to the person(s) at the center of it—will also notice your lack of response. Given a comment that warrants attention, they will likely join in and amplify it and will themselves draw a similarly negative conclusion if there is no substantive response from your firm or organization.

To be fair, a great use of listening *at the start* of your social media capability development is to bring your organization up to speed on what people are saying about your brand, product, or service. Use the listening tools to do this *before* you actively engage your customers through social technologies so that you can develop an effective engagement strategy. *This will help you build the internal constituency that you'll ultimately need.* But remember: Ultimately, *not* responding sends a message to your customers. Plan to participate not too long after you've started listening.

Workflow and Prioritization

If you've ever looked at conversational data pulled from the Social Web—perhaps you've tried one or more of the basic listening tools—you're no doubt thinking "Sounds great, but who's going to filter through all of this?" If you have a small brand or you're in an industry that isn't talked about a lot, you may have relatively few conversations that are of interest to you or require your attention, so a basic listening tool with some ability to respond may be sufficient. If you're Coke or Boeing or Bank of America, and in particular if your product has complex or frequent service needs or your industry finds itself in the news currently on a regular basis, you'll likely find yourself facing thousands of conversations daily.

To get an idea of just how seriously businesses are taking social analytics, use Google to search for "social media mission control." These are becoming central to the social customer experience management challenge and as such are a solid testament to just how important social analytics and understanding what is happening on the Social Web have become.

And there's a catch to all of this free data. For well-known brands or cause-related groups, and increasingly for many smaller brands and organizations, the amount of data can be overwhelming. Someone has to review this data, filter it, and then act on it! Very likely that means creating a social team that is staffed and run more like your call center than your marketing or PR team: productivity measures, SLAs, the whole nine yards. As you begin to plan your social customer experience strategy, think through the requirements for an engagement platform that make it easy to prioritize and address the conversations that are important to you so that you can respond efficiently.

Just as a social analytics dashboard will save you work by automatically displaying selected KPIs related to your handling of conversations in an organized and revealing manner, a proper social customer experience platform will automatically route customer conversations to the specific departments or service teams where they can be acted upon. Automated routing and prioritization based on your business rules is essential in efficiently responding to conversational data. Advanced capabilities—routing, prioritization, workflow—mark the transition from listening to engagement. Figure 5.2 shows schematically how all of this fits together, around a typical conversation.

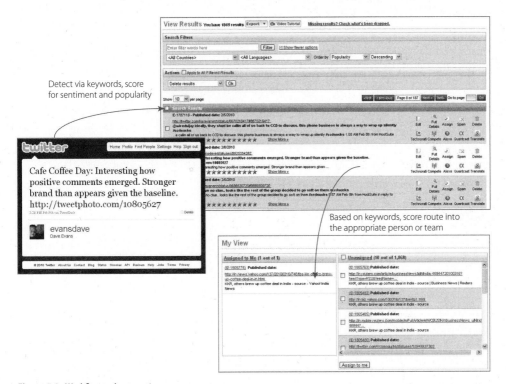

Figure 5.2 Workflow and automation

Active Listening

Active listening, a term coined by Rohit Bhargava, means integrating what is being talked about *outside* of your organization with the processes *inside* your organization that are driving those conversations. In other words, it means listening intently enough that you actually understand not only what is being said but how and why it came about, and formulating at least a basic idea of what you will do next because of it. The implication here is deeper than what social media marketing would typically consider.

The ensuing analysis and response will more often than not involve the entire organization or the better part of it.

Rohit Bhargava

Consumer behavior expert Rohit Bhargava is the author of *Likeonomics* (Wiley, 2012) and *Personality Not Included* (McGraw-Hill, 2008). Rohit blogs actively and also teaches marketing at Georgetown University.

You can follow Rohit on Twitter (@rohitbhargava) and read his blog, aptly named the "Influential Marketing Blog," here:

www.rohitbhargava.com

Consider the case of Freshbooks, a small-business billing and time-tracking service. Freshbooks makes a practice of paying attention to its customers, including what they are saying on Twitter. One post in particular caught their attention: Freshbooks customer Michelle Wolverton had been stood up on a date. Freshbooks' response, shown in Figure 5.3, taken from social media pro Erica O'Grady's series on using Twitter in business, got right to the point: "*We* would never stand you up." But then they did one better: Michelle is a Freshbooks customer, so Freshbooks sent Michelle fresh flowers. The result is near-legend status on the Web. Google it.

Figure 5.3 Freshbooks would never stand her up.

The point of the Freshbooks example is this: Listening alone didn't win Freshbooks praise. Instead, there was a process inside Freshbooks—at an operational level—that flexibly provided for an appropriate response to customer conversations. It is the combination of listening, understanding customers, and enabling the organization to respond effectively and in a talkworthy manner that is really at the heart of the Freshbooks example.

One may argue that Freshbooks is a small business or that if they sent flowers to everyone, they'd be out of business. The counter to the first objection is that plenty of small businesses could not have done this *even if they had wanted to*. Freshbooks actually did it and in a timely manner. Freshbooks' internal process—not their marketing campaigns—facilitated their talkworthy response. The counter to the second point is *they only have to do it once in a while* to advance in the eyes (and hearts) of many of their customers. There is no expectation that every Freshbooks customer will get flowers. Instead, there is an expectation that Freshbooks consistently recognizes and cares about its customers. Freshbooks is free to express this in any way it wants, whenever it chooses. Consider the similar practices at Zappos: They've built a billion-dollar business by doing things that were sometimes more expensive—free shipping in *both* directions and occasionally even overnight shipping upgrades—"just because." Creating customer delight is a proven business builder.

Touchpoint Analysis

Touchpoints are a passion for Dave. As a product manager, he was immediately drawn to the simple reality that everything he did in terms of product design came down to one customer moment. That moment is, of course, the one when a customer uses and experiences some aspect of the product you've designed or brought to market. That moment, and only that moment, is the single truth that exists from the customer's perspective: *what happens* when your customer plugs it in, turns it on, calls with a question, or shifts it into drive.

These points of intersection between the customer's world and the brand, product, or service are *touchpoints*. They include marketing touchpoints—a commercial that someone sees on TV that elicits an emotional response (as a dad, Dave still gets happy tears when he sees the original Sea World spots created at GSD&M)—as well as operational touchpoints, such as the feeling you get walking into a Whole Foods Market.

Touchpoint analysis is often presented from a marketing perspective but is applicable nonetheless across the organization and in particular to customer care. The key to applying this analytical methodology lies in understanding how your firm or business operates and in knowing what your customers consider important and talkworthy.

The combination of talkworthiness and importance comes about because conversations don't happen when no one cares to start them. Recognize here that some aspects of any product or service may not be talkworthy: Customers may not recognize or attribute significance to them, but they are still required by law or regulatory rule, for example. But for the aspects of your product or service that are both important *and* talkworthy, touchpoint analysis provides a method to analyze and prioritize how you go about applying what you learn on the Social Web to building your business.

Look more deeply into touchpoint analysis. Dave's airline experience that we opened the book with and his experiences at the Bengaluru International Airport in Bangalore, India, are great examples of touchpoints done right. Add to that the Freshbooks example and the general customer delight practices at Zappos. It's important to understand that across these very different businesses—of very different sizes and operating environments—the same basic practice exists: an emphasis on creating specific, tangible moments of delight that customers are very likely to talk about.

In the discipline of touchpoint analysis, we encourage plotting the defining attributes of important touchpoints—perceived performance and evident talkworthiness—against each other. The resulting plot will show you quickly where to focus. Figure 5.4 visualizes this concept.

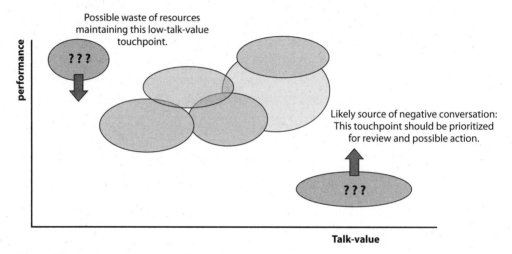

Figure 5.4 Touchpoint analysis and response prioritization

In the case of Freshbooks, they sent flowers—$50 and change—to a customer who may spend $500 on Freshbooks services. In the case of Zappos, they provide free shipping—maybe $10 plus an occasional upgrade (at a cost of perhaps $20) for customers with an average purchase of $100 to $200. In the case of United Airlines, change fees and fare differences that may have totaled $1,000 or more were waived for a customer who had spent something like 20 times that *with United* in six months on either side of those events. None of these are trivial decisions, and all require an understanding of business fundamentals: objectives, capabilities, constraints, and similar. Yet each drives—measurably—favorable brand sentiment and purchase consideration.

Consider the return on investment at Freshbooks: Even a conservative valuation of the positive, unpaid media coverage around its "We would never stand you up" response greatly exceeds what it spent. Zappos clearly runs a profitable business, all the while providing branded moments of delight. Because United has won Dave's loyalty through their acts of consideration, Dave has personally spent—from his own pocket, and *not* the reimbursed charges paid by his company or clients—more than $1,000 in fare differentials simply because he chooses first to fly with United even in cases where it is *not* the lowest cost option.

Active listening and engagement combined with a formal discipline like touchpoint analysis inevitably leads to insights into the business processes that drive marketplace conversations. The difficulty that is exposed, first with social media marketing and then with engagement, is that it becomes quickly apparent that controlling *what customers say* (as if you could) necessarily gives way to the more informed strategy of controlling *the business processes that drive the conversations* (which you certainly can).

Creating brand ambassadors—at the heart of methodologies like the Net Promoter Score—is a powerful strategy that is greatly advanced by smart use of social technology to understand precisely how your own business processes create the conversations you see on the Social Web. This is the contemporary challenge of business. It is not something that can be faked and not something that is undertaken lightly. It requires a specific, whole-business strategy and is rooted in active listening, engagement, and rigorous analysis of conversations.

Touchpoint Analysis: Bengaluru International Airport

In the course of traveling, Dave had a remarkable experience at Bengaluru International Airport, located in Bangalore, India: On arrival from New Delhi, his checked bags were waiting for him on the baggage carousel less than 10 minutes after the plane landed. Coincidentally, Dave met Anjana Kher Murray, the airport's director of public relations, the next day in one of his workshops in Bangalore, where, to her delight, Dave used the baggage example in the workshop during his discussion of touchpoint analysis.

Dave was interested in how the airport had created this experience and was invited to tour the airport. In Figure 5.5, airport CEO Marcel Hungerbuehler (right) explains the baggage process to Dave (center) as Anjana (left) also listens. Dave came away with a detailed understanding of just how his baggage experience happened. As you read through the following interview with Anjana, think about how each specific design consideration translates into a specific customer experience. Whether you do this upfront or you use this type of process in remediation efforts, one thing is clear: The experience of your customers at a given touchpoint is the experience you designed (or failed to design) into the process supporting that touchpoint.

Figure 5.5 Dave's behind-the-scenes tour of Bengaluru International Airport with Anjana Kher Murray (left) and Marcel Hungerbuehler (right)

When Dave first asked Anjana about the overall design of the airport, she replied:

We are committed to establishing the Bengaluru International Airport as India's leading airport in terms of quality and efficiency, to set a benchmark for the future commercial development of Indian airports. One of the pioneering concepts that were kept at the forefront while designing the Bengaluru International Airport was short walkways. This simple, functional terminal building is designed to ensure passengers don't have to walk till they drop. Short walkways take the passenger quickly from the entrance to the check-in counters and into the aircraft and the reverse for arriving passengers.

Compare that with the endless walks (or runs) as you change planes in some of the airports you frequent. Having been through the Bengaluru International Airport a number of times, I now expect to be through security and comfortably seated within about 10 minutes of having stepped out of the taxicab when leaving the airport and about the same when arriving.

Next, Dave asked Anjana specifically about his baggage experience. What were the design goals, and how were they measured? Here is her reply:

The following elements are critical in maintaining the baggage delivery standards: people, processes, and systems. The prompt delivery of arriving passengers' baggage is an important element of an enjoyable travel process and the aim is to provide high standards of efficiency in this area on a consistent basis. While the passenger reaches the baggage carrousel faster due to the short walkways, a long wait for the baggage could be disappointing. Upon arrival, it has been observed that passengers take about 6–10 minutes to reach the baggage claim area. Hence, it has been determined that the ideal time for baggage delivery should be between 7–10 minutes.

Important in Anjana's response is this: Each process is designed in the context of the processes that surround it. Baggage delivery standards are not set in a vacuum but rather in the context of precisely when disembarking passengers expect the bags to be available. This is naturally the point at which the passenger first approaches the baggage carousel. For some arriving flights—for example, with international flights where passengers must clear customs *before* retrieving bags—the first bags are not placed onto the carousel until those passengers are likely to be heading for the carousel. Recall the touchpoint diagram (Figure 5.4). There is no sense in expending resources to have bags on the carousel *before* passengers get to it. That incremental money and human effort can be better applied at some other passenger touchpoint.

Finally, Dave got into the operations issues. Designing a process that is supposed to delight customers and actually delighting them are two different things. So, how does the airport actually do it? Again, Anjana's reply:

A total of seven baggage carousels have been installed at Bengaluru International Airport, three for domestic and two for international arrivals; in addition, two carousels can be used for either domestic or international, depending on the peak hour requirement. Also known as a swing area, it enables flexibility and maximizes utilization of available infrastructure. The baggage delivery time is applicable to arriving passengers and is tracked on a first bag–last bag basis. First bag is defined as the time taken for the first baggage to be placed on the baggage belt. The same goes for the last baggage dropped on the conveyer belt and is defined as last bag.

As with the maintenance of any customer experience, measurement is a key aspect:

In order to ensure prompt baggage delivery on passenger arrival, we follow strict tracking methods: Ground handlers use radio communications, our Trunk Mobile Radio System (TMRS), to alert the airline ground staff on delivery of the first and last bags. This information is then sent to the Airport Operation Command Centre (AOCC) and recorded to monitor the time taken between the aircraft chock-on time (time when the chocks are placed under the aircraft wheels) to baggage delivery.

Periodic verification is done by the terminal team to confirm the baggage drop time for the first and last bag. We have also deployed special technology solutions such as Universal Flight Information Systems (UFIS) that help gather status information for the first and last bag. This system provides an alert if the first bag is not dropped on the conveyer belt within the specified minutes of flight arrival.

By this point it should be obvious that Dave's bags being ready promptly was no accident and that the multiple processes that contributed to this experience were all operating in parallel, under control of the AOCC. Just how important is the AOCC's role? Critical, as it turns out. It is the collaborative nerve center for the airport. When an airplane is delayed, for example, or when two flights are departing at the same time, the AOCC—which has airline representatives, ground staff, and other critical control personnel *physically* seated in the same room—calls for a quick conversation between affected parties. As a result, decisions are made in seconds rather than tens of minutes, and bottlenecks that would otherwise flare into actual flight delays are avoided. Anjana describes the AOCC and its purpose this way:

Our belief is that successful airport operations can only be achieved when all partners of the airport work closely together. This includes the processes and functions that ensure the baggage arrives on the correct belts within the set time frame. Hence, representatives of the Bengaluru International Airport's partners come together at the country's first 24/7 Airport Operation Command Centre. This is where crucial daily operations are streamlined for smooth, efficient, and well-coordinated airport functioning. As the nerve center of the entire airport, real-time data is being fed into it from diverse departments and collaborative decision-making process is facilitated.

As you consider your own business or organizational processes that drive customer experiences—and hence the conversations around your brand, product, or service—consider the practices of the Bengaluru International Airport in designing and measuring customer experiences with its facility. It should be clear that they are not simple, that they require a collaborative, cross-functional team to deliver, and that they do in fact produce very favorable conversations as a result.

There is another take-away from cases like the Bengaluru International Airport: Operations and infrastructure projects may not be as glamorous as a splashy Super Bowl ad. However, from your customer's perspective, how your business or organization actually runs is much more important. The Social Web is, in a sense, the great equalizer between large brands with big budgets and small brands that simply *do it better.* As a case in point, consider the new Dyson bladeless fans: If someone *needs* a fan, a standard 3-blade model can be purchased for under $20. But someone wants a bladeless fan that is quieter, works better, and looks better, it's a short step to a $300 Dyson bladeless. On top of that, the new owner will actually talk about the Dyson because it simply *is* a better fan, just as Dave has talked to anyone who will listen about the Bengaluru International Airport: It is simply a better airport, and its operations staff and infrastructure are big parts of what makes that so.

Social Technology and Decision Support

Just what is social customer experience management, and how do you build a strategy around it? In Chapter 3, "Social Customer Experience Management," you saw a quick overview and simple definition: "a way to think about how customers relate to companies and how satisfaction, loyalty and other business benefits really come about."

In this section, you'll build on this generalized idea of social customer experience management and see how to create a strategy that is specific to your business. You'll start with social CRM, since this is the connection between the Social Web and your marketing efforts.

Esteban Kolsky

Esteban Kolsky is a social strategist and consultant, and he is widely regarded as a thought leader in social CRM. You can follow Esteban on Twitter (@ekolsky) and read his blog here:

www.estebankolsky.com/

Social CRM includes the following five elements:

- A genuine effort on the part of the firm or organization to understand and consider the point of view of its customers and stakeholders, for whom the business or organization exists.

- A method to understand and map the social graphs, communities, and social applications that connect individuals within your overall audience to *each other* (rather than to you) and thereby provide an insight as to *how you fit into their world.*

- The identification of the *specific* difference between the activities your customers want to take ownership for versus those in which they look to you for guidance, relief, assistance, and similar contributions from you that improve their quality of life. See Table 5.1 for more on this.

- The optimization of your commerce or conversion processes given the role of customers and stakeholders in the conversations that impact conversion.

- The connections—*touchpoints*—between your activities and those of your customers with the internal business processes that drive the experience that occurs at those touchpoints.

The first column in Table 5.1 shows the basic decisional-support elements associated with social CRM. Take these five elements together and you have the basis for an enterprise-wide implementation of a feedback process based on customer insights gathered through active listening that can be harnessed and used to drive your business. This is what social CRM is all about.

Social CRM Element	Applicable Technique	Example Platform
Understanding the customer point of view	Social analytics and rigorous assessment of conversations	Alterian SM2, Nielsen | BuzzMetrics, Oxyme, Radian6, SAS Institute, Sysomos, TNS | Cymfony
Mapping social graphs	Source identification and social status	BuzzStream, Sysomos, Gephi
Differentiating control versus leadership	Support communities and expert identification	Lithium Technologies, Jive Software
Optimizing commerce	Quantifying and tracking ratings and reviews	Bazaarvoice, SAS Institute, IBM WebSphere
Quantifying customer touchpoints	Touchpoint analysis and prioritization of business activities	Create this yourself: See Chapter 6 of *Social Media Marketing: An Hour a Day* for more.

Table 5.1 provides a starting point for understanding and investigating some of the best-in-class tools that can be used to create the quantitative framework for your social customer experience strategy. By linking social analytics (conversation analysis) and source identification (social graph analysis) together with commerce feedback (ratings and reviews), you see an emerging end-to-end view of your commerce pipeline. Taking the further step—through touchpoint analysis or an equivalent process—of tying sources, conversations, and commerce data to the internal business or organizational processes that drive customers' experiences provides the business insights you need to evolve your business in alignment with your customers.

The Customer Point of View

Social analytics, even in their purely qualitative form, provide powerful insights into the personal views of your customers. Because analytics platforms collect large amounts of data, you can get beyond the anecdotes of focus groups. Because the tools are real time (or near real time) and ongoing, you can also move beyond one-off surveys. Going further, in exchange for your time spent configuring these tools—ranging from a few minutes to hours or days—they'll organize the relatively unstructured qualitative data into themes or categories so that you can make sense of the conversations. Figure 5.6 shows a typical social analytics dashboard and the way in which its data can be used to understand a conversation.

The insight gained into what customers are talking about—and hence how your product or service experience is perceived in the marketplace by your customers—is useful beyond marketing. This is an important point to note, in that many organizations adopting social-media-based programs place the marketing department at the focal point for this work.

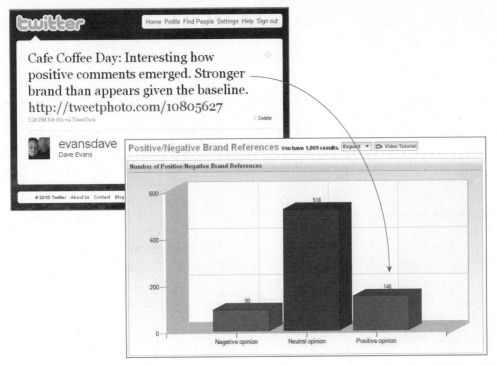

Figure 5.6 Social analytics

Here's why this happens and why it's important to see beyond marketing. Connecting social media with marketing makes sense if you consider the impact of a positive or negative post on sales. Clearly, these outside-of-brand-control comments, helpful or otherwise, keep sales managers and marketers up at night precisely because they cannot control those comments. However, when a business as a whole steps past marketing in its collective view of social customer experience, the conversations become more predictable, making it possible to manage them (in the direction of more favorable).

Looked at across the business or organization, the impact of social media extends far beyond marketing. Looking at the purchase funnel, shown in Figure 5.7, you can see that it's actually a better bet that social media has relatively little to do with marketing. Beyond creating a platform in which marketers—certain caveats respected—are welcome to participate along with everyone else in appropriate conversations, the origin of the conversations themselves has more to do with operations, HR, and customer care—all of which contribute in a tangible manner to what is talked about on the Social Web—and relatively less to do with marketing per se.

Social customer experience management (SCEM) picks up on this and formally recognizes that the conversations circulating on the Social Web *started* in, for example, operations but then exerted themselves upon marketing (by encouraging or dissuading sales). Again, this is a very different process from the more or less unidirectional flow of outbound messages associated with traditional campaigns.

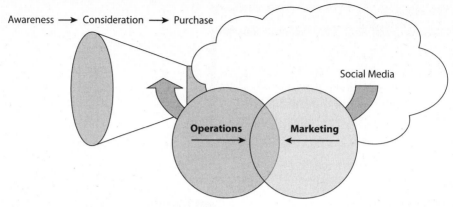

Awareness → **Consideration** → **Purchase**

Social Media

Operations → ← **Marketing**

Figure 5.7 The purchase funnel and operations

This is why SCEM is so powerful and so timely. Connecting customers into the business and understanding their perspective and what attracts them to or repels them from your brand, product, or service is a path to long-term success. SCEM combines the insights of Fred Reichheld's Net Promoter Score—itself a benchmark metric for long-term success—with quantitative tools and a flexible methodology for defining and evolving your business.

Map the Social Graph

Once you have a handle on what is being said, the next step in designing your social customer experience strategy is to understand *who* said it. By "who said it" we're not referencing the personal details of a specific individual, though you may in some cases be able to discern this information from actual customer data or a similar source.

Rather, we're referring to profile and social graph data, understanding who is talking about you by also understanding the other places where this same person publishes content and with whom it is shared. By seeing a profile in the context of that individual's social graph, you get a much more complete picture of individual motivation, influence, reach, and connectedness that allows you to prioritize your next steps in reaching out and responding (or not) to that specific individual.

The social graph itself—first covered in Chapter 2, "The Social Customer," and explored in detail later in Chapter 11, "The Social Graph"—defines the social links that exist between people within social networks. The social graph also includes pointers to the various other places where this individual publishes or otherwise participates. Social CRM and the more focused source identification tools navigate this social graph to create a map so that these relationships and linkages can be understood in a business context. Understanding where someone publishes and participates on the Social Web leads you to the additional relationships that can provide real insight into the conversations you've located that specifically reference your brand, product, or service. Figure 5.8 shows a typical map, generated by BuzzStream, for a potential contact based on an initial keyword search.

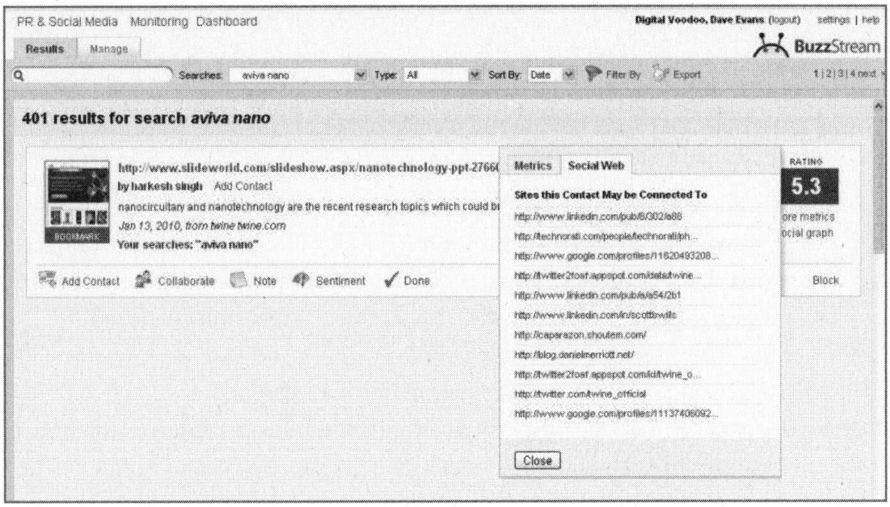

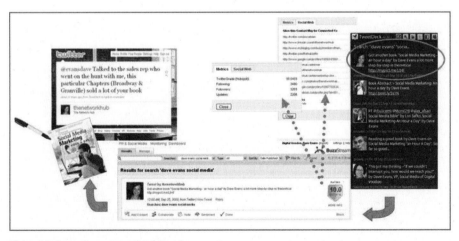

Figure 5.8 Mapping the social graph

As an example of how social analytics can be put to use in combination with an understanding of the social graph, consider what happens when you find a post that is favorable to your brand, product, or service on Twitter. Figure 5.9 shows a different example of social graph mapping, this time with the original tweet related to the map of the social graph. Using BuzzStream and a combination of basic search tools—SM2 from Alterian, now part of SDL, and TweetDeck (as a real-time search tool, and now a part of Twitter)—Dave was able to connect with the person who posted the original comment. The result is a new friend and business connection at The Network Hub in Vancouver. What if you could do this with everyone who mattered to your business? With a business-based SCEM strategy and an enterprise engagement platform, you can.

Figure 5.9 Connecting source and social graph

Tools like BuzzStream, TweetDeck, and HootSuite—none of which is break-the-bank expensive—provide simple and straightforward ways to implement these practices in your business or organization. For example, the combination of TweetDeck (available free of charge) and BuzzStream (under $100/month) enables you to actively monitor Twitter for mentions of your brand or a competitor's and ascertain the social influence of those talking about your products and services. This gives you precisely the data you need to prioritize your actual response effort (which is decidedly *not* free), given what is being said and who is saying it. This data translates directly into meaningful key performance indicators (KPIs) too: The number of mentions on Twitter, positives versus negatives, average influencer rankings, and mean response time are all examples of KPIs that you can add to your existing dashboards.

Stepping up, engagement platforms from Jive, Lithium Technologies, and others provide robust workflow and the ability to prioritize conversations—and even to route these to specific team members and to track response productivity. This allows you to efficiently connect more deeply with individual customers, be it a one-off interaction around a particularly delightful or upsetting experience or the development of a longer-term relationship with a significantly influential individual within your customer base.

If you've ever posted a favorable comment—or any comment, for that matter—about a brand, product, or service, think about what it would feel like if you were personally acknowledged by the brand manager as a result. In general, people post because they have something to say—and because they want to be recognized for having said it. In particular, when people post positive comments they are expressions of appreciation for the experience that led to the post. While a compliment to the person standing next to you is typically answered with a response like "Thank you," the sad fact is that most brand compliments go unanswered. These are lost opportunities to understand what drove the compliments and create a solid fan based on them.

Integration of the Customer Experience

In the previous section we illustrated how using a simple listening platform (for example, using TweetDeck as a real-time monitor for Twitter in combination with BuzzStream for social graph mapping) can yield valuable KPIs. The step-up in business value from listening/monitoring to engagement and response along with call-center-grade metrics is seen in the usefulness of these tools. They are enablers of business processes that connect what is learned on the Social Web with the way the business operates. This is how your ability to strategically manage the customer experience enables you to manage the customer conversations.

This combination of engagement and response, whether through use of a set of tools like TweetDeck along with BuzzStream or integrated tools like the Lithium Technologies' social customer experience platform, Sysomos' Heartbeat or Radian6 with Salesforce.com's social graph add-ons ought to be a formal part of your business toolset. And why not? Where else do you find customer conversations, served up and categorized, labeled by level of potential influence, all presented in the context of an historical baseline?

The engagement process is depicted in Figure 5.10. The integration with your business or organization occurs first in the routing processes and then in tracking. Of course, the act of responding itself is a business process, but that is really a function of having or not having a listening program and does not in itself imply a social business orientation. To be sure, listening is better than not listening, and listening combined with responding is a solid idea. But to really see the benefit of a social customer experience program within your organization, you have to take a further step.

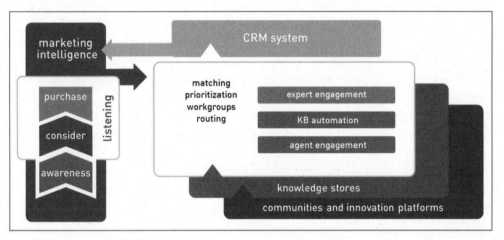

Figure 5.10 The engagement process

That further step is reviewing what you discover, tracking the issues—the positives and negatives—and then using this information to inform, change, and innovate inside your organization. This information can be used to develop a response strategy that includes elements of both customer response and internal business response and adaptation.

Susan Abbott

President and senior consultant and researcher at Abbott Research and Consulting, Susan Abbott helps clients discover insights and develop response strategies that support their business. Susan's down-to-earth take on the Social Web and social CRM is refreshing. You can follow Susan on Twitter (@SusanAbbott) and read her blog here:

        www.customercrossroads.com

Here's a great example, from Abbott Research and Consulting principal Susan Abbott:

I was mixing up some dip yesterday, and observed (for the hundredth time) that when you open the package, you rip off half the instructions.

—Susan Abbott, Customer Crossroads

Susan goes on to note that this is probably an avoidable accident. The barcode, she notes, is safely tucked out of the way. As they say in New York, "not sayin'…just sayin'." There is clearly an insight here, and trivial as it may seem—or not, depending on how critical those instructions were to successfully making whatever is in the package—these are the kinds of things that are within your control, that impact the customer experience, and that result in conversations.

Looking at Susan's packaging comment, what would you do if it were your dip and you had control over (or could influence) the packaging design? First, you could create a specific strategy, either as you discovered those comments for the first time (good) or before you began listening at all (better). The best practice here is clearly to have a response strategy in place before you start listening.

An effective response strategy considers several elements, including who will respond, how the associated workflow rules will be set up, and the threshold for response, set by the seriousness of the issue—"tore the instructions" versus "hate tiny print" versus "found something growing inside the sealed package." Your response strategy should be built around an assessment of timeliness standards—backed up with timely KPIs—and should also include an assessment of the effort required so that appropriate staffing plans can be created.

Digging into Susan's packaging comment further, by responding *and tracking,* you can tell the difference between a one-off case and an opportunity for process change that leads to better conversations on the Social Web. Maybe Susan—like more than a few of the professionals now tasked with social media responsibilities in addition to whatever was expected of them previously—is time pressured, resulting in this mishap. Or maybe, just maybe, the actual packaging process places the chip dip mix envelopes *upside down* in the box that Susan bought at Costco so that when Susan takes it out, she's actually holding the envelope in a way that guarantees ripping the bottom every time—and thereby destroying the instructions—instead of ripping across the top where you had intended.

This may seem like a trivial example, but scale it up across your own processes and the actual expectations you have of your customers: How many seemingly small but crazy things do you place into the marketplace every day? For example, how many times have you sprayed yourself with (pressurized) salad dressing when opening the little container on an airplane? Someone designed that package, someone oversaw the filling of it, and someone else sold cases of it to airline catering firms with *at least the opportunity* to understand what was likely to happen when it was opened inside an airplane. If you don't listen and track, you'll never know, and without an effective strategy and planned response, you won't be able to do anything about it.

These seemingly small things are actually important to identify and fix. Each, in its own way, contributes to a conversation, a parody, or a joke—or something far more serious that plays out on the Social Web. Rarely do any of these help you. The other great thing is that as you find these on your own or with help from customers, you can announce in channels like Twitter that you have fixed them. Not only does it send a nice message to customers like Susan, but it also says to anyone else listening that your business or organization actually pays attention to what is happening on the Social Web. At the least, this gives you an image bump; at most, it will help you spot a problem early as customers realize that *because you are present and listening,* it is worth their time to let you know about some particular service or product issue.

Here's the take-away: Social customer experience management and the strategic integration of what you learn into your business processes form a solid pathway to better customer experiences and thereby to the conversations that you really want. The program can be lightweight—basic listening combined with a triage process that picks off the big issues and makes sure they don't escalate—or it can be a deeply embedded and formalized source of continuous feedback that provides a customer-feedback heartbeat. Either way, by building strategically sound active listening into your *internal* processes, you've successfully connected your business to your customers. Further, you've done it in a way that they are sure to notice and appreciate. That will not only further solidify your relationship with your customers but will also result in their spreading your good word.

Nathan Gilliatt, Workflow and Social Media

Nathan Gilliatt, principal, Social Target, provides analysis and services supporting the implementation of active listening and supporting business strategy. You can read Nathan's blog here:

    http://net-savvy.com/executive/

Customer Support and SCEM

Salesmanship begins when the customer says no. Support begins when the customer says yes. In a sort of basic truth about business, this view of customer support clarifies one of the biggest opportunities a firm or organization will ever have: the opportunity to make those who were happy to buy from you even happier that they did. We point this out because in too many businesses, whether by accident or actual design, customer support feels to customers like an obligation whose cost is to be minimized.

A different orientation—viewing a call from a customer as an opportunity to create a moment of delight—is what defines firms like Zappos, though they are hardly alone. Beth Thomas-Kim, director of consumer services at Nestlé, took exactly this view when she transformed a cost center—customer service—into a brand-building touchpoint. By viewing each call as an opportunity and measuring the outcomes of the calls, the customer service objectives morphed from optimizing (that is, reducing) call time to creating happier customers who are more likely to make subsequent purchases as a result.

Beyond the support tools themselves, the essential practices that connect the conversations occurring within them have to do with tracking and quantifying the specific themes that recur. Issues in design, production, clarity of instructions, and a lot more can be identified and corrected by examining these themes in detail. Tracking service issues through associated tools like JIRA is an easy way to identify candidate activities for process improvement, just as looking at delivery or inventory issues leads to improvement in supply chain processes.

Beyond directly addressing support and related issues, what else can you do with a support forum? Along with product or service-related findings, support forums can also yield valuable insights into the hidden experts that exist within your customer base.

This is precisely what Dell discovered as it acted on its own belief that the discussions in and around its prior support structure indicated the presence of brand advocates and subject matter experts within its customer base. By turning some aspects of support over to its customers—by offering peer-to-peer options in a support forum while making use of the reputation management tools that are available in best-of-class support platforms—Dell was able to not only reduce its support costs while improving the overall levels of customer satisfaction with its support services but also identify the customer experts who existed in the support networks. This recognition drove higher levels of engagement from these experts, in support of Dell's overall efforts to respond to the issues that Jeff Jarvis had called out in his 2007 post calling Dell to task.

When evaluating a support platform, pay particular attention to its reputation management and expert identification tools. Support platforms from Lithium Technologies (providing the support platform for Dell referenced in the prior section) are particularly good in this regard: Expert identification is the core strength of this particular platform. When considering the use of a branded support community, look for ways to identify and reward members who are providing above-average value.

Activate Your Customers: Control vs. Leadership

Consider customer/product interactions like those described in the case of Dell and in particular the roles played by the customer versus the business or organization. The people creating and posting the content (for example, customers uploading pictures) have *immediate* control of the content and hence control over their side of the conversation.

It's immediate because it applies to this particular interaction: They get to define what is being said right now and to influence others who are listening right now.

By comparison, brand teams, product managers, organization fundraisers, and similar have control only as far as the design of the experiences that led to the conversations. In this sense, understanding the specifics that surround a conversation—who said it, what was said, and who (else) this conversation is likely to influence—provides the proof points for the business decisions and processes that gave rise to the conversations observed. These conversations close the loop—beyond the *immediate* sale—with regard to efficacy of business programs intended to drive *long-term* sales and profits.

The net impact is that the product manager, for example, is in more of a leadership role (as in leadership of the conversation) than a control role, a point worth noting for product team leads interested in understanding the impact of social technology on their own business. By shifting from a control mindset to one of collaborative leadership, you can achieve a more productive approach to product development that incorporates customer-led innovation. The end objective is, of course, to create the experiences that lead to the conversations you want and in turn drive the sales and innovation (or other conversions) that contribute to business success.

Review and Hands-On

This chapter covered the key decisions you need to make to undertake a social customer experience effort. It also covered integration of active listening and formalized social customer experience management into the business decision-making processes that drive an organization.

Most important is to recognize that the source of customer or constituent conversations—the specific things about your brand, product, service, or cause that people will convey to others through social media—are driven more by your organizational processes acting in concert than by marketing acting alone. This is a departure from traditional PR and advertising. While traditional channels remain vitally important in anchoring and promoting what you offer, it is the actual experience—created deep inside your organization—that drives the conversation that can significantly amplify your message and more fundamentally drive long-term success.

Review of the Main Points

The main points covered in this chapter are summarized here:

- Most companies mistakenly focus first on what social technology to deploy and which channels (where) they should engage.

- A better starting point asks why (goals) and who (customer segments and internal groups) will be involved.

- Organizations pursue social technology applications for three reasons: to sell, to save, and to learn.

- Learning means bringing a new, customer-driven capability to the decision-making activities inside your organization.

- Active listening is the core mechanism for tapping the Social Web as a decision-making tool, powered by the quantitative application of formalized social CRM.

- Social customer experience management is built around fundamental components, all of which must be present: direct customer input, influencer and expert identification, ideation and feedback gathered through organized customer support services, and a process-driven internal culture of collaboration.

- Decision making benefits directly from the integration of social technologies, applied at the levels of customers (social media), the organization (internal collaboration), and the connection between customers and the organization.

This chapter sets out a framework for applying what can be learned and applied to business decision making through the use of social technologies. This has an impact on tactical issues—responding to a localized negative event—as well as long-term strategic planning and product innovation.

Hands-On: Review These Resources

Review each of the following and connect them to your business.

1. Check out the website for award programs like Forrester's Groundswell Awards and Lithium's Lithys Social Customer Excellence Awards to read cases on how companies are aligning goals with strategies across different industries.

   a. http://groundswelldiscussion.com/groundswell/awards/

   b. http://lithosphere.lithium.com/t5/lithys-social-customer/idb-p/Awards

2. Spend time reading Esteban Kolsky's blog, and in particular search for and read the entries on "analytics engines." As a hands-on exercise, create a plan for integrating social analytics into your operational (not marketing) processes.

   a. www.estebankolsky.com/

3. Review the product innovation cycle (Figure 5.1), and map this onto your business and identify the specific areas or functions within your business that contribute to innovation. Think about the Bengaluru International Airport example as you do this. How can you design in the experiences you want your customers or stakeholders to talk about?

Hands-On: Apply What You've Learned

Apply what you've learned in this chapter through the following exercises to create your own social customer experience strategy:

1. Define the why, who, what, and where for your current social customer experience efforts, if any. How easy or difficult was it?

2. Visit with the IT, marketing, or operations teams that use your existing CRM data. Explore ways of incorporating social data into these processes and connecting that information to your business or organization.

3. Building on your exercises in Chapter 1, define one or more internal collaboration points based on what you discovered in exercise 1.

4. Building on your exercises in Chapters 2 and 3, create a workflow path for social data (for example, conversations) that carries this information to the points inside your organization that can act on it. Include a method for tracking results.

5. Build your touchpoint map, and identify the critical customer experiences that create the conversations that show up on the Social Web.

6. Combine the previous exercises and create a requirements list for the toolset that you will need to manage the social experience of your customers as it relates to your business objectives.

Social Analytics, Metrics, and Measurement

6

Chapter 6 hits our personal passion with regard to social media and business: measurement. This chapter covers the question that keeps most decision makers and change/process champions up at night: "How do I measure this and make sense of it?" It takes a hard look at the rationale for establishing specific metrics along with the tools and platforms that provide and analyze these metrics in the context of your objectives.

Chapter contents:
Why we measure
Social analytics
Know your influencers
Web analytics
Business analytics

Why We Measure

Before looking at how companies measure and analyze their social efforts, let's look at a more fundamental question: Why does measurement matter?

Measure to Inform: Numbers and Stories

At the most general level, measurement informs your teams, departments, and other stakeholders about the state and outcomes of some process or effort, in this case programs related to the social customer experience. Measurement enables you to see—and to share with others in your firm—how current metrics compare with yesterday's, last week's, last month's, and so forth. For example, how many customers asked for help on Twitter today? Was it higher or lower than yesterday? It's a comparative exercise. When you measure these outcomes, you're able to see how well the effort you've undertaken is accomplishing its goals. Of those customers on Twitter, how satisfied were they with the help provided? This is often a comparative exercise too, but the comparison may be to a future target or goal as easily as to an historical number.

Note that measurement is also intended to inform. Measurement is inseparable from communication. When you think about measurement, it's important to reflect not only on *what* you're measuring but also on *how* you will communicate those measurements and to *whom*. In business, we talk about measurement and reporting. But keep in mind that reporting has a purpose: It helps get things done. Good reporting not only informs; it inspires useful action.

Good measurement and reporting are always a mix of qualitative and quantitative. Metrics may tell you *what* happened, but qualitative insights can point out *why* it happened, *how* it happened, or *what it means*. Sometimes those qualitative insights are a product of analysis, such as the process of breaking data down to better understand it, and sometimes they are inherent in the data itself—the expressed opinions of a customer, for example. In fact, social data is much richer than traditional forms of business data in terms of the qualitative insights it offers based on quantitative metrics, and it's important to take advantage of that richness.

Finally, measurement is about *stories*. Note here that we do not mean "made up stories that pervert or obfuscate the truth" but rather the combination of objectively observed data and your professional insight which provides meaning. It's all the more puzzling, therefore, that so much social reporting inside companies consists of datasheets filled with numbers, absent accompanying text to explain or interpret what the numbers are saying and what actions may be indicated as a result. On this point, consider the following quote:

Power corrupts. PowerPoint corrupts absolutely.

—Edward Tufte, *professor emeritus of political science, computer science and statistics, and graphic design at Yale*

For more on the *effective and objective* use of data and the importance of stories particularly when using slide software, see:

www.edwardtufte.com/tufte/powerpoint

To put it simply, effective reporting is about numbers and stories. Think about how things get done—when they get done—in the U.S. Congress. Generally, Congress sponsors a study to better understand how significant and widespread a certain problem is. Thousands of pages of data are then delivered. But the data alone doesn't drive action. To get action, you also need citizens who are willing to testify about the impact of the problem on their lives. With data alone, nothing gets done.

The same is true in a business or any other organization. In fact, if you provide numbers without supporting stories—often called use cases or customer scenarios— you'll find that the decision makers on whom you depend will make up their own story— and perhaps not to your liking. We've all had the experience of seeing an executive latch on to a seemingly random metric in a report and then make that metric an all-important focus. You can help prevent this by *never* delivering a number *without* a story.

Performance, Return, and Insight

Another way to answer the question "why measure" is to ask, "What is the purpose of this measure, and how will this measure be used?" In social customer experience, business-related measurements generally apply to performance, return, or insight.

Performance

First, measurement is used help people understand how well social channels are performing. How many customers arrived via this or that channel today? What did they do? What did your organization do to drive customer activity? What did your team do to manage or respond? These metrics typically include visits, views, posts, and the like. Note that these metrics are often denigrated as meaningless or fluffy compared to more established measures like sales or margin or headcount. In fact, if you run an SCE effort, these metrics are critical to understanding what's happening in your channels today. They are often referred to as operational metrics, which is a good way to distinguish them from financial metrics. When sufficiently meaningful on their own, or when used in combination, for example, as a ratio of current to prior visits, they are often called key performance indicators (KPIs).

Return

Beyond performance (the state of what is happening) you can measure to understand the financial return (the impact of the change in state) or other benefits that your SCE efforts are having on your business. As noted in Chapter 5, "Social Technology and Business Decisions," return might be expressed as increased sales or reduced cost relative to the expense of the SCE program or some portion of it. It might be increased loyalty, measured by surveys (for example, NPS) or customer churn. Or it might be increased effectiveness of current programs, such as online advertising. This is commonly referred to as return on investment (ROI), discussed in detail in the final section of this chapter.

Insight

Finally, measurement helps you to better understand customers and markets, the drivers and nuanced characteristics that enable or constrain performance and return. These insights enable you to drive toward higher value or to avoid otherwise hard-to-spot challenges. They can also be of intrinsic value in themselves when directed to the right parties within the organization. For instance, they can tell the PR group which messages are getting the most traction among customers online or inform your development group how much (or how little) customers liked the product launched last week. They can make clear to the support group which emerging issues may be contributing to support requests, useful data in planning for future capacity. At the individual-customer level, they can even help the organization deliver the right offers to specific customers at the moment they are ready to receive them.

Performance, insight and return: It may be tempting to trade one of these objectives off against another: Stakeholders often have a favorite and will insist that only one really matters. The truth is that every SCE measurement program must encompass all three.

Sources of Data

"That's all fine," you say, "but where do I get the data I need?" To create an effective measurement and reporting program, you need access to the data contained in your social platforms, web analytics tools, and business systems.

Social Platforms

First, there's the data that comes from the social platform itself. This may mean collecting data from more than platform, or pehaps you are using a single platfrom that covers both on-domain (your website or a support forum you own) and off-domain (for example, the number of posts on a specific social network that is relevant to your business). Either way, you need to understand all the metrics that are available from the systems you use to power social interaction on your website, and you need to understand the continuously evolving set of tools that social networks like Facebook and Twitter make available to you. There's no substitute for this knowledge; make an effort to identify and understand everything that's available, and then choose the metrics that are most meaningful to you.

Web Analytics

Second, there's the data that comes from web analytics platforms. SCE exists within the larger context of the digital experience you are creating for your customers. The website is the heart of that digital experience, and web analytics measures what happens on the website. Most social platforms stop short of providing all of the capabilities offered within your website, so you may need to add web analytics skills and tools to your toolkit.

Business Systems

Finally, there's the data that exists in business systems. This data is critical to providing context to the prior sources of data: You can't measure the impact of your social efforts on sales if you don't have sales data. Likewise, you can't measure cost savings if you don't have cost data. You can't tell whether social participants are customers without connecting to your CRM system. Unless you have transaction history, you can't tell whether social customers are buying more, less, or the same as other customers.

Measuring return is always a process of combining social data with business data, relating what you are doing to the business results—generally measured in dollars—accruing as a result. Note here the importance of tying social measurement to financial measurement: As this book's co-author Joe Cothrel likes to say, "It's important to connect your metrics to your business objectives: In an expression like 'A * B = C' if neither A nor B has a dollar sign associated with it, then C won't either. If that's the case, you should be worried."

In the remaining sections of this chapter, you'll explore these data sources in detail. When you've completed this chapter, you'll be well on your way to becoming a social measurement pro!

Social Analytics

Social platform measurement and analytics have improved considerably over the past 10 years, as organizations increasingly treat their social efforts as part of the business strategy and operations disciplines rather than as one-off experiments. Every platform maker, from enterprise platforms like Lithium Technologies, Oracle, and Microsoft to large social networks like Google+, Facebook, and Twitter, is in constant dialogue with business users to better understand the specific types of information needed to properly manage and measure SCE.

As noted previously, there are quantitative and qualitative aspects to social analytics. Consider first the quantitative side.

Quantitative Social Analytics

Every social platform produces metrics, and every social manager uses them to measure and report. An example of a typical social trend chart is shown in Figure 6.1.

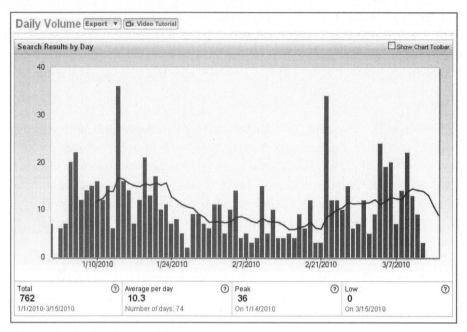

Figure 6.1 Social media analytics: trend chart

The social metrics that are available to you depend on the platforms you are using: a word to the wise when *selecting* your platform! Of course, there are some commonalities between platforms. Table 6.1 lists the five major types of social metrics and some of the specific metrics included in each type. Note that "amplification" and "applause" as used here are terms coined by Avinash Kaushik, featured in the sidebar that follows.

▶ **Table 6.1** Five major types of social metrics

Metric Type	Activity Examples	Metric Examples
Membership	Members who have joined your channel	Registrations, follows, likes (of brand pages), subscriptions
Contribution	Content posted by your customers or agents	Posts, comments, updates, tweets
Curation	Organized or classified content	Tags, labels, pins
Amplification	Shared content with others	Shares, retweets
Applause	Endorsed content	Kudos, likes (of content or users), +1s, friends

These five are likely a subset of the metrics available to you. In fact, a typical platform for on-domain SCE includes hundreds of metrics that you can use for measurement and reporting. *But we don't we recommend that you use every metric at your disposal.* Why not?

Avinash Kaushik

Author of *Web Analytics: An Hour a Day* (Sybex, 2007) and *Web Analytics 2.0* (Sybex, 2009), Avinash Kaushik publishes the blog Occam's Razor. You can follow Avinash on Twitter (@avinashkaushik) and read his blog here:

www.kaushik.net/

First, the metrics available in any platform aren't necessarily the ones available for your use. Your available metrics depend on the specific applications and features you are using in your channel. For example, if you are using an ideation application, you will have a metric related to the absolute count of ideas. This is a unique type of content that the application invites and tracks. If you don't use ideation, that metric won't be available to you.

The second reason for not using every metric in your system is that not all metrics are alike. Some metrics—total posts, for example—provide an understanding of a basic fact about the channel you are using. In this book and in the industry generally, these are called *pulse* metrics—they help you track the basic health and growth of a specific channel, as well as your overall community or networks. Other metrics—referred to as *diagnostic* metrics—are more useful for answering specific questions you might have about what's happening in your community. You need to strike a balance in using these types of metrics, and as a result you'll likely find yourself "choosing one from column A and one from column B" rather than everything on the menu. The important thing is selecting the metrics that help, over the long run, to articulate and punctuate the story you are telling. Again, we don't mean choose the measures that make you look good but rather choose the most concise set of measures needed to guide you toward success in the context of your business objectives.

For example, in a forum, member behavior around *posts* can be broken down into two component metrics: new threads and replies. If you see total posts decline and you want to investigate why, you might pull these two component metrics. If you see that new threads declined more than replies, then you probably have an issue with how new users are finding your community, because new users contribute a disproportionate number of new threads. If the reverse is true—if replies declined more than new threads—then you likely have a problem with your superfans or superusers, who in most communities contribute a disproportionate number of replies. Over the course of a year, you may use many of the hundreds of metrics in a system in this way, even though on a weekly basis you look at a much smaller number of metrics in addition to your fundamental success measures.

There's a third reason as well: Not all of the available metrics matter. The metrics you track should align with your SCE effort and for your business objectives overall. For example, if you are using your Facebook channel to publish content with the goal of driving engagement, then comments will be a pulse metric for you. Or, if what's important to you is that you respond promptly to comments on your brand page (assuming you've enabled replies), then replies and reply timeliness will be of interest.

Putting your measurements into the context of your business may seem an obvious first step, yet too often businesses and organizations fail to make this connection and therefore fail to formally recognize and measure the impact of social media on the business. Without such measurement, it is a stretch to think that a social business program will ever take hold, let alone thrive in a run-by-the-numbers culture. The result is that your social media efforts may plateau at *social media marketing* and in particular at using social channels for outbound campaigns.

This is really unfortunate, because purely *outbound* marketing is probably the *least* effective application of social media and social technology. Remember, the Social Web—unlike TV or radio—is not fundamentally a broadcast medium. Rather, it is more of a forum or place for conversations, some of which may be of interest to you as they impact your brand, product, or service. This creates an opportunity to talk, participate, and gain influence that, to be sure, can be helpful in marketing but can also provide benefits to more general business objectives. *Measurement* forms the basis for quantifying this work: *Your story* connects it to your business.

It's often instructive to see how other companies are using and interpreting quantitative social metrics. You'll see specific examples in Chapter 8, "Customer Engagement."

Webtrends for Facebook

Facebook provides a comprehensive analytics package that offers an excellent starting point for understanding the performance of your Facebook business page. Webtrends builds on that, adding additional capabilities and metrics not available through the basic Facebook tools. For more information, visit Webtrends:

http://help.webtrends.com/en/analytics10/facebook_about.html

Qualitative Social Analytics

A note of warning: When we say *qualitative social analytics*, we don't mean that there are no numerical values in the upcoming section. Rather, what we mean is that the focus of our analysis here is qualitative data, that is, on conversations, the meaning of those conversations, and the sources (people) behind those conversations. The reporting of this analysis typically includes both text and numbers. However, unlike quantitative social analysis—answering questions like "What are people doing?"—the starting point of qualitative social analysis is to answer questions like "What are people saying?" and "Why?" Again, too, note the importance of stories.

Good qualitative analysis transforms the Social Web from a source of largely unstructured qualitative data to a conversational framework that can be viewed and tracked quantitatively. It is this discipline that enables two essential best practices when it comes to applying social media to your business or organization:

- Making sense of what people are talking about in a way that leads to *prioritized* insights in the context of competing capital efforts

- Connecting these conversations and the results of your programs designed to change these conversations for the better by addressing adverse conversations and building on beneficial ones

In traditional communications, the activities that parallel the study of conversations via social media analytics include press clipping and reporting, focus groups and consumer research, so-called pre- and post-campaign marketplace surveys, and similar. In each of these, there is a specific collection/identification/result process that underlies a fundamental learning process. This learning process is designed to anchor a brand, product, or service in the desires, needs, and reactions of customers, influencers, and others whose opinions about what is talked about in the marketplace matter. In each of these measurement practices, there is a distinct set of metrics or an accepted method of stating a learned or observed outcome.

Start with What You Know

Qualitative social analytics is built around many of the basic practices applied to traditional media—who's talking, what are they saying—now applied to the (digital) conversations happening on the Social Web. So what's different? For starters, social media leverages the massively scalable publishing capabilities afforded to each Social Web participant—in simple terms, recognizing that it is easy for reasonably well-connected people to command a reach that rivals TV within local markets or to reach more accurately defined niches and social circles. This means that the well-connected homemaker, or the hobbyist blogger, or anyone else with a defined passion and a basic command of social media publishing can amass a real audience and can exert real influence within it.

Measuring this reach and impact is just as important on the Social Web as it is any place else. Further, because each conversation is time and date stamped, signed by a real person and accessible with a specific URL that is forever discoverable via search, these conversations form a robust body of information that is very useful in managing your business. This is what social analytics is all about.

Sentiment, Source, and Volume

As a starting point in social media analytics, among the most commonly cited metrics are sentiment (also known as *polarity),* source, and volume—measures of the origin and overall level of the conversations you are tracking. Start with these, but then push beyond them and understand the processes that drive what you observe.

As a starting point in social analytics, consider sentiment, source, and volume (Figure 6.2). *Sentiment* is the measure of the polarity of the conversation—positive versus negative with regard to the subject—and is useful in understanding not only the immediate issue of "Do people like _____?" but also the degree to which they feel this way. This is helpful, for example, in refining a brand advocacy initiative.

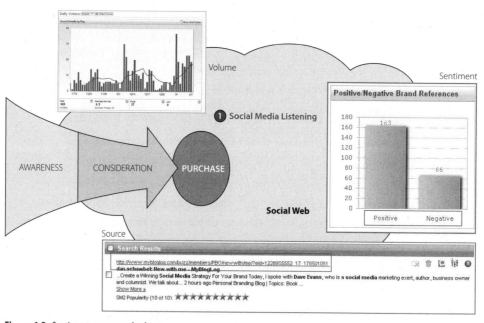

Figure 6.2 Sentiment, source, and volume

Source analysis—understanding the *who*—includes the identification and understanding of the author. In this context, "author" refers to the person creating the post, review, or comment. Source analysis also includes gaining an understanding of *what* is being posted *where*: on-domain in your support forums and company blog or off-domain on Twitter versus Pinterest or Facebook versus Tumblr. This combined view of the source of social content leads to an understanding of where you should be participating on the Social Web, information that is essential in planning a brand outpost program.

Volume measures are used to assess the overall level of conversation about your brand, product, or service: How many people are talking about a particular topic or picking up and reposting information, and is that changing? Volume analysis is most typically associated with conversational trends—the relative levels of positive versus negative over time, the number of conversations over time, or the sudden spiking of an adverse rumor.

Source and Sentiment Analysis

In Chapter 2, "The Social Customer," you saw the Autodesk and Barclaycard Ring cases, where the ideas that led to the innovations represented in these cases were presented right alongside the measurements—customer retention, life cycle via CRM, and similar, for example—that were used to validate these efforts. You also read about BuzzStream, an example of the tools that provide insight into the sources of influence within an area of interest. This is useful so that you can create relationships with the people talking about you. Your active listening program takes this one step further by connecting these sources with the actual business impact of the conversations in which they are a part.

Knowing who is talking is an important part of understanding the meaning of what is being said and then applying this in a useful manner within your business or organization. Combining the sources of the conversation—especially when the sources are actual (or potential) customers—with your listening data provides insights into how you can evolve your product, how you can reshape the customer experience, and where you *and your competitors* have points of relative vulnerability. As you consider specific listening tools and listening programs, consider how the data provided facilitates connecting the source of the conversation, along with the actual conversation and what it means, to your business processes that are driving the conversations in the first place.

NetBase: Customer Measurement and Analysis

NetBase offers a comprehensive measurement platform that supports source identification, content and topic trending, and sentiment analysis for larger brands:

www.netbase.com/

One aspect of listening—known as *sentiment analysis*—deserves specific mention. Sentiment analysis is one of the meaning-related processes by which conversations are categorized. It's also one of the most talked about and one of the most troublesome. Without belaboring the point, human communication is complex. Anecdotal examples of the issues around sentiment analysis can be summed up in two words: "Dyson sucks!" Odds are, this a positive comment—perhaps an expression of joy by a new customer first using these amazing vacuum cleaners.

Sentiment analysis, important enough in its own right, is not an end in and of itself, though many would love it if it were. How great it would be if instead of actively listening all you needed to do was read a report and respond to eight negative posts or send thank-you notes to a dozen loyal fans. Unfortunately, there's more to it—a lot more.

Like the tip of an iceberg, sentiment analysis—and more specifically tracking and trending sentiment—gives an indication of what is happening below the surface. Unlike the tip of an iceberg—which is a good indicator that there is more *ice* underneath the surface—in the case of sentiment analysis you generally have to go back to the original posts, to the original context of the conversations, to sort out what is really happening: You may find more ice, or you may find rocks. A strong negative comment may originate from a dedicated fan or a dedicated detractor. You must dig in and understand the differences rather than skim the surface with a sentiment score.

The challenge with automated sentiment—and one of three primary motivators for the consideration of workflow tools as a part of your listening program (the other two being data conditioning and noise elimination, along with scalable and trackable routing and follow-up) is that *meaning* is almost entirely context driven. One of the shortcomings of the automated listening tools is that they tend to consider the post—in which keywords of interest are embedded—in isolation. In other words, they see the immediate conversation but not the back-story.

Consider Twitter: Because of its highly fluid and distributed nature, the short posts that define Twitter are actually interlinked conversations. One person says, "I bought a new Dyson—I love it," and another, seeing that post, replies, "Me too. My Dyson really sucks!" as a humorous affirmation of the product, resulting in the "negative" post referenced earlier. Because replies are not always linked (in the technical sense) to their originating posts, a typical listening tool sees "Dyson sucks" in isolation, applies its rule base accordingly, and flags the post as negative. With the launch of the new Dyson bladeless fans and commercial hand dryers, a whole new round of sentiment issues arises for Dyson as posts like "Dyson really blows!" will start circulating. Make sure your listening tool is up to the task so that you always know what your customers really mean.

More seriously, none of this is a knock on sentiment analysis as an idea, nor is it intended as commentary on listening tools that include sentiment analysis in particular.

The fact is that using the current tools—with all their attendant shortcomings—still provides more value than not using them. The challenge—and your responsibility—is to ensure that you are, at some level, tying the conversations you discover back to their original context so that you can actually deduce the intended meaning. This is also important from the perspective of workflow (prioritization and routing) and the elimination of *noise*—those results that while they match your keywords are not related to your actual search. Referencing the Dyson products example, conversations mentioning Esther Dyson are likely not relevant to the concerns of the Dyson product marketing team. The effort required to winnow the results to those that are relevant to your specific interests must be considered as an integral part of any listening program.

Here's a twist on sentiment analysis: You can, if you're savvy, get your fans to do at least some of the work for you. Jake McKee, while at LEGO, often turned to key people within the communities he worked with for insights into brand sentiment. Fans would often let Jake know—via IM, where Jake maintained an active, open presence with fans—that there was something or other that he needed to pay attention to, adding within their posts whether this was a good thing needing more attention or otherwise. This is one more reason—as if you needed one more—to actively build a base of loyal and alert supporters.

Know Your Influencers

There's a particular kind of qualitative analysis that deserves to be examined in more detail because of its important role in SCE. It's called *influencer analysis.*

Parallel to traditional PR and the associated marketing and advertising concepts relating to influentials, there are metrics related to the social graph—the connective links, profiles, and updates connecting people on the Social Web—that define the sources of the conversations you are tracking with your social analytics tools. Just as with measuring any other communications channel, understanding how a particular source (typically an individual) fits into your overall intelligence and outreach program is essential to getting the most out of it.

From Journalists to Enthusiasts

In traditional PR in particular, there is an established practice of identifying and developing relationships with key journalists and industry experts. These media connections are useful, for example, when rolling out a new product. By communicating in advance with these contacts, you can seed the general market awareness with comments from these individuals as they begin writing about your product launch. Sometimes this is done confidentially—for example, you may embargo a press release when you want your closest contacts to have this information and be aware of what is coming but not actually talk about it before a certain date. Or, you may want these advance recipients to talk about it first, conveying to them a certain scoop value. As a tip, include in your press releases a 140-character statement intended for reuse on Twitter, what Brian Solis calls a Twitter pitch.

However you do it, the basic process involves identifying and building relationships with the journalists and experts who write about your product or service or focus on issues relating to your markets. The same process applies on the Social Web, with one big difference: The people you want to reach and build a relationship with quite often don't wear nametags.

For any specific interest, cause, lifestyle, product, or service, there are people who blog about it, who post about it on Twitter, and who convey this information to those who follow or subscribe to the blogs of these people. This includes the wider public audience that extends beyond media professionals and specific analysts and influencers.

The challenge, of course, is picking out the influencers who are of interest to you by using tools like Buzzstream and Sysomos, now part of Marketwire, along with Vocus and Cision, and then measuring your progress in building a relationship with them. Table 6.2 shows a selected set of core metrics related to influencer relations and relationship development.

▶ **Table 6.2** Examples of core influencer analytics

Measurement	Typical Tools and Services	What It Shows
Social Influence	BuzzStream, Sysomos MAP, Klout, and similar tools	Provides insight into profile connections revealed by examination of social graph
Reach	Facebook (fan count), Twitter Grader, Klout, and similar tools	Provides an indication of connectedness within a community relating to an individual profile or page
Frequency of Posts	Alterian SM2, Radian6, BuzzStream, Sysomos Heartbeat, and similar tools	Provides an indication of how active a particular person or source is

Metrics like social influence are returned directly through tools like BuzzStream. Figure 6.3 shows the BuzzStream dashboard and the social influence ranking that is applied. Tracking this type of metric over time, as well as across influencers, allows you to develop a profile of the people likely to be helpful to you as you go about the task of quantifying what is being said and affixing a numerical score to the likely impact of who is saying it. This helps you in two ways: You can build relationships with your influencers, and you can better understand the larger social graph that is connecting participants in the conversations around your brand, product, or service.

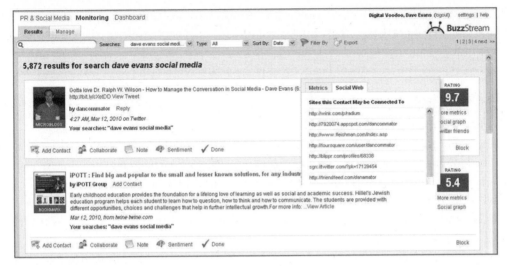

Figure 6.3 Influencer identification

Identify Your Influencers

Understanding your influencers requires more than simple tracking: You need to know *who* specifically is influencing others in your markets. By identifying them and then building an actual relationship with them, you can get into the subtleties of what drives the commentary they produce. This is an important insight, but it raises a question: How do you go about building these relationships?

Simply, you meet these influencers. As you discover influencers, you can connect with them. You can dig into their conversations and understand in detail what they like about your brand, product, or service and what they don't. Based on that, you can build a stronger relationship and understand why key influencers post what they post.

The first step in identifying influencers is to sort out who is connected to whom, who is influential, and who is not. It's not a fully automated process, so your gut instinct and skill will pay off as you sort through the quantitative information that is available and then combine that with your own industry knowledge, for example. Take advantage, too, of personal relationships that you may be able to build: If a conversation in a particular community is of interest to you, introduce yourself (in the real-world sense, for example, through email or Twitter) to the webmaster or community manager in charge. Share your point of interest, and see if this person or team will help you understand the other influencers within that community. More information is better, and if nothing else you'll build a nice connection with a community manager that may pay off later.

Look back at Figure 6.3, which shows a typical view of influencers through BuzzStream. BuzzStream gathers influencer information by crawling the social graphs of the people identified as the sources of specific conversations. What is presented to you is a summary of all of the possible publishing points associated with this person. You can then quickly scan these publishing sites for the people you are particularly interested in and refine the list. Drop the information you've gathered into a contact database, and you're ready to begin building an actual relationship.

The Role of Trust

Creating a trusted relationship is clearly important: Figure 6.4 shows the relative degree of trust across various sources of consumer information compiled by survey. It's worth noting that the gap, while it exists, between survey participants according to age is not especially large; trust and its origins are a relative constant in business transactions. More interesting is that in general the sources associated with higher trust tended to be written by others for consumption in a social (think "two way") context, while the least trusted were largely advertisements (think "one way"). Trust is built with influencers through participation; your participation in social channels is therefore a key to building strong influencer relations.

Global Average - Percent of Completely/Somewhat Trust

FORM OF ADVERTISING	2013	2007	DIFFERENCE 2013 VS. 2007
Recommendations from people I know	84%	78%	6%
Branded websites	69%	60%	9%
Consumer opinions posted online	68%	61%	7%
Editorial content such as newspaper articles	67%	*	*
Ads on TV	62%	56%	6%
Brand sponsorships	61%	49%	12%
Ads in newspapers	61%	63%	-2%
Ads in magazines	60%	56%	4%
Billboards and other outdoor advertising	57%	*	*
Ads on radio	57%	54%	3%
Emails I signed up for	56%	49%	7%
Ads before movies	56%	38%	18%
TV program product placements	55%	*	*
Ads served in search engine results	48%	34%	14%
Online video ads	48%	*	*
Ads on social networks	48%	*	*
Display ads on mobile devices	45%	*	*
Online banner ads	42%	26%	16%
Text ads on mobile phones	37%	18%	19%

*Not included in Nielsen 2007 Global Survey.
Source: Nielsen Global Survey of Trust in Advertising, Q3 2007 and Q1 2013

nielsen AN UNCOMMON SENSE OF THE CONSUMER™

Figure 6.4 Relative trust in sources of information

Trust manifests itself in a related concept: *social capital*. Social capital, briefly, is to social media and the reputation of your brand (and you!) what economic capital is to your CFO and your organization. Social capital plays a role in influencer relations: By understanding who your likely influencers are, and by then taking a genuine interest in understanding their points of view, not only do you learn more about how your brand, product, or service is perceived in the marketplace, but you also create the opportunity to gain social capital.

Here's an example: An influencer contacts you about a speaking date, but you are busy. You can rearrange your schedule, you can simply and politely decline, or you can refer a qualified professional you happen to know, however who is employed by competitor. If you can rearrange your schedule, that's great. If you can't, the best social option is to refer someone else who is qualified, because it is this act versus the simple declination that actually helps the person seeking your assistance. It's like the old retail cliché: "Do you have this shirt in blue?" A response like "We don't, but I know where you can get it" is the one that is remembered and appreciated. Building social capital works the same way, and it most definitely applies to building strong influencer relations.

Social Capital

Author and thought leader Brian Solis offers a clear, concise view on social capital and its importance in business. You can follow Brian on Twitter (@briansolis) and read his post on social capital here:

www.briansolis.com/2010/03/social-capital-the-currency-of-digital-citizens/

Apply Your New Influencer Knowledge

Once you understand the people in the marketplace or stakeholders who matter to your firm or organization, you'll want to do something with this information. Much of what can be done with influencer knowledge involves the use of the social graph and the tools that help you understand it in the context of your business objectives. You can combine this with information that highlights the interconnections between people to create an assessment of how influence actually flows. This can be tracked over time and tied back to your social-media-based marketing efforts; in other words, you can measure the impact of your influencers program.

Influence ranking further allows you to prioritize your tactical efforts. The cost of undertaking a program can be measured in terms of other opportunities foregone. The same applies to building relationships—with one caveat. When using influencer scores to prioritize your efforts, it's important to use more than the numerical influence score. While it's good to have highly influential people in your contacts database, it's also important to recognize that influence doesn't necessarily flow from the most influential directly to your prospects or others whom you have an interest in reaching. Instead, a significant amount of influence actually flows along what are called *weak ties*.

Weak ties are the casual bonds that exist across members of a community. Think of weak ties as "knowing someone who knows someone who...." For example, in a typical LinkedIn network there are people you know directly and people who are connected to the people you know directly. These weaker bonds are extremely important in helping information pass through a network, ultimately reaching the people who are considering some aspect of your offer.

By taking care to understand not only who your influencers are but also how they are connected to smaller—but collectively important—customer segments within your market to which you may not have a direct connection, you can significantly increase the likelihood that the conversations you participate in will ultimately reach more people. This information is especially useful in tuning an *outreach* program: Whether the goal is spreading your message further—think blogger outreach efforts— or building up your customer-driven intelligence program, knowing who is talking about the issues that matter to you and how these people are connected to others is vital.

Web Analytics

Prior sections define the basic metrics of social analytics. But social analytics are themselves a subset of, and deeply intertwined with, web analytics in general. What's more, connecting social analytics with web analytics is an important step in connecting social analytics to your business.

Website Performance

Web analytics are concerned largely with the performance of your website and related online applications. What is generally meant by performance is how well your website converts visitors into customers, people supportive of your cause into donors or enlisted volunteers, or some similar transition that carries them all the way through your purchase or acquisition funnel.

Web analytics offer a number of measurement points. Table 6.3 lists a representative set of the more popular metrics associated with the performance of a website in a business context: These metrics are available through common sources including Webtrends, Google analytics, Omniture, and similar measurement platforms. The key to getting the most out of your web analytics program is understanding the individual quantitative measures shown in Table 6.3 and then creating the qualitative story that links these to your business objectives. Far too many firms track the basics—bounce rate, time spent, page views—but fail to move beyond these basic counts and into the actual analysis: refining and extracting the insights that are essential in applying analytics to business.

▶ **Table 6.3** Web analytics

Measurement	Details and Notes
Unique visitors/visits	Compare with membership (registered visitors) levels
Bounce rate	Indicates the degree to which your landing page pulls visitors into your site
Time spent, pages viewed	Indicates the degree of engagement when used in combination with other measures of activity
Referrer URL	Provides indication of which social channels are sending visitors to your site, and which channels are likely to be most effective for social customer care

Beyond the Basics

What's beyond the basics? Although simply counting and reporting is an important first step, understanding what is driving the measurements you collect is essential to running your social media program and connecting what you learn to your business. The application of web analytics to your business should provide insights into how your online assets—your website, blog, or community site, for example—are driving your business and contributing to the achievement of business objectives.

By connecting the measurements to business processes, and by understanding how the process results drive the measurements themselves, you can use the trends you observe to steer your business or organization in ways that ensure achieving your business objectives. The necessary requirement here—especially as teams that span functional areas of a business or organization are brought under the increasingly large umbrella of social customer experience—is a quantitatively based understanding of how processes translate into results. The measurements you observe are indicators of results but are not themselves *business* results. By taking the steps to connect the measures to the business objectives, you ensure that you are tying what you've observed or learned through listening, for example, to the processes that create the conversations in the first place. In this way your Social Web efforts—whether outreach, listening, participation, or other forms of engagement—become measurably tied to the ongoing operation of your business or organization.

Don't Overcomplicate

Note here that going beyond the basics doesn't necessarily mean moving to advanced or exotic measurements. It means combining core metrics in ways that provide deeper insights and show you how to tie actions and results to your business objectives. Again, the key is taking the time to understand how relatively simple measurements can be combined, trended, and reinterpreted to provide useful information in the form of an effective story.

It is important, especially in the early stages of your social customer experience, to measure aggressively. You may end up discontinuing the collection of some items, but you will surely discover the sources of data you need to make sense of newer Social Web–based consumer behaviors.

Consider as an example *unique visitors*—a simple metric defined as the number of unique people who visited your channel at least once during a specified time interval (generally, one month). Particularly for on-domain SCE channels, this is a master metric, one that you should know for any channel for which you are responsible.

Starting with unique visitors you can begin to build a mathematical model for how conversions work in your channel. For example, what percentage of people who register will contribute? What percentage will return for a second visit? How many will become active users or superfans? You'll want to understand the basic relationships that exist between these metrics so that you can extrapolate the impact that each additional registration will have (on average) with every other metric in the system. If that sounds like a lot, consider that it all came from one metric! *Social measurement*, while based in numbers, is largely about extracting insights and creating a compelling story that connects your social technology efforts to your business objectives.

Beyond unique visitors, consider *bounce rate*, the relative measure of visitors who land on your site and then leave immediately, without looking at anything else. As you did with unique visitors, dig into bounce rate, slice it by source, slice it by date, trend it over time, and run correlation analysis against it. What's driving it? Do adjacent trends in blog activity or conversations on Twitter correlate strongly with the trends in bounce rate that you observe? *These* are the questions you really want to answer because when you know what is driving your bounce rate (rather than simply knowing the number itself), you can develop a plan to manage it, whether to further reduce it or to understand that further reduction has only a diminishing economic payback.

Connect the Dots

Moving beyond the basics of data collection is the difference between "12,357 people visited last week, up from 8,264 the week before" and "qualified visitors to our site increased following the release of the latest podcast program." Counting visitors is important, no doubt about it. So is studying the ways in which people traverse your site before they choose to make an actual purchase. Combined, these metrics prove the quantitative basis to help you spot qualified visitors earlier in the process and thereby implement steps in a timely manner that drives these conversions further. Connecting trends and changes in qualified traffic to specific Social Web–based programs enables an understanding of ROI: As a sort of lingua franca, ROI helps you make the case across your organization for meaningful spending on social business efforts.

To see how the data collected through a Social Web listening program is connected to the data collected in a web analytics program, it's important to understand correlation and causation. Figure 6.5 shows a visualization of correlation. The data represented by Data Set 1 (solid squares) appears to be correlated—note how it falls along a common line. By comparison, the relationship in the data contained in Data Set 2 (depicted by the dots) is more scattered over the chart. *Correlation* is the study of sets of observations, with the end goal being the detection of a possible connection between the sets of data.

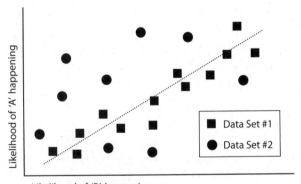

Figure 6.5 A visual chart of correlation

Correlation implies that whenever *A* is observed, *B* is also observed. An example of correlation is the observation that "People who bought dog food on the Petco website also bought dog leashes." Purchasing one does not in itself *cause* the purchase of the other. However, the two tend to occur together more often than, say, people buying dog food and a bowling ball, something that may well be observed on occasion in the checkout line at a local Walmart.

Causation, by comparison, is a direct cause-effect relationship between *A* and *B*. When *A* happens, *B* results. Acquiring a dog, for example, fairly certainly *causes* the purchase of both dog food and a dog bowl. Cause and effect can be seen in things like the increased numbers of items in online shopping carts that result when online shoppers are prompted to consider additional items based on what they have currently placed in their shopping carts: When people are told "Others who bought dog bowls also bought dog leashes," they tend to go look for a new leash.

The study of correlation can help connect social media analytics and other web and business analytics. Good news here: It's easy to do. Collect your listening results, clean them to remove noise and irrelevant results, and then attempt to correlate the listening results, plotting, for example, volume and sentiment against with web traffic. If the patterns match—if the correlation is high—you've got an indication that some deeper connection may exist. *This is not **proof** of such a connection!* But it is an indication that looking further might be worthwhile. Consider how this technique might be used to uncover relationships that are not immediately obvious.

Try shifting the dates, too: Lag the website traffic by a day or two days or a week and see if the relative measure of correlation improves. If you have reason to believe that some action today has some impact two days from now, shift the impact measure by two days and then see if correlation improves. If you see an improved correlation, you may be seeing an indication that what happens on the Social Web takes a certain amount of time to propagate across the Social Web. That's useful.

The observation of a propagation time is certainly the case with brand advertising, for example, where a build-up time in awareness is observed. This is very different from, say, TV-based direct response or impulse buying (think QVC) where running a spot immediately triggers a known (or certainly knowable) buying response. It makes sense that these same conditions apply between the Social Web and your online purchase points or conversion funnels. It's worth your time to sort out the relationships.

What about *causation*? If correlation is important, causation is the Holy Grail. When you nail down causation, you've got real power because the implication is that you can actually drive a particular outcome. The test for causation is tougher and more rigorous; systematic testing should be at the core of your analytics practices because of it. This is as applicable to your use of the Social Web as it is to your use of any other marketing technology that can be optimized. By testing and comparing, you'll separate cause from correlation and identify the key activities and practices that will drive your business.

Take the time to examine the "usual suspects" in the context of web analytics—bounce rate, page views, time spent, and unique users—and connect these to your social media program by selectively changing elements of the social media program and noting the results. Building on what you learn, add your conversion results to the mix. Using Google Analytics, for example, set up conversion goals and then compare the results of your testing around your social programs with your conversions. The result will be a quantitative understanding of your business and the way in which your social programs support your overall business objectives.

Business Analytics

The application of social media to business is driven by the connection between the posting, sharing, and collaboration that happen on the Social Web and the underlying business objectives of the firm or organization. In the previous sections, the links between social media analytics and web analytics were examined, with the result being a systematic review process aimed at finding the relationships (correlation) that drive results and then extracting the key practices (causation) that you can replicate to grow your business.

Initially, these techniques may be limited to marketing and your use of the Social Web as a marketing platform, as is often the case with social media marketing programs designed to create additional outreach points or places where people within your organization can participate with customers on behalf of the brand. The next section—where the focus turns to business analytics—takes the techniques that are useful in marketing and applies them to the business as a whole. In particular, in the case of social media and the Social Web, there is a measurable connection to business, expressed through a result against a set of established business objectives. That level of understanding needs to be the end goal, and you need to be relentless about getting there.

It's All about Results

When building a social business, *the connection between the Social Web and your business objectives is your starting point.* At a fundamental level, Operations drives the conversation more than Marketing. Therefore, the way in which the business is managed, what its end-output actually is, or the experience it creates becomes the focus. Compare this with business 10 or 20 years prior (not that long ago as macro trends are concerned) when the primary driver of success was how well the product or service was marketed.

Partly as a result, contemporary social customer experience and the software or technology that supports them are more likely to be paid for by the operations or information systems budgets than they are by the Marketing department. The Marketing department, by comparison, may pay for the programs associated with talking about the ways in which customers are benefiting from the implementation of a social business program or in building the outreach or listening platforms that drive them. Social technology is spreading out from marketing.

Why does this matter? Because when social business and software are seen as a business infrastructure investment rather than a marketing expense, it changes the ways in which the analytics are *required* to roll up. Social media analytics, web analytics, and influencer assessments must all be viewed in the context of their relationship to fundamental business analytics because they are the metrics that matter to the owners of the budgets and cost centers that are increasingly likely to pay for the costs of implementing a social customer experience program.

Because business analytics relates to the actual business operation, connecting business analytics to social and web analytics provides an end-to-end picture of the customer experience—manifesting itself as conversations on the Social Web—with the internal business processes that created the conversations.

Offline and Non-business Processes

For organizations that do not have an online commerce process—for example, for a cause that is collecting signatures—the thought process and the approach to business analytics are still largely the same. The commerce pipeline is simply replaced with the defined conversion process. Tools like Google Analytics offer well-developed conversion analysis support that you can use to refine your online programs in the same ways you would any commerce process. The objective remains pulling together the various sources of data that support measurement against your KPIs along with the process metrics around your established business goals, closing the feedback loop that the Social Web sets in place.

Mind What You Measure

Kate Niederhoffer, cofounder of Knowable Research, offers her perspective on what to measure and why in the following post. You can follow Kate on Twitter (@katenieder) as well.

www.dachisgroup.com/2009/11/three-masquerades-of-metrics/

If you are interested in understanding how measurement and research can lead to a more a social business, check out Kate here:

http://knowableresearch.com/social-technology/

Sources of Business Analytics

When creating a social business program, start with the following analytic sources: *commerce analytics*—after all, at the end of the day we are generally in business to sell something—along with measures of acceptance or rejection.

Commerce and Pipeline Analytics

Commerce and pipeline analytics are an obvious starting point, because these measures help tie social media analytics and (where applicable) and web analytics to actual sales. The study of correlation and causation—identifying the underlying relationships between various measurements and the economic performance of the business—will yield a fundamental set of metrics that can be used to guide your business vis-à-vis social media analytics.

What about non-business applications of social technology or the task of assessing its use in organizations where the direct connections are less obvious? This is where the studies of correlation and causation, combined with your own domain expertise around the processes that drive your organization, are valuable. You can employ correlation, for example, to literally find or discover useful quantitative measurements and to then press deeper into the understanding of *why* these particular observations are correlated. Not only is this directly useful, you can often find new business fundamentals—especially as they relate to the emerging marketplace defined by the Social Web—that will help ensure that you achieve your business or organizational objectives.

Measures of Acceptance or Rejection

Acceptance and rejection measures—for example, defect reports or call abandonment rates—provide a second and equally rich measurement area. Defect reports highlight the issues that result in difficult or repeated service calls and are likely a root cause for negative conversations on the Social Web. Likewise, call satisfaction—knowing how happy your customers are with the support experience—is very powerful in identifying the root cause of sentiment as well as the specific aspects of a product or service that are likely to be talked about.

Applied Business Analytics

In the prior sections we discussed the sources and potential application of data; we covered social, web and business analytics. In the next two sections we'll show how these concepts can be applied in ways that reach far beyond the ordinary aggregate trend and sentiment charts and into what really matters: business results.

Agent Productivity

One of the primary applications of social analytics as it relates to social customer experience is understanding how your social response team—your customer service agents more so than marketing professionals—is managing the inflow of customer requests in social channels. Working with a platform that provides deep analytics and workflow visibility it is well within your ability to measure and manage agent performance. Note that the following discussion and figures are based on the analytics available via Lithium Social Web, the workflow and engagement component of an overall social customer experience platform.

Figure 6.6 shows the number of posts handled by a customer service team during its first week, and then in the subsequent weeks following its initial launch of Lithium Social Web. As with the implementation of any new software or workflow process there is a training component that leads to agent mastery of the particular tool.

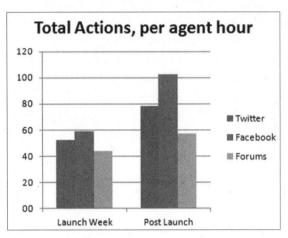

Figure 6.6 Agent performance following launch

The challenge facing the team is understanding how well training has been received and how effectively agents are performing against expectations. Across social channels gains in agent productivity are noted comparing the initial week with subsequent weeks, with a particular gain in Twitter-based customer inquiry productivity.

While gains in productivity are always good and successive gains in the early implementation of new tools is expected, the real business value that leads to ROI is in understanding how these gains were realized. This, by the way, is why understanding, prior to platform selection, the detailed metrics available in any specific social customer experience is so important: you can't manage what you can't measure!

To understand what's really happening and to see how the significant gain in agent productivity was achieved you need to be able to see the details of the workflow, at both an agent and team level. One way to do this is to use a normal analysis, in which the actual agent results are compared with a standard normal distribution. In productivity analysis, a normal distribution is desired: In simple terms, it says all of your agents are doing about the same thing, plus or minus random process variation. This technique was pioneered by Edwards Deming and is well worth understanding.

Looking at Figure 6.7, the productivity data has been charted against a normal distribution. However, Figure 6.7 clearly shows that the smooth normal distribution—the bell-shaped curve enveloping the actual data—does not neatly fit the data itself. Instead, the data has two distinct peaks, indicating that the agent behaviors are different, with one group (A) operating at a lower efficiency that than the other (B). What would be great would be if you could understand why and then take corrective action based on that knowledge.

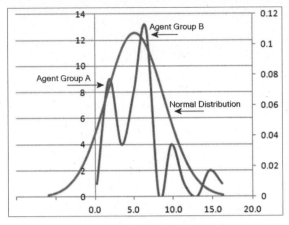

Figure 6.7 Agent performance vs. normal distribution

Robust analytics provide the ability to look into specific workflow behaviors. Turning to Figure 6.8, you can see that there is marked reduction in the number of agent-assigned posts—the queue length, as it is called within the Lithium data set—that are being held open by agents rather than closed following issue resolution when comparing the first weeks' results versus later weeks. Being able to see this granular data alerted supervisors to the fact that one group of agents had misunderstood a critical point in training regarding case resolution and case closing: This was corrected through retraining during the first week, and as a result in the later weeks the queue length dropped to expected levels after which productivity improved.

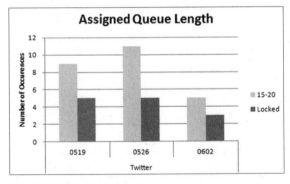

Figure 6.8 Agent workflow behavior

Turning back to Figure 6.6, following retraining the productivity across all agents improved in subsequent weeks, with agents now working at expected efficiency levels. Again, this is an example of the kind of immediate, data-based process management that is possible when the social customer experience platform you select provides the data you need to run your business. How you run your team is of course up to you: The take-away here is that you'll want to ensure that the data *available* in the social customer experience platform you choose matches the data *requirements* for your business.

Customer Likelihood to Recommend

Beyond using social media for outreach or promotion—for example, in creating a brand outpost or using a channel like Twitter to convey sales information or collect customer comments—the Social Web can be used as part of a real-time feedback system that keeps your firm or organization on track. You do it; they talk about it. You do it a different way, and they talk about it in a different way. At the root of your interest is, or should be, one fundamental question: How likely is it that what is happening on the social web is helping your business?

As a starting point, consider the Net Promoter score (NPS). Created by Fred Reichheld at Bain Consulting, the Net Promoter score is straightforward, well documented (a benefit to you when presenting social technology and gaining internal support for its use), and easy to apply. Built around a 0–10 scale and the single question "How likely are you to recommend my brand, product, or service?" the Net Promoter Score nicely captures in a single metric what underlies the majority of the significant connections between the Social Web and your brand, product, or service.

How can the NPS methodology help you? Consider the application of NPS by Austin-based B2B technical and lab furniture manufacturer Formaspace. Implemented in earnest in 2009, NPS provided a whole-business marketplace view that was fully auditable. It was implemented at the C level and is now followed by every department at Formaspace.

Co-author Dave Evans spoke with Formaspace CEO Jeff Turk about the implementation of the Net Promoter Score. Jeff described the effort like this:

We don't really look at NPS in terms of expecting a single great leap forward. We had a formal and frequently measured quality assurance and customer satisfaction system long before implementing NPS. We also know our most vocal customers quite well, so we had a very good idea what they would have to say about us before implementing NPS. We look at NPS as a source of continual incremental improvements.

The NPS system gives us a lot of small bits of feedback that incrementally add up to very high customer satisfaction. Some suggestions have included specific changes to furniture assembly instructions, asking for emails at certain times in the delivery process, and letting us know when we need to give kudos to a particular staff member.

Look back at the implementation and you'll see that the company knew its customers and what they would say. NPS was used in the context of a larger measurement program. NPS was used to drive continuous improvement and thereby loyalty. The implementation of NPS at Formaspace exemplifies exactly the processes articulated in this book thus far, and it has paid off. Formaspace was originally acquired as a turnaround opportunity in 2006. Recovering and rebuilding customer loyalty was absolutely a key measure of whether its new owners were turning the company around. Based on prior customer satisfaction and loyalty surveys, Jeff and his team estimated that its NPS score would have been negative in 2006 and in the 30 to 50 range between 2007 and 2008. The measured score was 77 in 2009, and the company's goal is to surpass 80 in 2010. That is impressive.

There's a bigger insight here too: Paying attention, in detail, to customer conversations and measuring and tracking results doesn't just boost measures like the Net Promoter Score; it actually drives business. Again, listen to Formaspace CEO Jeff Turk:

When we took over the company, it was doing so poorly at servicing customers that it sprouted competitors left and right. Today it would not be an exaggeration to say that Formaspace is the go-to resource for companies that use technical and laboratory furniture. We are rapidly becoming known as the "it" brand—so much so that our furniture is on the Discovery Channel, ABC's Grey's Anatomy, in NASA's mission control center in Houston, and will soon be seen on the sets of more than one major motion picture. Many people import furniture from China: Ours is in sufficient demand that we send it the other way.

Because Dave is a former product manager, this last exchange really hit home. When he served in this role at Progressive Insurance Company, before the firm turned fully toward a *customer* orientation, it was planting the seeds for its early competitors. Nearly all of Progressive's early competition came from former Progressive product managers and executives who simply copied the Progressive rate books and undercut the prices. Whether it's extreme price sensitivity (technically referred to as high elasticity), such as was the case at Progressive, or poor quality or bad service, negative factors like these are invitations to more competition and lower margins. Formaspace engaged its customers, turned high quality to its advantage, and put itself—in brand-speak—on a different ladder. To learn more about Formaspace—and to see the great products they build—check out Formaspace.com.

As an important note, the Net Promoter score may not be for everyone (see sidebar), nor is it the only metric available to you (although if you had to choose only one, it would be a very good choice). Instead, the Net Promoter score is a great place to start if you don't have a central dashboard or other in-place methodology for measuring success in creating an excellent social customer experience because it provides an understandable basis for linking the experiences you create in the marketplace with your organization as a whole, where these experiences are (largely) created.

Alternatives to the Net Promoter score

As the Net Promoter score has gained in popularity, so have discussions of its potential limitations; alternatives have arisen. As you are reviewing specific metrics and in particular the use of the NPS methodology, consider searching the Web for "alternatives to Net Promoter score" as well.

The Net Promoter score—or your preferred equivalent—provides a quantitative assessment through which you can capture and track the degree to which your customers will recommend you to others in the market for your product or service. In a marketing environment that is increasingly driven by trust in "others like me" and by the recommendations of people "nearby" in the sense of the social graph, adopting the Net Promoter score and supporting methodology can help in the following ways:

- It creates a consistent, trackable metric that can be presented and placed into context across an organization.

- It is naturally aligned with the conversational dynamics on the Social Web. If most people would highly recommend your brand, product, or service, then the conversations about your brand, product, or service will reflect that.

- It is quantitative. The Net Promoter score "translates" unstructured data like the characterization of the recommendations that people might give on your behalf into a number. You can work with numbers.

Having a consistent metric that can be shared across an organization is vital: It enables everyone in your firm to "speak the same language" when it comes to assessing performance. Recall the Formaspace case: The context of a single metric like NPS is as important as the metric itself, and the verbatim responses (that is, individually detailed conversations with clients) that are often gathered as part of an NPS implementation are extremely valuable as well.

The net of the measurement discussion is this: Given that you already have a solid understanding of your business and your business objectives, begin an aggressive measurement program that ties social media analytics to your business. The eye candy—the sentiment charts, trend lines, and radar plots—are all cool. But the connection to business is what matters: Connect web analytics with business analytics to get more out of your social media measurements and more out of your social media and social customer experience programs.

Review and Hands-On

This chapter covered the fundamentals of measurement and then showed how to take the basic metrics that are readily available further. By moving beyond counts and trends and into correlation and causation and by aligning social media analytics with business metrics, you can move your use of the Social Web in business to a whole new level.

Review of the Main Points

The main points covered in this chapter are summarized in the points that follow. The essence of Chapter 6, with credit to Katie Paine, is "Yes We Can! (measure social media)."

- Understand quantitatively what is happening on the Social Web, on your website, and in your business.

- Tie these measures together to create a complete feedback loop that includes the delivery of what is learned to the functional areas within your business or organization that can act on and respond to this information.

- Use quantitative techniques such as correlation to find relationships in available metrics that you may not have considered and that once identified can lead you to new understanding of what the impact of social media and Web 2.0 really is.

- Move beyond basic metrics in all of your measurement areas, and press into a complete understanding how these metrics indicate where you are heading rather than simply where you have been.

By taking the time to connect the dots, to link together the fundamental sources of data that are available to you, you can significantly increase the likelihood of gaining acceptance and support for the organization-wide adoption of social business practices. This sets up the truly collaborative relationships between your business and customers, or between your organization and its constituents, that drive long-term success.

Hands-On: Review These Resources

Review each of the following, and consider subscribing to those that you find especially useful or relevant to your business or organization:

Avinash Kaushik's blog, Occam's Razor

www.kaushik.net/

Kate Niedehoffer

http://socialabacus.blogspot.com/

Edwards Deming and Business Process Measurement

http://en.wikipedia.org/wiki/W._Edwards_Deming

Fred Reichheld and the Net Promoter community

www.netpromoter.com/netpromoter_community

Hands-On: Apply What You've Learned

Apply what you've learned in this chapter through the following exercises:

1. Identify the primary social, web, and business analytics that matter to you.

2. Run a correlation analysis on metrics you've identified, and then investigate why certain metrics are correlated more strongly than others and how this correlation might be used to further your understanding of how the Social Web is impacting your business or organization.

3. Develop a basic dashboard, or incorporate one or two new business fundamentals that you identify through the previous exercises into your current business scorecard.

Five Key Trends

This chapter covers five key trends that are driving the adoption of social technology in business, trends that as a result are forcing organizations to change and adapt. This chapter takes a look at significant consumer technology trends, ranging from engaging right here, right now, to making a game of everything, and places each into the context of a business that is setting itself up for success in the face of seemingly constant change.

7

Chapter contents

Real-time engagement

Mobile computing

Co-creation

Crowdsourcing

Gamification

Real-Time Engagement

Right here, right now. What's going on, and what do your customers need? More importantly, if you know the answers to these questions, what can you do about it?

Listening is often the starting point for the adoption of social technology. Listening is the basis for tangible, measurable connections between your business and your marketplace. It's also a direct link to your customers. Beyond knowing who said what, listening helps you develop a *baseline* so that you can more quickly spot irregularities. If a sudden new interest or accidental or unpaid celebrity endorsement kicks off a wave of excitement, or a negative event or rumor around your product or service is suddenly running through the market, you'll see it in time to take relevant action. Combined with a response strategy and a current understanding of marketplace conversations, you can build on the positive conversations and effectively address those that are negative.

Careful listening—in the context of the Social Web, meaning listening, analyzing, and thereby understanding both the subject and the source—enables you to make sense of conversations and join into them. Rohit Bhargava, principal with Influential Marketing Group, refers to this process as *active listening.* In simple terms, *active listening* is built around paying attention to conversations and then responding based on a combination of strategy and measurement.

Active listening is a key to understanding what to do and why on the Social Web, because doing so says to your customers, employees (for internal social technology implementations), or other stakeholders (the larger collection of members, staff, or persons served, as with nonprofits or municipal organizations, for example) that you are truly interested in their ideas and what they have to say about your brand, product, or service.

By establishing listening as a core practice and using what is learned to shape your response, you invite your customers into the processes that lead to higher-value interactions and ultimately to co-creation and collaboration. Given the opportunity and the tools, your customers will readily work together to create a better understanding among themselves with regard to what you offer. The Social Web provides the infrastructure for these conversations: Off-domain social applications and social networks enable content sharing and similar participative actions that occur in and around online marketplaces. On-domain applications, support forums, ratings, reviews, recommendations, and content showing your product or service in use help inform others' decisions, in a context that you can directly manage.

Create a Baseline

The first step in creating a baseline is active listening, using the information that is being shared for your own intelligence. Given the relative newness of the Social Web, there is a lack of guiding metrics that answer basic questions such as how much conversation should one expect or how many negative posts is too many negatives? Some would say one negative is too many, but that's probably not realistic. In any marketplace for any product or service, there will always be a range of opinions. Think about this: If you are reading a set of reviews and *everything* you see is positive, do you believe it? It is, therefore, essential to establish your own baseline—recognizing the value of both positive and negative conversations—and build your response strategy off of that.

Beyond the practical problem of developing an accepted baseline, the common or best practices that might provide guidance when starting out are likewise just emerging. But even more, as your brand or organization moves toward a social customer experience orientation, the unique differentiators that apply to a specific product or service, for example, begin to dominate in importance across conversations. Rather than the generic metrics—like number of units sold—social customer experience management is about understanding the specific ways your customers are talking about, using, and imagining your products, again making it mandatory that you dig in and discover the metrics that govern your business.

As an example, you may find little or no mention of your brand on the Social Web. In this case, your objective may be to build a conversation, and your baseline is the background measure against which you can assess success. Or, there may be substantial conversation, with some relative distribution between positive, neutral, and negative. Tools like the Net Promoter® score factor in here: A score near zero indicates a roughly equal balance between promoters and detractors, something you should be able to validate (through measurement) on the Social Web. In this case, your baseline is the relatively equal distribution of promoters and detractors, and your response strategy may be directed toward increasing the measured share of promoters and/or openly addressing the issues contributing to negative conversations.

Whatever your specific starting point, it needs to combine active listening and influencer identification with a marketplace performance assessment such as the Net Promoter® score so that you can both tell what's happening now and be able to assess performance against business objectives as you progress. That is, you need to begin with some data—what customers are saying, what they are concerned with, and so forth. Later, through collaboration you'll convert that to the knowledge you need to truly engage with your customers. At the outset, however, what matters is extracting enough *data* to sort out exactly where you are *right now*. Here's the good news: Most of the commercial (meaning paid) listening services provide historical information ranging from a few months of history to two years. You can use these tools to construct conversational baselines immediately.

Conversational baselines are obviously handy when you want to act now (as if that's ever not the case!). Historical data provides the context for many of the programs that you'll implement going forward. Using a basic listening platform—whether a service like Google Alerts, a DIY (do it yourself) toolset like SDL|Alterian SM2 or Radian6, or a full-service offering from your agency—you can establish a conversational *baseline*. Figure 7.1 shows such a baseline. In the example, the listening program was started January 1, and a social media effort to encourage conversation was started shortly after. The listening platform provides historical data against which any change in conversational levels can be measured. The practice of creating your own baselines and understanding their significance—along with any changes that happen over time—is essential in making sense of the conversations that you are interested in.

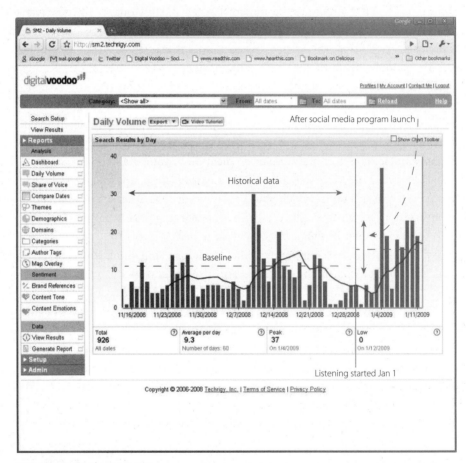

Figure 7.1 Baseline for conversation

As an important side note, *establishing a listening baseline can help you spot and manage a crisis before it's too late.* Whether it's a rumor about your brand or an actual (negative) event that takes place with your product or within your industry, trying to sort out who is talking and how the conversation is connected to your organization after it has become widespread is too late. Instead of fighting the fire, you'll be swamped trying to figure out where it's coming from, losing valuable time at a point in the crisis-management process when *minutes* may count. With an effective baseline program in place and an understanding of who your influencers are, as soon as you detect a rise in comments or the presence of a new and potentially damaging thread, you can be ready with a response that is directed to those who can help you.

In addition to establishing a solid baseline, create a strong internal policy that governs your organization and its application of social computing. Include notification rules, disclosure, topics that are off-limits (trade secrets, for example), and expectations for conduct. This will give significant comfort to your legal and HR groups, and it will make your social-media-based marketing and business programs more likely to succeed. Refer to Chapter 3, "Social Customer Experience Management," and Chapter 4, "The Social Customer Experience Ecosystem," for more on the use of social computing policies and in particular for pointers to IBM and other great starting points when developing your own social computing policies.

The New Role for Marketing

Managing (or leading) change while getting your organization ready to adopt social technologies is very often among the most challenging aspects of implementing an effective social media strategy. Realizing that effectively adopting social technology is larger than marketing presents a new opportunity. The savvy CMO or marketing director can take a much wider view of the customer processes that contribute to brand health.

The initial entry point for social media in business *is often marketing*—probably because the initial social applications are promotional or advertising related or focused on the Social Web and its impact to the brand. As a result, much of the initial social media seems most related to marketing and sales, and in the context of the purchase funnel it's certainly noticed there! However, the application of social media in *business* carries far beyond marketing. This is evident in the expanded view of the purchase funnel and the role of the conversations following purchase as they impact the marketing function—think sales or membership or donor campaigns here—within your organization. It's what happens after the sale, so to speak, that makes clear how far beyond marketing social media and social technologies can be applied.

Moving the application of social media beyond marketing requires that you anchor your programs in your business strategy. Social technology and technology applications must be aligned with the overall business objectives and strategic efforts, picking up on the dynamics of the purchase funnel and feedback cycle and then applying what is learned across the entire organization, beyond the purely promotional activities of product marketing.

The power of a metric like the Net Promoter Score is that it puts everyone in the business on the same page of customer accountability. The question to the customer is, "Would you recommend us?" The customer's response is based on all of the moving parts that resulted in a particular experience, upon which the likelihood of a recommendation is predicated. When an entire organization is looking at a holistic satisfaction metric, *questions get asked that wouldn't otherwise be asked*. Innovations arise that would not otherwise arise. The business actually runs—from the ground up—in ways that delight the customer.

While Dave was product manager at Progressive, one of the operation metrics that made it easy to understand the health of a particular product line was a universal metric called the combined operating ratio (COR), a basic measure of financial performance that everyone understood. It predated the Net Promoter Score and was a *fundamentally different* measure to be sure. While the COR was a business operations performance metric instead of a customer experience metric, *sharing the COR across the entire organization focused everyone on their specific impact to the proper operation of Progressive's business*. The result was an organization that worked like a single, cohesive team and thus advanced to the upper tier of its industry.

In summary, you can use listening to build the real-time social connections between your organization and your marketplace by first understanding what is being said and how it impacts you. You can leverage basic listening to shape your organization so that when the time comes it is able to respond effectively and efficiently. You can further leverage this basic data to encourage interest and involvement across the *internal processes* that span work teams or functional groups, again building the cross-functional discipline that you will ultimately need to be effective in your use of social technology.

Mobile Computing

Mobile computing will force every consumer-facing company to establish a direct linkage with its customers.

> Michael Saylor, cofounder and CEO,
> MicroStrategy, and author of The Mobile Wave

The future is social, and it is inextricably linked to mobile. *Mobile* means "right here, right now," and *social* means "with the people around me, the people like me." This changes everything.

Embracing change, and preparing your organization for the impact of that change, is part of successfully implementing social technology. Inside your firm, this preparation includes instilling a culture of learning so that new collaborative tools such as wikis, Salesforce's Chatter, and Microsoft's Yammer or enterprise platforms like SocialText are embraced rather than pushed off. Outside your firm it means recognizing the power of social technology and mobile computing, both of which are inextricably linked. Along with a culture of openness (so that employees are comfortable suggesting what may seem like wacky ideas to others in the organization) these measures can drive positive change, recognizing that dynamic is the new static.

Real Time, Meet Real Space

Perhaps more than any recent technology advance, with the exception of the Internet itself, the rise of mobile computing and its relationship to social technology is changing the world. Mobile computing, given ubiquitous network connectivity, means that anyone with the means has at their immediate disposal the ability to connect, evaluate, act, and influence others. And, driven by the relentless increase in technological capability coupled with a continuous decrease in cost, "with the means" more and more translates into an ever-wider reach of mobile social computing. Health care, education, commerce, and entertainment are all being reshaped.

If that's the macro, what's the micro? What's the part of this that affects you, in your business? To start, your customers expect you to be present in the critical moments in their lives when what you do intersects with what they are doing. And they expect your involvement to make sense *in their current location*. Real time, meet real space. Imagine that you own a restaurant, and a business traveler lands in your city for a conference: That person expects to be able to book a table at your restaurant, if one is available, *from the cab on the way in to the city from the airport*. Why? Because that same customer, after checking in or updating personal status, has found three friends also in town with whom to share a meal. Or maybe you run a hospital: Imagine a new patient, sitting in the waiting room at your hospital. Your patient expects to be able to talk about what's happening with friends or remote caregivers *in order to feel more comfortable* and will probably reach for a smartphone and the Social Web to do it. The list of mobile use cases goes on, each driven by the combination of peer dialog (for example, with other customers) and expert dialog (for example, with your social agents or other subject-matter experts) in the context of the present situation *and location*.

That intersection of content and location, of participants and settings, means your business needs to reach beyond your physical bounds: Cloud-based SaaS (software as a service) applications that provide data visualization (facts relevant to the current context) and enable choices (the applicable set of responses given those facts and the local context) through smartphone apps provide exactly this. Smartphone apps are an expression of the power of the individual in shaping the deployment and use of personal technology. As they proliferate, expect significant changes in the way you go to market, win business, and build brand advocates.

Flip back to Chapter 1, "Social Media and Customer Engagement," and see the sidebar reference for the USAF/Altimeter response matrix—*listen first* in order to understand what is being said. Build an understanding of how your brand, product, or service is viewed on the Social Web—and based on that, create your roadmap for engagement. Be prepared to use social technology for outreach, marketing, hiring, and especially to respond in the event of a crisis.

As an example of the latter, suppose that an isolated issue, enabled by mobile technology, results in a fast-growing negative conversation. In January 2010, India's

Café Coffee Day, a higher-end chain coffee outlet, caught the full force of just such an attack when a group of bloggers meeting in a Café Coffee Day were asked to pay a cover charge (presumably for sitting and talking in a coffee shop) in addition to the drinks and snacks they had already purchased. Understanding the role of mobile and the fact that this event played out in a highly localized context that then spilled onto the Web, makes obvious the need to grasp and plan for the impact of mobile at every brand touchpoint.

In the case of Café Coffee Day, consider the business's point of view: Restaurants and cafes need to balance the needs of sitting customers—enjoying conversation after a nice meal—with the needs of those waiting for an open table. In this case, there were open seats and the group was spending money, so predictably the request for a cover charge resulted in a localized uproar (the event occurred within a single store) that quickly moved onto the Social Web. The brand team's preexisting participation and in-place crisis plans specific to the Social Web and social media saved it.

Café Coffee Day's social team typically fielded, at the time, about 10 posts per day from customers on Twitter. Suddenly, a large spike followed by numerous posts in the following 24-hour period as more people jumped in—in technical terms, piled on—to the conversation. The brand team actually handled the event pretty well. Because they were already listening (again, credit to them for participation in social channels in the first place), they were able to spot this and respond quickly. They took action publicly (reviewing, for example, the motivation of the store owner in requesting a cover charge when no such corporate policy existed). The online team issued an apology, made amends, and wrapped it up.

But the piling on continued, and that's what brought the brand advocates, who were also seeing what was happening, out in support of the brand. The advocates saw the event, saw what to them appeared an appropriate response from Café Coffee Day, and then took action as others seeking to cash in on the notoriety of the thread kept reposting, after the fact. *The advocates defended the brand.* You can see the positive (up) and negative (down) comments in Figure 7.2, and you can see that the positive comments rose as fast as the negatives. The primary event was over in a few hours, and the online storm died out not long after.

Two things in the Café Coffee Day event are important to recognize. First, the brand was present in the social channels and so they quickly recognized what was happening. Second, *they knew how to respond*: listen, acknowledge, correct, and move on. The result was the emergence of a supportive crowd as the brand advocates moved in and a fairly balanced conversation resulted—for every hater there was roughly one lover. Had the brand team not been involved, the event would have simply gone out of control, unanswered, *because without the brand's public recognition of the actual wrong and the apology from the brand team to the bloggers involved directly, the defenders would have had no ground on which to stand.*

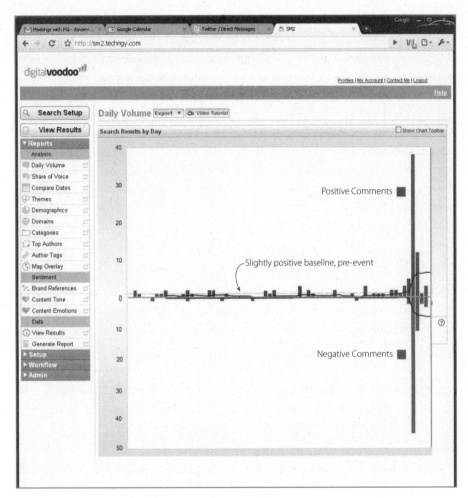

Figure 7.2 We're listening: Café Coffee Day

Co-creation

Collaborative activities sit at the top of the engagement processes. As such, moving your customers, members, and employees toward collaboration is a definite must-do in your list of both marketing and (larger) business goals. Collaboration, whether internally across functional work teams or externally (involving customers in product and service design, for example), is the inflection point on the path to becoming a social business.

Collaboration in the context of your business begins by connecting the off-domain conversations of customers—sharing photos taken with the newest model camera phone your company has launched or talking about one of your new shows on a network like GetGlue—with your on-domain application. On-domain includes your forums, idea exchanges, and the network itself in the case of the relaunched MySpace. By bringing these off-domain conversations onto your network and into your forums or your mobile applications, you move your online customers into a place where you can directly engage and encourage collaborative behavior.

Encourage Collaboration Everywhere

As a basic framework for an organization-wide path toward collaboration (meaning driving high levels of engagement, as defined in the social context), consider the following set of steps developed at Ant's Eye View, now part of PwC:

1. Define your objectives.

Begin with a clear view of your *business* objectives and an understanding of your primary customer base or applicable segment of it.

2. Listen.

Implement a listening program to understand the specific conversations around your brand, product, or service. Use this same program to validate the actions you are considering and then use it to measure or otherwise understand the impact of those actions.

3. Organize.

Organize internally and externally around what you learn through listening. Create cross-functional teams, for example, that respond fully to the customer need rather than just the functional issues you discover.

4. Engage.

Engage the customer through participation. Respond in the channels in which your customers are talking, implement the collaborative solutions that result, and then give your customers credit because this will encourage them to participate more.

5. Measure.

Aggressively measure everything until you have adequate baselines to assess the impact of the programs you embark on. You can always discontinue the collection of unneeded or uninformative data later. You can't, however, make decisions based on information you don't have.

Taking these steps together, collaboration occurs—or at the least is facilitated—in the fourth step; engagement is a direct result of the preceding three steps. Collaboration, in this context, requires the active participation of both the customers and the employees—of the marketplace and the organization itself.

It's About Me...and It's About Us

Referring back to the process leading to collaboration—content consumption, creation, curation, and then collaboration—compare content consumption as applied to traditional marketing and business processes with its social counterpart. Consumption—whether of your mass market communication or the video assets you've placed on your website—is often described in a traditional media sense in terms of engagement. Look more closely, though, and what's happening in most forms of traditional media is actually a relatively passive and in most cases solo activity. Call this traditional consumption for lack of a better term. Whatever the term, this type of engagement is a relatively low-involvement form.

Now move to the social sense of engagement: What does it really mean for customers to be engaged in ways that engender conversation or sharing or the creation of new content? As people become more connected, their desire to be part of something larger increases. When someone posts "I am standing in line at Starbucks" or "Waking up to a beautiful day in Austin" on Twitter, the motivation is not sharing the fact that some particular activity is happening right now. Instead, it's all about telling *yourself* that *you are part of a larger community* and telling that community that you *appreciate* its being around you. Ultimately, you are asking that community to appreciate you back, so to speak. It's what humans do.

This is the kind of expressed ownership or belonging that manifests itself in the relatively higher levels of socially inspired engagement—and in collaboration between community members, for example. If you see Twitter (and social media in general) as a big, meaningless, narcissism-fest, think about that last point again: Participants truly value their communities and the tangible expressions of belonging. When one *belongs* to something, one takes personal ownership for it. This shows up in member-to-member curation, in solutions posted in help forums, in the entries developed over time in Wikipedia, and through many other similar expressions on the Social Web. This sense of participation and belonging is more encompassing than it may seem: It's not just my own needs expressed through my own activities. It's about us.

To be sure, to an extent social participation is "all about me," but this includes knowing who's (also) in line at Starbucks. Whether connected through SMS, Twitter, Foursquare, or whatever, it's about your knowing what is happening around you and in particular with and among the people you are connected to through your entire (meaning across networks) social graph. It's about a larger, social view of what's around and your specific role within it as a participant.

In a resounding setback, Facebook was called out when it botched its privacy changes in mid-2010 and similarly faced pushback following its acquisition of Instagram. That said, the fact is that people willingly and knowingly share a *lot* more personal information than ever before, precisely so that *they can see* some sort of reflection in the world around them that they exist. The consequences and pushback for mass marketing are huge as the coincident drive toward alignment with brands that recognize individuals accelerates. Again, this observation:

As people take control over their data while spreading their Web presence, they are not looking for privacy, but for recognition as individuals. This will eventually change the whole world of advertising.

Esther Dyson, 2008

Across multiple forms of media—social media being no exception—*consumption of content* is typically the most likely activity. However, beware! Whether you're reading the paper, watching TV, or listening to the radio or a podcast, consumption is by all counts a passive activity. Even when the activity involves social media (reading blogs, for example), 80 to 90 percent of the audience limits its activity to consumption. This is the heart of the 90/9/1 rule we discussed in Chapter 1: 90% watch, 9% participate casually, and 1% participate frequently. Your mileage may vary, but the underlying behavior is well established.

While this can be helpful from a marketing (awareness) perspective, it doesn't directly connect customers around the brand, product, or service in the kind of social context that leads to the higher forms of engagement.

It's important to get beyond content consumption and bring your audience to the level of a genuine connection. This means participating with them, getting them into the game, and placing yourself in it with them. The easiest way is to do this through social activities—not unlike real life—and to do it in the online social spots where your audience is already present.

As a starting activity, consider *curation*. Curation is built around activities such as rating, reviewing, and otherwise passing judgment on the content (or conduct!) of others in the community. Because this content has been made available in a social setting, curation is a natural next step. What does curation look like? It can be as simple as rating a post as useful (or not!).

Curation matters for two reasons. First, it is a reflection of the sensibilities and value system of the audience and/or community members. Curation and the general act of evaluating and rating content—videos, posts, articles, and so forth—make it easy for others to quickly find what's valuable and learn about what the community values. Curation drives positive community experiences for the benefit of community members. Curation in the community and membership context helps provide a better experience for members and thereby encourages the collaborative activities seen in the higher forms of engagement. Recall that these higher forms of engagement are what one is after through the adoption of social technologies. In consumer products, for example, these higher forms of engagement lead to better products and to better understandings among customers as to why these are in fact better products.

Pepsi, looking to expand its highly integrated program in the direction of increasingly social connection points, launched its Refresh project, built on cash donations from Pepsi directed to social projects that Pepsi consumers suggested and voted on. This program directly defines the Pepsi brand according to the lifestyles, passions, and causes of its customers. Pepsi's Refresh project, shown in Figure 7.3, is an example of participant-controlled marketing by a brand built around participation and collaboration.

Figure 7.3 The Pepsi Refresh project

Social programs that go beyond awareness (consumption) and instead push for collaboration between the businesses and their marketplace stakeholders are becoming more common. They are part of an overall, holistic marketing program. Programs like Pepsi's Refresh and Starbucks's My Starbucks Ideas, though different in their approaches to and use of social technology, both connect the brands into the specific interests of the company's customers. Curation, along with basic content creation, occurs naturally in these efforts, making them ideal for participative marketing efforts and the use of social technology.

Building on consumption, curation, and content creation, collaboration is the main objective when creating advocates, evangelists, and brand ambassadors. Getting people in your audience to work together collaboratively is very powerful. Working together to produce a common outcome, participants around your brand, product, or service bond with each other; and as they do, they develop a strong loyalty for the communities in which they are able to collaborate.

Find Your Influencers

Moving deeper into collaboration and its connection to listening, *who* is participating in the conversation is often as important as *what* is actually being said. Being able to identify participants who are more broadly connected or who have a specific connection in your marketplace is clearly important. In PR, for example, you connect with media influencers and similar professionals by researching or subscribing to a database of known journalists, writers, analysts, media influencers, and so on. These people sit at the entry points of the media channels that convey your message to large, defined audiences. In this setting, getting your information to specific people is as easy (or as hard) as the readiness of your own contacts database enables. Getting them to use that information the way you want them to is, of course, much more difficult.

By comparison, one of the aspects of the Social Web that makes it more challenging than traditional channels of communication is that the influencers—in the conversational leadership and direction or tone-setting sense—can be literally anyone. *How do you find them?* Sure, there are A-list bloggers who actively cover larger industrial and social/lifestyle verticals, just as there known media pundits and subject-matter experts who blog, write columns, host news shows, or produce similar commentary. While you may not be able to influence them directly, at least you can spot them and build appropriate relationships with them.

But what about the smaller-scale or niche bloggers whose 1,000 or 10,000 or 50,000 subscribers also comprise a meaningful slice of your customer base? Influencer identification—as a part of your overall listening program—is all about spotting and building functional, productive relationships with these individuals. This means taking an additional look into your influencers to pick out specific behaviors—what is a particular blogger focused on within the larger industry covered, and what are the larger industry or cause-related issues that most or all of the bloggers you are following are themselves focused on? Understanding the interests and hot buttons of groups or specific types of bloggers that matter to you is as important as picking out specific bloggers. These people too are influenced by their peers and operate with the benefit of their own collective knowledge. That means you need to understand this as well. The tools used to develop marketplace and specific influencer profiles—recall Buzzstream from Chapter 2, "The Social Customer"—include crawlers that navigate the Social

Web looking for connections *between* people, so they can be used to spot both individual and group behaviors.

In a socially connected setting, the influencers in a decision process are very often the actual users of the product or service who have also established a meaningful presence for themselves online. This is exactly who you want to be engaging with as you set out on a strategic path toward collaboration and co-creation, the subject of the next section. This person might be a homemaker who blogs about health, nutrition, or family vacation planning or a photographer who publishes reviews of cameras along with techniques for lighting and subject composition. These are otherwise ordinary people, with a specific passion or interest, who have also made it a habit to publish and share what they love, hate, find useful, or otherwise want others like themselves to know about. These are precisely the people you want to find and build relationships with.

With the combination of listening and influencer identification programs in place, you can take a big step toward designing your business based on what your customers want. It's important to understand that this goes beyond "designing the products they ask for." Sometimes customers don't know what they want, or they don't know what is possible, or they want the wrong things. Don't confuse listening and influencer identification with the wholesale turning over of your business design to your customers. At least as regards your brand, product, or service, it's still your ship, but your customers are the crew, and so they can make or break the voyage.

Bring Social Learning (and Technology) on Domain

Using your listening program to discover and track important memes (thoughts and trends) and to spot influencers and create valuable relationships is step 1. Connecting these to your business by bringing these conversations on domain—to your support forums or your idea and innovation applications—is step 2.

The process of understanding and managing the social customer experience is highly focused on the combination of getting marketplace information where it needs to go and ensuring that you have the kind of organization that can benefit from it. Internally, this means connecting your teams with social applications like SocialText, Lotus Connections, SharePoint, or Jive. Externally, it means building powerful customer communities on platforms that support social customer experience management like those from Lithium Technologies and Salesforce.com. Dell's Employee Storm and Philips's use of Socialcast are examples of social technology applied internally to create powerful connections to customers. HP, Time Warner Cable, Comcast, BSkyB, and Sephora are all examples of businesses that have connected external off-domain customer interactions with on-domain collaborative and community resources. These connections were built to implement effective responses to conversations wherever they occur and to ensure that, within the organization, a specific customer's question is directed to the right person, so the right response happens at the right time. This kind of efficient, timely response is critical to collaborative behavior.

Connect Collaboration to Your Business

With a collaborative context defined, the challenge is to connect the engagement process as defined in the social context to your business or organization's objectives. Starbucks and Dell, using a range of social technologies, accomplished this early on and remain great case studies precisely because of the history since. They have used consumption, curation, and creation through their ideas platforms as a way to *invite* collaboration and then used what they learned to improve their products and product experiences. Searching the Web will produce plenty of analysis and commentary on these cases. Check them out to see how their implementation of what amounts to a suggestion box—done right—has changed their businesses.

Collaboration extends into tactical marketing programs as well: Pepsi's Refresh is one way of involving customers directly in building a relevant brand, clearly a long-term strategic social-media-based proposition. By comparison, in early 2010 announcements from other big consumer brands like Unilever and Coke indicated that they too would be de-emphasizing branded microsites and similar media programs as components of online marketing. Instead, they increased investments in building a presence in globally significant social networks like Facebook. Coke, for example, has literally millions of fans collected around its Facebook business page.

In 2007, building on the Salesforce.com Ideas platform, Dell launched IdeaStorm. Like the My Starbucks Idea program, IdeaStorm is a transparent adaptation of the classic suggestion box, humorously depicted in Figure 7.4. What makes this updated suggestion box work is the fact that voting—done by customers and potential customers—is out in the open. The better ideas move up as they are discussed. Ideas faring less well sometimes get combined in the process, strengthening their chance of making it into the idea pool from which Dell's product managers ultimately pull ideas.

The suggestions implemented through the IdeaStorm platform were significant, including Dell offering the Linux Ubuntu operating system as a preinstalled option. Additional ideas receiving higher than average attention include aspects of customer service, suggestions regarding the website (a primary source of income for Dell), and suggestions that preinstalled promotional software be optional. Looking at these ideas, it's clear that social technologies have applicability and impact that extend beyond marketing.

Beyond consumer businesses, business-to-business brands—like Element 14, American Express, HSBC, and Indium—are using purpose-built communities, business-oriented networks like LinkedIn, and blogging to get closer to their own customers. In all of these efforts, the rationale is simple: Respect your audience by getting involved in the activities that they are themselves involved in. Become part of their community by bringing your brand to them. Combined with a longer-term strategic plan, these types of real-world, tactical efforts, built around platforms that already exist, are a great way to get started.

Figure 7.4 What's wrong with this picture? Everything!

Crowdsourcing

Stepping up from co-creation, crowdsourcing tips in favor of your customers having an outright hand in design and the advancement of specific solutions or in similar roles. Crowdsourcing is an important source for innovation: As you saw with Dell's IdeaStorm, the task of trying to make sense of 10,000 ideas randomly submitted is considerably easier if you let your customers sort the submissions for you. They'll vote for what they want and pass on the rest. You can focus on what they want. How much faster can problems be solved when everyone involved—including your customers and your employees—work together to solve them? Collectively solving problems is a great way to show your customers you love them.

Crowdspring: Crowdsourcing

If you've never tried a true crowdsourcing application, here's your chance. For a couple of hundred dollars, you can get a snappy new logo and card design for your upcoming birthday party—or just about any other event that you wanted branded. Of course, if your business needs a visual makeover, you can use Crowdspring to do that too.

Crowdspring attracts artists—designers, typographers, CSS wizards, and more—who compete for projects. Unlike eLance, where project awards are made *before* the actual deliverable is prepared, Crowdspring participants see the actual designs as they are evolving—in public and in view of competing designers—as the process occurs. You pay after the fact.

What really makes Crowdspring work, however, is the participation of the buyer in collaboration with the designers. Take a logo design as an example: Imagine that you want a logo for your new business. First, you create an account and define what you want—color preferences, style choices, and maybe some examples of logos you like. At this point the designers review the project, and those wishing to compete jump in and start offering design ideas.

Now, if the buyer doesn't participate beyond this point, the designers will offer a range of styles and the buyer may pick one, but this isn't the optimal path. One of the Crowdspring rules is that buyers have to pick a winner based on what is offered: This means it's in the direct interest of the buyer to improve what's offered. The best way to do this is to participate alongside the designers, not as a designer but rather through feedback on the designs being produced. As the buyer actively signals which of the submitted designs is favored, the existing pool of designers will all start shifting in that direction, and new designers, seeing the activity, will jump in, increasing both the pool and the range of choices. After 10 days, buyers choose the design they like, and the logo (or whatever design work you requested) is delivered. It's really quite amazing how well Crowdspring works.

Here's a great insight on crowdsourcing: The more you participate, the more the crowd will participate. Disclosure: Dave has used Crowdspring multiple times, and each time has seen the number of participating designers go up, directly in response to his participation. If you want people to participate—in any social application—show them you are serious by participating yourself.

Crowdspring

You can check out Crowdspring and see how it works and what others have used it for here:

www.crowdspring.com

Threadless.com: Crowd-Sourced Design

What happens when you build your business around a crowd-sourced process? For starters, your customers get involved in your products and services right from the start, which in turn can give you a continuous source of innovative suggestions on how to evolve. In addition, directly involved customers can become your most ardent supporters—or most vocal detractors.

Threadless.com—shown in Figure 7.5—offers T-shirts for sale. That sounds simple enough, but Threadless does it one better. Rather than selling their designs (or worse, designs that people could buy elsewhere), Threadless sells only the designs that its own customers create.

Figure 7.5 Crowd-sourced design: Threadless

The Threadless model works like this: People submit T-shirt designs, which are then reviewed and put to public vote. The winning designs are produced and sold, and the creators of the selected designs receive a cash reward as well as additional cash on future reprints. Threadless customers—through collaboration with each other and with the business itself—have a direct hand in shaping the product.

Threadless is a great example of a collaborative business. Founded in 2000, Threadless is also a testament to the viability of a collaborative business. According to the Small Business Administration, on average new businesses have slightly less than a 50/50 chance of making it five years, let alone twice that.

> **Threadless**
>
> You can learn more about Threadless and its history by visiting Wikipedia:
>
> http://en.wikipedia.org/wiki/Threadless

HARO: Knowledge Exchange

HARO—an acronym for Help a Reporter Out—is a knowledge exchange that was created by Peter Shankman. The basic proposition of HARO is that for every person who has a question, somewhere there is a person with an answer. The trick is to put them together, and this is what HARO does.

The context for HARO is news reporting. Reporters are often in the predicament of having to report on something they themselves don't fully understand. This is *not* a knock on reporters; it is simply the reality of a technically complex world. Even if a reporter is the science journalist for a magazine or paper, it's unrealistic to think that this person would simultaneously fully understand a nuclear power reactor, the inner workings of a rocket motor, and the various competing ideas and technical underpinnings for what to do about global warming. Yet, in the course of a week, that reporter may be asked to cover all three.

This is the classic expertise-sharing problem that led Dr. Vannevar Bush to conceive of the memex, the theorized mechanical device that provided the fundamental insight in creating the World Wide Web. Peter Shankman has applied this same thought to the job of the reporter and the challenges they face in getting accurate information about a variety of topics, even within a chosen focus area.

On one side of HARO are reporters. Reporters need information. Typically, information costs money, except online where everything is assumed to be free (not)! So here's the dilemma: How do you get reporters the information they need without paying for it, at least directly in cash, since that would introduce a whole host of issues with regard to reporting?

The insight was this: Experts seek recognition, and being cited as an expert in a publication can be very valuable as a way to advance the career of an engineer, doctor, sociologist, prosumer (a sort of professional-grade hobbyist), and a lot of other people. HARO puts these two needs together through a searchable exchange. Reporters go looking for experts, and the experts—who have signed up and completed detailed profiles about their expertise—are thereby available for interviews by those reporters. Rather than paying in cash, people get paid in social capital and they see their own contributions gain public notice.

HARO

You can learn more about HARO—and perhaps even sign up yourself—here:

> www.helpareporter.com

You may also want to learn more about Peter Shankman, who developed HARO. Peter is the author of *Customer Service: New Rules for a Social-Enabled World* (Que Biz-Tech, 2010). You can follow Peter on Twitter (@skydiver).

Gamification

In recent years few buzzwords have been as hot as *gamification*; predictably, the concept is widely misused and misunderstood. *Gamification is the adaptation of the principles of online games to social applications, in this context to add interest to programs supporting social customer experience.* When properly used, the point of gamification is not simply to entertain—nor is it to trick your customers into doing things they don't want to do. In fact, it's close to the opposite: It's about enabling them to tap into what they love, what's fun—and to thereby encourage them to do for your business what anyone playing a game would do for themselves. Read on to learn more.

Social Technologies and Gaming

Social technologies and online gaming have long been intertwined. Some of the earliest and most vibrant communities on the commercial Web were built by and for gamers. As an example, brothers Lyle and Dennis Fong, champion online gamers, created Gamers.com in 1998 as a place where fanatical fans of games like Quake and Doom could get together and share their passion and knowledge of these games. As it happened, some early users of Gamers.com happened to be employees of Dell and SONY, who individually approached the brothers with the idea of adapting the Gamers platform to the goals of an enterprise business. In Dell's case it was customer support, while SONY wanted to bring together enthusiastic users of its gaming console.

The Fongs—seeing the clear business benefit of gaming behavior applied to business—decided to create a stand-alone company to serve large enterprises like Dell and SONY. That company, Lithium Technologies, now powers social customer experience for hundreds of companies around the world. Lithium's customers—brands like SONY, Best Buy, and Caterpillar—now have gaming in their social DNA.

Social customer experience takes more from gamers than just technology: Much of the knowledge and expertise in managing online communities came from gaming too. Meet a Fortune 500 or global brand's community manager and you're likely to have met a gaming enthusiast, gaming site moderator, or admin. Gamification, then, is not something new being added to customer communities; it's been there all along.

Building Communities on the Web

The first and best book on online community management, *Community Building on the Web*, was written by Amy Jo Kim.

Not surprisingly, Amy Jo Kim is a recognized expert in gaming and game systems!

Elements of Gamification

Today, it seems like everything is being gamified. In 2013, the City of Chicago gamified the city parks. Visit a park, get a badge. Collect them all! And people did just that.

The city's goal was to help citizens discover and use all the great park resources—beaches, pools, tennis courts, nature paths, and so forth—in America's third largest city. The *higher purpose* was to promote both civic and individual health. Whether you believe that people need such motivation to jump in a swimming pool, or that two pools are better than one, is beside the point. The point is that this example illustrates three common themes in gamification at its best:

- By adding an element of fun, it encourages people to do more of what they would like to do.

- At its best, it helps people achieve a goal that is meaningful to them.

- As a result, the brand—in this case the City of Chicago—achieves the business objectives associated with this particular program in an excellent and sustainable manner. The game encourages participation, and the game itself carries forward naturally as new parks and other points of interest are added.

In short, good gamification in a business context is built on human motivations that are intrinsic, rather than extrinsic, and that lend themselves to the future of the game itself.

But what does it mean to gamify a system? Specifically, what elements make a system gamified? A gamified system has one or more of the following four elements:

- Points
- Ranks or levels
- Badges
- Missions or journeys

Remember the video games you played as a kid? When you finished a game, you got a point score. If the score was high enough, you showed up on a leaderboard. Point scores accomplish the minimum that gamification should achieve: They make progress visible and measurable and thereby inspire efforts at improvement. The downside of point systems is that they are easy to manipulate, to game. Compared to other gamification elements, points can be harder to align with intrinsic motivations: Not everyone describes himself or herself as competitive, for example, so points alone do not make a game.

Again, back to the games you played as a kid: When you played more advanced games, you typically got another kind of reward. When you succeeded in negotiating a challenge, winning a battle, or solving a problem, *you moved up a level*. Levels or ranks are among the earliest and most fundamental elements of gamification. Not coincidentally, the difference between early message boards and later community platforms was built around rank: Community platforms adopted reputation systems—usually featuring ranks—that motivated people to continue to stay active over time.

Good rank structures for social customer experience share some common characteristics. First, they are flattering, not punishing; every rank title, even the lowest, should make the user feel good. (No "newbies" here.) Second, they are intuitively progressive; users will immediately know it's better to be a king than a knight. By comparison, few will understand the hierarchical ordering of ranks like *apple* versus *banana*. Finally, they are progressively more difficult; going from level 9 to level 10 is much harder than moving from 2 to 3.

Well-designed social platforms allow you to combine online data with activities or credentials from the real world, like loyalty or education programs. As a result, ranks are often based on a variety of activities. And unlike a position on a temporary leaderboard, a rank is something lasting. Once you earn it, it's yours. Some people put such permanent ranks in their email signature or LinkedIn profile; some even put them on their resume!

There's a problem with ranks, however: As an individual you can generally have only one within any given social network. What if you want to give a user more than one reward, perhaps for a very specific activity, or for a limited period of time? That's where the third element of gamification comes in: badging. With badges, customers can be rewarded for many different activities, typically with a distinctive graphic that appears on their user profile.

Badges can be awarded for any behavior that you want to encourage. In customer communities, badges are typically awarded for four things:

- Activity: Performing a particular activity at an exceptional level or for a specific period of time. Example: a badge for contributing 10,000 comments.

- Attendance: Being present or taking part in an event. Example: a silver badge for attending a user conference, and gold badge for attending 3 years in a row.

- Affiliation/certification: Earning or otherwise possessing a relationship with the brand. Example: a badge showing that you are an employee of the brand.

- Achievement: Accomplishing a set of activities. Example: a badge for viewing all the videos in a specific topic area.

Consider airline status, which may at first glance appear to be a rank. Airline status is really a form of badging. Look back at the previous criteria and you'll see why:

- Airline status is typically earned based on a specific set of activities, with successive badges being earned as additional specific accomplishments—flights flown, for example—are accumulated.

- Status lasts only for a preset time. High-status flyers who participate less in the next year typically lose status—moving down to a lower status the following year.

By comparison, earning a "million mile flyer" designation is a true rank; once completed, it's done and you own it forever. United Airlines' MileagePlus program—not coincidentally voted the best frequent flyer program 10 years running—offers customers who achieve 1 million miles or more *lifetime* benefits; at 1 million miles, that customer is Gold for life (and of course can earn higher status in any given year). At 2 million miles, that customer is Platinum for life. At 3 and 4 million miles, additional lifetime levels are awarded.

What exists in addition to rank and badging? And specifically, what gaming provision rewards and motivates the absolute highest levels of participation? We're glad you asked.

When a set of activities is significant enough, it qualifies as the fourth element of gamification: *missions and journeys*. Missions and journeys have been common in online gaming starting with the primitive text-based games of the 1980s, and they remain a powerful element in contemporary games. Missions and journeys align well with the basic notion of building a (gamified) community or other social application around passion, lifestyle, and cause.

Grand Theft Auto V generated more than $1B in revenue in the first three days after its release in September 2013. Why? Certainly the violent and salacious content didn't hurt, but that's actually not the success factor. Instead, the commercial success of games like Grand Theft Auto is connected to a basic human need *to face a series of challenges and emerge victorious*. We all want to win *at something*.

Now imagine harnessing the power of missions to the goals of your brand, your community, and your customer. Companies are increasingly thinking of their social customer experience channels not just as mechanisms to drive cost savings, satisfaction, and transactions but as *platforms for driving change, learning, and transformation*.

In this way, the fourth element of gamification—mission and journey—may ultimately be the most important. As we noted previously, gamification at its best helps people accomplish goals that are meaningful to them and that produce outcomes aligned with your business objectives. Things that have meaning are often hard and require commitment; therefore, missions and journeys, with their built-in difficulty, are an ideal vehicle for building social brand advocates.

Loyalty, Location, and Mobile

You may have noticed that the discussion about ways to earn a badge was not limited to activities that happen online. Your customers interact with you online and off, and it's important to recognize this fact when you create your gamification strategy. Recognizing offline activities can be tricky, though unlike in the online world what happens offline isn't always recorded and accessible. A visit to a shop or restaurant doesn't show up on any server log; a purchase may be recorded at the cash register, but point-of-sale data isn't always available to your social customer experience (SCE) systems. How do you unite your SCE efforts with your offline customer experience? Take a look at the following examples.

Foursquare: Mobile Game-Based Sharing

Beginning with phones that include GPS or similar location tracking, early applications such as Brightkite, Dodgeball, Loopt, and Latitude have made the simple act of being someplace talkworthy. (Just how talkworthy they are is, of course, left to the participants in any given conversation to decide!)

Each of these tools in some way traded on the value of knowing where others to whom you have connected are right now. Fast-forward to the contemporary location-based (aka, mobile) services like Google Maps and wearable products like Glass and Pebble that bring right-here, right-now interactions with brands within reach of a wide range of consumers. Add gaming, and stand back.

Early mobile applications included things like meetups, coffee shops, and dinner dates. Depending on your motivations, the ability to see where your friends are can be useful information. But beyond basic location awareness, these early applications didn't do much. That was a problem.

Enter Foursquare. Foursquare combines location awareness with collective knowledge to produce an order of magnitude more useful (and more rewarding) experience. Using Foursquare, upon arriving someplace you check in. The GPS in your phone knows where you are, and Foursquare tells you what's around you. Typically, you see the name of the place where you are and some others that are nearby, and you simply click Check In. As an additional nod to gaming, and recalling the discussions of badging and rank, Foursquare will evaluate your Klout score and let you know how you rank in your current location.

What makes Foursquare relatively more popular compared with earlier mobile check-in applications is its game-based functionality. As you check in, you accumulate points. Check in someplace new and add that venue to the Foursquare database—there's a form for this right on your phone-based app—and you get six points. Even better, hit three places in the same day, and you get a Traveler badge. Go out on a weeknight, and you'll earn the School Night badge. Co-author Dave does this too: Dave is a Level 10 Trainspotter (45 different stations), and has most every flight-related badge that exists. You can see your points and badges when you log in online or open Foursquare on your phone (see Figure 7.6).

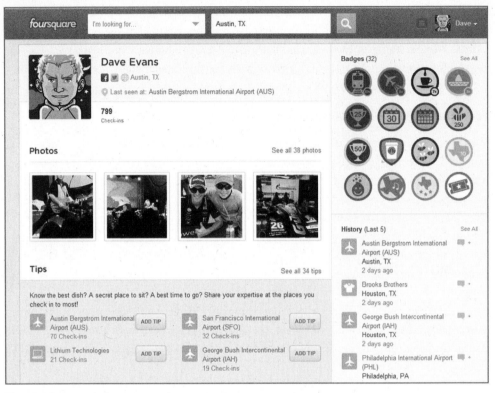

Figure 7.6 Foursquare badges

Once you check in, you see a list of your friends *also using Foursquare* who are nearby, along with tips about the place you've checked into. The tips are one of the first big-value adds of Foursquare: Dave now advocates for the SBB (Swiss Rail) mobile app, which he learned about while climbing the Trainspotter ranks. Checking into a restaurant, you can see what's good (or alternatively, what's good that is right across the street). Checking in at a grocery store alerts others in your friends list that you're there—and they can ping you to ask you to pick up some milk (since you actually know each other, the relative tolerance for such an imposition is known by both parties) and thereby save your friend a needless trip in the car.

Foursquare: Beyond Meetups

Peter Kim takes the possible social business applications for Foursquare further, extending the application well beyond simple meetups and check-ins. You can read more about Peter and Foursquare here:

www.beingpeterkim.com/2009/11/foursquare-social-business-design.html

> ### Sharing Location Data
>
> Foursquare and Twitter both allow you to follow people and allow others to follow you. Unlike Twitter's basic posting features, however, that let followers know what you are doing, Foursquare tells them *where* you are. This means it's also telling people where you *aren't*. If you check in at a movie theater, it means you aren't going to be home for about 2 hours.
>
> Rather than uninstalling the application, think about your own follower/following and friending policies. Location-sharing applications raise the bar in this regard. Dave's good friend Susan Bratton talked of the "gluttonous social behavior" many have engaged in—amassing thousands of followers simply because they could. Many are now rethinking that behavior.
>
> Before accepting a follow request with location-sharing tools, take a minute (or more!) to think through the potential impact of what you are sharing. Twitter has taught that not everyone really wants to know what everyone else is doing right now. Foursquare may teach that even fewer people want *anyone* to know *where* they are doing it.

Review and Hands-On

Applying social media principles effectively in business is both straightforward and challenging. It is straightforward because there is actually a process around which you can organize your efforts. It is challenging because much like the rethinking that occurs when applying social media in pure marketing applications, applying social technologies at a business level may require a redesign of the business itself.

Review of the Main Points

The five key trends covered in this chapter are summarized in the points that follow. Get these things right and you're on your way to a solid implementation of social technology in business.

Real Time

Listen and engage with your customers, in and around the channels that they prefer. Immediate response is now the norm: Your customers expect a direct linkage to your company. Take advantage of off-domain social applications by listening to what is being talked about and connecting these people to your on-domain social applications.

Mobile

Real time essentially implies mobile: Think of mobile as the platform for "real-space" applications. In the way that real time means right now, at this moment, real space means right here, at this place. This is where your customers are heading. Meet them there.

Co-creation

Customer-driven design and lightweight customer participation (ratings and reviews, for example) lead to businesses built on co-creation models. Co-creation speeds innovation and positively links your business to the market.

Crowdsourcing

The follow-on to co-creation, crowdsourcing adds peer content, turning control over to customers and opening up business opportunities in the new sharing economy.

Gamification

By making it fun, by making it a challenge, and by making it a game, you can encourage your customers to participate in co-creation and crowdsourcing and orient these activities on a positive track that helps you build your business.

Hands-On: Review These Resources

Review each of the following, and ensure that you have a complete understanding of how social media and social technology are used.

Dell Ideastorm

`www.ideastorm.com/`

Threadless

`www.threadless.com`

Foursquare (You will need an account with Foursquare and a GPS-capable phone or similar hand-held device for this.)

`http://foursquare.com`

HARO

`www.helpareporter.com`

Hands-On: Apply What You've Learned

Apply what you've learned in this chapter through the following exercises:

1. Assess the real-time capability of your organization. How long does it take you to respond to customers online? Can you reduce that time?

2. Understand your company's mobile strategy. Is your website mobile-friendly? Are there mobile apps that you could deploy? (Tip: Look at your competitors too!) This will help you understand whether you can integrate social with existing efforts or need to develop on your own.

3. Prepare a short presentation using Threadless or a similar crowdsourced enterprise as the subject or any other collaborative business design application that

you choose. Talk to your team about what makes the application work and how social technology has been built into the business.

4. Looking at your own firm or organization, list three ways that your customers could collaborate directly with each other to improve some aspect of your product or service.

5. Develop an outline for a business plan based on exercise 2 that involves multiple departments or functions to implement. Win the support of those people.

Social Customer Experience Building Blocks

III

In Part III, we dig deeper into the five building blocks of social customer experience: organization, platform, content, people, and tools. What does successful customer engagement look like? How do all the various platform elements come together? How do you and your customers get the most out of the content, networks, and tools you assemble?

Customer Engagement

All the plans, programs, and platforms we've discussed depend on one thing: customer engagement. While you create the experience you want customers to have, that experience is powered by customers themselves, every day, by how they engage with your brand, product, or service and with each other. To succeed you need to understand why customers engage and which channels are best for that engagement. Done right, your value to your customers—and their value to you—increases dramatically.

8

Chapter contents

Hierarchy of Types

When you take the applications we detailed in Chapter 4, "The Social Customer Experience Ecosystem," and apply them to a particular purpose, you get an *engagement type*. Choosing an engagement type—or types, since an enterprise social effort usually includes more than one—is a key decision in creating your social customer experience. It's important to customers because it determines the ways they can participate with your organization. It's important to you as an organization because different engagement types impose different opportunities, responsibilities, and risks. Successful social customer experience efforts don't begin by choosing an application or platform and then seeing how customers decide to use it. Successful efforts determine first what purpose the effort will fulfill, for both customer and company, and then choose and deploy the application to serve that purpose.

The most common engagement types are these:

- Support: Customers give and receive help and advice related to the use of a product.
- Sales: Customers signal needs or share experiences in the context of purchasing a product.
- Innovation: Customers share ideas and experiences to help companies improve products or processes.

Table 8.1 provides examples of company programs related to these different engagement types.

▶ **Table 8.1** Engagement programs

Brand	Engagement Activity	Engagement Platform
Starbucks	**Innovation:** Transparent suggestion box seeking innovative ideas, with visible participation by the Starbucks team.	My Starbucks Idea
HP	**Support:** Member-driven answers to technical questions, with HP playing a supporting (participative) rather than primary (controlling) role.	HP Support Forums HP Facebook and Twitter presence
Indium	**Sales:** Executive and engineering blogs used as a platform for thought leadership; invites discussion and creates loyalty.	Indium.com
PGi	**Support:** Developers speak openly with each other as they develop applications using PGi's programming tools and thereby drive demand for PGi's services.	PGiConnect Developer's Community

When selecting an engagement type, it is useful to think simultaneously in terms of value to your business and value to your customer. From a business perspective, the value may be increased revenues, lower costs, or valuable customer insights. From the customer's perspective, it looks different: It's about finding products that are of higher quality and more suited to your needs. It's also about getting the most out of the products you buy and maybe—in the best case—finding brand communities that you're proud to be a part of. As a company, how do you align these so that you simultaneously achieve your objectives and satisfy your customers?

It's easier than you might think. That's because there's a hierarchy (Figure 8.1) that links your objectives with the motives and perspective of your customers. The hierarchy begins with customer care and the importance of satisfied customers. Built on top of satisfaction is loyalty, which is built around pre-sales support aimed at getting customers connected with the right products. With satisfaction and loyalty in place, your organization is now in a position to enlist your customers in collaboration and co-creation.

Figure 8.1 Engagement hierarchy

The hierarchy shown in Figure 8.1 provides an insightful look into the experiential mechanics of effective engagement at scale: The hierarchy relates satisfaction (care), loyalty (sales), and advocacy (innovation). It's also easy to see how connectedness on the Social Web impacts the purchase funnel: If you cannot address in a meaningful, visible manner the majority of your *visible* (Social Web!) customer requests for service, how can you expect to sell a premium service? At the innovation and advocacy levels farther up the hierarchy, if customer satisfaction is low, then asking for customer ideas is likely to yield gems like "I've got an idea: Don't lie to me! This product doesn't do what you claimed it would!" rather than thoughtful suggestions that lead to real and sustained innovation.

Instead, by ensuring that customers are basically satisfied—meaning that most customers would say that what you delivered matched the promise you offered and that they generally get reasonable, visible answers to their questions in a reasonable amount of time—you are more likely to build advocates, the kinds of customers who will contribute important, new ideas that lead to innovation, as well as encouraging vocal brand advocates to rally to your defense as they did for Café Coffee Day.

Level 1: Support

The most powerful motivator in social customer experience can be summarized as simple as "How do I _____ ?" Customers ask this question millions of times every day: How do I find, how do I buy, how do I use? While there are other motivations that spur use of social channels—curiosity, a sense of community, even boredom—the "how do I" motivation is especially important because it brings people to social channels with a need to fulfill. If you can fulfill that need well, you can inspire gratitude and even delight. If you don't meet that need, your relationship with the customer winds down.

Years ago, Joe provided advice to a Marketing department in one of the world's largest software companies. Their goal was to use online dialogue to discuss how technology was transforming business. They knew that their customers were thinking deeply about the changes brought about by Internet technologies, and they wanted to tap into that knowledge. When they launched their effort, however, their customers delivered a strong message: We need support! Because of the lack of online social tools available for support, customer flooded the new channel with support-related requests—despite the clear signposts that this channel had been created for strategic discussions. The lesson is that you have to meet basic needs first. Some people quite rightly compare this to Maslow's hierarchy of needs, beloved of psychology students. If people don't have food and shelter, they're unlikely to appreciate a new art museum.

So, it's important to meet basic needs (support) first. Basic, though, doesn't mean simple. Getting social support right is hard work. Successful social support engagement requires organizations to have the people, processes, and technology in place to engage appropriately, to meet customers seeking support on the channels through which they seek that support. To see what that means consider next two primary variations of social support: peer-to-peer support and agent-based support.

Peer Support

Peer support is an engagement type in which customers help customers. Dave relates the following story:

I was on my way to Gold's Gym one morning. It was about 4:30 a.m., and I had a full day planned including a conference call at 10:00 a.m.. As I was checking my calendar, my newly updated Google G1 froze up. I tried the obvious: I turned the phone off and then turned it back on. Halfway through the startup sequence, the process hung on the

Android logo. I was stuck in about the worst situation a digital nomad can be in: My connection to the Internet was gone! I was outside the spacecraft, without a tether.

At about 6:30 a.m., between workout sessions, I visited a nearby Starbucks, opened my laptop, and searched via Google for "g1 frozen android cupcake," because this seemed like a reasonable starting point. (I included "cupcake" because this was the operating system update that had been installed a day or two prior.) Near the top of the search results was an entry whose visible description read "freezes with android logo following cupcake upgrade...."

That looked promising, so I clicked into the result and found myself in the T-Mobile support forum. About five posts down I saw the recovery process for a frozen G1, outlined in detail. I followed the steps, and in less than 3 minutes my phone was functioning, albeit in its basic (default) configuration. After I finished my conference call I reinstalled my needed apps. Problem solved.

The point is this: At 6:30 a.m., much less 4:30 a.m., it would have been a stretch to expect live phone support. But in this case, Dave wouldn't have been able to call anyway: His phone was dead, and he'd long forgotten how to use a pay phone! (Do they even exist?) Because T-Mobile had created an online community for Android support, he was able to quickly self-serve and resolve his own problem. Had he not had his laptop, he could have done the same thing from any library or other municipal facility in Austin. And he wouldn't be alone—about 70,000,000 Americans regularly access the Internet from public libraries, schools, and similar public facilities in public, government, and municipal buildings.

Not only did T-Mobile save itself the cost of a call, Dave was delighted, even in the face of a failure. As an occasional user of first-generation devices, he expects a few bumps when using them. Hey, even Apples freeze, right? What's delightful is when the recovery from such bumps occurs in minutes and without disrupting the rest of an otherwise fully booked day. Dave's conference call went off as planned, and yes, he recounted this story at the start of the call.

Peer support is arguably the original form of social support. Autodesk, mentioned in Chapter 2, "The Social Customer," began its social efforts with support discussions ("boards") in the late 1980s on the commercial online service, CompuServe, at the time also used by home computer hobbyists.

In the early days of peer support, such communities were truly peer driven and often peer created; the company that made the product wasn't involved at all. Up until the end of the 1990s, in fact, the conventional wisdom was that companies *shouldn't* participate. The community, built by the customers, definitely belonged to them as well. Even if the company did organize and fund the community, the general rule was "Hands off." When companies launched a community, they would say, "Welcome to our community! This is a place where customers help customers. If you'd like an answer from us, please write or call." It seemed funny not to be involved, but the experts said stay away, so companies did just that.

Over time, companies realized that even in the best support forums, customers never answered 100 percent of the questions. It was obvious that many questions could never be answered by a customer; they required access to information that existed only inside the company. What's more, when questions went unanswered, people complained! Surely that's not what should be happening.

As a result, companies began to equip themselves to participate in their own peer support forums. This meant a change in roles. Where early communities were staffed only by a community manager and a moderator, support staff now needed to be involved. The role of the moderator—the person who enforces the rules and helps people use the application successfully—began to merge with that of support agent. By 2005, most peer support communities had some percentage of questions—generally around 5 percent—answered by employees.

Today, employees—often as members of a formal support team—answer an increasing number of questions posed by customers, but make no mistake: The thrust now is still to empower customers to answer other customers in these forums directly. In fact, the *customers* of UK-based telco giffgaff and France-based telco Joe Mobile, shown in Figure 8.2, provide 100 percent of the support in community-type social applications.

Figure 8.2 Joe Mobile

Even for firms that will ultimately deliver a combination of phone and social support, in the early stage of product launch, before customers arrive in large numbers, a significant share of the support-type questions are often resolved in social support forums. On balance this has been a good change: When you participate overtly, your customers see that you are part of the community too, helping you build stronger customer relationships. They don't just tolerate your presence—they expect it.

Successful Communities Start Here

So what does it take to make peer support successful? In 2008, co-author Joe Cothrel defined 10 keys that have been used by hundreds of companies since then:

- A business sponsor who sets direction and allocates budget
- A community manager who conducts planning and day-to-day decision-making
- A moderator who maintains positive tone, enforces rules, and helps users have a good experience
- Well-defined roles for staff and users, and software that supports those roles
- A set of comprehensive user guidelines
- Well-defined procedures for resolving or escalating issues that arise
- Good promotion and visibility to potential users
- The proper page and topical structures to spur participation
- A well-managed group of superusers
- A strong measurement program focused on value

Take a look at Joe's presentation, available on Slideshare:

www.slideshare.net/joecothrel/successful-communities-start-here-lithium-technologies

As you can see from the list of practices, a successful peer support effort is a marriage of good policy, procedure, and technologies. On the technology front, most successful peer support efforts by large organizations are powered by a relatively small set of technology platforms—most common among them Lithium and Jive. You might ask why so many organizations so often select the same vendors. The answer is that while social functionality like forums is relatively easy to *offer*, it isn't easy to bring functionality into a platform that is *manageable, measureable, secure, scalable, and available.*

Manageable means a company has control over what happens in the community at all times, generally through a robust set of permissions.

Measureable means the platform provides data that managers need to assess community health and measure community value.

Secure has an obvious meaning; no company wants to expose itself or its customers to the risk of having their data compromised.

Scalability and availability are also part of the ante—if your customers can't use the system, it doesn't matter what its features or virtues are.

What's nice about these applications and implementations is this: You can focus on building relationships and managing the processes that support them rather than designing and maintaining the technical environment. This affords you the time to build trust—the product of good relationships and reliable processes—and helps you set an entire context for the conversations that involve your brand, product, or service. Your customers will sort out many of the conversations for you so that you don't have to respond to every single comment, suggestion, or idea. When you do choose to respond—or when it's clear that you are expected to respond—you can focus on the requests and suggestions that have a large following or that, if left alone, may generate one. If you can't implement a specific idea, you can explain it once and move on. And, if you think you *might* be able to do it given an internal process change, design change, or similar effort, you have at least the beginnings of the *customer* support you need to make the business case inside your organization for pressing for the required change or innovation.

This brings up an additional point about true engagement solutions: When you connect with your customers and participate with them in conversations—inviting them to collaborate with you and placing an *appropriate* degree of trust and control in them—your customers will actually enable you to take up their case inside your firm or organization. Rather than stopping at the first no from your legal team or the C-suite, for example, you'll actually find yourself championing the cause on behalf of your customers. That's the point where you know you are on the way to a social technology–driven business and to long-term success.

Collaboration and peer support extends beyond commercial business, too: Nonprofits, NGOs, and governmental agencies themselves are all part of the social business evolution. In an especially insightful remark, Ian Wilson, Librarian and Archivist of Canada Emeritus, noted the following:

Governments will collaborate with experts, lobbyists, trade organizations, and service partners. Policy will therefore evolve and the citizen will become more engaged in the political process. To my mind social media will deliver one of the greatest leaps forward in democratic participation seen yet in our world. Government had better be ready.

Agent Support

Another important factor causes companies to take a more active role in their peer support communities: the rise of social networks. Communities are centered on shared interest; therefore, if you create a community around your products, your customers will find you. Personal social networks—you and your specific friends on Facebook, for example—are different. Because personal networks are centered on people rather than interests, specific expertise around specialized questions may not exist, and as a result questions often go unanswered. As a practical matter, no one's personal network is likely to have all the answers to the how-to questions they might have.

To address the challenge of highly specialized questions—how do I use this particular app on this particular phone?—support-type engagements on social networks have taken on a very different character compared with those in support communities. In social networks, it's often the company—through team agents trained in specific aspects of technical or sales support—that generally provides the help and advice. Twitter, in particular, has become a significant focus for many companies. Most large companies today have their own Twitter handle, and many companies have a Twitter handle specifically for accepting and answering support and service questions.

Your organization, and in particular your customer team and internal (employee) sources of domain expertise (people who know a lot about how your customers use your product or service), provide *an effective liaison of the brand and its values.* If you thought this was the lead-up to *an important front line when managing customer requests,* you'd hardly be alone: Too many organizations still see customer care as the first line of defense in keeping customers from interfering with the otherwise smooth flow of business. In a social context this point of view and operational strategies built around it no longer work.

How do companies engage successfully? You need a strategy, a platform, and a workflow that does for social what your call routing and similar technologies do for your call centers.

Start with automated listening: In Chapter 7, "Five Key Trends," we talked about active listening. Automated listening goes one step further: Using a platform like Lithium Social Web, Sysomos Heartbeat, or Radian6, you can selectively identify posts on the Social Web that reference your brand or other content that you are specifically interested in. Platforms like Lithium Social Web, Conversocial, and Sprinklr can then take an added step, routing those posts automatically to teams that are specifically skilled in responding to certain questions. For example, posts about current orders or posts about warranty service can be routed to specific social agents with the training to respond to shipping and warranty questions. This enables you to respond efficiently and visibly and to thereby send a message to your customer and (if/as appropriate) to the friends and followers of your customers who may be watching.

Beyond your full-time social agents—typically found in your customer support unit—there are others in your organization also able to assist in response, to help you reduce and manage the combined load of social requests. Experts in other areas—product managers, HR and legal resources, and others—are all appropriately tasked with selected customer requests. This not only provides a better experience for customers—getting to talk to the "source" is often a satisfying experience for advanced or highly technical customers—but it also connects your organization more deeply with your customers. Dell has upward of 5,000 trained, certified employees *outside* of customer care, each of whom is empowered to talk about Dell issues using social media.

Level 2: Sales

Sales engagement is the second level of the social engagement hierarchy, and it may be surprising to find sales activities covered by a platform typically associated with support.

Brand managers approaching social technology may consider ratings, recommendations, and product reviews as the primary social content that influences product purchases. And while it's true that product reviews play an important role in supporting online sales, think about how you make buying decisions. In all likelihood, your purchases involve online research, and most online research includes a product review.

Bazaarvoice Social Commerce Statistics

The website of product ratings and review vendor Bazaarvoice has long been an excellent source of statistics on social commerce. Check out the following page for statistics you can use to assess the potential of peer content in driving sales:

```
www.bazaarvoice.com/research-and-insight/social-commerce-
statistics/
```

It's important to understand that any peer content can support a purchase decision. Peer support forums are a common location for potential buyers to see what customers are saying about the products they are considering. Purchase intentions are often conveyed directly in the questions people ask, such as

I'm thinking about buying a new 42-inch LCD flat-screen TV. Can anyone recommend one with excellent picture quality?

If you aren't shopping yourself, you may not notice how common such buying signals are in discussions that have been created for support-type engagement. It's not uncommon for 25–30 percent of the content in support discussions to contain signals like this. If you have customer discussions today, select a sample and analyze it for signals that participants are sending in a purchase process. Even if only a small percentage of those individuals ultimately make a purchase, the numbers can be meaningful.

The number of retailers who include peer discussion on their websites testifies to the power of customer content to influence purchase behavior. For example, Canadian electronics retailer Future Shop, a unit of Best Buy, includes a host of social applications under a navigation item called Ask & Learn. News, blogs, discussions, reviews, and videos in this section blend customer contributions with those of employee experts and even representatives from vendors like Sony.

Perhaps the most common form of sales engagement today happens in off-domain channels like Facebook, where companies are publishing content in the hopes of generating comments or clicks that result in revenue. We talk more about that in Chapter 10, "Social Objects."

Level 3: Innovation

The prior sections covered social technology as an empowering channel through which your customers help each other. This section is about your customers helping *you*: It shows you how to connect your customer with the process and priorities of your marketing and product development teams. Market research—up until the introduction of online social technology an activity largely confined to focus groups and market surveys—can now be undertaken using a purpose-built social application: a research community.

Imagine inviting selected customers to participate in a peer-to-peer, long-term innovation program. How much would you learn, and how special and how connected would they feel to your product or service that they helped design? Research communities are one of the ways that you can begin to engage customers and constituents in a collaborative process. Because participants know that they are engaged in a research and learning effort, they are already in the mode of sharing what they think with you. Unlike focus groups—typically one-off events, too often with only a small number of screened participants—research communities provide a context for more natural participation. This is not a criticism of focus group methodology. Clearly, they are one of the tools that remain important in the discovery and design processes for marketing campaigns, product features, and a lot more. Research communities combine the basics of focus group research with the social structures and potential for collaboration found in social networks.

The business advantage of a research community over a focus group is in its longevity and continuity. Participants may be involved for months or even years. This gives you the opportunity to develop real relationships with participants and for the research community members themselves to become very familiar with the brand, products, or services being evaluated. As a result, the level of feedback—and the insights that you can carry back into your business—can be quite substantial.

Research communities can be launched using services that provide turnkey implementation as well as participant recruitment and community management, or they can be built up from the ground just as you would build any other community. Service providers such as Ipsos and Communispace offer these types of purpose-built communities as turnkey services. Take a look at these offerings if you are interested in this type of collaborative social application.

Research Communities

Using a community platform for extended research can provide in-depth insights into brands, products, and services and the ways in which customers are likely to perceive them. One big caveat: Because these are often fixed-time programs, be sure that participants understand the terms, expectations, and when (if) their stay in the community will end.

Ipsos, Communispace, and Passenger are among the leading providers of research communities. You can learn more about them here:

www.ipsos-na.com/products-tools/ipsos-panels/social-spaces/

www.communispace.com/

www.thinkpassenger.com

Hierarchy of Value

The hierarchy of engagement types reflects increasing levels of value for the company. Support engagement reduces cost, sales engagement drives revenue, and innovation engagement produces improvements that offer returns on into the future. But equally, these types of engagement offer customers increasing value as well. Support engagement produces satisfaction, sales engagement can engender loyalty, and engagement around innovation can result in the highest level of bond between customer and company: advocacy.

At the heart of engagement is a fundamental connection between businesses and customers, a relationship in which the customer is an equal partner, not a target. This connection extends to employees, who collectively represent a largely untapped resource in building brand advocates. The requirement to manage this for *all* of your customers, for *all* of your stakeholders, and for *all* of your employees in turn requires that you approach engagement as applied to social customer experience using strategies and processes that are closer to those of your call centers than those of your PR and communications team. Simply, as you scale up for engagement, you are addressing the many rather than just the influential few.

This shift in perspective, from central command and control to a multidisciplinary and participative orientation that scales across your organization, is significant and will be difficult for many businesses to fully embrace. Altimeter's Jeremiah Owyang put it this way:

Companies know the problem will get worse before it gets better. Organizations realize they are no longer in charge. They often lack a credible strategy that empowers their employees to catch up with their customers.

What the Social Web really does—and the reason that traditional measures or views of things like engagement are shifting—is driven by the need to involve customers meaningfully in the processes that produce and deliver the products and services that they buy from your firm, not to cede full control to them. So, when a customer says "jump," you should ask "why?" and then *listen* to the answer and evaluate it jointly with that customer in the context of your business objectives.

This realization shapes the firm or organization's response to ideation, support, and similar social engagement applications. Suppose, for example, that customers ask for something that you *cannot* legally or responsibly do. For example, regulated businesses like airlines, pharmaceutical firms, and banking and investment firms are sometimes governed by processes that may not be evident to customers. In such firms, as a product manager or marketing director you may find yourself bound by regulations that may be at odds with what customers are requesting. If that is your business and your customer is making the request, what do you do?

You must address the customer's concern or risk alienating (to put it nicely) your audience. The only viable response—which by default makes it the best response—is to clearly explain why this particular request can't be entertained and to offer instead an alternative if one is available. When customers have the information they need to understand *why* something is happening (or can't happen), they generally end up supporting you. This is where the combination of participation and transparency can really pay off. Honest, open conversation includes "We're not allowed to do this, or to talk about this, by law" or "Our company has made a strategic and top-secret call." This kind of frank honesty—simply put, sometimes the answer *is* no—is especially applicable in regulated industries where social media and the adoption of social technology are nevertheless expected by customers and stakeholders. Importantly, your practice of *consistently* transparent, forthright participation on each and every interaction is essential in building trust: Trust happens not on the first interaction, but on the second, fifth, or hundredth interaction. Building a relationship is done by working at it over time.

As an example of the difference that the right information shared at the right time can make, consider the following: Dave was on a flight heading for Cleveland one evening, and as his plane approached the airport, it began circling. If you've flown more than once you know that planes fly relatively direct routes between cities, and so circling generally means only one thing: You are being delayed. Tensions on the plane started rising as it circled for 5 minutes, then 10, then 15.

At this point the pilot came on, explained that in fact this was a delay, *and asked the passengers what they wanted to do*: The choices offered were either circle for another hour—the estimated time of delay—or divert to Milwaukee and spend the night there. In a unanimous cry, the plane's passengers opted to circle for *an hour or more*. However, the pilot then continued explaining the choices more completely: Dinner and rooms would be provided if the plane diverted to Milwaukee rather than circling for the expected hour, at which point he also added that the plane had *less than 45 minutes of fuel* remaining. Everyone yelled "Let's go to Milwaukee!" and off they went.

What's important in this somewhat humorous example is that regardless of how the decision was actually made, the passengers—*the customers*—were given the opportunity to participate, to be included in the process, early on. This is not to say that airlines should let passengers fly planes, any more than you should let your customers run your business. Instead, it's about recognizing that even a small role for your customers can often make a huge difference in the acceptability of an otherwise suboptimal choice.

Imagine how different this would have been if the pilot had said, "We are being diverted to Milwaukee; someone will give you more info when we land." Same basic outcome (we *went* to Milwaukee), but with essentially no choice. When given all of the information needed to make a decision and the option to actually play a role in that decision, customers are generally a pretty reasonable group. *We chose Milwaukee.* When customers are kept in the dark and looked at as objects to be controlled, managed, or optimized, predictable problems arise. No one likes to be told what to do and even less so in a dictatorial manner. Yet, that is exactly how too many customers are treated. Engagement in a social technology context depends on active participation and collaboration, not control.

The point is this: When implementing an engagement strategy on the Social Web, you will ultimately present yourself (or your brand) as a *participant* and as such you will have to participate alongside your customers or constituents. *How* you participate is up to you: It's not an all-or-nothing deal. Just because a customer demands something, it does not in itself mean it has to be delivered. What it does mean is that a response is needed and that this response needs to affirm in the minds of your customers or stakeholders that they have been heard and that their point of view has been considered. If the request made in a support forum is in line with the existing community policies—if the suggestion for a process change made via an ideation or support platform is not inflammatory or otherwise at odds with the stated Terms of Use that govern everyone's conduct within the application—then a response that indicates review, consideration, and thought is expected in return. This includes the possibility of politely, accurately, and clearly explaining why a particular request *can't* be honored, or at least not in its present form.

Creating Customer Advocates

Ultimately, engagement is all about driving collaboration and the development of brand advocates. It may be reserved or casual, or it may be spontaneous and enthusiastic. But in the end what you are after as part of the leadership team within a business or cause-related organization—and especially so as a marketer—is a customer base that spreads beneficial word of mouth for you. Peter Drucker noted that "the purpose of business is to create and keep a customer." With the advent of social technology, the objective now includes the notion that customers will (also) create (more) customers.

Looking at the awareness-driven purchase funnel and connecting it to the Social Web creates a closed-loop feedback path. Cyclical behaviors that surround social media and the purchase funnel feedback loop often resist definition in terms of starting and ending points: It's an iterative process, not a line with an end point. Listening leads to innovation and product or service design that delights customers and in turn drives beneficial word of mouth that shows up as favorable posts in listening exercises and social media analytics. Life's a circle, right? So is business.

To make it simple, assume that if at some point in the cycle customers are actively promoting a brand, product, or service, then this is the "result" desired. In other words, as a marketer it's less about creating awareness (though awareness still matters and is the right focus of your advertising efforts) and more about creating advocates and evangelists. Imagine the delight of our fisherman friend if the first fish that spied that lure told three others, "Hey, you've got to check this out." That's what you want on the Social Web, too.

What Drives Advocacy?

Collaborative activities, in a business context, are designed to move current and potential customers up and through the engagement process toward true brand advocacy. Brand advocates are an essential factor in a brand's overall success: Not only do they promote the brand and its associated products or services, but they will defend the brand when it is being attacked. The earlier example of India's Café Coffee Day made clear the beneficial impact of brand advocates.

There is a larger play to be made, however, using social technologies. Similar to the diffusion that is observed in PR (where easily identified journalists or industry experts active in traditional media give way to lesser-known but nonetheless important brand enthusiasts present on the Social Web), the development of brand advocates requires a deeper dive into the conversations that surround a brand, product, or service so that the advocates—and the topics around which advocates may form—can be identified and nurtured.

Most useful is the following realization: Whether social activity drives business success or business success provides a context for an active social presence is not the issue. Instead, the connection between the social activity associated *with* successful brands and the business success *of* those brands arises out of the combination of business acumen and significant time spent in defined, measurable activities that engage customers. The result is a higher-than-average generation of brand advocates, further driving this (positive) cycle! In other words, it's not the social activity that matters per se; it's what happens in and around a business or organization and its marketplace as a result of this social activity. More engagement + better experiences = more advocates.

Consider a successful business—in the profit and loss sense—that largely ignores the conversational (social) issues that surround it. Walmart in the early nineties comes to mind, with issues ranging from hiring and pay differentials to product pricing practices and controversial new store locations. While Walmart was being attacked on all sides, its public policy, summed up, seemed to be "We can't hear you." As businesses took to the Social Web, Walmart tried as well—unsuccessfully—to create an early presence in places like Facebook. Each time it tried it was overrun by hard-core detractors, or worse stumbled over its own efforts to control social media.

Compare this with Walmart now: Stores are changing, becoming more open, designed and located with more input from communities, with attention to the kinds of products stocked and the quality of these products. Walmart has introduced organic foods and worked with Bazaarvoice to implement a comprehensive ratings and reviews program across its product lines. These are all efforts that would be widely praised if just about any other retailer were to have implemented them. A few years ago, if you searched Google for "Walmart brand advocates," the top results returned were things like "Why do some people advocate boycotting Walmart?" Today, you get information on Walmart's own brand advocacy programs.

The insight is this: Commercial success by itself does not translate into overnight Social Web success, particularly when a historical view of the business presents a picture that is counter to the norms associated with the successful use of social media and social technology. Furthermore, when such brands involve themselves in social media, the results are typically lackluster, or worse, actually contribute *at first* to the further negative perception of the brand. Tarnished reputations on the Social Web, correctly managed, do heal. Walmart appears committed to this and over time will benefit from a sustained effort to reinvent itself. As noted earlier, building a new reputation takes time. Walmart is certainly on the right path and will ultimately get there. It is an organization built on clear goals that serve the needs of its customers, and it is run by smart people.

Back to advocates: It really is about the combination of business savvy and a genuine intent to place customers—and not the brand—at the center of the social experience. Brands like Starbucks (which openly and deliberately called on customers to help it find its way forward) and Zappos, eBay, Microsoft, Google, Nike, and SAP have all undertaken specific programs to overtly reach out and connect—to engage—with customers and constituents. The result is increased momentum—call it brand mojo if you want—that places a further distance between these firms and their competitors while decreasing the separation between the businesses and their customers. The overall result is the emergence of brand advocates and, in particular, brand advocates that are unexpected and/or nearly invisible (except to the potential customers they influence!).

When Comcast championed the industry's first Twitter-based customer service program, the initial observation was simply "A lot of people are complaining about us on Twitter—maybe we should pay attention to that." This is a really insightful first step. It was not a corporate strategy to do something about the firm's image problem on Twitter but rather a decision to *engage customers where they are*, a point stressed by Jeff Jarvis in his work relating to creating a social business. Based on what they found, and what the firm's internal customer advocates did next, the result was profound: In the words of Comcast CEO Brian Roberts, "It has changed the culture of our company."

In addition to looking at social technology as a marketing application, and beyond the actually engagement points—support forums, communities, ratings platforms, and similar—that help shape a social business, look to your own purposeful and decided participation as a way to build a force of advocates. Combined with a decent business model, an orientation that positions your firm as the advocate for your customer is a smart play.

Create Advocates through Engagement

Having established the path from *consumption*—think traditional media and traditional-media-like activities in a digital context (banner ads or video pre-rolls, for example)—to collaboration and advocacy as a sort of process template or design guide for your social business engagement programs, the next step is connecting the resulting expressions of *advocacy* to your business.

Recall Fred Reichheld and the Net Promoter Score: A base of customers or constituents that are highly likely to strongly recommend a brand, product, or service is a fundamental condition for driving long-term profits and sustained growth. This is precisely what advocacy is all about. Advocates will readily and favorably recommend brands, products, services, and causes, which in turn leads to a competitive advantage by reducing expenditures required to overcome a lack of referrals or worse (detractors, for example). Offering price breaks, discounts, rebates, or similar concessions intended to offset inferior quality inevitably eats away at margins. Over the long term, any unnecessary expense and the associated deterioration of margins will obviously hurt the business or organization.

What is perhaps less clear (though equally valid) is that sustainable higher profit margins—think Whole Foods versus the other food stores against which it competes even if not directly—lead to enhanced opportunities to innovate, to the ability to attract and retain higher-quality employees, to support higher-quality suppliers, to use better raw materials, and to realize other similar business benefits. Each of these has a distinct, measurable payback of its own.

Consider innovation and the ability of a firm to afford the programs that support and drive innovation. An enhanced ability to innovate means your business or cause or program is less likely to be stymied by a change in the legal or business environment (as when AT&T was forced to open up its local lines to upstart MCI) or technology (say, from horse-drawn to horseless carriages). The latter example may seem obsolete, but Fisher Body is the classic case of innovation and survival after its core business—depicted in its logo (shown in Figure 8.3)—dried up in the face of technological and industrial change.

Figure 8.3 Body by Fisher

Fisher began by making horse-drawn carriages. Seeing the opportunity for innovation as Ford and other auto manufacturers sprang up and having access to working capital, they adapted what they knew about *carriage* building to become a premiere *auto* body builder. The result was a firm that became a household name building car bodies for General Motors long after horse-drawn carriages and the firms that made them had disappeared. The point is this: Innovation is the lifeblood of business, and the opportunity to innovate rapidly is enhanced through the engagement and collaboration with customers through social technologies.

While much of the interest in social media *marketing* is driven by sales and demand generation, innovation as a result of the adoption of social customer experience processes can pay an additional dividend: higher sustainable margins that enhance your ability to attract and retain higher caliber employees. Investing in better employees across the board pays big dividends when your firm or organization sets out to transform itself—for example, into a social business that is connected more directly to its customers. This type of transformation can be upsetting, so you need employees who will buy into the change and who have the innate ability to step up to a more complex job.

Superior employees are both more capable and more willing to learn new skills, to consider different ways of doing things, and to look for and champion new solutions. This is critically important. When you connect your business to your customers, those customers will no doubt ask for things that your firm has not considered—or has even decided against. Your ability to innovate and address these suggestions and ideas, to rethink past decisions, and to question established practices will rest entirely on the willingness and capability of your employed or retained workforce. All other things being equal, better people will produce a better outcome.

Create Experiences That Drive Advocacy

As a practical example of the connection between operations, marketing, and social business, consider JetBlue's terminal, T5, at JFK. All airlines have delays—they are part of the trade-off between the reality of weather, a highly interconnected flight system, and the overriding concern for passenger safety. JetBlue's T5 is the kind of place one actually looks forward to visiting—shops, restaurants, plenty of free, robust Wi-Fi, and pleasant open space. Dave spent an extra few hours there one evening when ice had closed all but one of JFK's main runways. As Dave looked around, he was struck by the relative calm, with a large number of people watching Hulu on their laptops and patiently waiting.

The robust Wi-Fi in T5 is no accident. JetBlue actually takes a further step in ensuring that its T5 runs smoothly from the perspective of travelers by recognizing that Wi-Fi (along with food, drinks, and engaging activities in shops and restaurants) is essential to maintaining a sense of calm. When people are productive or happily diverted, things work better! Wi-Fi is also largely a function of external providers, so JetBlue works with its external Wi-Fi support services to ensure that their services, too, keep pace with the needs of its customers while in T5.

Social customer experience management is all about connecting customer feedback and business processes, about using what is learned and building on responses and engagement, and finally about creating systems—in the case of JetBlue, direct customer experiences in T5—that trigger and cultivate advocacy. Recovering from a near meltdown following a severe storm, JetBlue did the hard work: They reexamined and rebuilt operations-driven processes to match their differentiating marketing prowess. The result is the steady rise in the creation of JetBlue advocates.

Here again, social technology (used to connect employees and passengers to drive service innovation) comes into play. The combination of active listening—understanding what is happening (positive or negative) right now—and collaborative systems that facilitate ideation and innovation inside of JetBlue as it grows is a large part of what defines its successful approach to business in a socially connected marketplace.

If you're wondering about how powerful the combination of operations and marketing really is and about the kinds of conversations this kind of alignment can generate, go to Twitter and search "JetBlue T5." Figure 8.4 shows the typical results. My favorites? "T5 is by far one of the greatest terminals ever." And how about Adam Greenwald, evidently planning to get married in T5! Kind of makes you want to Fly JetBlue to New York, doesn't it? That's not a coincidence. It's a business decision, designed to create a great social customer experience.

Figure 8.4 JetBlue's T5 drives advocacy.

The combination of active listening, touchpoint analysis, and collaboration (via engagement) makes obvious the root causes of dissatisfaction and the potential solutions (ideation and innovation) that drive enhanced satisfaction. More than anything else, what makes airline travelers nuts is the feeling of an almost total loss of personal control from the moment you contemplate purchasing a ticket until the moment you successfully retrieve your bags on the return flight. At the same time—and again very much the subject of social business—consider the *employees* of the airlines and their role in all of this: They have ideas, too. The motivated and consumer-oriented professionals at Southwest Airlines, Alaska Airlines, and United Airlines or Dubai's Emirates—to name just a few—have a significant impact on the business success of their organizations.

Review and Hands-On

This chapter, the first of the "social customer experience building blocks" chapters, covers engagement in detail, viewing it from the company's and the customer's perspectives. The latter is critical: Analogous to catching more fish by learning to think like one, getting it right in social business means engaging your customers from their point of view. In short, it means becoming their advocate so that they might become yours.

Review of the Main Points

The key points covered in this chapter are summarized in the following list. Review these and develop your own practical definition for *engagement* in the context of a social business:

- Engagement is a customer-centric activity.
- Think about engagement types: support, sales, and innovation.
- Think about engagement value: satisfaction, loyalty, and advocacy.
- Implement a strategic approach to social business that specifies a plan to create advocates and then measure your performance.
- Finally, it's still your business. Placing customers at the center of what you do doesn't mean handing them the wheel.

Chapter 8 sets up the primary activity that differentiates social customer experience from other things you do as a business. A business that steadily builds its own base of advocates is a business that steadily and surely wins over the long term.

Hands-On: Review These Resources

Review the following and apply them to your business or organization as you create your plan for integrating social technology into your fundamental processes:

The case studies in Lithium's online case study library contain well-documented examples of a variety of social applications that result in both advocacy and positive ROI.

`www.lithium.com/customer-stories`

The whitepapers in Jive Software's resources library, in particular Social Business Software Adoption Strategies.

`www.jivesoftware.com/resources`

Hands-On: Apply What You've Learned

Apply what you've learned in this chapter through the following exercises:

1. Make a note of every recommendation you give or receive over the next week. Rank them according to the degree of enthusiasm on the part of the recommender.
2. Starting with the resources listed previously, develop your own library. Look for the similar resources offered by other social business software firms, and add those to your library.

3. Review your own engagement programs, and carefully examine how you are measuring or evaluating engagement and from whose perspective you are defining engagement.

4. Assuming that you have an appropriate social computing and social media use policy for employee use in place now, design a plan for an ideation, support, or discussion platform that will actively solicit customer-led conversations about your firm or organization or about your brand, product, or service.

Social CRM and Social Customer Experience

We've talked a lot about how social customer experience (SCE) looks from the customer side, the new experiences that customers want from companies, and the ways those experiences change the relationship between companies and customers. In Chapter 2 we talked about how the concepts of SCE relate to the ideas behind CRM and social CRM, and in Chapter 5 we discussed what the SCE ecosystems look like both on-domain and off-domain. Now we're going to dig down into how organizations create a platform that brings SCE to life. Yes, SCE is more than technology, but technology makes SCE possible. And that technology today is as much about how all your customer-facing systems come together as it is about what specific social applications actually do.

9

CRM, Social CRM, and SCE

Not long ago, when companies talked about social technology and behavior, they talked in terms of individual initiatives. "We're creating a community," they would say, and they added forums, blogs, or other social elements to their website. Or they would say, "We're creating a Facebook page," and they created a branded presence on that network that included marketing content and the opportunity for customers to post content or show their interest by liking that page. Mostly, these initiatives were located in a specific function like marketing or support or a specific part of the business, for a specific product or brand. These efforts were mostly experimental—the product of an individual or a small group of people who believed that social was important to customers and important to the future of the business.

Over time these efforts grew. Communities attracted thousands, hundreds of thousands, or even millions of users. Social network efforts grew as well and began to attract more attention from the public and from media. In a real sense, social business has grown up, which has led companies to ask a whole set of new questions:

- How do we make it easier for our customers to access and use our social channels?

- How do we use social content to enrich our larger digital experience, rather than treating it as a separate silo?

- How do we recognize and serve customers in social channels appropriately, based on their status or history with the company?

- How do we make sure that users in our social channels have the quality of experience they expect from our company and our brand?

- How do we ensure that social channels are coordinated with other customer-facing channels so that messages and information don't differ from channel to channel?

- How do we make sure that the insights we gain from social channels inform the way we create products and processes every day?

In other words, companies are asking the question: How do we transform our organizations to truly take advantage of the potential that social technologies offer? Sometimes people make the mistake of thinking that this transformation is just about culture. They think that organizations that don't adopt social technologies or don't use them effectively are simply those that don't care or don't get it. In fact, it's not enough to care or to understand. No matter how much your executives or employees care about customers, they need the processes in place to allow them to carry out those good intentions, every day. What's more, they need the technology that supports and automates those processes, so those intentions can be delivered consistently and efficiently at a high level of quality, in the way today's customers want and expect.

SCE is the latest evolution of technology innovations around managing our relationships with customers. To better understand how and where social fits into existing infrastructures, consider CRM, social CRM, and SCE, covered in the following sections.

The Evolution of CRM

Customer relationship management (CRM) began with a simple question: How can a large organization interacting with thousands or millions of customers at a distance replicate the kind of service that is provided by a local business that knows its customers personally? The idea was to capture information about each customer and then put that information to work in every interaction you have with that customer. This is important in service and support, where customers requesting help own a set of products or services. How does a customer service rep come to an interaction armed with information about what products or services that customer owns? Even better, how do they come with all the information about past interactions with customers, so they know the history of the customer's interactions with the company?

It's also important in sales: How does the sales rep interacting with a prospect understand what products that prospect has purchased in the past or what interactions that prospect has had with the organization in the course of discovering, evaluating, and selecting a product to buy? This information is critical to the experience the customer or prospect has with the company. It's the difference between feeling like you have a relationship with the company rather than a series of disconnected transactions.

When you talk to people in your organization about CRM, what they say may sound like the proverbial blind men and the elephant. (The blind men described an elephant as resembling a wall, snake, tree, or other object, depending on which part of the elephant they were touching at the time.) Some will say, "CRM, yes—that's what our sales organization uses to track leads." Others will say, "Oh, CRM—that's what our customer service agents use to track customer issues." Still others will say, "Our CRM system is what powers our support portal." That's because CRM as a product category includes companies that do one, two, or all three of these things.

A CRM suite is a product that combines multiple strands of CRM tools into a single solution. Table 9.1 lists the most common CRM suites and the associated delivery methods—installed as on-premise software or delivered as a cloud-based solution—in use in organizations today.

▶ **Table 9.1** Typical CRM suites

Vendor	Primary Market	Delivery Method
SAP	Large enterprises	On-premise and SaaS
Oracle	Large enterprises	On premise and SaaS
Salesforce.com	Large and medium-sized companies	SaaS
Microsoft	Medium-sized companies	On premise and SaaS

While a good number of CRM implementations have produced solid business results, many have failed to deliver hoped-for benefits. In 2009, a survey of analyst reports over the previous eight years found that failure rates for CRM implementations ranged from a low of 18 percent to a high of 70 percent. Why is this? To start with, projects that fail typically suffer the flaws of many large-scale enterprise software implementations: vague goals, poor project planning, lack of user adoption, and inconsistent approach across the organization. Organizations also didn't foresee the problems they would encounter when they acquired new businesses with their own CRM systems in place. In many organizations, the result has been multiple CRM systems implemented within a single large enterprise: a different system in support than is used in sales, different systems used in different divisions or businesses. Even today, when you ask a company about their CRM system, the answer is often "Which one do you mean?" Point taken.

On top of these challenges, CRM vendors are trying to navigate three major transformations in their industry today:

- *The movement from on premise to SaaS.* The largest CRM vendors began with solutions that were installed on premise—that is, onsite at a customer location, behind the corporate firewall. However, while CRM solutions were getting footholds inside large organizations, the enterprise software industry was transforming to a new model: software as a service (SaaS). SaaS solutions are not installed at a corporate site behind the firewall. They are hosted in a data center and accessed via the Web. Rather than spending money, time, and effort installing software, companies are increasingly choosing to buy their software on a subscription model, from a SaaS vendor. A new entrant in the field, Salesforce.com, began as a SaaS company and quickly made inroads. Companies like SAP and Oracle were faced with creating competitive SaaS solutions as well. That process is ongoing today.

- *The continued expansion of the CRM solution.* As CRM systems matured, they expanded: CRM vendors were faced with adding new products to the suite to compete effectively with vendors who sold just one best-of-breed solution. And so, on top of creating a new SaaS offering, CRM vendors continued to add products to their suites, which then needed to be integrated into overall suites. That process too is ongoing.

- *The arrival of social technologies.* The arrival of social technologies complicated the challenge for CRM vendors as well. Suddenly new interactions, many of them not only not behind the firewall but also not even on the web domain, needed to be encompassed in CRM to fulfill the original vision of CRM to provide a 360-degree view of the customer.

If you're responsible for SCE in your organization, why does this matter? It matters because *you can't truly achieve SCE without meaningfully integrating your social technologies with your company's CRM effort.* And today, for most organizations, CRM is in a state of fragmentation—many systems, not one—or in a state of transition. This need not derail your efforts, but it's something important to know in order to create realistic plans and timelines.

The Evolution of Social CRM

In late 2008, Gartner research analyst Sharon Mertz noted that "looking forward, social networking, collaborative technologies, and social software are producing a major impact on the CRM market." Within the next two years, news items on Google for social CRM went from none in August 2008 to more than 100 in November 2012.

The idea of social CRM was to tie together three things that then existed as completely separate worlds: CRM, social media, and on-domain social communities. It made sense: These things existed as separate silos of customer interaction and information, and none of them integrated or talked to one another in any meaningful way. Interest was driven largely by sales organizations, which wanted to tap the potential of social media to identify prospects and deliver relevant offers to relevant individuals on the Web. Support was quick to follow, which made sense. In fact, service and support approached social media channels with much more of an operational mindset, which required tools to support.

There was a challenge in the provisioning of social CRM, however: Social vendors included in the category were not CRM vendors, and CRM vendors included in the category were not meaningfully social. Social CRM experts helped customers bridge this gap, defining social CRM as a philosophy more than a product, as Paul Greenberg noted:

Social CRM is a philosophy and a business strategy, supported by a technology platform, business rules, workflow, processes and social characteristics, designed to engage the customer in a collaborative conversation in order to provide mutually beneficial value in a trusted and transparent business environment. It's the company's response to the customer's ownership of the conversation.

Paul Greenberg, July, 2009

Without such expert guidance, companies seeking to implement social CRM were often challenged: Is SCRM a solution or an approach?

Fortunately CRM products have matured and made this adoption a bit easier: nonetheless, mentions of social CRM in news items have declined every year since 2011. To a great extent, the debate about social CRM has been subsumed in today's conversation about SCE.

What does this mean to you? It means that SCE likely provides a fuller conceptual framework for your efforts than social CRM alone. *It recognizes that the end of your efforts is not a new platform or system but rather a new kind of customer experience.* It ties into the new energy around customer experience and the emerging discipline that's growing around that concept. Maybe most importantly, it links directly to the message that resonates with most senior executives—that social technologies create a unique opportunity to place customers at the center of your business.

"Social CRM Is Dead"

For more information on why social customer experience has succeeded social CRM as a concept and framework, read Bob Thompson's excellent article: "'Social CRM Is Dead: Long Live the Social Customer Experience," on the *Customer Think* news and community website:

```
http://customerthink.com/social_crm_is_dead_long_live_social_
customer_experience/
```

But this chapter is supposed to be about platforms, right? So let's get back to creating a platform for SCE.

The Case for Integration

A key take-away from this chapter is that no single platform will do everything you need to create your social customer experience. This is true today and, we think, will be true for the foreseeable future. Given that, you have one major challenge: integration.

Today, companies are integrating their social technologies in the following primary ways:

- Into the website, with web links, content, and widgets
- In the web registration system, with single sign-on (SSO)
- Into website search, with federated search
- Into the support infrastructure, with auto-escalation and integration with the agent dashboard
- Into the enterprise dashboards and analytics tools, via APIs
- Into email campaign and marketing automation systems
- Between on-domain and off-domain social technologies, with integrated social suites

Website

Integration of social concepts into websites now approaches 100 percent adoption: Adding social media content into enterprise websites is a clear best practice. The simplest kind of integration consists of links to social channels directly from the company domain. Look for an example at the website for Caterpillar.com. Scroll to the bottom of the page and click Social Media. You'll see a full page of links, organized by the eight major divisions of the company plus other key areas, that provide direct access to every social channel that the company supports.

It makes sense: More customers typically use the company website than use any individual digital channel. Therefore, advertising social channels on the website just makes sense. For website-based social applications in particular, links on key pages of the site—such as the home page or support home page—are often the single largest source of traffic to those applications in the early weeks and months after a new community or support forum is launched. Eventually, search engines drive the majority of traffic to those channels. But that can't happen without a successful launch that creates content that search engines can index and deliver to potential users.

A second common integration is to embed social content directly into web pages. While this can simply be static quotes or snippets included on relevant pages, it's more powerful to actually embed a widget that shows the most recent customer content related to the subject of that page. Linksys, for example, has a page for every product that contains help and support content related to that product. But those pages also include a widget showing real-time updates of content from their support forums, to put great peer content at the disposal of those who might not know the forums exist. Retail firms take it a step further, with some offering social interactions on product pages, enabling customers to ask questions of their peers or to share relevant content directly from the product page.

Don't think that this dynamic content has to be limited just to content from on-domain social applications: The best social platforms also enable two-way flows of content from and to off-domain social channels.

Web Registration

Single sign-on is the second most common integration between social applications and the corporate or commerce website. Building strong social engagement is all about breaking down the barriers to participation—so allowing registered users to participate in on-domain social channels automatically, without registering again, just makes sense. Plus, managing multiple registrations is one of the things that annoy customers: SSO makes participation easy.

There are two things to think about when doing SSO. First, the registration system on your website may or may not be designed to permit registration by people who are not already customers of your organization. Think about it—for many companies, the only area of the website that requires registration is the one where customers access their own account information. Don't underestimate this task when you're pushing to get social applications integrated with your registration system. You need the web team to understand the value of allowing non-customers (that is, prospects) to *quickly* register and participate on your site.

A second consideration relates to future directions in this same area. Today, most websites have a two-step registration process for their on-domain social applications. First, you register at the website. Second, when you navigate to a social channel and try to participate, you are prompted to complete a second step: selecting a username to identify your comments. Every additional step will lead to abandons—in other words, a loss of potential participants. Instead, consider integrating username selection with your initial registration process. Because really, every customer and every interested prospect are already part of the real community around your products. Why not make it formal?

Website Search

Web usability expert Jakob Nielsen describes search as "the user's lifeline for mastering complex websites." It therefore makes sense to ensure that when people use the search box on your website, they get not only the best editorial content on your website but also the best social content from your forums, blogs, or other on-domain social elements.

There are three ways that this type of search, commonly referred to as federated search, is usually accomplished. First, you might pull social content into your search results using the APIs offered by your social platform. This is one reason to make sure any social platform you implement has robust APIs. Second, you might integrate the search capability in your support solution—for example, a knowledge base search—with the search feature in your social platform. Finally, if you use a tool like Google Search Appliance, you might simply configure the appliance to index your social applications as well as the rest of your web content.

Support Infrastructure

2007 saw the first integration between an enterprise social platform and a CRM system. Keyboard and mouse maker Logitech brought together its support CRM vendor, RightNow (now part of Oracle), and its enterprise social platform vendor, Lithium Technologies, and worked together to create an integration that helped the company make sure that its contact center operation was taking full advantage of the help and support being provided by peers and employees in the support community.

Following that early model, integrations between support CRM and social platforms tend to have some common elements:

- Auto-escalation: the ability to make sure that questions that don't receive answers are escalated, after a configurable period of time, to the contact center for response
- Search integration: the ability for someone searching a support knowledge base to also get the best peer content from the forums

- Integrated agent dashboard: the ability of an agent to see customers' social interactions to be better informed about them when they call and even to respond directly to customers in peer channels from within the agent dashboard

Where early integrations focused on on-domain social channels, today's social customer efforts include both on-domain and off-domain. The appearance of robust platforms for managing off-domain social channels has added a new complication. It remains to be seen whether the future of social response lies within incumbent support solutions or this new generation of engagement and response consoles, which are listed in Table 4.3.

Enterprise Dashboards and Analytics

As use of social channels grows, one of the top demands from executives is better visibility over what's happening there. Social listening platforms, which were designed for use by marketing organizations to monitor social mentions, significantly underserve this need particularly as social behavior grows into a mature enterprise business process. Web analytics tools offer ways to track visits and views but provide little insight into what those visits and views mean.

Social platforms include increasingly sophisticated analytics and reporting features, which may help meet the broader needs of companies to understand and respond to social channels. For today, however, it's mostly a do-it-yourself world, where companies pull data from their various systems into custom dashboards, using platform APIs. Among the most interesting recent developments is the creation of social command centers, where data from social channels is aggregated and displayed in real time, and executives and other managers can get an up-to-the-moment view of what their customers are doing and saying on the Social Web. You can imagine how powerful this is for executives who have long had customers filtered through many layers of management or relied on static product reports weeks after the events took place. There's no doubt in our minds that such command centers will soon be as common in corporate headquarters as boardrooms are today.

Email and Marketing Automation

Integration between social channels and marketing campaigns is often a manual process of feeding social user data into marketing systems. This is an area that is ripe for change.

Integrating On and Off-domain Social Systems

While we've been talking mostly about integration of social processes into traditional or non-social systems, there's another kind of integration that's arguably more critical today: integration between on-domain and off-domain social systems. In the past, when on-domain and off-domain efforts were managed independently—most often by the support and marketing organizations, respectively—such integrations were not a priority. Now, however, customers insist on using every channel to its maximum purpose.

Customers don't know or care that Facebook is owned by the marketing organization: If they need customer service, they'll expect it to be available right there, on Facebook. Customers increasingly have the same expectations of on-domain channels and no longer accept that peer channels don't include employees willing and able to help.

As a result, companies are struggling to create operational models that allow them to manage social channels in a sustainable way. If you think that companies are going to add hundreds of personnel to staff new contact centers focusing on Twitter, you are wrong. If you are planning such a new contact center, you're wrong too. Sustainable social support will help customers help themselves rather than simply delivering the old service in a new channel. Engagement platforms that integrate on-domain and off-domain are critical to helping companies get there.

Where This Is All Going

Social customer experience begins with observing, measuring, and connecting what is learned via the Social Web to those places within your business where the underlying experiences that are talked about are created. As customers begin to connect, they will form and publish opinions and put forth suggestions about what they like or dislike about a specific brand, product, or service. With that comes also what they'd *like to see* or what *could have been better.* Integrating social channels with CRM and other systems provides an organized way to take that information through to the next step, driving process improvement, innovation, and more.

The challenge that the higher levels of engagement—like content creation and collaboration—present from the perspective of a business or organization is in sorting out what to do with this *newly accessible* information, along with how to do it. This is the challenge of efforts related to the social customer experience: Your customers expect meaningful engagement on the Social Web—after all, you're already on their TV sets and radios and billboards along their highways, and you're already in their magazines and wrapped around the online content they view. As you develop a social media *marketing* presence, your customers will also expect you to be active in the related social places where *they* are talking about *you,* about your products or services, the places where they exchange ideas about your business (and how it might serve them better) with others who share that same interest.

What all of this adds up to is an opportunity to participate—something you may already be doing in some form through a social media marketing program—that leads to an opportunity to learn and adapt your products and services according to the experiences and desires of your customers.

Note that the customer owns the conversation and that the conversation is happening *in public*. From the perspective of a marketing manager or chief executive officer, entrepreneur, or associate director, this ownership and visibility effectively mandates a response and thereby suggests a formalized process supporting social customer experience.

From a business perspective, the essential point is that an intelligent, relevant response is now a typical expectation—even perhaps a requirement—in many Social Web settings and certainly from the perspective of your customers. This is the connection point between the Social Web, social media marketing (SMM), and SCE: The experience created in the presentation, delivery, and use of a product or service drives a conversation. This sequence implies a connection between that conversation and the business or organization that created it. Social CRM and SCE provide a framework for measuring, connecting, and leveraging this entire conversation cycle.

SCE: Engagement Drives Innovation

Social customer experience processes can drive change and innovation, in particular when built around a well-defined SCRM-based *engagement* (response) process. Beginning with listening, filtering, measuring, and routing the conversations happening on the Social Web that are relevant to your brand, product, or service, SCE is decidedly customer and constituent focused. Rather than using technology solely to identify the next sales opportunity—which is a great business goal and direct benefit of traditional CRM—the SCRM/SCE combination seeks to understand what customers really want and to take that information and prioritize it, route it, and track it across your organization as it is translated into new, superior products and services. Starbucks' Splash Stick (Figure 9.1) is a well-known example of just this sort of customer-driven innovation.

Figure 9.1 Starbucks' Splash Stick

Australia's Telstra, India's Café Coffee Day and the *Hindustan Times,* Swiss retailer Migros, Germany's Tchibo, IBM's IdeaJam, and other businesses including Comcast, HP, Dell, Starbucks, and dozens of others around the globe are using social channels to take listening a step further: These firms and many others are using social software like support forums—perhaps recast as ideation platforms—along with existing social communities like Twitter and Facebook to build robust *customer service and engagement platforms.* Whether responding to ideas, crises, calls for help, or requests for information, these response systems serve to connect these businesses to their customers in ways that are fundamentally more compelling to those customers than are the more common—and highly controlled—traditional feedback channels.

Getsatisfaction.com: the Company-Customer Pact

Get Satisfaction provides a spot-on Company-Customer Pact that establishes the ground rules for support programs that begins with this simple reality: "We, customers and companies alike, need to trust the people with whom we do business."

You can read the entire pact here:

```
http://getsatisfaction.com/ccpact/
```

In addition to creating a closed-loop feedback and engagement process, the firms and organizations adopting SCE practices are measuring these social activities and tying the results to their business objectives. This includes understanding and measuring *not just the transactional activities*—posting content, reading or writing a review, and similar activities—but also digging in and understanding *who* is involved. Identification of influencers, right along with conversational analytics, is fundamentally important.

SCE and the Bill of Rights for Users of the Social Web

Joseph Smarr, Marc Canter, Michael Arrington, and Robert Scoble offered a point of view on the use of personal data—not just identity but also their activity streams ("Bob just uploaded a photo…") and the relationships they form (part of their personal social graph). The Bill of Rights for Users of the Social Web is worth reviewing as you think through your SCE strategy.

You can read more about the Bill of Rights for Users of the Social Web here:

```
http://opensocialweb.org/2007/09/05/bill-of-rights/
```

Figure 9.2 shows the integrated SCRM and SCE processes, identifying the components covered in the prior section. As you look at Figure 9.2, consider how the combination elevates the role of social media internally—in collaborative processes that facilitate customer-driven innovation—as much as it does externally, where conversations circulate between customers themselves.

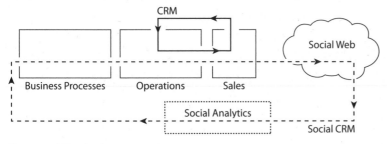

Figure 9.2 SCE in a business context

The New Know

Author Thornton May argues that analytics is needed by *all* enterprises to be successful. This is most certainly an underlying reality and end objective of an SCE program. You'll want to read Thornton's book, *The New Know* (Wiley and SAS Press, 2009).

Hope Is Not a Strategy

As you begin to craft your program, the guiding idea is this: An effective program begins not with hope but with a grounded, well-defined social media strategy *that extends across the organization.*

This is not to say that there is no room for experimentation; there certainly is. It is to say instead that the stakes are significantly higher with social business and investments in social technology than the similar entry costs (in time, dollars, and opportunity cost) for social media marketing. Where social media marketing can be "trialed" in places like Facebook or Twitter or backed into via a discrete listening program using a free tool like Google Alerts, an SCRM/SCE program—even a light-duty implementation—directly involves your customers and brings them into your business. By opening up the formal listening/response/collaboration channels with customers, you are making a significant commitment to the formal inclusion of your customers as a component of your business.

A solid social media marketing program begins with business objectives, an understanding of the audience, and a thought-through measurement program or success-assessment methodology. SCE is no different, and it adds the requirements of creating a cross-functional team within your organization to deal with the feedback, ideas, and suggestions when they start flowing. In Chapter 2, "The Social Customer," we talked about workflow and the routing of critical information—at scale—directly into the parts of your organization that need to see it. These kinds of considerations and more are the added requirements in building a social business and SCE program. Without the ability to effectively route and track potentially large amounts of conversational data (workflow), your SCE efforts will quickly bog down.

Integrate the Social Experience

BatchBlue Software provides Batchbook as an integration tool aimed specifically at small businesses using Google applications. Batchbook connects social data with your in-house data and the Google apps you are using now.

www.batchbook.com/google/

Gigya provides integration tools across registration, social activities, and measurement as a part of its social business solution set.

www.gigya.com/solutions/

Your Social Customer Experience Plan

Creating a social CRM and social customer experience plan is a *technically* straightforward process. The challenge is organizational buy-in. This section takes you through the process of building a team around you to get this done.

As with social media marketing, you start your business plan with your *business objectives*. What do you want to achieve from your business or organizational perspective? *What do you want your customers to gain* as a result of this program? Be clear as well in identifying which of your customers or audience will be the focus of your initial efforts. Plan accordingly, allow time to do this prep work correctly, and provide plenty of opportunity for others in your organization who may be similarly interested to join with you. Here's why: One way or another, you will need the support of your entire organization. What is talked about on the Social Web is the net result of the actions of your entire organization, and there is no getting around that. If you charge into social technology adoption *alone*, you risk alienating the very people you need to succeed.

Begin with a team and an initial plan based on your business objectives; combine that with your listening program results. Use the conversations circulating now to shape your early programs. If you have not undertaken a best-practices-driven listening program, you'll want to initiate one. Add to this a set of metrics that are relevant to your firm or organization and define how you will recognize success. The following questions take you through the balance of the considerations as you undertake development of a project specification for your SCE program:

What are your business objectives? For example, are you looking to improve your organization's innovation processes, effect service improvements, understand and respond more quickly to competitive offerings, or develop a customer-based influencers' program? Watch out if you answered this question "all of the above." Start with a manageable objective.

What is your organizational culture? This matters because you are potentially pressing for internal and operational changes. If you've read *Who Moved My Cheese?* (G. P. Putnam's Sons, 1998), you understand the significance of accounting for culture and planning for change. If you haven't read it, from the title alone you can guess the issue and why this matters (and, why the book was a best seller!).

What drives your delivery experiences? Regardless of whether you are manufacturer, a service firm, a nonprofit, a municipality, or something else altogether, if your organization serves someone—and we're assuming it does because otherwise you probably wouldn't be reading this—then there is a process by which you create the experiences that drive their conversations about your brand, product, or service.

Who else needs to be a part of your team? At one level, the answer is "your entire organization." However, this answer doesn't really help you at a planning stage or early implementation. Who are your allies in Operations, Marketing, Customer Service, Human Resources, and Legal? What are the roles and expectations for each? Build that team.

Do you have social computing policies in place? If not, add this to your task list. With employees directly participating in your firm's social technology programs, ensuring that they understand how to communicate outside the organization (and when/when not to) through social channels is essential. Think back to the reference of IBM and its established social computing policies as a great example how one firm has managed this challenge.

How will you measure success? Effectively tapping results will necessarily involve tying business analytics to social data. What are your primary social and business KPIs, and how will you use them to tune your program and demonstrate—quantitatively—success?

Take a look back at these items. The kickoff for SCE programs is like that of any other marketing or business program: You start with your business objectives, combine them with the behaviors and interests of your expected participants, and use this to plan and implement your program.

One of the easiest ways to sort out which types of solutions are right for your applications is by posing and answering questions like the following: Are your primary business objectives related to addressing an existing condition, improving margins through the work of brand advocates or through expense reductions, or focused on innovating and creating something new? Formulate your own additional questions like these for your specific situation as well.

If you are addressing an existing condition, then at the top of your list might be tools like a listening platform and influencer identification, combined with a participative channel such as Twitter or similar. Gather and analyze relevant conversations, and then use a simple conversational channel to keep that dialogue going. This combination provides the intelligence and precise targeting that you need. You can use do-it-yourself listening platforms like SDL|Alterian's SM2 or Sysomos, along with an influencer identification tool like BuzzStream or Rapleaf, to gather the background information you need to develop a conversational baseline and then track your progress. When creating your tool checklist, look for the ways in which one activity (listening, for example) informs another (like internal product review meetings and product design efforts), and then ensure that any potential solution meets your business requirements.

Alternatively, if you are looking for margin improvement through cost savings, then your focus might be the Web 2.0 tools and technologies that enable delegation of work to your customers. Dell's support forums exemplify this: Relatively few moderators and community managers acting together manage literally millions of customers (translation: cost savings), while the customers themselves bear the real load—much to their liking—in addressing the actual technical support issues that are the subject of the support community.

SCE efforts often force internal considerations as well. The same triage process used to identify and connect an external program around business objectives can also be applied to internal process change and innovation. If you are seeking ideas for improved future products or radically new designs or are looking for insights on how your organization might restructure itself (including virtually), then consider ideation platforms from Lithium Technologies or Salesforce.com. *They can be applied internally*, as Dell did with its Employee Storm platform, the internal counterpart to its customer-facing Idea Storm. Be sure to connect the outputs of external efforts to your internal work process!

Looking back at Table 9.1 and Table 9.2, use your business objectives to refine the available technologies. After using your business objectives to narrow the choice of solution providers, ask the solution providers themselves to come back with a report or proposal on how they would approach your situation and how their tools and methods apply. They'll be happy to do this and to share their case studies with you. Nothing like spreading the workload! Plus, it's a really smart way to generate a wide range of options quickly and to gain a broad perspective on what is available. Although this book will slowly go out of date, your good habits of due diligence and self-education won't.

Review and Hands-On

Chapter 9 built on customer engagement and collaboration—the building blocks covered in Chapter 8—wrapping these concepts around your business and bringing social customer experience processes inside the organization. Collaboration is a key factor in creating the strong linkages that connect engaged customers and constituents with the organizations that create the product and service-related experiences that are the subject of the conversations on the Social Web. Connecting these conversations with the organization defines the connective tissue that enables customer-business collaboration.

Review of the Main Points

The key points covered in Chapter 9 are summarized here. Review these and develop your own vision and plan for a social CRM program:

- Social CRM is less about a CRM than it is a fusion of social technology—Web 2.0—and the business-centric analytical processes associated with CRM.
- Social customer experience connects with social customer experience concepts through external conversations and ideas—for example, off-domain posts or the end-product of your on-domain innovation community—to internal functions and personnel who are able to act on this information to improve the customer or constituent experience.
- Social customer experience can't be created without an integration of your processes, systems, and platforms already in place.

Going back to the purchase funnel plus feedback concept that powers social-media-based marketing, social customer experience is the primary set of technologies that draw this feedback—measurably—down into the business. It is through CRM that a planned, replicable program for managing the conversations that occur on the Social Web can be implemented.

Hands-On: Review These Resources

Review both of the following and apply these to your business or organization as you create your plan for integrating social technology into your fundamental processes:

1. Review cases noted in this chapter. The principles of social CRM are sufficiently well demonstrated that they can be applied to almost any business.
2. Review the general toolsets in the tables in this chapter, and take note of the order in which specific tools or technologies are applied. As with social-media-based marketing in general, the implementation process begins *not* with technology but rather with business objectives and strategy.

Hands-On: Apply What You've Learned

Apply what you've learned in this chapter through the following exercises:

1. If you haven't done so already, look at the social computing policy examples at the Altimeter site or those of IBM or Dell. In addition, visit the sites of firms or organizations like yours to see what they have done. Imitation—followed with an in-house legal review—is the sincerest form of getting there faster!

2. Work with your IT or other applicable department to design a pilot program for internal collaboration. The exercise will challenge your organization, so choose a small project and recruit enthusiastic volunteers.

3. After completing the first two exercises, prepare and deliver a starting plan for social customer experience management to your colleagues (or customers, if you are a consulting firm or agency).

Social Objects

Networks and communities are made up of people, of course, but they are also made of something else: content. In fact, as a customer the first thing you probably notice about any social channel is the content: Is it interesting? Is it useful? Can you rely on it? If you're creating a social experience for your customers, you want them to answer yes to all of those questions.

But what kind of content do customers want? What's the best balance between brand-published content versus customer-generated content? What's the most effective form for content: text, image, video, or something else? To answer those questions, we need to look at social content in broader context. We'll do that through the powerful concept of social objects.

10

What Is a Social Object?

A *social object* is something that is inherently talkworthy, something around which people will naturally congregate and converse. In the current context of social media—after all, social objects have existed since humans began socializing—a social object forms the link between participants at the center of an online conversation. Social objects anchor the online communities in which conversations take place. Simply put, the social object is the "what" that people talk about.

Social objects can be as small and specific as a blog post, a photo, or a comment. Objects can vary by network or channel: On Twitter it's usually a text update; on Facebook or Google+ it's a link; on Pinterest it's an image. The object might itself be trivial (have you seen this funny cat photo?) or important (please sign my petition!). In either case the act of sharing can be more significant than what is shared. You need look no further than one of these networks to see the unlikely objects that spur vibrant and long-lasting discussion. In a funny way, one lesson seems to be that who, or when, or how social objects circulate is always at least as important as what the object actually is.

Definition: A Social Object is some "thing" we share with others as part of our social media experience on the social web.

Glenn Assheton-Smith, 2009

Social objects don't have to be small and specific. They can be, well, very large and general. They can be areas of interest, such as the environment, politics, or art. Your business, your industry, your individual products—these can be thought of as social objects too. These types of social objects can also sit at the center of community, drawing people together, not at just one instant but over time.

What are some examples of the kinds of social objects that will pull large groups together? National pastimes and sports like soccer, baseball, cricket, NASCAR, and Formula 1 are just the sorts of activities that tens or hundreds of millions of people around the world will readily associate with and talk about. They'll form fantasy leagues—clearly a social construct—in order to extend their own level of participation. Fans gather around celebrity sites to share stories and feel a part of the excitement, while retirees readily join up with others in the same life stage in AARP's online community (www.aarp.org/online_community/) to talk about what the future may hold. Social objects extend to the more ordinary as well—a new mobile phone, a programming language, and a vacation destination can all be viewed as social objects. Oh, and did I mention pets and babies? They're good candidates too!

A constellation of social objects surrounds every company and every organization. Every customer or customer segment has relevant objects too. To a great extent, our previous comments about defining the relevant topics and themes can be thought of as exercises in mapping the constellation of objects you want in your community or channel.

Channels can often dictate the type of objects to be shared, just by the nature of what they permit or enable. Twitter, for example, is built around short posts, or updates, usually of a timely nature. It's great for sharing brief nuggets of information or opinion. Nowhere is the impact greater than on media channels: If you're an online music station like San Francisco–based SomaFM (@somafm) or a radio station like Amsterdam's KINK FM, you might use Twitter to push your playlists along with news and events to listeners. And, your customers can use these same channels to push a steady stream of updates to *you*—updates about the experiences they are having with your products or services or your support desk or the staff in your retail outlets. You can use these updates to open a new channel of customer service—as so many companies have, from Comcast to Dell to BSkyB—or you can begin by merely harvesting these insights via a listening tool and using the data to improve products or processes.

Other kinds of social objects lend themselves to the specific purpose of enabling customers to complete a task or mission that they've set for themselves. Three examples from France illustrate this well. Hardware and building supply chain Leroy Merlin uses customer-authored product reviews, shown in Figure 10.1, to help customers in the consideration phase of a purchase process to make fact-based decisions on what product to buy.

Figure 10.1 Leroy Merlin product ratings and review

When customers are ready to buy—except perhaps for one or two specific questions—mobile phone service provider Joe Mobile uses question-and-answer pairs, shown in Figure 10.2, derived from past customer interactions to help speed the process.

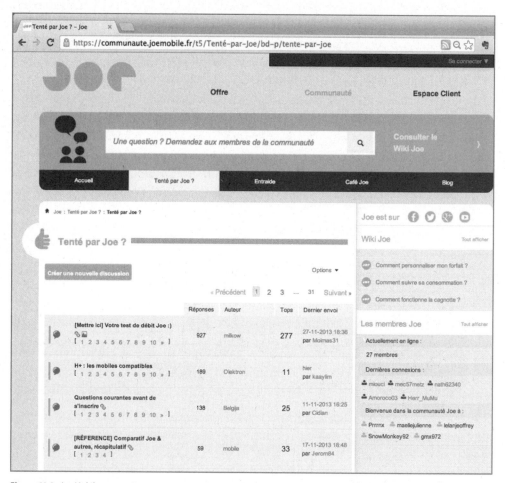

Figure 10.2 Joe Mobile community

When customers of French grocer Groupe Casino don't find their favorite products on the shelf of the local store, they can use C'Vous, the company's ideation community shown in Figure 10.3, to suggest it be added to stock—or perhaps to add their vote to a suggestion already made. Different objects, different purposes, but a common goal—to enable customers to do something they want to get done.

Figure 10.3 Groupe Casino's C'Vous community

While these three examples illustrate several innovative approaches to the use of the social technology in transactional business processes, your business or organization might have a larger goal. You might aspire to use social channels to help customers fulfill their personal objectives—to improve themselves or their lives or their own businesses. This generally means that you'll be working with larger social objects—passions, avocations, lifestyles, or causes—and ones that are related to the products or mission of your organization.

A great example of the use of these larger social objects is myFICO, the consumer division of an organization that helps banks and other businesses determine the creditworthiness of individual consumers. If you've ever bought a house in the United States, you know what a FICO score is—you generally can't get a home without it! MyFICO sells products to consumers to help them understand their own credit history and ratings. But the organization, like its parent company, also has an interest in educating consumers on how to use the credit wisely.

Since 2007, social media has played an important role in fulfilling this mission. In 2007, myFICO created an online community, shown in Figure 10.4, for consumers to share experiences and help one another navigate the complexities of credit use in the United States. Thinking of the constellation of social objects around credit, they focused the community on two topics—credit cards and mortgages—in order to target the areas where consumers struggled the most to make good, informed decisions.

256

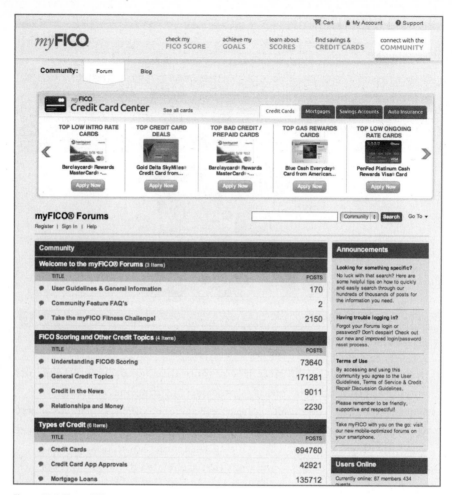

Figure 10.4 The myFICO community

The myFICO community has expanded to cover auto loans, student loans, and even business credit. More importantly, it has generated more than a million contributions from individual consumers, both those seeking help and those with help to offer. Often the latter include people who had credit problems in the past and worked to restore their reputation. Their passion is now to help others do the same.

The reward for myFICO? The company finds that community users show a 40 percent higher spend for myFICO's credit-monitoring and reporting products. It's no surprise that they buy more—they're better informed and as a result see the value in the FICO products. But as the keeper of the scores, the company can also see the positive impact that community use has on individual credit scores. Companies talk about measuring the ROI they get from social; FICO can measure the *customer's* ROI as well!

Taken together, social objects are essential elements in the design of a social media marketing program built around a sense of community. Social objects are the anchor points for these efforts and as such are the magnets that attract participants and then hold a community together. While it may seem like so much semantics, when compared to the way in which people are connected or to whom they are connected, the social object provides the underlying rationale or motive for being connected at all. In short, without the social object, there is no social.

Jyri Engeström

Sociologist, Jaiku cofounder, and now Google product manager, Jyri Engeström coined the term *social object* as a label for the things that people socialize around. Jyri provides a nice discussion of social objects in this video, on Vimeo:

> http://vimeo.com/4071624

You can follow Jyri on Twitter (@jyri) and read his blog here:

> www.zengestrom.com/

Take a look at the operational definition of social object at the start of this section again. What it really says is this: People will congregate around the things *they* are most interested in and will talk about them with *others who share that interest*. This is what lies at the heart of the Social Web.

By looking at the larger objects—human interests and pursuits—it's easier to identify and build an SCE strategy that helps the participants in that community be better at the things they love or are interested in. People look to spend time with others like themselves, talking about the things in which they have a shared, common interest or purpose as an enrichment of their own existence. Your challenge is to connect those interests to the things you provide through your business or organization that facilitate their pursuit. Getting this right essentially ensures that the conversations that follow will help you grow your business over the long term.

Why Social Objects Matter

What is it about the Social Web and social media that engages people, and why do they congregate around specific activities or sites? There are actually two answers to this: First, people have in general—and now at least in some manner in most parts of the world—adopted social technologies as a means of keeping in touch. To be sure, it is only a minority of the global population that is involved, for a variety of reasons, but it is also steadily increasing. Sooner or later, the conversations in your markets will flow onto the Social Web. More likely, given that you are reading this, your market is already involved, whether through basic mobile services like SMS—aka "text"—or always-on, always-with-you broadband social applications.

Second, the relationships created via the Social Web have become real for the participants involved. This includes aspects of relationships like identity, reputation, trust, and participation. Do not underestimate this, because it strongly suggests the norms for your own online social conduct and it suggests how powerful the relationships you ultimately build online can actually become.

The combination of the increasingly real-world aspect of social computing—participation in social networks and the engagement in personal and professional life in collaborative, online tasks—along with the emergence of meaningful social objects in that same context creates a social space where real interest flourishes. Creating these experiences and then connecting them to a business objective is an important factor in building a strong and durable social presence online.

Social Objects: Types and Uses

When you begin formulating the plan for your use of social technology in your business, the perspective shifts to that of your customers and stakeholders (or employees, for internal social platforms). What are *they* interested in? What are the things that they are passionate about or want to know more about? This almost always raises the question of the value of social objects—usually referred to as content but used here with the specific requirement that this content be both rated and shared by and between your customers—as an element of your business plan.

Using Social Objects

Building a presence with social objects is a straightforward—but not necessarily simple—process. The following steps define the process. Each is explained in more detail.

1. Identify suitable social objects.

2. Create and plan the way you will encourage the development spread (sharing) of these objects.

3. Use these objects to build interest and participation in your community specifically and in your social presence in general.

Identify a Social Object

The first step in anchoring your brand, product, or service is sorting out where to actually connect to a preexisting community. The main questions to ask yourself (or your agency or work team, if the overall social strategy is in the hands of a distributed team) are the following:

- What do the people you want to participate with have in common with each other?
- Why are they participating in this activity?
- What do they like to do, and what is it about these activities that they find naturally talkworthy?
- How does your firm or organization fit into the previous points?
- Specifically, how can you improve the experience of the current participants as a result of your being there?

Armed with the answers to the previous questions, you are ready to plan your own presence in that community, and you have the beginnings of how this involvement can be tied to your own business objectives as you simultaneously become a genuine participant in this community.

What are some of the social objects that successful community participation has been built around? Table 10.1 provides a handful to get you started. More will be said about these in the sections that follow.

▶ **Table 10.1** Social objects that support communities

Brand	Social Object	Participant/Brand Connection
Dell	Entrepreneurship	Entrepreneurs and small businesses use Dell hardware.
Petco, Pet360	Pets and pet owners	Petco and Pet360 provide everything needed by pets and the people who love them.
Pampers	Babies	Babies and diapers go together.
Red Bull	Action sports	If two people are competing anywhere on the planet, one is wearing a Red Bull logo.

Looking at the brands and social objects in Table 10.1, you can see that the main take-away at this point is that each brand has identified for itself an existing social object around which to place itself in an existing social context. This is directly analogous to the process through which a brand is mapped to a core consumer value or articulated business purpose in traditional advertising: Where the advertising anchor points provide a context for communicating what a brand is or what it stands for, the social object provides the context for consumer and stakeholder participation in the activities that are related to the functional aspects of a brand, product, or service.

Create and Plan Your Use of Social Objects

Once you've identified a viable social object, the next step is to connect to it. You have choices in how you attach a particular business process to a social object: You may create a service that you offer, for example, that can itself become part of the way your audience pursues its involvement with the social object. Nike+ accomplishes this by connecting runners with its shoes through a service that connects runners with other runners.

Look at the Pampers community, shown in Figure 10.5, as an example. Called Pampers Village, the community allows parents to ask questions and share knowledge about the most common challenges encountered by new parents. You'll note a feature of this community that has grown more common over the years—the presence of expert content alongside content contributed by customers. In the Pampers Village, a doctor or other relevant professional will respond to the question, and other registered members are free to chime in as well.

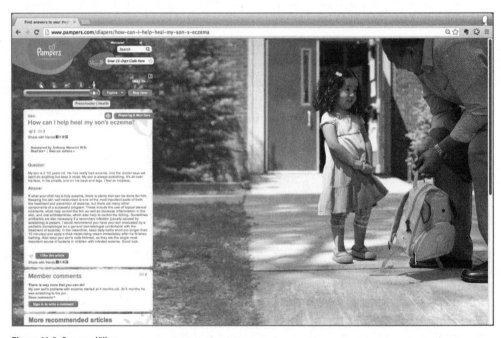

Figure 10.5 Pampers Village

Content Rules

Expert and other brand-contributed content in social channels can vary widely in effectiveness. Every community and social media manager should be conversant with best practices in content marketing, to make sure that content has the desired impacts. One of the best books on the subject is *Content Rules*, by Ann Handley and C.C. Chapman (Wiley, 2012). Handley and Chapman offer the following rules for effective online content:

- Embrace that you are a publisher.
- Insight inspires originality.
- Build momentum.
- Speak (like a) human.
- Reimagine, don't recycle.
- Share or solve, don't shill.
- Show, don't just tell.
- Do something unexpected.
- Stoke the campfire.
- Create wings and roots.
- Play to your strengths.

You can read more about these rules and how they can be applied to your business here:

```
http://contentrulesbook.com
```

Another interesting dimension of the Pampers example is the integration of the community with the loyalty and rewards program. When customers register for the community, they are automatically included in Pampers Gifts to Grow, which entitles members to discounts and other special offers.

Another great example of specific social objects tied to larger social objects is Sephora's BeautyTalk community. The larger object is beauty and the desire of Sephora's customers to find the best cosmetics products for their skin type and other attributes and to use those products effectively to enhance their personal attractiveness.

Since the advent of Pinterest, all of us are more aware of the power of image sharing, particularly in helping drive enthusiasm and ultimately commercial activity. Sephora too has embraced images in their on-domain social channels. As you can see in Figures 10.6 and 10.7, customers can choose to experience the community in a style similar to the Facebook feed (Figure 10.6) or as visually appealing grid, à la Pinterest (Figure 10.7).

Figure 10.6 Sephora feed view

Figure 10.7 Sephora image grid view

Naturally, where a photo can accurately show appearances, a video can do that and more. In the best case, it can effectively convey emotion. As a breakthrough communication platform, Skype connects millions worldwide. And while a large footprint in a global market is good, that kind of market coverage sets up being seen as a commodity player rather than a unique provider of a specific service. To help defend against the value erosion associated with commoditization, Skype launched a social program around Skype Moments, shown in Figure 10.8, inviting its customers to create and share content that shows how they use Skype uniquely to make little parts of a day that might otherwise go unnoticed stand out. In the process, Skype's customers are both reminded of and enlisted in sharing what makes Skype special.

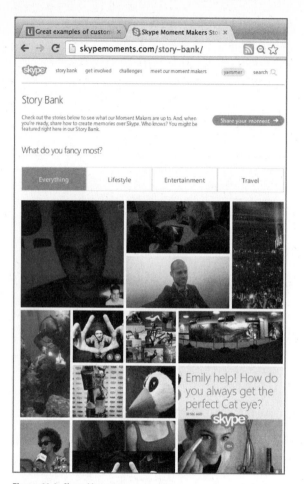

Figure 10.8 Skype Moments

Video is, of course, just one example of how social content is expanding beyond the discussion-based interactions that have typified online social content for so many years. Another recent development is the proliferation of customer-populated knowledge repositories. Customer knowledge is increasingly being harvested from other formats—discussion being the primary one—and imported to page-oriented formats like wikis and knowledge bases.

There's another trend in social objects that is well worth noting. It used to be that almost all the objects shared in social networks—article, videos, and so forth—were objects created by publishers. The commentary around the object was from consumers, but the object itself came from a brand. Today, the objects themselves are increasingly created by consumers. Box-opening videos are a great example: Consumers excited about acquiring a new product film the process of undoing the packaging and examining what's inside. The same trend is happening with other kinds of content. Today, if you visit the website for Lenovo, you'll find a great knowledge base of articles about

Lenovo laptops and mobile devices. That in itself is not surprising, but look closely: Alongside technical articles written by Lenovo's experts, you'll find articles written by customers! Lenovo knows that customers often know as much about its products as employees do, so why not give their knowledge top billing as well?

Peer-created knowledge—not just conversations—is a hot topic in service and support today. One big reason is that putting customer knowledge in article form—not just buried in a discussion thread—is a great way to make that knowledge more accessible. While some customers are eager to learn the ins and outs of a problem by taking part in discussion, others say, "Just give me the answer!" This is particularly true when the requests for help come from Twitter or Facebook. At BSkyB in the UK, peer-generated support content—articles and solutions generated by customers—are used in conjunction with its social media engagement platform to serve this content directly to off-domain customers seeking answers that unbeknownst to them already exist, because they were created by community members.

It's just conceivable that in the future the home page of customer support communities might look more like a knowledge library than a set of discussions. Look at the Unboxed community at Bestbuy.com, and you'll see that day has arrived.

We can't complete the conversation around social objects without talking about ideas. At giffgaff, a UK-based telecom firm, the company uses peer articles and comments in its ideation (innovation) community as sharable content that is itself directly rated as it is reviewed, allowing giffgaff to easily see which ideas have real traction with customers. The giffgaff innovation forum is shown in Figure 10.9.

The Rise of Short-Form Video

The growth of mobile means that every social manager needs to think about how to deliver content and experiences to this most challenging of channels. In the November/December 2013 issue of *Target Marketing* magazine, Fernando Espejel, director of digital platforms for DraftFCB in Chicago, argues that short-form videos, enabled by the appearance of Vine along with recent changes to the YouTube and Instagram platforms, are becoming a standard content element in social channels. Espejel recommends three uses for short-form video:

- Bring awareness to an existing product or brand (basically a short TV spot with no media spend).

- Drive users to a larger video format (to get the most out of investment in long-form video).

- Aggregate consumer-generated video (short-form is easier for consumers to create and contribute).

You can read more about short-form social video here:

```
www.targetmarketingmag.com/article/the-rise-short-form-video-
mobile-channel/1
```

Figure 10.9 giffgaff and consumer innovation

You may be thinking that the social object has to be large or that larger brands—perhaps because they are perceived (not always correctly) to have more resources (they have profit and loss pressures, too)—have an easier time. Not true. Social objects come in all sizes, and you can generally find one that applies to just about any business audience segment of interest. Look again at the examples in Table 10.1: businesses focused on pets, babies, and action sports are all powerful social objects. As a result, not only is each of these a social connector—you could easily throw a social event around any one of these topics—they are also perfect alignment points between these businesses and their customers. This is what social objects are all about: They form the common-interest-based connection between your brand, product, or service and your customers, constituents, and employees.

Build Interest and Participation

With your social objects identified and an activation program that connects your business to that activity built around it, attention turns to growing and supporting the community. Think about showing up at a friend's party. Unless specifically told otherwise, you'd likely bring a small gift to share: an appetizer or dessert, or maybe a bottle of wine if the setting is appropriate. The point is this: This sort of value exchange is recognition that a social gathering among friends is a collective activity, one that *is made better* as more participants contribute and share.

Your business presence in a community or activity built around a social object works the same way. Since you're but one of the participants—remember that the activity centers around the social object and not you—your program will generally work better if you are an equal co-contributor to the general well-being of the community and its specific participants.

The result—looking back on the overall process—is that you have created a space for, or joined into, the interests, lifestyles, passions, and causes that matter to your customers and stakeholders. By practicing full disclosure and by taking care to contribute as much or more than you gain, you have successfully anchored your business in what matters to your customers, made things better for them, and created a durable supporting link that ties back to your business.

However you choose to integrate social objects into your social customer experience strategy, building a community based on your brand implies that the brand itself is big enough—or has been made big enough—to anchor the social interactions of that community. For brands that are either sufficiently big themselves (such as GM) or sufficiently novel or talkworthy (such as Cannondale's commitment to cyclists or Tesla Motors and its electric automobiles), a brand-based community may well be viable. Tesla, GM, and Cannondale all connect to their customers in sufficient ways to support social interaction. Cannondale might build a discussion forum around terrain exploration and riding safety, while Tesla and GM might build around their own insight and innovation programs for future personal transportation using an ideation platform. For business-to-business applications, a company like EDS (now HP Enterprise Services) might build a community of suppliers and contractors, for example, who have a direct stake in the benefits of collaboration aimed at process improvement in the delivery of higher-valued IT services.

In each of these examples, the key is placing the community participant at the center and encouraging interaction between participants that offers a dividend—like learning, insight, and a spreading of the brand presence—to the company or organization. If your strategic plan for a brand-based social community includes this specific provision, you are on solid ground. Note the nuance here: The community (in this case) is built to emphasize a specific aspect of the brand. However, it is the participant, and not the brand, that is at the center of design and the activity that follows.

By thinking about participants as the central element—rather than your brand, product, or service—you avoid one of the biggest mistakes made when approaching social media marketing from a business perspective. That mistake is putting the brand, product, or service at the center of the social effort and then spending money—very often a lot of money—pulling people toward what amounts to a promotional program in the hopes that they will talk about it and maybe even make it go viral. This rarely if ever works over the long term, and even when it does it still fails to drive the sustainable social bonding and engagement behaviors that result in collaboration and ultimately advocacy. Be especially careful of this when implementing a community at the product or service level: focus on the customer experience and the delivery of benefits to customers

Beyond content, larger objects—a whole business, an idea, a passion, a lifestyle, or a cause—can also be effectively tapped as social objects. Found Animals, based in Los Angeles, California (www.foundanimals.org), provides a great example of how a powerful social object—the love of pets and concern for their care—combined with a thought-out presence and community participation come together to create a successful organization. Found Animals became an operating foundation in March 2008, hiring its first employee, Executive Director Aimee Gilbreath, at that same time. The foundation is committed to increasing the rate and quality of pet adoptions, thereby lowering pet euthanasia. To succeed, Found Animals provides financial and business-model support to the Los Angeles municipal animal care facilities with a focus on adoption, spay/neuter programs, microchipping, and licensing. Clearly, the love, care, and concern for animals—of any type, especially companion animals—is a natural, powerful social object around which a community can be created.

Dave Evans spoke with Andrew Barrett, director of marketing for Found Animals, about how social media factored into the overall outreach and awareness programs:

We have several key messages intended for current and future animal adopters and we want our audience to trust us as their partner. These messages include adopt your pet, rather than going to a store, spay/neuter your pet to prevent pet overpopulation, microchip your pet so they can be returned if lost, and license your pet—it's the law. We are very active on Facebook and Twitter, and these channels have proven excellent tools for us to reach our intended audience and bring awareness to our programs and message in an efficient and popular method. To achieve this, we have an internal, full-time digital-media program coordinator responsible for the strategic and creative development and implementation of our social marketing across all digital channels.

Found Animals maintains an active Facebook presence in addition to its website. Dave asked Andrew about the experience with Facebook:

We have built a relationship with over 7,000 fans on Facebook. We engage them through traditional uses of Facebook and social media: polls, surveys, wall-post discussion, and so on. Many times we use incentives to increase participation, like gift cards for pet-related spending. Currently, we are working to build on our social media success by developing metrics: comparing the amount of participation against the number of new adoptions or current adopters who rely on us as a direct result of our social media program. We will also be measuring the impact of social media on our other initiatives: spay/neuter services, microchipping, and licensing.

Finally, Dave asked Andrew about the growth of Found Animals' Pet Club and its future plans to continue building its programs around the care and concern for animals:

Let me preface this by saying in most cities once you adopt a pet and leave the animal care facility you're on your own. Your vet is available by appointment and for a fee. Your friends, family, and neighbors who have pet experience are available as well, when you can get their attention. Generally, there is no single, centralized resource with trusted information and a knowledge base built on personal experiences of thousands of pet owners. The goal of Found Animals and our Pet Club is to serve that need. Through social media, we've listened to our community, and they have clearly expressed a desire for a tool like this that is not linked to an exclusive commercial product or line of products or a corporation with commercial goals. Our Pet Club will be a living, breathing, and very personal online experience that will rely on medical and professional experts, as well as the expertise of pet owners like you and me.

What is particularly impressive about Found Animals is the way they have naturally integrated social-media-based marketing and community participation (both online and off) into the operational design and marketing of the foundation. Carrying this further, by listening carefully to their customers and community stakeholders, Found Animals has identified a clear need and a larger, more valued service offering that it is now building into. That's social business in action.

Lifestyles make great social objects: People naturally tend to associate based on lifestyle choices—values, preferences, care, and concerns—and the ways these personal choices are made visible. Lifestyle is closely related to things like personal identity and culture. The Catalan culture in Spain, the Sikh traditions in India, the Cajun culture of Louisiana, the historical interests that power the Daughters of the American Revolution, or the surf lifestyle (complete with Dick Dale's Lebanese-inspired surf sound) of California are all at the centers of powerful, compelling, and long-standing communities. Can your brand compete with these, or would it better to join them and bring some unique benefits that connect the participants in communities like these to your business or organization?

Lifestyle-based social objects include action sports—skiing, kart racing, wakeboarding, and kite surfing—along with quilting, cooking, and online gaming. World of Warcraft, for example, is a great example of the kinds of activities that will spawn significant followings. For small businesses—and the businesses and organizations that serve them—there is plenty of interest around the small business ownership lifestyle. Figure 10.10 shows the American Express OPEN Forum, a business community that is built around the needs and interests of small businesses. Lifestyle associations are a great place to start when planning your Social Web presence. They provide natural places for you to participate and, assuming relevance, easy ways for your brand, product, or service to become a valued part of these communities.

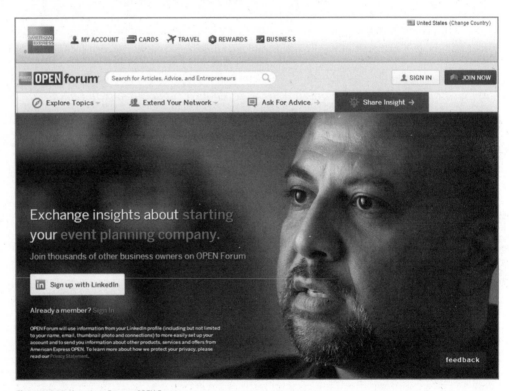

Figure 10.10 American Express OPEN Forum

Passions are another rich area when you're looking for existing social objects. Shown in Figure 10.11, Red Bull University is a community built for enthusiasts interested in taking their passion for action sports to the next level. Beyond the program's entry point, student brand managers are connected to exchange best practices and tips and to generally assist each other in the development of a variety of Red Bull's promotional activities, in part by sharing information through the online social channels that form around action sports.

How could you use a program like this in your organization? Could you actually *teach* your enthusiasts to become advocates? The real insight here is not so much having a brand university—although that's a pretty innovative step on its own. The big insight is in recognizing that for nearly any fan base, there is a thirst for getting closer to the action, for becoming part of the team. Fans don logo wear for a reason: It's an act of *inclusion*. Be sure you consider this when planning your social media program, and more specifically, consider how you can *empower* your fans to become evangelists.

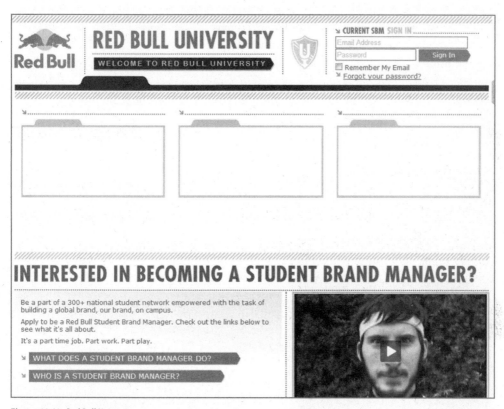

Figure 10.11 Red Bull University

Right along with passions and lifestyles, *causes*—such as ending child hunger or advocating the humane treatment of animals—are natural social objects. Not only are causes easy to identify—after all, they generally form around issues that command attention—but the people involved are predisposed to talk about them, driven out of direct, personal interest. This makes cause-related social objects great vehicles for business programs as well as a natural focal point for cause-related organizations, for two reasons.

Number one, by getting involved in a genuine and meaningful way, your business or organization brings more brains, muscle, and capital to the table. Your contributions, along with those of all others involved, make it that much more likely that the ultimate goal of the organization will be met and that the participants in the effort will feel good about the process as a result.

Number two, you are able to create an additional and appreciated connection point between your brand, product, and service and the markets you serve. On this point, a social presence built around a cause-related social object is distinctly different from corporate social responsibility and similar philanthropic programs. Straight-up giving is absolutely appreciated by—and vital to—many cause-based organizations; corporate donations and in-kind contributions help them deliver their services or benefits to society.

Figure 10.12 shows the Tyson Foods Hunger All-Stars program, a cause-based effort that taps the company's unique capabilities across a number of social channels and additionally highlights the individual contributions of its Hunger All-Stars. This point is a big one: Highlighting the individual contributions—making the participants the stars rather than the brand—is an absolute best practice in social business.

Figure 10.12 Tyson Foods' Hunger All-Stars

Figure 10.13 shows Aircel's efforts in raising awareness of the near-extinction of India's Bengal tigers. The campaign goal, beyond awareness, is in its partnership with the World Wildlife Fund. The program is aimed at moving people to act in support of the protection of the Bengal tiger. In both the Tyson and Aircel programs, the community-building goal is fundamentally the cause and is intended to build on awareness and to move people to action. These programs—whether working in local hunger relief efforts or demanding that existing but overlooked laws regarding tiger poaching are actually upheld—tap the potential in the associated cause-related communities that exist around these social objects.

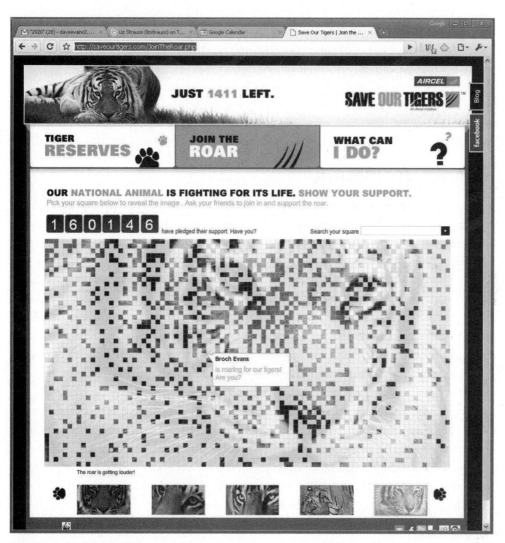

Figure 10.13 Aircel's Save Our Tigers

Worth noting in both of these examples is that they aren't so much examples of marketing alignments with popular issues as they are legitimate efforts to address worthy causes that are aligned with the values and missions of the companies involved and the people in the markets they serve. Tyson feeds families, and so feeding families that are sometimes unable to feed themselves is directly related to its own operations. Aircel describes itself as a pioneer and is clearly part of the next generation of India's social adopters. That this next generation should also be able to witness first-hand—and not in a zoo, or worse, an encyclopedia—the amazing presence of India's national symbol fits right into that.

Here's a great test that you can apply when thinking about building around a cause: Poll 10 random employees in your business as to how some specific cause is connected to your business. If you get nine decent responses, you're onto something. If not, keep looking (for causes, not employees to quiz).

Finally, one word of caution: If you choose to create a community around a cause, make sure the business is committed to the idea long-term. In general, if your business doesn't already support the cause in a meaningful way, it's unlikely to make the kind of long-term commitment to supporting a community and helping it grow.

The Future of Social Objects

The most basic role of the social object is driving conversation. In the business applications discussed previously, the social object brings participants together based on a common interest around which a conversation occurs. It also provides a relevant context for a brand, product, or service.

This clear connection is important: Recall that a basic fact of social media is that in comparison with traditional media, it is harder to interrupt. This differentiator plays out in two ways: First, because it is harder to interrupt the activities of participants directly—like the way you can interrupt a TV program with an ad or an online page view with a pop-up—your activities with regard to your business objectives have to have an obvious relevance. Otherwise, you'll be ignored (best case) or asked to leave (worst case). The Social Web isn't a marketing venue, though it is a very powerful marketing platform.

Second, because it is harder to interrupt (if not impossible), your message, your value, and your contributions to the community must be delivered within the existing conversation. In an analogy to TV, think about the difference between product advertising on TV versus product placement within the TV program. In the case of product advertising, there is a clear distinction between the program and the ad. In the case of product placement, the product becomes part of the program.

Trusted Content

Beyond the basic requirements outlines—clear connection to your business and a rallying point that is generally larger than the brand itself—vibrant social strategies are built with or around social objects that are overtly *trusted*. Simply put, this means that not only do your customers need to find the content that underlies your social programs to be engaging, but they also have to trust it. An easy way to see this is to think about an experience on YouTube, where content engagement is generally high. High engagement does not imply high trust, as time spent watching entertaining but not necessarily useful video content makes clear. To be sure, there is useful and trusted content on YouTube, so the question "what makes content trusted?" is relevant to your formulation of an overall content plan.

In the context of social customer experience, trusted often means contributed by your peers. Survey research by Nielsen in September 2013 found that 84 percent of consumers trust recommendations from friends, and 68 percent trust consumer opinions they see online. By contrast, less than half of consumers trust the most common types of online ads, including those found in social networks, search results, banners, and mobile. This does not mean that consumers generally distrust brands; in fact, they don't. Company websites are trusted by 68 percent. But it does mean is that in the drive to become smarter consumers, your customers are turning to each other to vet what you claim, to validate what you say. "The best phone for under $100" ought to be evident to those consumers who have actually purchased one or more under-$100 phones. And those comments—immediately discoverable—can be used to validate specific claims. To the extent that comments, ratings, reviews, articles, and so forth are marked as accepted or highly recommended by others, the trust in the content itself increases. By extension, as the trust in the content rises and the alignment with the brand's own claims is validated, the trust in the brand increases, adding to the value of the SCE program.

This becomes more important as more consumers adopt social technology and increasingly take part in social commerce. You need to be part of the community rather than an interruption. Note that this *does not* mean hidden and certainly does not mean covert, but rather that you participate in a transparent, disclosed manner. Above all, your participation should appear as a natural element of the surrounding conversation.

SEO: Get Found

With the social object in place, the next objective is building your audience. This means being findable through search. Author Brian Solis, known for his work at the intersection of social media and public relations, has often stressed the importance of using the Social Web and social media as a part of your overall search optimization program. Because the photos, videos, blog posts, and similar content associated with social media can be tagged, described, and linked, they can all be optimized for search. Don't make the mistake of dismissing this as little more than a tip, trick, or technique to be implemented by search engine optimization (SEO) firms (although a good SEO specialist can really help you here). Instead, step back and consider the larger idea that Brian and others making this same point are conveying: People search for things, and they discover relevant content in this way. If great content—and the community that has been built around it—can't be found, then that content effectively does not exist. In that case, the community won't be found.

This much larger view of SEO makes clear that SEO applies to everything you do on the Social Web. Too often SEO is applied in a more narrowly focused application of page optimization or site optimization against a specific set of commerce-related keywords. This works, and it's better than nothing, but the real gain comes when each piece of social content is optimized in a way that promotes self-discovery and, therefore, discovery of the entire social community. As portals and branded starting pages give way to a search box or a running discussion, how people find things on the Web is changing dramatically. In the portal context or the big, branded community, the assumption is that a preexisting awareness—perhaps driven by advertising—brings people to the content, after which specific items are discovered. For example, I may see a spot on TV that advertises the continuation of the story unfolding in the spot and find at that site lots of interesting discussion around that spot and the associated product or service. More likely, however, people will find that community by searching for the content itself and discovering the community, working backward to the online version of the original TV spot, posted on YouTube.

It's really important to catch the significance of this. A common approach to promotion typically uses an ad of some type to drive people to a microsite or social presence point where the audience in turn discovers the content that ultimately encourages individuals to join, visit, or otherwise participate. This is not how the increasing use of search engines—everywhere, and increasingly on mobile devices—works. Instead, people search for specific things—often at a very granular level in searches for things like "wakeboard" rather than "action sports watercraft." With the emergence of ubiquitous search boxes, it is imperative that each single piece of content—each social object in the very narrow sense of the term—be optimized. By optimizing the individual social objects, you greatly increase the likelihood that the larger community will be discovered, since that community is the container for those objects. The "Hands-On" section of this chapter has an exercise that shows you how important this is.

This all gets to the larger point of optimizing social media and social objects in particular. In a world with less interruption, in a medium that is driven by search and powered by direct personal interest along with sharing and recommendations, it is the *details* (the small items and pieces of content) that are the most desired and hence are the things most likely to searched for and the most likely to be appreciated, shared, and *talked about* upon discovery. Tags, titles, categories, and other forms of applicable metadata (for example, the *description* of your company video posted on YouTube) that apply to the content—to the social object—and not just the web page must be keyword rich and must perform as well as search attractors as they do as attention holders. Be aware here: It's quite common to focus (appropriately) on the content—good content matters, after all—and to completely ignore the tags, titles, and other meta information at the object level and instead focus SEO efforts at the website or page level only. Don't make this mistake: Work with your SEO team to optimize *everything*.

Review and Hands-On

Chapter 10 explored the social object in detail. While social objects are in general anything around which a conversation may form (a photo, a short post, or a lifestyle), Chapter 10 focused mostly on the larger social objects (lifestyles, passions, and causes), how they relate to the smaller social objects that customer share online, and the ways in which these larger and smaller objects can be used to encourage conversations around your business or organization.

Review of the Main Points

The main points covered in Chapter 10 are listed here. Review these and develop your own list of social objects around which to plan your social presence:

- Social objects are central to developing trust and trusted content—the customer-approved subset of social and branded content is most valuable.

- Social objects are the center of social activity. Without the social object, no meaningful conversation forms.

- Social objects are often built on lifestyles, passions, and causes, because these are universal areas of commonality and discussion.

- Social objects include talkworthy aspects of your business or organization or unique features of your product or service.

- Social objects, like any other type of online content, should be optimized for search and discoverability. Social objects are very much the connectors between a community and the people who enjoy or find value in being part of it.

Social objects are a building block of online social communities, and as such they are an essential consideration in the development of your social business and social media marketing programs. Built around areas of shared interest, your participation in existing or purpose-built communities gives you a powerful connection point between your business or organization and the people with whom you'd like to build stronger relationships.

Hands-On: Review These Resources

Review each of the following and connect them to your business.

1. Look at the work of Jyri Engeström, beginning with this video (`http://vimeo.com/4071624`) and his blog (`www.zengestrom.com/blog`).

2. Make a list of the social sites you are currently a member of (all of them). Connect each with the social object around which it is built, and then consider how your connection to this object drives (or fails to drive) your participation in that site.

3. Visit your own brand or organization website and brand outposts. Is a social object readily identifiable? Does this social object connect your audience to your business?

Hands-On: Apply What You've Learned

Apply what you've learned in this chapter through the following exercises:

1. Create an inventory of communities applicable to your brand, product, or service. Once you've compiled it, join a manageable set and understand the interest areas and social norms for each. Develop a plan for how you might integrate your own activities into these communities.

 Note: Always practice full disclosure, and refrain from test-driving active communities.

2. Using Google, search for a lifestyle, passion, or cause that you are interested in. Note the documents that come back, and review a subset of them. Then do the same content search again but this time select only image results. Review the images and note the number of images that lead you to a social site of some type.

3. Define three core social objects for your business or organization around which you could build or enhance your social presence. Create a touchpoint map to help guide your selection.

The Social Graph

11

We've talked about the Social Web as consisting of people and content, but it's the connections among people arising from their shared interest in that content that make the Social Web so attractive. A key concept in understanding those connections, and the subject of this chapter, is the social graph.

Chapter contents

What Is a Social Graph?

Social graph can be a confusing term. Sometimes people use it interchangeably with *social network*. But social network is itself confusing: Is a social network a group of connected people or a platform that people use to connect? When people call Facebook a social network, they clearly intend both meanings, but they also understand that the individuals connected on Facebook constitute a social network even without the platform.

You may recall a related problem from the early days of social interaction on the Web: Is a community a group of people or a place online where people connect? As with social network, the answer is it's both.

Fortunately, social graph has a meaning that is distinct from social network. Consider the following definition:

Definition: The Social Graph is the representation of our relationships. In present day context, these graphs define our personal, family, or business communities on social networking websites.

Jeremiah Owyang, 2007

The key word here is *representation*. A social graph is a social network, *as represented in terms of its connections, generally either visually or in computer code.* Figure 11.1 shows an example of a social network represented visually in a social graph.

While visual representations can be useful, not to mention beautiful, representations in code can be extremely powerful. These representations, often without being explicitly called out, power much of our experience on the Web today.

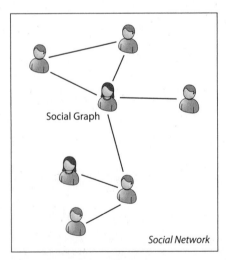

Figure 11.1 A simple social graph

Consider the following, all of which are powered by graphs:

- Book recommendations on Amazon, under the heading "Customers who bought this also bought"
- Suggestions for photos, movies, and places that your friends like, available via Facebook's Graph Search
- Recommendations you receive from Twitter, after you follow someone new ("Suggestions based on John Doe")

You may have noticed that only the last example is based on a social graph alone. The first two are based on a social graph *and* a knowledge graph. Knowledge graphs are like social graphs except the nodes of the graph are content, not people. Often, knowledge graphs and social graphs are mixed. In the case of Facebook, my recommendations are based on my connections to people (social graph) and their connection to knowledge (movies, photos, and so on).

You probably used a knowledge graph before you ever used a social one. After all, that's how Google decides what content to serve up in response to your search request. When knowledge objects are highly connected (that is, linked), Google gives them preference over those that are not. If other sites link to a site, it's likely you will find that site useful too. Of course, Google doesn't ignore the social graph (see the sidebar "Google and the Social Graph").

The knowledge graph that powers Google is arguably the largest in the world. Microsoft's search engine Bing also relies on a knowledge graph, to deliver summarized or relevant knowledge in the snapshot pane of the Bing results page. Neither Google nor Bing contains all the knowledge in the world, of course. Each relies on its own knowledge graph to represent—in an always partial but ever improving way—the network of knowledge in the world.

Just as there is no single, all-compassing knowledge graph, there is no single social graph. But unlike the world of search, where competitive platforms are few in number, the social world contains many platforms. Each of these platforms relies on a social graph of its own, a social graph imported from another platform, or both. So there are more social graphs in the world than there are knowledge graphs. Social networks like Facebook, Google+, LinkedIn, and Pinterest; photo messaging apps like SnapChat and Instagram; text messaging apps like WeChat, WhatsApp, and LiNE; and enterprise social platforms like Lithium, Jive, and Telligent all rely on social graphs, since they all permit users to friend, follow, or connect.

Google and the Social Graph

Reviewing patent filings can be a great way to see where technologies are going. David Harry, CEO of Reliable SEO, read Google filings to understand how they thought about social. His 2013 article on the Searchmetrics CEO Blog titled "Google and the Social Graph: More Data to Feed the Beast" is full of interesting insights. Among them are the four kinds of connections Google might take into account when looking at social data:

- Explicit—designation as friends, colleagues, fans, blog feed followers
- Implicit—friends in common, messages sent between users, viewing another user's profile page
- Common groups—membership in a group related to a particular interest, membership in a group related to a particular geographic area
- Common activities—users posting messages to the same forum, users playing an online game together

Harry suggests that Google may be heading toward a kind of TrustRank concept in which social connections are used to improve the results generated today by the link graph.

```
http://blog.searchmetrics.com/us/2013/01/07/google-and-the-social-
graph-more-data-to-feed-the-beast/
```

Still, all social graphs are not alike. At more than 1 billion users worldwide, Facebook's social graph is the largest. In an increasingly social world, where every site and application on the Web wants to be social, having access to Facebook's graph is a huge leg up. Think of all the applications that ask you if you want to find your friends when you first register. They may ask for access to your contact list in Yahoo, Gmail, or other mail applications, but increasingly they connect to the social graph of one or more large social networks.

Access to social graphs of large public networks used to be open. If you wanted your users to be able to find their friends or followers on your site or application, you just used the APIs to do it. Over the years, however, these networks have started to move to requiring consent to link to their graphs—and consent is not always granted. In 2010, Facebook blocked Twitter from connecting to Facebook's graph. In 2012, Google closed the API to the social graph that powers Google+. Later the same year, Twitter blocked Instagram, signaling a new scrutiny of companies wishing to leverage its network. While it's still possible for Instagram users to share photos on Twitter, it's no longer possible to find your Twitter fans within Instagram automatically. While better use of network resources may be part of the reason, there's little doubt that networks want to avoid sharing such a valuable asset with companies that may compete against them.

What does this mean if you're running a social customer experience effort? We think it means three things:

- Understand the access permissions and requirements of all the applications you are using.
- Prepare for a landscape that has changed and is continuing to change.
- If you are pulling directly from social network APIs, understand that your access may only be temporary.

This fast-changing environment is one of the major motivators driving the adoption of software as a service (SaaS) social software solutions as discussed in Chapter 9, "Social CRM and Social Customer Experience." Companies understand the importance of connection to the Social Web at large, and they are rightly wary of taking on the responsibility for ensuring that their connections are always live and operational. SaaS vendors promise that ensuring those connections will be their problem, not their customers' problem. While the vendors are also subject to changes in policy from the big social networks, their membership in partner or certification programs means they have better visibility over coming changes and perhaps even some influence over the changes that occur.

Will there eventually be open standards to permit the sharing of social data? Google helped initiate such an effort, back in 2007, with the creation of the Open Social initiative, but that effort today focuses on social sharing in social networks inside large corporations. A larger, open public standard seems very far away.

The Social Web Bill of Privacy Rights

Beginning with the right to make an informed choice, the Electronic Frontier Foundation has suggested an initial Bill of Privacy Rights for people using social networking services and the use of the information by businesses—including information contained in members' social graphs. It's thought-provoking and likely an eventual reality. Check it out, and see how many of its suggested practices you can build into your social applications now.

www.eff.org/deeplinks/2010/05/bill-privacy-rights-social-network-users

A final word about social graphs, definitions, and standards: We've been talking here exclusively about collective social networks, but social networks exist on the personal level as well. Your network of friends and associates can be represented visually too. If you use Gmail, Yahoo, or Outlook, see MIT's immersion tool to create a visualization of your email network, `https://immersion.media.mit.edu`. There's a movement today toward greater control by individuals of their own online identity, content, and history. As you access applications on the Social Web that ask for permission to access your friends list, do you ever wonder, "Am I doing something some of my friends might object to?" Facebook's Graph Search evoked an immediate reaction from privacy advocates—does this make it too easy to parse and analyze an individual's behavior? We believe that individual control over social data will increase, not decrease, over the coming years. It's another topic about which those running social customer experience (SCE) programs should stay aware and informed. Feeling lost? It's not surprising—this is a complex area that's changing every day. For a refresher on the basics, see the sidebar "A Social Graph Primer."

A Social Graph Primer

ReadWriteWeb author Alex Iskold published an article in 2007 that outlines the basic concepts underlying the social graph and its use in business. You'll find the post here:

`www.readwriteweb.com/archives/social_graph_concepts_and_issues.php`

Characteristics of Social Graphs

In the physical world, sociologists sometimes distinguish between different kinds of network relationships that an individual might possess. These include trust networks, which consist of the people whom you rely on and trust; communication networks, consisting of people who keep you informed and up to date; and advice networks, those individuals whom you turn to when you need guidance in decision-making. Social network expert Rob Cross of the University of Virginia, who has studied such networks in large organizations, has determined that you might even have something called an energy network, which consists of people who energize you as a byproduct of your interactions. In an era of declining employee engagement, his research provides one potential clue for getting employees back in the game. Each of these networks can be graphed to provide insight into their formation and operation.

Types of Social Networks

Online, different kinds of networks are emerging as well. In addition to the friend networks we see on Facebook, people are united by common location, interests, values, and status. It's simple: People like to connect with others like themselves. Social applications like Meetup and Twellow, shown in Figure 11.2, build on an existing social graph based on common values, location, or other shared interests among Twitter members.

We all know what a *friend network* is; Facebook is probably the largest and most familiar example. That doesn't mean that people don't have many motivations for connecting on Facebook. It just means that they mostly connect because they are friends offline.

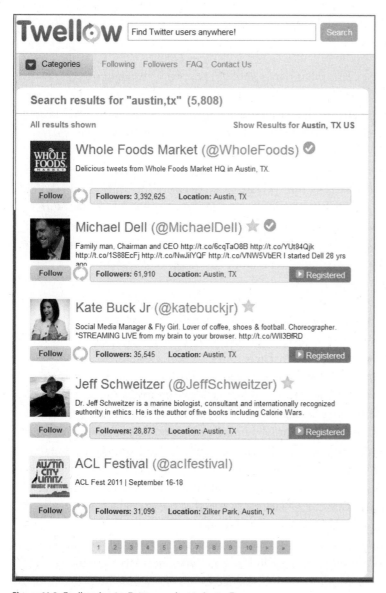

Figure 11.2 Twellow showing Twitter members in Austin, Texas

Location Networks

Location networks are exactly what they sound like: networks brought together by people in the same location. For example, on any day of the week, you're likely to see hashtags in your Twitter stream that clearly relate to a conference taking place in some city or town. These are location networks, albeit temporary ones, that form when people share the same location for a period of time.

Location networks also exist around cities and towns and neighborhoods. Nextdoor (`https://nextdoor.com`), the "private social network for your neighborhood," leverages the common interests of people who live in a geographical location. With a focus on real identities, Nextdoor hopes to realize the vision of earlier location-based efforts like Everyblock. While location grows increasingly important every year, it's interesting to see companies struggle to take full advantage of its potential.

Interest Networks

Interest networks are in some ways the most exciting networks today. Many classify Pinterest as an interest network, since the focus is not on members themselves as much as it is on the things that interest them. There's an interesting connection here with communities, which are often distinguished from social networks because of their focus on common interest rather than social bonds. We were struck to observe Tara Hunt, social media expert, and Bridget Dolan, head of social programs at Sephora, make almost identical comments about why interest networks and communities provide something social networks don't. "Facebook is about who I am," Dolan noted. "Community is who I want to be." Likewise, Hunt has observed, "Facebook is who I am. Pinterest is who I want to be." Both Dolan and Hunt point to an aspirational element to interest networks that can be lacking in social networks, which are grounded in one's current activities, relationships, and lifestyle.

But there's another reason why interest networks have generated so much excitement. They have shown a much stronger link to commercial activity than have other kinds of social networks. According to BI Intelligence, Pinterest alone accounted for 23 percent of social-mediated e-commerce sales in the second quarter of 2013.

Jon Elvekrog, blogging on Forbes CIO Network, broadened the value proposition for interest networks by identifying "five ways they will transform the Web":

- Ad matching—using interest graph data, advertisers can compose more accurate segments to improve ad click rates.

- E-commerce recommendations—interest data can help improve poor performance from history alone.

- Customer relationship management—interest data can tell companies what a consumer values the most, insight that can be used to incent or reward.

- Entertainment applications—interest data can help improve movie or book recommendations.

- Marketing and promotions—in summary, more relevant offers.

While it may seem obvious, this tendency to connect around interest actually has a significant impact on the way connections between members—and hence conversations—propagate. The tendency to associate based on interests can manifest itself in the formation of a social graph in distinct and important ways. It's worth understanding the tendency to preferentially connect with people sharing overt similarity when designing your social media and social business programs. For example, if you are after new ideas and are looking to a customer community to generate and discuss them, be sure that your participants haven't formed cliques and instead are making connections based on more than specific personal interest. Otherwise, instead of collaboration you're more likely to end up with competing factions.

Visualizing Partisanship

The tendency for like people to act together is nowhere more evident than in partisan politics. Using social graph visualization tools, Forbes contributor Erica Swallow offers a look into the increasingly polarized connectedness of the U.S. Senate. You'll find the article here:

www.forbes.com/sites/ericaswallow/2013/11/17/senate-voting-relationships-data/

Value Networks

In contrast to interest networks, value networks rely on association based on shared interest, lifestyle, passion, or cause. An entire community—in real life—coming together to stack sandbags against a flooding river is a real-life example of a value network. Regardless of social status, the collective community shares in the immediate goal of protecting itself. This plays out online in a social context when women across diverse walks of life come together to talk about common issues and challenges in places like the BlogHer Community. This sort of democratized social interaction is actually at the root of a lot of what happens on the Social Web.

The tendency for people to come together and organize around common issues, given diversity, is particularly important when designing a community application. When people are gathering around large social objects—lifestyles, passions, and causes—it is very likely that it is the shared values and purposes associated with these larger objects that are bringing together a variety of different people, in addition to the primary common interest itself (the specific passion, lifestyle, or cause that is shared). This in turn means that the shared outcomes, activities, and intellectual content produced within the community need to flow back in some form to *everyone,* regardless of who the actual contributor is. Otherwise, the individual interests will take over and the community will fragment.

Status Networks

The last type of network we've observed is a status network. This type of network takes advantage of what's referred to technically as status homophily—the tendency of similarly credentialed or titled individuals to associate with each other. A CMO's group on Facebook or a list of social media experts on Little Bird (http://getlittlebird.com/) is examples of relationships built on shared titles or occupations. Networks that encourage this type of relationship development include professional associations, skill-specific support forums—for example, a CIO discussion board or forum—and similar.

The status community, by comparison, is very likely to be driven by the reputation management system within a community, forum, or other social application. The reputation management system provides many of the cues that alert members to their own status or that of others within that community. CTOs joining a C-level tech community know already that the title of CTO or its equivalent is a shared credential. What engages them (in that community) are the solutions, tips, referrals, and best practices that they can pick up and apply in their work. The reputation management system—which provides a visible indication of which members are most likely to have offered viable solutions, for example—will quickly sort out the relative *status* ranking, beyond title, within this type of community.

Reputation management plays a role in the development of values-based communities too. Status differentiation can and does occur as some contributors within a shared value–driven community will produce more or more useful content than other members. That's a natural condition, and members expect recognition for their efforts. What's important, though, is that the community as a whole does not lose sight of the overall values connection as some members are elevated as a result of their greater contribution and participation.

Influencers and the Social Graph

Within any community or social construct—the kind of social space that is defined by the existence of a social graph—some participants are more influential or more valuable than others in any given situation. Reputation management—touched on earlier and in Chapter 4, "The Social Customer Experience Ecosystem"—governs the *visible* aspects, the signals or markers that identify the influencers, the leaders, and the experts within a social network, generally based on content contribution and the ratings or recommendations of other participants within that community.

Examining a particular member's social graph on its own provides a potentially different—and not always consistent—view of influence within a social network. The social graph provides insight into influence and reputation through a study of how participants are connected. Somewhat esoteric terms like *adjacency* (the relative connectedness of individuals in a network) or *centrality* (the relative importance of an individual in a network) can also be used to determine who matters, to whom, and why within a social network. If you could walk into a party and see this kind of information in your augmented reality browser (neatly displayed behind your sunglasses), how much more effective could you be as a networker? The same principle applies—in much more realistic terms—to your business or organizational use of social graph analysis and visualization tools today.

Understanding "who matters" is great information for a wide range of social applications. However, this type of information is absolutely critical in one broad class of applications: support networks. In a support network, participants depend on each other for solutions, and the consequences of bad information can be much worse than, say, getting bad advice on a movie or a meal out. In a support forum, spotting, elevating, and otherwise ensuring that the experts remain engaged is essential to the long-term success of that support platform.

By examining the social graph, you can locate, groom, and cater to the experts. This ensures that they

- Have what they need to consistently deliver the best answers
- Feel that the time they spend is noted and valued

When expert candidates are identified—for example, by high centrality, that is, having a relatively large number of followers, the community managers might invite them to attend a special training event or to become a part of an insiders program to ensure that they continue to have access to the information they need to deliver quality solutions within the support community.

Adjacency (who is connected to whom) is equally important. Think about how LinkedIn adds value by showing its members the direct or potential path(s) from the people they know to the people they want to know. Indeed, a deeper study or observation of the social graph of your customers and constituents can be very beneficial.

Like participation, *influence* can also be measured inside the social network using the visible indicators described in Table 11.1 and network-specific tools such as netvizz (a Facebook application). The analytical tools provided natively within Facebook can be used to measure the quality of interactions and activity data overall that is associated with business pages. Influence can also be measured through the use of external tools.

Additional measures of behavior—for example, behaviors that connect what is happening on one particular network with the larger discussions happening elsewhere on the Social Web—include influencer analysis through the use of tools like BuzzStream. Tools designed to spot influencers as they act *inside* the community are also valuable. Lithium Technologies offers a particularly robust set of expert identification tools that are very helpful in spotting and supporting the experts that emerge (naturally) in a support or similar type of community. Klout (see sidebar) offers an interesting, for-pay service in addition to its free service. Interested individuals can visit Klout and calculate the influence score for their own social presence. On top of that, Klout offers—via its own API—a for-pay service that allows anyone to calculate the relative influence scores for participants in their own social networks.

Measure Your Influence: Klout.com

Klout offers an assessment of social influence—similar to what Twitter Grader does with Twitter—but then provides an additional for-pay service that returns the influence of individual members within a given social network.

www.klout.com

▶ **Table 11.1** Measures of influence

Metric	What It Means
Average number of friends	The degree to which people are connecting to others is useful in understanding the ease with which relationships form. If this is low relative to expectations, look at the mechanism for friending or consider adding automated suggestions for relationships.
"Top 10" by friend count	Who are the most connected, and does this change over time? This will help you identify your community leaders.
Popular group or topic themes	What are the big interest areas? Knowing this is fundamental to encouraging the development of new applications.

Continues

Metric	What It Means
Most popular brands, products, services	What are the common interests, focused on marketing and business? What are people talking about that is important (business-wise) to you?
Most viewed events and members	What are the popular activities? Combined with popular groups and conversational themes, this information provides specific guidance in ongoing activity development.

Social Graphs Spread Information

Beyond linking people within a social network, the relationships that are present within a social graph play an important role in the spread of information throughout that social graph and hence play a direct role in the sharing of content across a social network. Looked at another way, without sharing, a social network is a largely theoretical construct: *What difference do a thousand connections make if nothing of value is flowing between them?* Consider, for example, the value to you, personally, of a network that you may have joined without understanding why—except perhaps that everyone else was joining it—and as a result rarely find yourself using it. You have connections within this network, but of what use are they?

When Dave first joined Twitter he admittedly did not get it. Dave started using Twitter in 2007 at SXSW; he is member number 12,556,112. According to Dave, "Half of my motivation for joining was that everyone else I knew had already joined." Given a bit of time, however, Dave started to develop actual relationships with people and began linking with people that he knew, or knew of, and with people interested in working on some of the same things he was interested in. *And that's when Twitter made sense*—when he was able to use his social graph as it existed within Twitter in ways that benefited not only him but also the growing Twitter community.

The take-away is that only with a meaningful social graph—only with connections between people with shared interests—do the social networks that people belong to become relevant.

The applications built around the direct use of the social graph are important. Dave spoke with Rapleaf's Michael Hsu—at the time Michael was part of Rapleaf's marketing team—about applications that mine or otherwise tap the information exposed through the study of a particular social graph. Michael noted applications ranging from driving participation in online gaming—in one application, players with more than five friends in the game were significantly more engaged than those with four or fewer—to the observation that the spread of movie reviews across a network is directly related to the strength and connectedness of the graphs of the individuals who publish reviews. All of this suggests the value of knowing, through measurement, who is connected to whom and how these connections can therefore be used to encourage additional connections.

In a specific example, Rapleaf worked with an online university to identify opportunities to increase engagement (more direct participation in classes) and encourage recommendations to friends for specific classes (new business growth). Using Rapleaf to identify the friends of prospective students who were already students themselves—all with explicit permission—they found a significant increase in the likelihood of new student conversion (320 percent) associated with having a friend who is also a student. This quantitative knowledge, gained through study of the social graph, resulted in the implementation of a bring-a-friend-to-class promotion (your friend gets to attend class with you for free, for one week), an online student center where prospective students can talk with current students, and a formal new student-referral recognition program.

Dave spoke further with Michael, asking about what Michael saw in the near future for applications of social graph analytics and measurement tools:

What's becoming clear is that an experience that is more "social" and connected for people is an experience that is more rewarding and engaging. It's one where both customers and businesses win. For customers, this means more relevance, more fun, and more meaningful activity. For businesses, this means more activity, more repeated engagement, better retention, faster word of mouth, and faster acquisition (through all the sharing).

What we're really going to see is a big push from consumer-facing companies to connect "friends" into their offering. Movie/food review sites, shopping sites, media/newspaper sites, hotels, movie studios, restaurants, and more—everyone will start to integrate friendships and the social graph in creative ways in order to provide more relevance and to personalize content for the user.

Remarketing: Decoding the Social Graph for Business

Remarketing is the industry term given to the use of existing customer data to create a more complete picture of customers for the purpose of improving marketing efficiency. While remarketing began with and often involves email data, the general practice now includes social points of contact and expressed interests as well. *Any such application must be undertaken with proper respect for consumer privacy.* Firms like Rapleaf, mBLAST, and Pick1 provide remarketing services; check them out here:

http://rapleaf.com

http://pick1.com

http://mblast.com

Ultimately, the social graph—combined with tools that encourage or facilitate content creation and sharing—powers a social network. Think back to the engagement process—consumption, curation, creation, and collaboration. The tools that support the sharing of information through the social graph drive the engagement process. Ultimately, collaboration is driven by relationships, and the relationships themselves are what form the social graph.

The Tools That Power a Social Graph

The tools that drive the formation of relationships and the engagement process itself range from essentially passive to highly active. During the design phase of your communities, ideation platforms, support forums, and similar, an important concept to remember is that *the more active the relationship encouragement is, the stronger in general the resulting social experiences that link participants will be.*

In a basic social-software platform—an entry-level discussion or community platform, for example—deployed straight out of the box, participants are generally able to create basic profiles and engage in topic-oriented discussions. These basic social platforms may also include built-in support for photo uploading, creating profile pictures, writing individual blog posts, group formation and discussion, and so on. Note here that these are features that enable members to do things that relate primarily to consumption, curation, and creation. Members of a woodworking forum might be creating and publishing pictures of cabinets, tables, and other projects they have completed or a review of new table saw that has been recently purchased.

We might think these platforms don't promote social connections as readily as social networks do, but look again: The networks formed here are around content (for example, interest), not personal relationships. The challenge for these platforms as we move into the networked age is not to merely emulate large social network sites by adding tools for building one-to-one relationships but rather to make the relationships being formed around content more salient. If I rate something you contributed, you should readily see that. Moreover, you should see the fate of all your content as it is consumed, rated, and responded to by other members of the community.

These platforms have also lagged social networks in terms of personalization. Some progress has been made with suggested content (related content widgets are becoming standard), but suggested member widgets (given your interest in these topics, you may be interested in these members) are relatively rare. Sorting out precisely who would be good to connect with is left to the participants.

In addition to the rules that power potential relationships (friending suggestions, for example) and engagement in the community, members need ways to find each other, to find people with whom a relationship might be beneficial. At an even more basic level, Facebook's activity feed and Twitter's retweet capability—RT in

Twitter parlance: the act of forwarding a tweet that you have received from someone you follow to all of your own followers—are themselves useful in discovering potential relationships.

The retweet in Twitter works to build one's social graph like this: Say Chris follows Pat, and Pat posts something interesting that Chris sees. Chris retweets Pat's post—a lot like forwarding an email—and as a result *Chris's* followers (including those who may not have known of Pat) now see Pat's post. Chris's followers discover and follow Pat in this way—potentially increasing the size and reach of *Pat's* social graph, all because Chris thought Pat's post was interesting and simply passed it along.

In this example, it was Chris's social graph that acted as the conduit for Pat's post. The ability to easily retweet enabled Chris to share Pat's post, building Pat's social graph in the process. The process by which tweets propagate and drive expansion of the social graph within Twitter is shown in Figure 11.3. Pat's tweet, "something notable," is retweeted by Chris, one of whose followers sees it and decides to start following *Pat* as a result. Driving Twitter's success, among other factors, is the extreme ease with which one can grow a large social graph. As a result, Twitter gets sticky, fast.

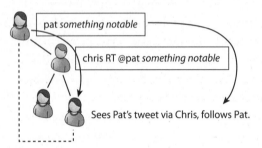

Figure 11.3 Growing the social graph

Beyond passing messages along, tools that enable searching, filtering, and aggregating content and sharing it between members serve to expand and refine personal social graphs. Facebook offers this capability through the combination of search and suggested friends (recommendations). Twitter introduced lists of specific members—a feature that built on and has since replaced the popular groups feature in TweetDeck (now owned by Twitter)—that people create and (optionally) share. Someone interested in horseback riding might build a list of riding coaches or professional equestrians to simply keep track of the posts from (just) these people. Twitter then provides the additional ability to share this entire list with others, making it very easy for others to further build their own social graph by following that entire list.

Spread Content Further

In addition to connecting people (members and participants) outright, the social graph is also useful as a conduit in spreading content—thoughts, ideas, words, pictures, and videos—across social networks. In the earlier Twitter example, Chris picked up

Pat's tweet and retweeted it, expanding Pat's social graph and spreading Pat's content beyond Pat's own immediate social graph in the process. Not only was Pat's social graph expanded in the process, but Pat's content was spread further when Pat's and Chris's individual social graphs were momentarily merged through Chris's retweet of Pat's content.

In this way, the social graphs of members can be used to spread content further, to and between members across distinct social networks whose social graphs intersect. What does it mean to say that two social networks—or the individual social graphs contained within them—*intersect*? Simply, it means that two members, each with their own social graph, have someone (generally, another person) in common. Looked at a different way, if Marcia is a member of both Facebook and Twitter, then Marcia's personal social graph actually spans two networks, and you can describe Marcia as a *point of intersection* between these distinct graphs.

Going further into the larger graphs that span social networks, Facebook introduced a set of tools built around its API that makes it easy to connect content (and hence participants) in social networks or content sites *outside* of Facebook with its members *inside* of Facebook. It works like this: Using a small code block that can be automatically generated on the Facebook Developers pages (see the sidebar "Social Graph APIs"), content developers on almost any network can introduce Facebook's Like function to their content that is outside the Facebook social network. When someone clicks a Like button associated with a specific piece of content that is *outside* of Facebook, a status update is published *inside* Facebook, alerting others who are themselves Facebook members that this content exists and that someone they know likes it. As people inside (and outside) of Facebook see these notices, and as a result click the Like button that is associated with that same content, the like rating of that content goes up, furthering its spread.

The kinds of connections and content visibility offered via Facebook's Like plugin can be a very powerful way to increase the visibility of content outside of Facebook. For example, you may have a blog or a branded community; the content created for those applications can be shared onto your Facebook business page. This capability drives social graph growth through content spreading and exposure. This sharing can also drive friending based on the common likes of specific content, again adding to the value of your social technology implementation. This extends as well to recommendations and other forms of content that can also be personalized as they are shared, adding an additional element of clutter-cutting credibility to the entire process.

By extension, what works for published content (across networks) also works for content served into networks (content like ads, for example). Using the social graph, content that is being syndicated or published into a social network can be optimized based on the likes and dislikes of those in a particular member's social graph. Going a step further, advertisements that leverage the social graph can actually display the fact that others within a particular person's social graph like this advertised product or service. It's a sort of 2.0 version of "All your friends are doing it, so perhaps you'd like to try it as well."

Measure Content Spread

One final measure may be of interest: Referring back to the discussion of homophily—the tendency for like-minded individuals to link together in a social network—there are ways to measure the degree to which this is happening. This is useful to know because it suggests, for example, the degree to which a particular site is bringing individuals together at a rate that is different from what would happen by chance.

In other words, by studying the effects of homophily in a social setting, the degree to which the social network itself is successfully driving friendships or other relationships over and above what would be expected provides an indication of the value and performance of the relationship tools—the ability to search and discover interesting connections, for example—and hence a measure of how likely the community is to grow and the degree to which it is delivering social (versus purely functional) value to its members.

The Social Graph and Social Customer Experience

The social graph—and navigating and investigating it—are central to using social technology in business. Contained within the social graph are the relationships and structures that define influencers, the connections that suggest shared interests, and the pathways over which content, ratings, and reviews can be spread throughout a social network. So, the first step in creating a robust network or social application is to ensure that as members connect with each other, relationships form and thereby enable social actions.

Make Sure People Connect

So how can you encourage participants in your social projects to connect? There are a few basics to consider, and you can always take a tip or two from the best practices used by other social networks in encouraging members' development of their own social graphs.

Recall the importance of *profile completion*. If members can't identify each other, they won't connect and build relationships. Think about it: Would you accept a LinkedIn connection request from "asdf ghjkl" in "anytown, usa"? (Dave actually received that request and promptly moved it to the trash.) If members are not completing profiles, add the tools that help them to do this, as is done on LinkedIn. LinkedIn shows you, as a member, the specific steps to take next to complete your social profile. Ensure that the networking platform you select supports something similar, either out of the box or easily added by you. Many social applications offer a programming extension or an API to enable you to extend the capabilities of the core platform.

Tip: Figure out the capabilities you need in regard to how much you want to assist or suggest connections and similar friending activities, and then make sure you know how to implement them *before* you select a platform. When you know what you want, it's lots easier to find it.

In addition to the tools that focus directly on social interactions and the things that facilitate them, consider contests, reputation and profile completion bonuses, and other incentives that encourage profile completion and social interaction. Think back to Chapter 7, "Five Key Trends," and the discussion of gamification to understand the importance of encouraging this kind of behavior. Relationships are possibly the single most important gating factor in the development of a strong community experience. Figure 11.4 shows LinkedIn's profile page and the tools available to continuously improve and strengthen profiles to encourage connections (LinkedIn's primary business value). As noted, relationships and the content sharing they enable are absolutely key to the progression toward engagement with your brand, product, or service.

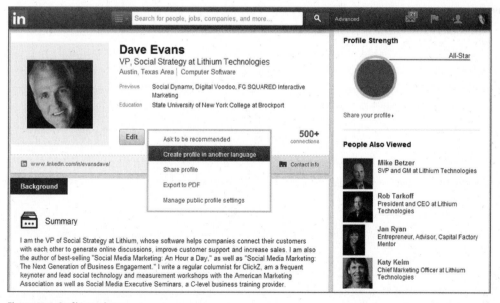

Figure 11.4 Profile completion

Make Sure Activity Is Visible

Very few want to party alone; translated, it means that building a vibrant social presence is accelerated when activity, lots of activity, is obvious. This activity takes the form of posts, comments, contribution, and connections. Facebook, for example, regularly recommends that friend requests be sent between members who are not currently friends but have a number of mutual friends within the network. If Tom knows Jane, and Jane knows Mike, maybe Tom would have common interests with Mike as well. Note that this is not always the case. More than a few ill-advised friend suggestions have occurred as a result! But don't let that stop you. The underlying point is that through the analysis of how people are connected, reasonable suggestions can be made as to who else might benefit from also being connected. Offering that bit of helpful connection advice can make a big difference in how well your community applications develop over time.

In addition to recommending friends, Facebook also uses its awareness of its members' own social graphs to encourage engagement between current friends—for example, to keep "everyone involved in the party." Facebook community managers noticed that more than a few members had, as they described it, dropped out. After an initial period of activity following their joining Facebook, the activity levels of some individuals declined to near zero.

To counter this decline in activity noted with some of its members, in 2009 Facebook introduced its reactivation program, called Reconnect, as an initiative to rekindle activity. However, rather than simply sending an email that said, "Hey, what's up? We haven't heard from you in a while," Facebook turned to the social graphs of its members.

The Reconnect initiative worked like this: First, Facebook looked for people in your social graph whom you hadn't talked to in a while. Then, it prompted you to reach out and share something with them. After some growing pains—suggesting, for example, that someone reconnect with an ex—the program effectively increased the overall member participation. With access to the social graph in the community networks that you create and a bit of programming work, you can add the same capability to your own social efforts. Figure 11.5 shows Facebook's recommended activities, including a suggested friend and a suggestion to reach out to someone.

More recently, and to the same end, Facebook added its timeline feature. By providing members with an easy way to look back and rediscover prior content, Facebook has made evergreen articles (content that has a longer than usual lifespan, for example, a post about infant care) and similar posts relatively more important in the otherwise immediate context of most social networks.

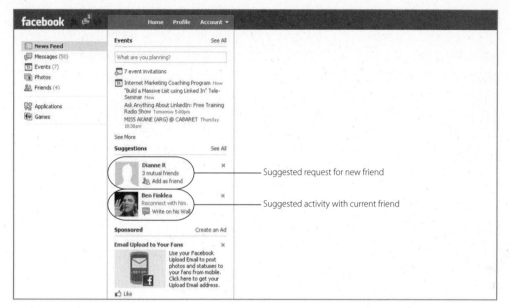

Suggested request for new friend

Suggested activity with current friend

Figure 11.5 Suggested activities

An even simpler method of encouraging relationships and participation can be borrowed from Twitter and the way it encourages profile completion: Encourage the provision of data that will help members *find each other*. Look at the profile data that has been entered across *your* social network. Pay attention to what is required and what is optional and to the information you may *not be asking for* that is common in other networks. If people are accustomed to providing specific information in other networks, they may also be willing to provide it within yours. Take the time to find out. More information is generally better when it comes to encouraging relationships.

In particular, take steps to encourage members to responsibly provide *personally identifiable information*. You'll want to clearly explain why and clearly disclose how it will be used and be sure this is reflected in your privacy policy. Likely too you'll need the underlying trust of your members. The big note here is that you are *not* doing this to share this information *directly* with others but rather to provide others who already have this information an additional, easy way to discover friends. Got that? Here's an example: If you include an option for entering an email address in the profile—and keep it private, hidden from general view—it can still be used for *member discovery* by someone who knows that (person's) email address, providing an additional (and very efficient) method of finding friends already on Twitter. Figure 11.6 shows the email and similar data that can be used to help connect people on Twitter.

Taking this one step further, by including an option for email addresses your social site—through built-in or built-on software extensions—you can look into a new member's address book *with explicitly granted permission* and then suggest automatically friending or following any discovered matches between the new member's address book entries and those of other members on your site.

For marketing purposes, having a business presence on professional networks like LinkedIn can make sense, and in fact this is now considered entry stakes for most businesses and organizations, in the same way that having a website is considered for most as a must-have. Stepping up from the basics, accessing and putting social graphs to work is the basis for more substantive business applications built on or around personal and professional networks.

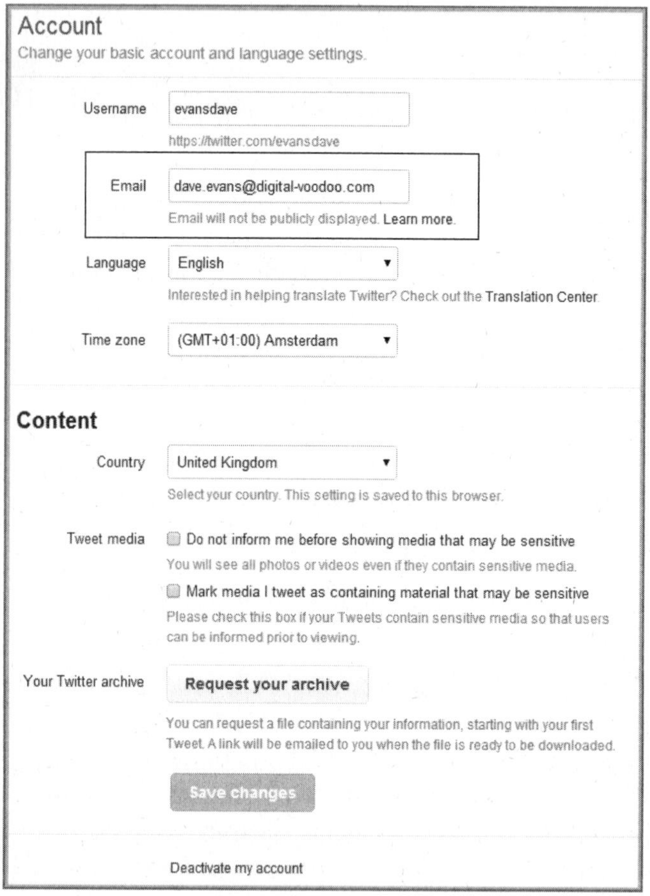

Figure 11.6 Twitter: getting found

Figure 11.7 shows an application of the LinkedIn social graph API, developed at 2020 Social in New Delhi. Using the combination of the LinkedIn display ads and the LinkedIn API, the application looks at the first-degree connections of the person exposed to the display ad in LinkedIn. If the LinkedIn member clicks the ad, the landing page then lists the names of the employees of 2020 Social *who are also first-degree connections* of the member. If you click it, you see the employees of 2020 Social that you know. Taken together, the ability to examine the LinkedIn social graph and present relevant social data (first-degree connections who are also employees of 2020 Social) creates a very powerful landing page experience and one that taps directly the value of the relationships contained in LinkedIn connections via the social graphs of its members.

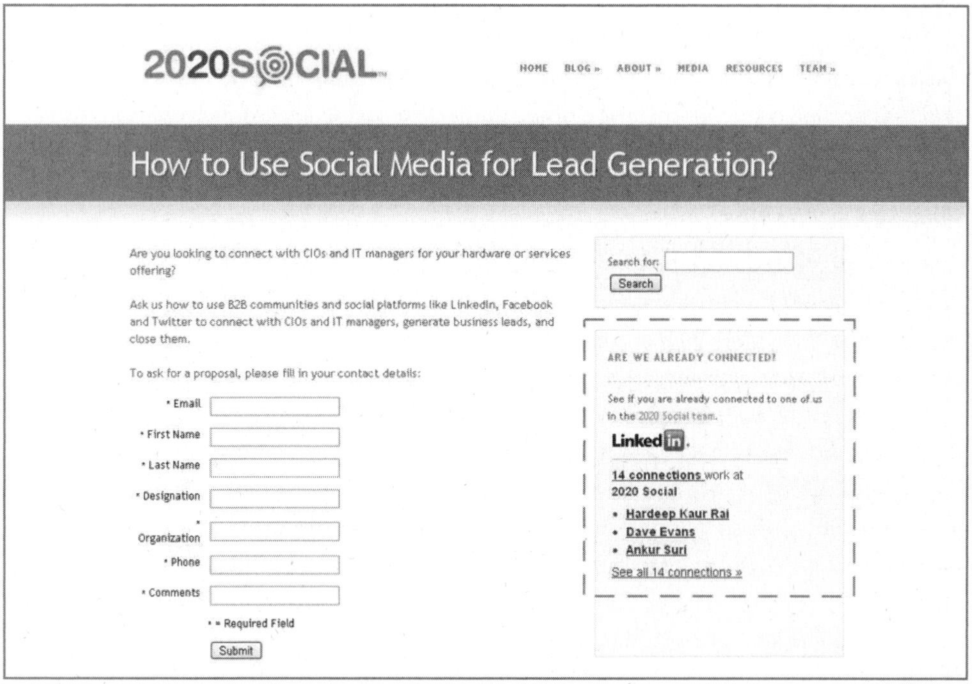

Figure 11.7 2020 Social's LinkedIn landing page

Mapping Social Networks: LinkedIn and Gephi

LinkedIn chief scientist DJ Patil walks through his own LinkedIn profile using Gephi, a visual analysis tool that you can use to look at the connection patterns and other structural details within social networks. You can follow DJ Patil on Twitter (@dpatil) and watch his video presentation here:

```
http://gephi.org/2010/dj-patil-explaining-linkedin-social-graph-
visualizations/
```

On-Domain: Community and the Social Graph

Social networks form according to a variety of primary applications—for example, for personal or cause-related activities (think Facebook, whose core appeal is for personal social interaction) or business use (as in Element14's engineer community where electrical designers review and purchase semiconductor components). Personal networks can attract large numbers of people who then engage in conversations and share purchase experiences or discuss and form groups around the interests and causes they support. Purpose-built business networks, such as Element14's or the American Express Open Forum Small Business community, have clear business applications, built around the passions and lifestyles of the member professionals who use them.

KickApps, a community platform acquired by Perfect Sense Digital in 2012, built this exact capability into their platform. Called the KickApps Social Graph Engine, the functional value is the optimization of incoming advertising according to the collective likes and dislikes of the member's friends, expressed through an individual's social graph.

Connected Communities

As a final point in the application of the social graph, consider the imminent rise of the universal social graph and its potential impact on business and cause-based organizations. While the Social Web is certainly about connecting and sharing—and to a much greater degree than websites, whether business or personal, ever were—there is still an element of one winner must emerge. What was once AOL and then Friendster, then MySpace followed by Facebook and Twitter, and then…will continue to morph.

Off in the distance lies the universal social graph—the single-location collection of your various profiles and personas. Think of personas as tuned personal profiles, sort of like your accountant (one persona) who takes to the highway on a Harley-Davidson Softail every other weekend (a different persona, related to the same underlying individual, or profile). The universal social graph approaches the challenge of maintaining multiple profiles, friend lists, and activity feeds by collecting them all around an individual and then plugging an appropriate identity into specific social applications as needed.

Of more-than-trivial consequence, the fact that most social networks require individual participants to create an entire, complete profile for use exclusively inside that specific social network actually limits cross-network participation. As a practical matter, how many profiles do you really want to maintain? This is a question that more and more social networking participants are beginning to ask, and eventually you will have to address this in the design of your social business applications.

As an alternative to the network-centric profiles of Facebook and similar networks, consider Ning, now owned by Glam Media. Ning members create a single identity and then use that as the basis for membership across the various Ning communities that they choose to join. A Ning member may be associated with one or more sports communities, a professional group, a college alumni network, and one or more lifestyle- or cause-based Ning communities. Regardless, it's the same individual who is linked in all of these.

Very important here—and a key in understanding the differences in potential implementations between a Ning-based presence versus Facebook, for example—is that Ning is not simply a single sign-on protocol applied to a collection of individual networks. Instead, Ning is an example of an approach to social networking that begins with the personal profile and then attaches that profile to the various social applications that have relevance to the individual represented by that profile. This is definitely a trend to watch because it is yet another push in the movement away from centralized social hubs and "websites-as-islands" and toward a social experience that is defined first by the identity of the participants (via the profile) and then second by the context (specific social applications) in which they participate.

The take-away from this discussion is this: As you set out and plan your social technology, consider how (and if) members of your support forum, for example, will join it and share content as appropriate outside of that network—for example, in another community where they may be advocating the use of your products for which they are (also) seeking support through your support forum. Whether through a mechanism like Facebook's Open Graph, Ning's approach of "one identity, multiple communities," or the use of OpenSocial (a social networking toolset developed by Google, MySpace, and others), you will want to make it easy for your participants to share experiences and move content across social networks just as they do within a single network. As business applications involving social technology develop further, the ability to easily traverse intersecting social graphs will gain in importance.

Review and Hands-On

Chapter 11 provided a deeper look into the social graph and the role that it plays in connecting individuals, in driving new relationships, and in spreading content. Chapter 11 drew a subtle distinction between two other nearly interchangeable terms: a *social network* (an interconnected set of people, relationships, and activities built around a common theme or platform) and the *social graph* (as defined here as a social network as represented visually or in code).

Review of the Main Points

The key points covered in Chapter 11 are summarized here. How might you incorporate these points into the design or use of the social applications you are planning for your business or organization?

- The social graph is key to the sharing of content and the spreading of shared experiences across social networks.

- The social graph can be used in business, both as an indicator of who is connected to whom and as an indicator of who might like to meet whom or where specific content should be pushed.
- There are different kinds of social graphs, including those based on interests, and also different kinds of social networks.
- The behavioral aspects of the social graph can be measured and used to monitor and tune the larger social network.

The social graph—while not as immediately obvious or as visible as shared content or the direct use of a social application—is an absolute key in developing and maintaining a vibrant social experience for the benefit of the participants in that shared experience. The role of the moderators, the design of the interaction points, and the degree to which participants can discover potentially valuable relationships are all driven by the existence and makeup of a participant's social graph(s).

Hands-On: Review These Resources

Review each of the following, and then take note of what you learn and insights you gain. How can you apply (or specify the use of) these items in your own projects and the further development of your understanding of social technology?

Facebook Open Graph plug-ins for use in social-media-based marketing: http://developers.facebook.com/plugins

Tools, papers, and resources available through membership in the INSNA and the larger discussion of social network analysis: www.insna.org/

Hands-On: Apply What You've Learned

Apply what you've learned in this chapter through the following exercises:

1. Map your first-degree network in your office, and then do the same in some personal aspect of your life, a civic organization, for example. Who is in both networks? What content is shared between these networks as a result?

2. Look at your friends in some of the social networks you belong to. How many of these friends or people you follow are people you knew prior to joining versus the number you met after joining? How were those you met after joining referred or suggested?

3. Develop a set of specific metrics for your social business applications that involve the social graph. Create a regular report, and track these measures over time.

Social Applications

*Social applications combine the attraction of
social objects, the power of the social graph,
and the natural tendency for people to gather
and converse. Because social applications connect, enable, and coordinate the interactions of
participants, they offer a straightforward way
to realize a powerful business presence on the
Social Web. This chapter wraps up Part III with
a look at how to evaluate, define, and implement successful social applications as the core of
your social customer experience effort.*

12

Chapter contents

What is a social application?
Social applications drive engagement
Plan your social customer experience platform

What Is a Social Application?

Social applications, simply, are software components that facilitate interaction between members of a social network or community. Social applications are built around social objects—lifestyles, passions, and aspirations, along with myriad talkworthy smaller objects such as short posts (tweets, for example), photos, videos, and more. Social applications are driven by the connections embodied in the individual social graphs of participants, and as such they act as efficient conduits for the spread of information within the network. Skype's member community, shown in Figure 12.1, is a nice representative of the class of social applications that connect customers for the purpose of enhancing the social customer experience.

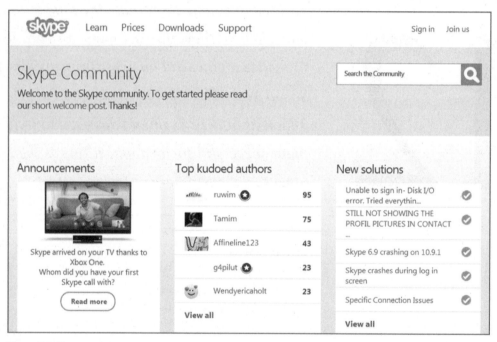

Figure 12.1 Skype member community

Throughout this chapter, the term *social application* refers to social software and embedded or installed applications within a social context that facilitate social interactions between participants within that network.

The central idea that a social application combines group interactions and capabilities "important to running your business or organization" is related to the focus of this book: the business use of social technology. Suffice it to say that if a particular social activity is not relevant to your business, it's probably not a good candidate for your social media and social business programs.

A second point to consider with regard to the effectiveness and usefulness of social applications is that they often depend on the treatment of *identity.* Recall the discussion around identity and the work of J. D. Lasica in Chapter 4, "The Social Customer Experience Ecosystem." Without identity in at least a general or contextual sense—and with the exception of specific applications that for a variety of reasons appropriately allow anonymity—sharing and collaboration are *much less* likely to occur, if they occur at all. For typical business applications of social technology, sharing and collaboration are among the primary goals. Identity—and details like profile completeness—really matter. On Facebook and Twitter, for example, there are no guarantees of claimed identity ("verified" accounts aside). However, with friends or followers in common across participants, it is fairly simple to assure yourself that users are who they say they are.

What kinds of social applications appropriately relax their identity requirements? Think about a nonprofit, for example, that might encourage participants to share stories about cancer survival, corporate noncompliance, or physical abuse: While identity (and protection of identity) is clearly important, enabling otherwise hesitant participants to take a first step by posting is also important. So, anonymous posts may be allowed with the caveat that prior to more substantive action a complete profile must be created. As well, a sporting goods company or one of its retailers may want submissions of experiences using its gear, but it may provide the option of not publishing the names of those submitting these stories. Social apps come in a variety of forms, and not all of them require that a full personal identity be provided. Of course, on the flip side, how much trust customers place in anonymous reviews or posts matters too.

How much needs to be included in order that your social application encourages participation by and among members? One way to answer this is to ask participants how much they are willing to share, taking care to explain the benefits of providing such information as well as exactly how it will be used.

What this all comes down to is the realization that the combination of *identity* and *functionality* supports high degrees of social interaction within a social application. Profile completeness and reputation management are important aspects in the design of social applications, right along with specific functional tools including those that support content uploading, friending, sharing, rating, tagging, and more. If participants don't know with whom they are sharing—or can't curate or share content easily—they are less likely to share at all, shutting down the higher levels of engagement like content creation and collaboration that are central to realizing value through the business applications of social technology.

Taken together, it's the combination of these that is important to your business or organization. Consider this within the context of a social network that involves participants and in so doing create the opportunity for highly specialized social applications that enable collaboration and content sharing. This is the overall approach that defines the successful social application in the business context.

Social Applications Drive Engagement

Examples of social applications that drive higher levels of engagement include Skype's member community (mentioned in the opening of the chapter), the use of Foursquare (a location-based social application) for location-based advertising as well as Foursquare's mayors program that rewards frequent visitors, and HP's use of Twitter as one of its many brand outposts. Twitter is itself a social network, made more useful with clever applications built on Twitter's API that facilitate business development and customer care applications: Twitter enables two-way interaction between a business and its customers (and between customer themselves). Dell's Small Business group, Comcast's customer service team, and Australian telecom firm Telstra all use Twitter as a conduit for information that connects their respective business programs with their customers. The majority of the cases and examples presented in this book have been, in some form or another, a type or instance of a social application.

Given the encompassing nature of social applications, how then does one segregate the various functions and uses of these tools for planning and design purposes? Clearly, lumping together Dell's IdeaStorm, a member community for support, and Foursquare's mayors program and saying "I want one of those" isn't likely to produce a successful outcome. What's needed is a way to categorize the various types of social applications so that they can be connected with business objectives. Business objectives, after all, drive the specification and development of social applications.

I Love You More Than My Dog

As an aside, read the book *I Love You More Than My Dog* (Portfolio Hardcover, 2009). Author Jeanne Bliss goes into detail in the processes that create amazing customer experiences. Not only are these the kinds of insights gained through collaborative social applications, but they also point out the degree that Operations and Marketing must work together to build long-term customer loyalty. You can follow Jeanne on Twitter (@jeannebliss) and read more about Jeanne and her work here:

```
http://customerbliss.com/
```

Important to note here is what is meant by a successful outcome. Josh Gordon, president of Selling 2.0, published a whitepaper in *Social Media Today* titled "The Coming Change in Social Media Business Applications: Separating the Biz from the Buzz." Josh points out the split between the use of social technology in business for branding (about 60 percent) versus *collaborative* applications (about 40 percent). While lots of businesses and organizations are using social media—recent CMO surveys have put adoption at something north of 80 percent—the majority of these uses are still rooted in a traditional approach to marketing. Given the numbers of people who collect around social sites, the appeal of marketing programs that are intended to push a message into these sites is understandable, but it misses the larger gains in engagement that come about through social applications that support content creation, sharing, and collaboration. Using social applications for *awareness* can provide a starting point, but more can be done.

For social-media-based marketing, the beneficial impacts to branding efforts, increased lead generation, and buzz are all success-oriented objectives. To be sure, however, these applications barely scratch the surface of social technology. What is of interest here—and what defines success—is the degree to which *collaboration* as a result of the implementation of social technology is achieved. The degree to which collaboration between participants is achieved is, therefore, one of the primary indicators of a successful outcome, again with the note that success is always measured within the context of the underlying business objectives.

Social Media Today

A highly recommended resource for marketers and similar business professionals interested in B2B application of social media and social technology is Social Media Today, cofounded by Jerry Bowles and Robin Carey. Social Media Today includes contributions by literally hundreds of the best social media/ B2B thinkers and practitioners.

http://socialmediatoday.com/

The take-away from the discussion around defining successful outcomes and the use of social technology is this: Social technology deployed in a business context drives higher levels of engagement (content creation and collaboration). Social applications serve as connectors between participants, as extensions of built-in social network functionality, and as crowdsourcing and content publishing tools within the communities they define or the social structures in which they are implemented. Sure, social technology can be used to drive awareness, but so can a dozen other channels. What social technology and social applications in particular are uniquely great at is driving participation—sharing, creating, and collaborating around content rooted in lifestyles, passions, and causes.

As an example of social applications driving engagement at higher levels like creation and collaboration, consider New Belgium Beer, makers of Fat Tire amber ale and other beers. The team at New Belgium laid out its business objectives:

- Engage New Belgium's existing fan base on Facebook and reach out to their friends.
- Pick up on the style, vernacular, and creative assets already used on the New Belgium website, and then reflect through the fans' voices.

- Create contests and similar engagement applications that fit the brand image and appeal to the underlying passions and interests of the fans.
- Ultimately, further grow New Belgium's Facebook fan count by attracting *true* fans, not just those looking for the next brand giveaway.

Working with Palo Alto–based Friend2Friend, they put an engagement program in place that connected New Belgium fans with the brand ethos by building around the passions and interests of those fans. *Disclosure: Dave is an advisor to Friend2Friend.*

Dave talked with Friend2Friend CEO Roger Katz about the New Belgium engagement program. When asked about the origin of the program, Roger described it like this:

New Belgium wanted to increase the number of fans on its Facebook Fan Page through entertaining social activities while staying true to the brand image. They also wanted to preferentially attract authentic New Belgium fans—real beer drinkers who enjoyed fine beer. The program team includes Backbone Media (agency of record for New Belgium) and Friend2Friend.

Dave then asked Roger about the Friend2Friend social application and what it was intended to do. Roger explained:

Friend2Friend picked up on the vernacular of the New Belgium website and created "What's Your Folly?" a contest where Facebook members can become a fan and describe their folly—their passion or interest—and thereby enter a weekly drawing for a limited edition New Belgium cruiser bike. The bicycle is also a part of the New Belgium brand ethos.

As fans read of others' follies (content consumption) and then declared their own personal follies (content creation), the interest in the contest grew, spreading through Facebook via the Friend2Friend social application. Roger added:

The resulting Folly Gallery of over 6,000 follies gives New Belgium a base of branded user-generated content to jump-start their next promotional programs.

Simply put, New Belgium's customers are, as a result, collaborating with the company and its agency to design the next round of engagement campaigns.

Now for the hard question: "What happened, and how was it measured?" Roger's response:

In a five-week period, almost 7,000 users downloaded the social application and submitted personal follies, generating over 1 million social impressions through news feeds, wall posts, and Fan Page visits. New Belgium gained 10,000 new fans. Contest participants spent an average of four minutes creating their entries and reviewing those of others.

Compared with a 30-second spot, that's a big gain in attention.

In summary, New Belgium built its engagement campaign around Facebook, using an existing social application (Friend2Friend) that was customized for this particular use. Higher levels of engagement were clearly seen, and the results were measured and successfully tied back to the original underlying business objectives.

As you look for ways to use social applications in your business, consider the specific type of applications that you can choose from. The New Belgium example of contest-driven engagement and fan recruitment is but one of the choices available to you. Following are the primary buckets into which social applications can be organized to simplify the process of creating a strategy that links your business objectives with the many types of social applications that are available or that can be built.

Social Applications Connect People

Social applications connect people. That much is obvious. It's what happens beyond the basic connection that matters, especially in business applications of social technology. Consider Twitter: It's possible—but rarely recommended—to buy followers (literally, for money). Prices run a hundred dollars, give or take, for a few thousand followers. The question is why—beyond *looking* popular—would you want to do this? We sure don't have the answer.

Why Money (Really) Can't Buy You Love

Dan Evon, senior writer for Social News Daily, offers an excellent insight into the folly of buying followers and why you may want to think twice before doing this.

    http://socialnewsdaily.com/17305/get-twitter-followers-buying-fake-
    followers-will-will/

You can follow Dan here (for free): @danieljevon.

Instead of buying followers, what generally makes more sense is to introduce into a social network the tools that make following happen naturally and spontaneously. Think back to touchpoint analysis: What is it about your brand, product, or service that makes it talkworthy? Now apply this same thinking to your social presence: What about it would make someone want to follow your brand on Twitter, join your business page on Facebook, or offer up their own ideas through an ideation application? Combining the answers to these questions with specific tools or applications that make it easy for the participants in your social application to connect will grow a stronger network than will buying one.

Facebook, Google+, Twitter, and similar social applications around the globe have functionality built into the platforms that encourages friending or recommends interaction between friends, both of which drive additional connections. A definite best practice offers an overt profile completeness indicator: A higher percentage of relatively more-complete profiles encourages more connections between social network participants. When planning and building a social application, it's a best practice to include explicit indications of profile completion—for example, indicating the current completeness level *and* advising members as to what else needs to be done to fully complete individual profiles.

> ### Twitter Marketing: An Hour a Day
>
> If you're interested in learning more about how Twitter can be applied to business, take a look at *Twitter Marketing: An Hour a Day* (Sybex, 2010) by Hollis Thomases. You can follow Hollis (@hollisthomases) on Twitter as well.

Whether you choose to create a social application of your own or join one that is already in place, the extent to which connections are *actively encouraged* and can be *efficiently managed* are important considerations. Look for tools, functions, and processes—along with the ability to build on them or modify them in ways that make it more likely that participants will create connections with each other. Not only will this result in increased use and stickiness of the community or larger social application, but it will also help participants create richer social graphs that facilitate content sharing and the general spread of ideas between people.

As you look at the ways in which you can encourage connections, consider adopting and trending specific metrics and KPIs (key performance indicators) that reflect the degree to which connections and two-way relationships are being created. These KPIs can help you evaluate the effects of connection-oriented tools that you may use, create, or add later. In addition, insisting on a focus on measurement right from the start puts your social business program on a solid base.

Social Network Extensions

When building a social network, whether from scratch or through a ready-to-use software as a service (SaaS) or proprietary platform, or instead building onto an existing social networking platform, there will be a set selection of prebuilt components and functions that you'll use to define your core participant interactions. Typical of these prebuilt functions are content ratings, member reputation, content uploading, blogging or posting, and similar functions. While these will likely cover the majority of what you'd like participants to be able to do within that application—creating a profile, friending, uploading content, and so on—there will also be a set of more specific activities driven by your business objectives that may not be immediately available. You'll have to specify and implement these features yourself.

Beyond creating a community or implementing an extension of the available functionality within a social network, how else can you use social technology to extend your own social points of presence—your blog or your website, for example? If your business objectives include expanding your presence, spreading awareness of your business or organization, or similar objectives built around visibility and participation, then one approach might be to *link* your current online content and popular presence points that are relevant to your customers or stakeholders. For example, using the Like plug-in, you can connect your website or blog content directly into Facebook. When someone visits your web page or blog and clicks the embedded Like button, that person is simultaneously (assuming this person is a member of Facebook) sharing this content with friends in Facebook. In Figure 12.2 you can see how this works: When Dave visits colleague Gaurav Mishra's blog, clicking the Like button results in a posting to Dave's wall in Facebook that his friends see, exposing them to Gaurav's posts.

Figure 12.2 Facebook's Like button

How else might you connect to a wider audience via the social graph and social applications that are built on it? Pandora uses Facebook's social graph applications to connect members who are also friends around shared interests in music: One member will be prompted to listen to a particular artist because the *friends* of this person are also listening to that artist. Whether or not this seems a bit "Big Brother-ish" is secondary (unless that aspect of these kinds of social applications directly conflicts with your brand values). What matters more is that it's becoming an acceptable way to spread content. As much as we all pride ourselves on being individuals, a lot of what we do (and therefore purchase) is driven by what we see others like ourselves doing.

Facebook Marketing: An Hour a Day

If you're interested in learning more about how you can use Facebook in business, check out the newest edition of Chris Treadaway and Mari Smith's *Facebook Marketing: An Hour a Day, Second Edition* (Sybex, 2012). You can follow Chris (@ctreada) and Mari (@marismith) on Twitter as well.

Finally, through the basic best practice of ensuring that everything you produce is easy to share, be sure to include links to the obvious: Content-sharing applications can make a big difference in the visibility of the content created by participants within your social applications. Include links to these services in everything you do and by extension to everything that is created in your applications. Be sure as well that you create your own presence, where appropriate, in existing social networks, especially if your customers or stakeholders spend time there. Known as *brand outposts,* these networks are an easy way to extend your presence into the places where your customers spend time.

In the previous examples, the firm's business objectives (being more relevant to more customers to drive more sales) and social technology strategy (being more relevant in the places where customers are already spending time) are what lead to the implementation of the respective applications. Extending the functionality of an existing social network in which you create an outpost or creating new functionality for a white-label or SaaS social application that you are building around can be an important aspect of a business or cause-related effort to both *build* (awareness) and *activate* (collaboration) customers and stakeholders.

Importantly, as you review and consider the examples presented throughout this book, do so with your own business objectives and the behaviors of your own audience in mind. Unless a specific example or social technology application was called out as something to avoid, you can assume that if it's in this book (or being talked about elsewhere on the Web) it is or was a good idea *for someone.* However, don't be led into the trap of chasing others' good ideas. Instead, link the applications you see here and elsewhere with the underlying business objectives that gave rise to them and then see if *your* business objectives (and the behaviors and capabilities of your audience) line up with them. If so, you have a potential match. If not, note the idea for possible future review (perhaps creating an entry for it on your internal "future ideas" application) and then move on.

Content Publishing and Sharing

In addition to outright social networks and the more tightly defined extensions and functional tools that enable participants to accomplish very specific goals, social applications include more generalized software services around which some form of social interaction takes place. Examples of these types of social applications include YouTube for general media sharing, along with services like Scribd, Google Docs, and SlideShare. Scribd and Google Docs, for example, both support publishing and *sharing* nearly any type of document; SlideShare is specific to—and therefore particularly good at—sharing slide presentations. SlideShare and Scribd are excellent places to publish thought-leadership content that your business or organization creates. You'll benefit from the social interaction (commenting and reviewing) and increased visibility (sharing) that these social sites provide.

YouTube offers the immediate usefulness of posting content (rather than hosting it yourself) and sharing it from that point both within YouTube and by embedding that video content elsewhere. YouTube is an ideal place to post content that is then shared through your other points of social presence (making content easier to manage, since you don't have copies floating about). YouTube also provides the built-in benefits of sharing and exposure in its own social contexts. YouTube offers branded business channels, for example, something you can use to organize and share sequences of related content.

What else can you with YouTube? A lot, as it turns out. Conduct interviews with customers and employees and then post them. Chapter 3, "Social Customer Experience Management," noted Freescale's use of YouTube for employment videos and product announcements. You can show customers using your products, offer testimonials, and provide coverage of your own presentations as a part of your outreach and thought leadership efforts. Figure 12.3 shows a video of a presentation with Intuit CEO Brad Smith, as he talks about what Intuit has learned as it embraces social technology as a business. You can find the video on YouTube by searching for its title, "User Generated Unemployment at Intuit." This video is definitely worth watching: Brad describes his firm's coming to grips with some of the very challenges that any organization implementing social technology is likely to face.

Figure 12.3 Intuit CEO Brad Smith's interview on YouTube

Using YouTube for Business

Interested in learning more on the use of YouTube in business? Following are the top three listed references. If you are looking specifically for B2B, check out the reference to the article by Meryl Evans (no relation to Dave), the third reference: It offers 34 ways that YouTube can be used as a part of a social media program in business.

http://socialmediatoday.com/sendible/1044831/8-effective-ways-use-youtube-business

http://socialmediatoday.com/shankarsoma/1613026/using-youtube-your-business

http://webworkerdaily.com/2009/07/28/34-ways-to-use-youtube-for-business/

While the benefits of sharing content through social applications like Twitter and YouTube are largely self-evident, there are additional applications for content-sharing social sites. If your business objectives include establishing a position as a thought leader or if you are looking for collaborative input around early ideas that are appropriate for sharing publicly, consider using applications like Scribd, Google Docs, and SlideShare. If you've hosted a webinar or developed a research paper around a topic of general interest, consider publishing it on these sites.

SlideShare and Scribd are particularly useful for small businesses, consultants, and anyone else regardless of the organization size or vertical specialty interested in thought leadership. Combined with a corporate blog, for example, SlideShare can be used as a sharable publishing point for past presentations as well as presentations created specifically for SlideShare to explain the use of a software service or impact a legislative debate. Figure 12.4 shows the use of Scribd in sharing the owner's manual for a Sony Ericsson mobile phone, along with a SlideShare-based presentation on healthcare, authored by Dan Roam and C. Anthony Jones, M.D. This presentation won SlideShare's World's Best Presentation of 2009 contest. It has been viewed more than 200,000 times, and it has been embedded in more than 600 other online locations.

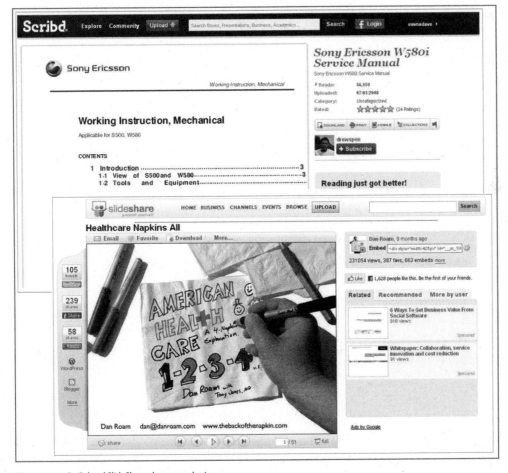

Figure 12.4 Scribd and SlideShare: document sharing

Social applications like YouTube, SlideShare, and Scribd offer simple ways to extend the reach of your existing content, and they provide a ready-for-sharing platform for your ideas, presentations, whitepapers, and similar content. YouTube, SlideShare, and Scribd support *embedding*—meaning *others* can place your presentation into *their* online site, with full credit automatically extended to you—and as such are excellent vehicles for a component of a thought leadership or similar program in addition to simply getting the word out about your brand, product, or service.

As you set out to plan and implement social applications, make note of the ways in which content-publishing sites like YouTube can be used. You don't have to reinvent content uploading, video storage, and streaming, nor do you have to build your own community to distribute thought-leadership materials. Take advantage of existing social applications like YouTube, Scribd, and SlideShare. Save your money (and time) for creating the very specific social applications—such as Aircel's Facebook-based recharge application or Penn State's Outreach platform for employee collaboration and knowledge sharing. And if you haven't already done so, develop and implement your social computing policies. Instead of reinventing what already exists, build on it and use your resources to fill in the gaps or bring unique value to your customers and stakeholders.

Curation and Reputation Management

So far, the social applications and tools covered have centered on extending the functionality of social networks, facilitating member connections within them, and using these platforms to publish and share content. In a simplified view, these applications have involved or enabled (further) content consumption, setting up the content-sharing process that leads to collaboration. The next sections cover the applications that you can use, build, or subscribe to in order to move site participants to these higher levels of engagement, to contribute their own thoughts and ideas, and to facilitate collaboration among participants and with your business.

The previously mentioned Facebook Like button is a simple implementation of a more sophisticated class of social applications that encourage curation, the basic act of voting something (or someone) up or down, rating, reviewing, and so on. For nearly any type of content, in nearly any application, one of the new realities of the Social Web is that people generally expect to be able to rate it, review it, or otherwise share it and indicate their own assessment of its worth in the process. This is a subtle but very important insight: Where not too many years ago a web page or online advertisement was largely assumed to be a one-way message, the expectation now exists for the *option* to participate. Posting an article without providing an easy way to rate it or comment on it effectively screams to your audience, "We'll talk, you'll listen."

Curation applies to social interactions—liking someone's wall post, for example—and to content itself. For these types of applications, there are as many choices for plug-ins and curation tools as there are platforms. In the general application of ratings and reviews as applied to *commerce* (the items being placed into a shopping basket), a common choice among online/offline retailers (for example, physical retailers with an online presence) is Bazaarvoice, and for good reason. Not only does Bazaarvoice offer a proven, easy-to-implement platform, they also provide a rich set of metrics that help their customers tune their online and offline commerce programs. In June 2010, Bazaarvoice introduced SocialConnect, a platform capability that integrates customers' comments between social networks like Facebook and the brand's own websites. SocialConnect supports the Facebook Like functionality as well, all of which adds up to enhanced engagement, potential gains in sales, and importantly a reduction in product returns. Best of all, it's measurable.

Ratings and Reviews Made Easy

If you'd like to add ratings and reviews to your commerce site, Bazaarvoice and Lithium offer components that can be used stand-alone and/or integrated within a community application.

www.bazaarvoice.com

www.lithium.com

If your business objectives call for adding ratings and reviews to a non-commerce site (a thought leadership blog, for example), look in particular at the ready-to-use components from providers like JS-Kit/Echo and Disqus.

http://aboutecho.com

http://disqus.com

Social technology providers offer plug-in modules for use in almost any application, as well as specific components for use with DIY favorites including WordPress, ExpressionEngine, Drupal, Joomla, and other social software platforms. For nearly any online social platform, there is an associated curation solution. If the platform you are using does not support curation (again, most do), strongly consider moving to one that does.

Absent the ability to curate, the progression to higher forms of engagement is effectively stopped. In nearly any act of sharing, for example, there is at least an implied sense of rating: "If I didn't think some particular piece of content was worth your time, then I would not have shared it with you." Beyond the polar share/don't share as a surrogate for curation, more finely grained ratings and reviews, testimonials, and other forms of direct, overt curation provide participants in social business applications with a direct pathway to collaboration. Providing the ability for customers and stakeholders to publicly comment and share opinions is essential in drawing people into your social applications and thereby moving participants ultimately toward collaborative involvement in your business or organization.

Crowdsourcing

Covered in Chapter 7, "Five Key Trends," crowdsourcing is a social activity that directly drives collaboration. Like ideation, presented separately in the next section, crowdsourcing not only makes everyone a participant but does so in a way that provides public credit for this participation. In doing so, crowdsourcing *encourages future participation* and builds stickiness with regard to that social application.

That crowdsourcing applications have the ability to grow and develop an audience over time is a significant plus. Crowdsourcing applications can be used as a part of a larger social business program not only to pull participants in but also to keep them involved over the longer term. This is especially helpful when your objectives include both the need to solve a problem or challenge that is suitable for crowdsourcing and to simultaneously build and sustain a community or similar social structure in the context of your business.

In business applications, crowdsourcing often takes the basic form of publicly asking for ideas or suggestions against a specific business objective. Building on consumption and curation, crowdsourcing is a viable method for accomplishing specific types of tasks that *appropriately* involve your customers or stakeholders. The development of confidential or proprietary processes, for example, is clearly an internal matter, so in these cases consider an internal crowdsourcing application: Dell's EmployeeStorm and Ford's use of the Covisint ideation and collaboration platform across its supplier network are solid examples.

Directly involving customers, stakeholders, potential customers, and others in appropriate collaborative activities conveys to these participants a sense of ownership and control—a stake in the brand, so to speak—that is not possible in a read-only context. Not only does crowdsourcing offer the potential of better outcomes—as defined by those who *participate* in such programs—but it also further moves these same participants up the engagement ladder, ultimately toward brand advocacy.

From Crowdsourcing to Ideation

Building on the general idea of crowdsourcing, social applications aimed at ideation can help your organization innovate faster by tapping into the ideas of your customers. Lithium offers the following resource on best practices for ideation and its use in business:

www.slideshare.net/LithiumTech/best-practices-ideation

Ideation

Ideation is a derivative of crowdsourcing built around generating, organizing, and applying fresh ideas to a specific set of business or organizational challenges. Unlike the promotion-oriented applications of social technology, ideation is often oriented toward operations and product development, where insights into process and product improvement can be translated through action into improved customer experiences.

Ideation platforms are a powerful class of social applications that lend themselves to both business management (again, for process, product, or service innovation) and the quantitative assessment of outcomes. Customer-driven ideation—the specific practice of pulling customers into the business-design process—is important on at least two fronts. First, as noted it is a source of innovation and competitive differentiation. When you've been making the same thing for years and years, certain established practices begin to shape every decision. Getting fresh eyes—and in particular the eyes of the people buying your product or service—applied to rethinking these accepted processes can be really beneficial.

Second, by opening up at least part of the responsibility for collective thinking outside of the current thought leaders, the entire pool of ideas is expanded, driving not only product and service-level change but also process change. Along with better things come better ways to make those things. These are exactly the results noted by Starbucks, Dell, German coffee retailer Tchibo, and Intuit's Small Business community, all of whom are using the ideation platforms as ways to improve their respective businesses by forging collaborative relationships with their customers.

What really makes an ideation platform work is not the idea solicitation per se. After all, how many people really believe that anything actually happens as a result of an anonymous note dropped in a suggestion box? The problem with the classic suggestion box—anonymous or not—is that the suggestion *acceptance* process and any actual outcomes are not visible to the person making the suggestion. In other words, there is a lack of transparency, a lack of accountability (on both sides), and therefore a lack of significance. "Why bother?" is the most common response, and the opportunity to gather real feedback is lost.

By comparison, on-domain ideation platforms—communities that you create for the purpose of gathering customer feedback and ideas that drive innovation—bring transparency and accountability to the suggestion and feedback processes. Ideas are publicly submitted where they are visible to everyone (content creation and consumption). Next, they are voted up or down by participants at large (curation). Finally, the business stakeholders—a product manager, for example—selects from the highest ranked items and offers various versions for implementation, *which are then reviewed again by the participant community* (collaboration). The resulting innovations become additional bonding points for customers as credit is given back to them. The entire process is visible, and the outcome—the actual disposition of any given suggestion—is clear to everyone.

Note that ideation comes in many forms. In addition to large-scale ideation platforms, small groups of personally invited participants can be very effective. As an example, consider the specifically invited LEGO fans who helped influence the design of LEGO Mindstorms or impromptu feedback sessions with larger groups as a part of existing industry events. Ideation, while it is the formal name given to this new-style transparent suggestion process, does not itself have to be formal.

The result of extreme transparency around ideation and innovation, combined with a clear process that steps through the engagement ladder—consumption, curation, creation, collaboration—is that rough ideas are readily provided and turned into solid product and service enhancements with credit flowing right back to customers. *That is a powerful loop.* Check out the My Starbucks Idea site or even better visit a store and look for "Inspired by You" No-Splash sticks or reusable Via cups or the recycling program piloted in the Seattle market or Dave's favorite—one-click Wi-Fi—and see for yourself how the brand is reconnecting itself with its customers by listening and implementing the ideas they gain as a result.

In addition to the benefits of new ideas, there's also the practical reality of customers being *less likely* to complain when their own ideas are put into practice, something that extends beyond the idea itself. Because they see their own ideas reflected in the brand (or, equivalently, other ideas from the ideation community to which they belong), actual credit is bestowed on these individuals and/or the community groups that drove the innovations.

Finally, when customers are also collaborators in the brand, product, or service, they are more likely to recommend it and defend it. They have ownership for the innovation, and they act accordingly. As they take "ownership" of the brand, instead of complaining they join *with* the brand and go to work on making their own experience better. See the sidebar "Building Competitive Advantage" for more on how ideation combined with touchpoint analysis can be used to drive competitive wins.

Building Competitive Advantage

Tapping Social Web conversations can lead to an understanding of the places where your customers—or those of your competitors—feel shortchanged. Combining this information with touchpoint analysis can lead to insights into building long-term competitive advantage, or as Dr. Natalie Petouhoff put it in her Forrester Research report, "Businesses that understand and execute on the competitive potential of technology to innovate customer experiences can easily blow away their competition." For more, you can follow Natalie on Twitter (@drnatalie) and read her blog here:

www.drnatalienews.com

Support Communities

If ideation is the fresh-thinking business application built around the practice of crowdsourcing that delivers ideas into business and organizations, then support communities—again, these are social applications—are the analogous tools that deliver needed information and solutions back to customers, based on the combined principles of crowdsourcing and direct customer empowerment.

Customers are often experts—at least as regards their use of a product or service—and as such are in collective possession of a sizeable body of knowledge. Properly applied, this collective body of knowledge can radically change their support and service experiences as customers. The problem is that this knowledge is largely unstructured, and it's distributed in ways that make actual bits of knowledge hard to spot when they are really needed.

Enter the support forum: Organized by topic and driven by the allure of brand support and the elevation in personal status (a form of social capital) for providing correct answers—in public, to other customers—support forums make it easy for customers to tap the larger collective, to self-serve and quickly solve their own problems. Customers can subscribe (typically via RSS) to specific topics—mobile applications or service issues for their particular laptop or TV set—and ask questions and/or offer answers as they are so moved. Over time, that extensive body of knowledge contained in the minds of customers is expressed in the support forum discussions where it is curated ("this solution works/this solution doesn't"), organized, and made available to customers seeking this information.

Participant-driven support forums provide the possibility of both improved service and the actual determination of ROI. Service may be improved, for example, because the support forum is available 24x7, including all day on gift-giving holidays when the need for support typically spikes, and because the larger body of participants will often have more answers for more issues. Customers themselves often possess a deep body of collective knowledge about how to fix, extend, or simply get more out of the products and services they buy—think about social applications like Skype's Customer Community, HP's Customer Support Forums, or LEGO's Mindstorms Community, where enthusiasts hack the internal control programs and publish their findings for use by the larger Mindstorms community. Each of these applications directly empowers users to get more out of the products and services offered by the respective firms: Support forums are now central to the redefined, collaborative customer experience of leading brands.

What about ROI? Support calls have a known cost. Support incidents that are fully resolved in a support forum represent a call-center cost *avoided*, leading directly to formal ROI measures and standards to which even the CFO will give two thumbs up.

Plan Your Social Customer Experience Platform

Active, participative engagement means that your customers and stakeholders are buying into your business or organization in ways that transcend any actual purchase or transaction. They are aligning around values—established, perhaps, through advertising but then proven through social applications like The Good Guide and Barclay's Your Bank ideation forum, part of Barclay's overall social technology program referenced in Chapter 2, "The Social Customer." In addition, your customers are offering their contributions freely as to how your brand, product, or service can evolve beyond the satisfaction of basic needs and wants and further align with their personal values, passions, and causes.

Closing the loop, the higher levels of engagement possible through social applications can be tapped as drivers of your business objectives. (If not, what's the point of any of this?) What's required is a planning methodology that at once recognizes the connection between business objectives, customer or stakeholder desires and behaviors, and the cross-functional nature of your internal collaborative teams to whom the task of delivering talk-worthy experiences will fall.

The Planning Process

The planning process leading to the successful deployment of a social application necessarily begins with business objectives. Along with them, it defines acts in service of customer and stakeholder behaviors. The planning process uses these same factors to shape the *organizational preparations* that precede the implementation of a social business effort.

Social Technology Implies Change Management

Caveat: This book is focused on the application of social technologies in the support of business objectives. As such, the viewpoint is decidedly "external" to the firm or organization. Recognize that more advanced applications of social technology in business will often require significant attention and organizational change with regard to internal processes that may exist. The short discussions of "workplace collaboration" and references throughout the book to Enterprise 2.0 and internal collaboration are intended to provide an entry point for your further study of this critical aspect of social business.

Beginning with social-media-based *marketing*—for U.S. brands in particular, typically the use of Twitter and Facebook as outbound channels, for example, or the implementation of a corporate blog and similar outreach activities—the required tools and skills can all be managed to great effect solely within the Marketing and Communications departments of nearly any organization. Social applications—and the *collaborative* processes associated with the higher forms of engagement—require a more developed strategy for customer involvement, and as a result an elevated response capability, and in general an organization that is able to act *holistically* rather than along functional lines (aka, silos).

If This Seems Difficult...

...it's because it is. Where creating and managing a basic social presence requires deciding how and where you'll participate, implementing social technology in your business can force efforts up to and including rebuilding your entire business. Articulating perfectly why social technology is becoming an imperative, Gartner's Michael Maoz put it this way: "It is more difficult to build a business case based on community participation, satisfaction, and loyalty metrics than on efficiency metrics, but loyalty and satisfaction are what drive revenue growth." For more from Gartner, follow Gartner on Twitter (@gartner_inc) or see the Gartner site here:

www.gartner.com

This does not, however, mean that massive organizational change is required to make effective use of social applications. What it does mean is that you need to pay specific attention to the portions of the planning process shown in Figure 12.5, wherein your larger working teams are defined. Simply put, when customers begin talking to you, you need to be ready to respond. Among other things, this will directly raise implementation decisions as to how to best use an agency or other intermediary as a blogging or response partner. Customers expect a timely, genuine response, and one way or another you'll need to staff for that.

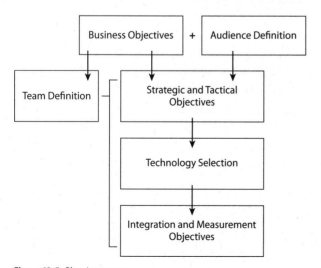

Figure 12.5 Planning process

Business Objectives and Audience Definition

The application of social technology is best anchored in business objectives, for several reasons:

- Throughout your firm or organization, while people may not agree on the virtues of social media and collaborative technology applied in business, they do agree on business objectives. If not, you have larger challenges that need to be addressed prior to implementing social technology. If you've ever witnessed a family feud in a restaurant, you have a good idea of what a business that doesn't know why it's in business looks like on the Social Web.

- By tying to business objectives, the likelihood is far greater that any social technology implementation will produce measurable, beneficial results. Experiments are fine—but then call them that and tie them to a business objective like "being seen by customers as innovative." Identifying an objective like the one in this example isn't a trick—it's a *start* down the best-practices pathway of *always* tying to business objectives.

- Understanding your business objectives and organizing your social technology planning process around them ensures that your approach is "business challenge and expected contribution first, choice of technology second." Note that this bullet item has an ROI of its own. If you doubt it, add up the costs in your own organization of technology implementations that failed because the chosen technology never matched the business. Cost avoidance—in this case, not making that mistake with social technology—has a knowable and legitimate ROI.

On this last point, in the 12 chapters of this book there have been references to a large number of technology platforms, partners, and solution options, all of which do basically the same thing: They support the development of conversations and ultimately encourage collaboration between participants in a defined network that is important to your business. Starting with business objectives ensures that you will correctly identify the technology *best suited* to your specific situation. When it comes to social technology, given all of the unknowns, there is one thing that is certain: You have lots of choices.

Right along with business objectives, consider next the participants (or lack thereof) that you expect to interact with or learn from. While the use of ratings and reviews is nearly a given across *all* age groups in nearly all global markets, this is not always the case, particularly in markets where technology adoption itself has a pronounced age factor. In India, for example, while there is a very important (and large) component of the marketplace that *is using social media* in substantially the same way as any other marketplace, the difference between those connected and those *not* connected to the Social Web is significant and therefore must be considered. When Godrej (a respected Indian manufacturer of a wide range of consumer goods) announced its plans for its online community called GoJiyo (meaning "Go Live"), Godrej patriarch Adi Godrej described the effort at a conference Dave spoke at in Bangalore as being intended to *reconnect* Godrej with the emerging Indian youth culture. The insight is this: Godrej has a much larger marketing effort supporting its entire marketplace. GoJiyo is *one component*, tied to a specific business objective and created for a specific (and growing) customer segment. That is smart thinking at Godrej, and it's the right approach anywhere.

Internal Readiness: Workflow and Your Response Plan

Coincident with your external social technology plan, begin early the process of identifying and recruiting colleagues across business units for the development of your cross-functional social technology team. Need help getting started? Go back to the identified business objectives: Who has profit responsibility associated with those objectives? Those are good people to start with. Add representatives from your legal team. They can help you create effective social media policies that are consistent with the culture of your firm or organization. HR and Finance/Compliance are part of this too: Sarbanes-Oxley, in the United States, and the unfettered employee use of social technology—including by employees when *outside* the workplace—can be a troublesome mix, to say the least. Customer Support is as well a great potential partner in your social technology planning process.

Workflow is an important factor in your implementation, so look for intelligence tools (for example, social media listening and analytics platforms) that offer robust workflow support, including automated prioritization, routing, and tracking. If this sounds more like a call-center requirement than it does listening features, that's not an accident: robust engagement requires the same attention to workflow and productivity measures as do call centers. Refer back to the flowchart (see Chapter 1, "Social Media and Customer Engagement") developed by the U.S. Air Force for systematizing your response efforts. In particular, consider who will actually respond, and create estimates for the amount of time a response to a tweet or blog post will require and then build this into your cost and effort plan for the upcoming period. Attention to details like this will pay huge dividends as you ramp up collaborative social media programs.

Social Web Presence

With your business objectives and audience(s) defined and a thought-through plan for how you'll manage conversations directly involving customers and stakeholders—for example, responding to tweets, managing and participating in comments on your blog, or keeping a Facebook business page updated—you can complete a basic specification for the kinds of activities you'd like to engage in.

Listening is always a great starting point (see Chapter 6, "Social Analytics, Measurement, and Business Decisions" and Chapter 7, "Five Key Trends"), especially for inputs to your planning process. You can estimate the workload associated with your response efforts by studying what is being said about your brand, product, or service in current social channels. Add to this your basic outreach channels—a business presence on Facebook, Google+, Twitter, YouTube, or LinkedIn—and then ask the bigger question: Given your business objectives, audience, and current social media programs, what needs to happen to move customers and stakeholders to higher levels of engagement, and what is it that you specifically want to accomplish as a result?

The higher forms of engagement—content creation and collaboration—are essential elements of contemporary marketing. Business objectives relating to the development of brand ambassadors and advocates, enhancing the value proposition of your product or service, inspiring and guiding innovation, and the improvement of brand image are parts of this planning process. Comcast uses Twitter not only to address its critics' negative posts about the firm's perceived lack of visible care for its customers but also to call attention to its own positive adoption of social technology and improved response capability in a public forum so that (offsetting) credit rightly flows to the brand as it works to build value in the eyes of its customers.

Initiate Your Plan

Once you've defined your goals and identified your audience, you can look at what applications make sense. Table 12.1 connects the broad classes of social applications to common objectives for social media in business.

▶ **Table 12.1** Social applications and tactical objectives

Social Application	Tactical Objective
Listening	Customer insights, influencer identification
Publishing and sharing	Knowledge creation, capture, and propagation
Facebook updates	Delivery of brand content, marketing announcements
Questions and answers	Rapid delivery of answers, engagement with employees and experts
Ideation	Collaborative innovation, improvement of existing products and services
Discussions and forums	Development of brand advocacy and sustained engagement

In selecting applications, think about which applications your customers might want and use. If you're considering an application on a social network, the first question is how many of your customers use that social network? A good conservative proxy might be the number of people who have liked your brand page. If you are considering an application for your community, how many people have joined your community to date? How many participate on a daily, weekly, or monthly basis?

If your community is small or new, you might consider general applications like forums and blogs, which can be used for many purposes, providing flexibility as you build your social customer experience platform. If you have an in-place community that is larger or more mature, you might consider specialized applications, for example, an ideation app. These specialized applications are optimized for one purpose—sharing ideas, for example—that not all people want to pursue.

Adding new features to an existing platform works the same way. A general feature like ratings or comments can be used for many purposes. When a user gives something a positive rating, it can mean a wide range of things, including "I like this content," "I like this user," "I found this funny," "I found this relevant," "I share this problem/opinion." By comparison, adding tagging, that is, enabling your customers to finely label and curate content, is more single-purpose—and therefore fewer of your customers will use it. Unless you expect thousands of customers to be using your community every day, it's best to start with general applications and then work into the specialized applications as your social customer experience program takes hold.

Building on the basic planning process, and with your internal workflow and response programs defined, the first step up from social media marketing—toward the higher levels of customer engagement like content creation and collaboration—depends on connecting your online presence socially into the communities and social activities of your customers and stakeholders. If you've taken—or are ready to take—the relatively hard steps of preparing your internal operations for the collaborative involvement of your customers, suppliers, partners, and stakeholders, you'll find that implementing and thereby benefiting from social tools is relatively easy by comparison.

Review and Hands-On

This chapter tied together the concepts of higher-level forms of engagement—content creation and collaboration for the purpose of driving advocacy—with the basic best practices around the use of social objects and the social graph. The discussion of social applications centered on enabling the kinds of activities that lead to conversation, new ideas, and innovations and provided suggestions to guide your continuous improvement programs.

Review of the Main Points

Review the main points covered in Chapter 12, listed here. Consider these as you begin to develop your overall plan for the integration of social technology in your business or organization.

- Social applications tie social objects and social graphs together. Simply put, people connect with other people around the things that interest them in order to accomplish tasks that improve their lives.
- Internal readiness—the capability to respond and to address business challenges holistically rather than functionally—is an element of your social technology implementation effort.
- Social technology begins with business objectives. Don't let the technology guide your implementation, but instead let your objectives guide the technology selection.

In summary, unless you are ready to tackle Enterprise 2.0 (or you are working in an organization that is already doing this), the starting point in applying social technology to business is *connecting your customers and stakeholders through collaborative processes* that link business objectives with the higher levels of engagement. You can speed this process within your own functional area with the assistance of informal cross-functional teams. Take the time to build support in other parts of your business, and you'll find the entire process significantly easier.

The typical starting point—after the implementation of a listening program— is generally connecting your business presence into the existing social spaces where customers spend time, setting up an effective listen-understand-respond process. This is followed by the implementation—as driven by your business objectives—of collaborative tools such as support and ideation platforms to drive a basic business norm of Listen, Understand, Evolve.

Hands-On: Review These Resources

Review each of the following, and then take note of what you've learned or gained insight into. How can you apply (or specify the use of) these items in your own projects?

- Visit the tutorials* and resource pages for the APIs and social plug-ins associated with Facebook, MySpace, Twitter, Foursquare, and similar platforms. Gain an understanding of the intended uses of each, and then look at the examples of how they have been used to create differentiated social technology solutions.

- Visit the websites of Jive Software, Lithium Technologies, GetSatisfaction, Microsoft SharePoint, Lotus Connections, Socialcast, and Socialtext. Gain an understanding of the intended uses of each, and then look at the examples of how they have been used to create branded social applications.

- Visit SlideShare and search for presentations on "Social Applications." You'll find great resources for almost any type of business.

  www.slideshare.com

Hands-On: Apply What You've Learned

Apply what you've learned in this chapter through the following exercises:

1. Articulate your business objectives, and define your audience.

2. Given the discussion of social applications, develop an idea for a social application that serves your business objectives and fits with your audience behaviors. Write a complete brief around its deployment. Include within this your development efforts supporting a cross-functional internal team.

3. Tie this plan to your existing marketing and business efforts and to your accepted business metrics. Define your guiding KPIs and if appropriate the basis for establishing ROI.

---

*If you are not a programmer, read the summaries and cases associated with each. The objective here is to obtain ideas on how these services and tools might be used.

IV Appendixes

The appendixes include definitions of key terms, lists of resources, and a summary of the hands-on material presented in the book.

Appendix A: **Terms and Definitions**

Appendix B: **Thought Leaders**

Appendix C: **Hands-On Exercises**

Note: You will find copies—including updates—as well as printable (PDF) versions of the appendixes at www.ReadThis.com.

Terms and Definitions

In any sufficiently precise study—and the application of social technology is certainly no exception—the need arises for specific terms that enable concepts to be translated into actions. The definitions of many of the terms that are core to social technology are still evolving; however, within this book the following have been adopted and used consistently. More important than agreement on specific terms—at a general level some of these are nearly interchangeable—is understanding the meaning of the following terms and then applying these meanings as you develop your social technology and business programs. This appendix presents the key definitions used in this book, in the order in which they build on each other.

Appendix Contents
Social Object
Social Application
Social Graph
Social Network
Social CRM and Social Customer Experience

Social Object

Definition: A Social Object *is some "thing" we* share *with others as part of our social media experience on the Social Web.*

Glenn Assheton-Smith, 2009

What It Means and Why It Matters

A *social object* is something that is inherently talkworthy, something around which people naturally congregate and converse. Social objects are an essential element in the implementation of social technology: Social objects are the anchor points for these efforts and as such are the magnets that hold a community together.

While it may seem like so much semantics, when viewed in the context of the way in which people are connected or to whom they are connected, the social object provides the underlying rationale or motive for being connected at all. In short, without the social object, there is no social.

Social Application

Social applications are software components that facilitate interaction between members of a social network or community. Social applications are built around social objects—lifestyles, passions, and aspirations, along with myriad talkworthy smaller objects such as short posts (tweets, for example), photos, videos, and more. Social applications are driven by the connections embodied in the individual social graphs of participants, and as such they act as efficient conduits for the spread of information within the network.

What It Means and Why It Matters

The term *social application* refers to the specific tools or functions available to participants in a social network—that is, the tools and functions that allow those participants to perform specific social tasks such as friending, connecting, sharing, and similar. In this sense, it's the social application that allows social activity to happen in a distributed (for example, virtual or online) context. In real life, the social application is the living room sofa, where conversation is facilitated, or the postal system, through which party invitations and RSVPs are exchanged. In online communities, this same type of social exchange is facilitated through software.

Social Graph

Definition: The Social Graph *is the representation of our relationships. In present day context, these graphs define our personal, family, or business communities on social networking websites.*

Jeremiah Owyang, 2007

What It Means and Why It Matters

The term *social graph* refers to the relationships between members of a social network and the details around the ways in which those members are connected. The social graph of an individual may extend beyond a single network, in which case this individual forms a link between adjacent networks.

The social graph is important in business applications. By understanding the ways in which participants in a social network are connected, you can predict how information will be transmitted through that network, and therefore the social graph forms the basis for optimizing business participation in social networks.

Social Network

A social network *is a social structure made up of individuals (or organizations) which are tied (connected) by one or more specific types of interdependency, such as friendship, kinship, common interest, financial exchange, dislike, sexual relationships, or relationships of beliefs, knowledge, or prestige.*

Wikipedia

What It Means and Why It Matters

The term *social network* refers to the collective facility—to Facebook or Orkut or the Intel Developer's Network and everyone contained within it.

In this sense, the term *social network* is a noun: It refers to a *place* (however virtual it may be) where social interactions—aka *social networking*—occurs.

Social CRM and Social Customer Experience

Consider this excerpt from Paul Greenberg's definition of social CRM, presented in Chapter 9, "Social CRM and Social Customer Experience":

Social CRM *is the company's response to the customer's control of the conversation.*

Paul Greenberg, 2009

Paul gets right to the heart of the matter: SCRM, and now SCE, is about how you choose to respond, how you choose to participate, given the customer's control—whether in whole or in part—of the conversation.

What It Means and Why It Matters

The idea of "your response given the customer's control" matters because you can't truly achieve SCE without meaningfully integrating your social technologies with your company's CRM effort.

This in turn means that SCE is a better conceptual framework for your efforts than social CRM alone. It recognizes that the end of your efforts is not a new platform or system but rather a new kind of *customer experience*, where customers are truly seen as central to your business.

Thought Leaders

B

The following people—listed alphabetically—are noted within the book and are collected here to provide a convenient reference to their ongoing work and thinking. Take the time to check them out: Consider following them on Twitter and subscribing to their blogs and podcasts.

Susan Abbott

President and senior consultant and researcher at Abbott Research, Susan Abbott helps clients discover insights and develop response strategies that support their business. You can follow Susan on Twitter (@SusanAbbott) and read her blog here:

www.customercrossroads.com/customercrossroads/

Glenn Assheton-Smith

Glenn Assheton-Smith describes himself as very curious. That alone makes his work worth reading: He has an excellent set of blog posts on applying social media to business and in particular to the media and journalism. You can follow Glenn on Twitter (@GlennAssh), and do read the set of posts he has created, beginning here:

http://glennas.wordpress.com

Rohit Bhargava

Rohit Bhargava is a consumer behavior expert and is the author of *Likeonomics* (Wiley, 2012) and *Personality Not Included* (McGraw-Hill, 2008). Rohit blogs actively and also teaches marketing at Georgetown University. You can follow Rohit on Twitter (@rohitbhargava) and read his blog here:

www.rohitbhargava.com

Jeanne Bliss

Author Jeanne Bliss (*I Love You More Than My Dog*, Portfolio Hardcover, 2009) is passionate about the processes that create amazing customer experiences. You can follow Jeanne on Twitter (@jeannebliss) and read more about Jeanne and her work here:

http://customerbliss.com/

Krishna De

Dublin, Ireland–based Krishna De blogs about social media and its application in business. You can follow Krishna on Twitter (@krishnade) and read more about Krishna and her work here:

http://krishnade.com/blog2/

Jyri Engeström

Sociologist, Jaiku cofounder, and now Google product manager, Jyri Engeström coined the term *social object* as a label for the things that people socialize around. You can follow Jyri on Twitter (@jyri) and read his blog here:

www.zengestrom.com/blog

Gautam Ghosh

Gautam Ghosh works for Philips India and has a passion for internal collaboration and knowledge management. You can follow Gautam on Twitter (@gautamghosh) and read his blog here:

http://gauteg.blogspot.in/

Nathan Gilliatt

Nathan Gilliatt, principal, Social Target, provides thinking and services supporting the implementation of active listening and business strategy. You can follow Nathan on Twitter (@gilliat) and read Nathan's blog here:

http://net-savvy.com/executive/

Paul Greenberg

Paul Greenberg is a recognized thought leader in Social CRM and the application of social technology in business. You can follow Paul on Twitter (@pgreenbe) and read more from Paul here:

http://the56group.typepad.com/

Rachel Happe and Jim Storer

Rachel Happe and Jim Storer are behind The Community Roundtable, a great resource for community managers. You can follow them on Twitter (@rhappe and @jimstorer), and read more about their work here:

www.communityroundtable.com/blog/

Jeff Jarvis

Well known partly for his work involving Dell, Jeff Jarvis is a recognized leader in the application of social technology in business and customer service. You can follow Jeff on Twitter (@jeffjarvis) and read his blog here:

www.buzzmachine.com/

Avinash Kaushik

Avinash Kaushik is the author of *Web Analytics: An Hour a Day* (Sybex, 2007) and *Web Analytics 2.0* (Wiley, 2009). Avinash publishes the blog Occam's Razor. You can follow Avinash on Twitter (@avinashkaushik) and read his blog here:

www.kaushik.net/

Peter Kim

Peter Kim works with Austin's Dachis Group. Formerly with Forrester Research, Peter focuses on social technology and its impact on business. You can follow Peter on Twitter (@peterkim) and read his blog here:

www.beingpeterkim.com/

Esteban Kolsky

Esteban Kolsky is a social strategist focused on the application of social technology to business. You can follow Esteban on Twitter (@ekolsky) and read his blog here:

www.estebankolsky.com/

J. D. Lasica

Writer J. D. Lasica offers his views on social technology, cloud computing, and more. You can follow him on Twitter (@jdlasica) and read his blog here:

www.socialmedia.biz

Brent Leary

Brent Leary is cofounder and partner of CRM Essentials LLC, a CRM consulting/advisory firm focused on small and midsize enterprises. You can follow Brent on Twitter (@BrentLeary) and read his blog here:

http://BrentLeary.com

Frank Leistner

Based in Zürich, Frank Leistner is the author of *Mastering Organizational Knowledge Flow* (Wiley, 2010). He is passionate about the flow of knowledge in large organizations. You can follow Frank on Twitter (@kmjuggler).

Charlene Li

Charlene Li is the author of *Open Leadership* and coauthor of *Groundswell*; she is the founder of Altimeter Group and a former analyst with Forrester Research. You can follow Charlene on Twitter (@charleneli) and read her blog here:

    www.charleneli.com/blog/

Ross Mayfield

Ross Mayfield is the founder of Socialtext. You can follow Ross on Twitter (@ross) and read his blog here:

    http://ross.typepad.com/

Gaurav Mishra

Gaurav Mishra is founder and CEO of FutureCrafting, based in Shanghai. Gaurav is now focused on the application of personal and social technology for wellness. You can follow Gaurav on Twitter (@Gauravonomics) and read more from him at his blog here:

    www.gauravonomics.com

Kate Niederhoffer

Dachis Group principal Kate Niederhoffer offers her perspective on social technology and its measurement. You can follow Kate on Twitter (@katenieder) and read her blog here:

    http://socialabacus.blogspot.com/

Nick O'Neill

Writer and industry analyst Nick O'Neill publishes a collection of reviews and commentary on a variety of social media topics including the use of analytics. You can follow Social Times on Twitter (@allnick), and you'll find the Nick's online commentary here:

    http://nickoneill.com

Jeremiah Owyang

Jeremiah Owyang is a recognized expert in the tools, technologies, and techniques that are essential when applying social concepts to business. You can follow Jeremiah on Twitter (@jowyang) and read his blog and learn about his new firm Crowd Companies here:

    www.web-strategist.com/blog/

    http://crowdcompanies.com/

K. D. Paine

Tired of hearing "The problem with social media is that you can't measure it"? Encourage people within your organization to look at K. D. Paine. You can follow her on Twitter (@kdpaine) and read more from her here:

www.painepublishing.com/what-we-do/

DJ Patil

DJ Patil, vice president of Product at RelateIQ, was formerly the chief scientist at LinkedIn. You can follow DJ on Twitter (@dpatil), where he often references topics and concepts related to the social graph.

Dr. Natalie Petouhoff

Consultant and speaker Dr. Natalie Petouhoff offers her views on the potential of social technology applied to business. You can follow Natalie on Twitter (@drnatalie) and read her blog here:

www.drnatalienews.com

Kaushal Sarda

Kaushal Sarda is the CEO of the enterprise applications and products firm Kuliza, based in Bangalore. You can follow Kaushal on Twitter (@ksarda) and read more about Kuliza here:

www.kuliza.com/

Susan Scrupski

Susan Scrupski is the founder of Change Agents Worldwide, a professional network that serves large enterprise organizations interested in adopting new behaviors and technologies for the 21st century. You can follow Susan on Twitter (@ITSinsider) and read more from Susan and Change Agents Worldwide here:

http://blog.changeagentsworldwide.com

www.changeagentsworldwide.com

Filberto Selvas

Filberto Selvas is a product planner and manager with experience and insight on social networking tools and technologies. You can follow Filberto on Twitter (@filbertosilvas) and read his social technology blog here:

www.socialcrm.net/

Ted Shelton

Ted Shelton is vice president, Consulting – Customer Solutions Practice at Cognizant Technology Solutions. You can follow Ted on Twitter (@tshelton) and read his blog here:

tedshelton.blogspot.com/

Hands-On Exercises

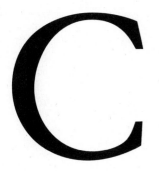

As Dave's college physics professor often declared, "You won't learn if you don't do the homework." Appendix C contains all of the review and applied exercises recommended throughout the book.

Note: You will find a printable (PDF) version of Appendix C at www.ReadThis.com.

Chapter 1: Social Media and Customer Engagement

Review each of the following, taking note of the main points covered in the chapter and the ways in which the following resources demonstrate or expand on these points:

- Search the Web for "Dell Hell" to understand what happened at Dell and how it inspired other companies to start on the social journey.

- Read the Nielsen Norman Group's report Social Media User Experience.

  www.nngroup.com/reports/social-media-user-experience/

- Review Starbucks's My Starbucks Idea ideation application:

  http://mystarbucksidea.com

- Read the Altimeter State of Social Business 2013 report to understand how companies are responding to the needs of their social customers.

  www.altimetergroup.com/research/reports/the_state_of_social_business_2013

- Look at the blog of Peter Kim, on the topic of social business:

  www.beingpeterkim.com

- Look at the work of Jeremiah Owyang, focused on the topic of social technology and collaboration applied to business:

  www.web-strategist.com/blog/

  http://crowdcompanies.com/

Apply what you've learned in this chapter through the following exercises:

1. Define the basic properties, objectives, and outcomes of social applications that connect your customers to your business and to your employees.

2. Define internal processes that enable efficient resolution of customer-generated ideas.

3. Map out your own customer engagement process and compare it with the engagement process defined in this chapter.

Chapter 2: The Social Customer

Review each of the following, combining the main points covered in the chapter and the ways in which the following resources expand on these points. Then tie each into your business or organization:

- Paul Greenberg's "Social CRM Comes of Age"

  www.oracle.com/us/036062.pdf

- Jeremiah Owyang's list of social CRM tools

  www.web-strategist.com/blog/2009/12/08/list-of-companies-providing-social-crm

- The Edelman Trust Barometer

  www.edelman.com/trust

Apply what you've learned in this chapter through the following exercises:

1. Find examples of where your customers are behaving like the new social customer today. What are they telling you about what they want and expect?

2. Find examples of bloggers or other social participants who are influential in ways related to your product or industry. Was it easy or hard to find these people?

3. Review the tools and platforms you use today to manage customer information and customer interactions. How socially aware are they? Where are the gaps?

Chapter 3: Social Customer Experience Management

Review each of the following, taking note of the main points covered in the chapter and the ways in which the following activities demonstrate these points:

- The Temkin Group website, including the Customer Experience Matters blog

  www.temkingroup.com/

- Michael Wu's e-books, *The Science of Social* and *The Science of Social 2*

  http://pages.lithium.com/science-of-social

  http://pages.lithium.com/science-of-social-2.html

- Chris Brogan's A Simple Presence Framework, which we adapted for this book

  www.chrisbrogan.com/a-simple-presence-framework/

- Consortium for Service Innovation website, how the practice of customer service is changing

  www.serviceinnovation.org/

Apply what you've learned in this chapter through the following exercises:

- Arrange a meeting with senior executives in your organization to talk about their views on collaborating with customers.

- Create an inventory of your current social media programs. List home bases, outposts, and passports (see the "Three Levels of Social Activities" sidebar for definitions of each) and then define the metrics and success measures for each.

- Meet with the leadership of your customer service and product design teams, and meet with Legal and HR to review the requirements or concerns about connecting employees more collaboratively or engaging more fully on the Social Web.

Chapter 4: The Social Customer Experience Ecosystem

Review each of the following, ensuring that you have a solid understanding of the concept being shown in the example:

- Brand outposts like Coca-Cola's Facebook page are viable alternatives to one-off microsites and branded communities:

  www.facebook.com/cocacola

- New Belgium Brewing's Facebook-based mobile photo and story contest taps readily available passions and interests. You don't have to reinvent wheels to create great social media points of presence. Check this and other social marketing efforts based on sharing and content collaboration created by Friend2Friend for New Belgium Brewing:

  www.friend2friend.com/client/new-belgium/

- Clearly articulated policies create a strong platform for collaboration and the adoption of social computing:

  www.ibm.com/blogs/zz/en/guidelines.html

  Apply what you've learned in this chapter through the following exercises:

1. If you use Twitter or LinkedIn, bring your personal profile up to 100 percent completion.

2. If your office or organization has a profile-driven knowledge-sharing application, repeat exercise 1 for your profile on that network. Then, get three colleagues to do the same.

3. List your favorite social communities, and describe an application that your business or organization might offer within that community. Connect it to your business objectives.

Chapter 5: Social Technology and Business Decisions

Review each of the following and connect them to your business.

- Check out the website for award programs like Forrester's Groundswell Awards and Lithium's Lithys Social Customer Excellence Awards to read cases on how companies are aligning goals with strategies across different industries.

  http://groundswelldiscussion.com/groundswell/awards/

  http://lithosphere.lithium.com/t5/lithys-social-customer/idb-p/Awards

- Spend time reading Esteban Kolsky's blog, and in particular search for and read the entries on "analytics engines." As a hands-on exercise, create a plan for integrating social analytics into your operational (not marketing) processes.

www.estebankolsky.com/

- Review the product innovation cycle (Figure 5.1), and map this onto your business and identify the specific areas or functions within your business that contribute to innovation. Think about the Bengaluru International Airport example as you do this. How can you design in the experiences you want your customers or stakeholders to talk about?

Apply what you've learned in this chapter through the following exercises to create your own social customer experience strategy:

1. Define the why, who, what, and where for your current social customer experience efforts, if any. How easy or difficult was it?

2. Visit with the IT, Marketing, or Operations teams that use your existing CRM data. Explore ways of incorporating social data into these processes and connecting that information to your business or organization.

3. Building on your exercises in Chapter 1, define one or more internal collaboration points based on what you discovered in exercise 1.

4. Building on your exercises in Chapters 2 and 3, create a workflow path for social data (for example, conversations) that carries this information to the points inside your organization that can act on it. Include a method for tracking results.

5. Build your touchpoint map, and identify the critical customer experiences that create the conversations that show up on the Social Web.

6. Combine the previous exercises and create a requirements list for the toolset that you will need to manage the social experience of your customers as it relates to your business objectives.

Chapter 6: Social Analytics, Metrics, and Measurement

Review each of the following, and consider subscribing to those that you find especially useful or relevant to your business or organization:

- Avinash Kaushik's blog, Occam's Razor

  www.kaushik.net/

- Kate Niedehoffer

  http://socialabacus.blogspot.com/

- Edwards Deming and Business Process Measurement

  http://en.wikipedia.org/wiki/W._Edwards_Deming

- Fred Reichheld and the Net Promoter community

  www.netpromoter.com/netpromoter_community

Apply what you've learned in this chapter through the following exercises:

1. Identify the primary social, web, and business analytics that matter to you.

2. Run a correlation analysis on metrics you've identified, and then investigate why certain metrics are correlated more strongly than others and how this correlation might be used to further your understanding of how the Social Web is impacting your business or organization.

3. Develop a basic dashboard, or incorporate one or two new business fundamentals that you identify through the previous exercises into your current business scorecard.

Chapter 7: Five Key Trends

Review each of the following, and ensure that you have a complete understanding of how social media and social technology are used.

- Dell Ideastorm

  www.ideastorm.com/

- Threadless

  www.threadless.com

- Foursquare (You will need an account with Foursquare and a GPS-capable phone or similar hand-held device for this.)

  http://foursquare.com

- HARO

  www.helpareporter.com

Apply what you've learned in this chapter through the following exercises:

1. Assess the real-time capability of your organization. How long does it take you to respond to customers online? Can you reduce that time?

2. Understand your company's mobile strategy. Is your website mobile-friendly? Are there mobile apps that you could deploy? (Tip: Look at your competitors too!) This will help you understand whether you can integrate social with existing efforts or need to develop on your own.

3. Prepare a short presentation using Threadless or a similar crowd-sourced enterprise as the subject or any other collaborative business design application that you choose. Talk to your team about what makes the application work and how social technology has been built into the business.

4. Looking at your own firm or organization, list three ways that your customers could collaborate directly with each other to improve some aspect of your product or service.

5. Develop an outline for a business plan based on exercise 2 that involves multiple departments or functions to implement. Win the support of those people.

Chapter 8: Customer Engagement

Review the following and apply them to your business or organization as you create your plan for integrating social technology into your fundamental processes:

- The case studies in Lithium's online case study library contain well-documented examples of a variety of social applications that result in both advocacy and positive ROI.

  www.lithium.com/customer-stories

- The whitepapers in Jive Software's resources library, in particular Social Business Software Adoption Strategies.

  www.jivesoftware.com/resources

  Apply what you've learned in this chapter through the following exercises:

1. Make a note of every recommendation you give or receive over the next week. Rank them according to the degree of enthusiasm on the part of the recommender.

2. Starting with the resources listed previously, develop your own library. Look for the similar resources offered by other social business software firms, and add those to your library.

3. Review your own engagement programs, and carefully examine how you are measuring or evaluating engagement and from whose perspective you are defining engagement.

4. Assuming that you have an appropriate social computing and social media use policy for employee use in place now, design a plan for an ideation, support, or discussion platform that will actively solicit customer-led conversations about your firm or organization or about your brand, product, or service.

Chapter 9: Social CRM and Social Customer Experience

Review both of the following and apply these to your business or organization as you create your plan for integrating social technology into your fundamental processes:

- Review cases noted in this chapter. The principles of social CRM are sufficiently well demonstrated that they can be applied to almost any business.

- Review the general toolsets in the tables in this chapter, and take note of the order in which specific tools or technologies are applied. As with social-media-based marketing in general, the implementation process begins *not* with technology but rather with business objectives and strategy.

Apply what you've learned in this chapter through the following exercises:

1. If you haven't done so already, look at the social computing policy examples at the Altimeter site or those of IBM or Dell. In addition, visit the sites of firms or organizations like yours to see what they have done. Imitation—followed with an in-house legal review—is the sincerest form of getting there faster!

2. Work with your IT or other applicable department to design a pilot program for internal collaboration. The exercise will challenge your organization, so choose a small project and recruit enthusiastic volunteers.

3. After completing the first two exercises, prepare and deliver a starting plan for social customer experience management to your colleagues (or customers, if you are a consulting firm or agency).

Chapter 10: Social Objects

Review each of the following and connect them to your business.

- Look at the work of Jyri Engeström, beginning with this video (http://vimeo.com/4071624) and his blog (www.zengestrom.com/blog).

- Make a list of the social sites you are currently a member of (all of them). Connect each with the social object around which it is built, and then consider how your connection to this object drives (or fails to drive) your participation in that site.

- Visit your own brand or organization website and brand outposts. Is a social object readily identifiable? Does this social object connect your audience to your business?

Apply what you've learned in this chapter through the following exercises:

1. Create an inventory of communities applicable to your brand, product, or service. Once you've compiled it, join a manageable set and understand the interest areas and social norms for each. Develop a plan for how you might integrate your own activities into these communities.

 Note: Always practice full disclosure, and refrain from test-driving communities.

2. Using Google, search for a lifestyle, passion, or cause that you are interested in. Note the documents that come back, and review a subset of them. Then do the same content search again, but this time select only image results. Review the images and note the number of images that lead you to a social site of some type.

3. Define three core social objects for your business or organization around which you could build or enhance your social presence. Create a touchpoint map to help guide your selection.

Chapter 11: The Social Graph

Review each of the following, and then take note of what you learn and insights you gain. How can you apply (or specify the use of) these items in your own projects and the further development of your understanding of social technology?

- Facebook Open Graph plug-ins for use in social-media-based marketing:

  http://developers.facebook.com/plugins

- Tools, papers, and resources available through membership in the INSNA and the larger discussion of social network analysis:

  www.insn/a.org

  Apply what you've learned in this chapter through the following exercises:

1. Map your first-degree network in your office, and then do the same in some personal aspect of your life, a civic organization, for example. Who is in both networks? What content is shared between these networks as a result?

2. Look at your friends in some of the social networks you belong to. How many of these friends or people you follow are people you knew prior to joining versus the number you met after joining? How were those you met after joining referred or suggested?

3. Develop a set of specific metrics for your social business applications that involve the social graph. Create a regular report, and track these measures over time.

Chapter 12: Social Applications

Review each of the following, and then take note of what you've learned or gained insight into. How can you apply (or specify the use of) these items in your own projects?

- Visit the tutorials* and resource pages for the APIs and social plug-ins associated with Facebook, MySpace, Twitter, Foursquare, and similar platforms. Gain an understanding of the intended uses of each, and then look at the examples of how they have been used to create differentiated social technology solutions.

*If you are not a programmer, read the summaries and cases associated with each. The objective here is to obtain ideas on how these services and tools might be used.

- Visit the websites of Jive Software, Lithium Technologies, GetSatisfaction, Microsoft SharePoint, Lotus Connections, Socialcast, and Socialtext. Gain an understanding of the intended uses of each, and then look at the examples of how they have been used to create branded social applications.

- Visit SlideShare and search for presentations on "Social Applications." You'll find great resources for almost any type of business.

  www.slideshare.com

Apply what you've learned in this chapter through the following exercises:

1. Articulate your business objectives, and define your audience.

2. Given the discussion of social applications, develop an idea for a social application that serves your business objectives and fits with your audience behaviors. Write a complete brief around its deployment. Include within this your development efforts supporting a cross-functional internal team.

3. Tie this plan to your existing marketing and business efforts and to your accepted business metrics. Define your guiding KPIs and if appropriate the basis for establishing ROI.

HANDS-ON EXERCISES ■

Index

Southwest Airlines Freedom Fighters, 60–61
stakeholders, SCEM and, 67
status updates, social applications, 90
Storer, Jim, 339
support
  communities, 117
  customer experience, agent support, 219–220
  engagement, peer support, 214–218
  SCEM and, 141–142
  social applications, 323

T

Telligent, 86
Telstra, 70
Terms of Service, 36–37
Thomases, Hollis, *Twitter Marketing: An Hour a Day,* 312
Threadless.com, 196–197
touchpoints, 127–129
  Bengaluru International Airport, 129–132
transparency, real names, 85
Treadaway, Chris, *Facebook Marketing: An Hour a Day,* 314
triggers, business as, 68–69
trust, influencer analysis, 162–163
Tupperware, 63
Twitter, employees and, 76–77
Twitter Marketing: An Hour a Day (Thomases), 312

U

UCG (user-generated content), 33
  Yelp and, 34
unique visitors, 166

V

value hierarchy, 222–230

value networks, status networks, 288
video, 265
viewing, 18
voice-of-customer channels, 42

W

Walker, John, 47
weak ties, 164
Web 2.0, 4
  as consumer, 106
  engagement and, 12–24
web analytics, website performance, 164–165
  bounce rate, 165
  causation, 168
  correlation, 167
  social measurement, 165
  unique visitors, 165
Web Analytics: An Hour a Day (Kaushik), 152–153
website performance, 164–165
  bounce rate, 165
  causation, 168
  correlation, 167
  social measurement, 165
  unique visitors, 165
websites, integration and, 238–239
  registration, 239–240
  searches, 240
white-label, 94
wiki pages, social applications, 90
workflow, 124–125
Wu, Michael, 73–74
  influence, 164

XYZ

Yelp, 34
Zappos, 25